THE NEW GERMANY

THE NEW GERMANY

At the Crossroads

by

DAVID MARSH

CENTURY

LONDON SYDNEY AUCKLAND JOHANNESBURG

First published in Great Britain in 1989 by Century
New edition in paperback published in 1990 by Century
An imprint of Random Century Ltd
20 Vauxhall Bridge Road, London SW1V 2SA

Century Hutchinson Australia (Pty) Ltd
89–91 Albion Street, Surry Hills, New South Wales
2010, Australia

Century Hutchinson New Zealand Ltd
PO Box 40–086, 32–34 View Road, Glenfield,
Auckland 10, New Zealand

Century Hutchinson South Africa (Pty) Ltd
PO Box 337, Bergvlei 2012, South Africa

Photoset in Ehrhardt by
Derek Doyle & Associates, Mold, Clwyd.
Printed and bound in Great Britain by
Mackays of Chatham Ltd, Chatham, Kent

British Library Cataloguing in Publication Data

Marsh, David
The Germans: Rich, Bothered and Divided.
1. Germany. Social conditions, from 1945
I. Title
943.087

ISBN 0-7126-3085-6

In Memory of My Father

Contents

Acknowledgements

The author is grateful for permission to reproduce excerpts from *The Complete Poems of Heinrich Heine*, translated by Hal Draper, published by Suhrkamp-Insel (1982), and *Heinrich Heine: Works of Prose* edited by Hermann Kesten, published by Secker and Warburg (1943). Thanks are also due to Roba Music Verlag for permission to reproduce part of the lyrics from a song by Udo Lindenberg.

Preface

Germany offers endless fascination, in good times and in bad. 'Foreigners stand astonished and attracted by the riddles revealed in the contradictions of the German soul,' wrote Friedrich Nietzsche in 1886. A preface in one American book on Germany, written in 1950, starts off: 'The answers to the great paradox of post-war Germany are inevitably paradoxical.'* In writing the first edition of this book, which was published in October 1989 under the title *The Germans: Rich, Bothered and Divided*, I was guided by the desire not to add to the paradoxes, but to explain them. The three primary aims, I wrote in the preface, were to explore the conundrum of the division of Germany in the light of dramatic changes in East-West relations; to investigate the influence of Germany's turbulent history on the make-up of the country today and its place in the world; and to provide an account of how modern Germany works. The final chapter in the book closed with these words: 'The challenge ahead is to find a solution to the growing dilemma over Germany's future before it captures the full attention of a watchful world.'

In the space of merely six months, in which the momentum to German reunification has built up at breakneck pace, the world has indeed woken up – with a mixture of surprise, hope and alarm – to the prospect of a new united German state. In this new edition I bring the reader an up to date account of the revolution in the eastern half of Germany in autumn 1989, which I was lucky enough to observe at close quarters. I describe the countdown to unity after the East German elections of March 1990. And, without changing the thrust of the analysis of the first edition, I explore the consequences of German unity on a continent in transition. Self-determination for the people of East Germany is a goal which has been proclaimed by the Federal Republic and its neighbours and partners for 40 years. Because, however, so few in East and West were prepared for it, the merger of the two German states is likely to be an exercise fraught with political, economic and psychological risks.

Many ideas and themes expounded on these pages have been

---

* *This is Germany*, edited by Arthur Settel, 1950.

developed in my work as a correspondent in Germany for the *Financial Times*. I am grateful to the newspaper for encouraging me to delve into the issues tackled in this book, and for giving me time to write it. Particular thanks go to Sir Geoffrey Owen, Richard Lambert, Jurek Martin and J.D.F. Jones.

Although parts of German life are undoubtedly opaque, this, on the whole, reflects complexity rather than secrecy. The Federal Republic is an open and rewarding place for a foreign correspondent. I am indebted to countless Germans from all fields who have given generously of their time, assistance and patience. Almost without exception, I have met courtesy, informativeness, and a sense of humour. This includes many of my experiences in East Germany, which I have been able to visit far more freely since summer 1989 than in previous years.

Many of those whose insights helped most – officials, experts of all kind, and 'ordinary' Germans – will remain anonymous. I would like to record my thanks to the following people who granted me extensive interviews, both in the course of my reporting for the *Financial Times* and in specific preparation for this book: in politics and public life: Egon Bahr, Kurt Biedenkopf, Norbert Blüm, Gerhard Boeden, Willy Brandt, Hans Daniels, Jutta Ditfurth, Alfred Dregger, Björn Engholm, Heinz Galinski, Hans-Dietrich Genscher, Hildegard Hamm-Brücher, Volker Hauff, Philipp Jenninger, Petra Kelly, Helmut Kohl, Bishop Martin Kruse, Otto Graf Lambsdorff, Alfred Mechtersheimer, Wolfgang Mischnick, Johannes Rau, Ludwig Rehlinger, Manfred Rommel, Wolfgang Schäuble, Otto Schily, Helmut Schmidt, Rupert Scholz, Lothar Späth, Gerhard Stoltenberg, Klaus Töpfer, Hans-Jochen Vogel, Wolfgang Vogel, Richard von Weizsäcker, Manfred Wörner; in economics, industry and finance: Hermann Josef Abs, Klaus Barthelt, Rudolf von Bennigsen-Foerder, Ernst Breit, Reiner Gohlke, Eckart van Hooven, Wilfried Guth, Prof. Wolfgang Kartte, Eberhard von Koerber, Manfred Lahnstein, Tyll Necker, Karl Otto Pöhl, Edzard Reuter, Prof. Karl Schiller, Prof. Helmut Schlesinger, Otto Schlecht, Ronaldo Schmitz, Hans Tietmeyer, Hanns Arnt Vogels, Burckard Wollschläger; in the media, creative and scientific worlds, Rudolf Augstein, Alfred Biolek, Klaus Bölling, Klaus Bresser, Daniel Cohn-Bendit, Joachim Fest, Michel Friedman, Prof. Ulrich Gabler, Karl-Günther von Hase, Wolfgang Herles, Werner Höfer, Werner Holzer, Josef Joffe, Horst Krüger, Friedhelm Kemna, Robert Leicht, Prof. Elisabeth Noelle-Neumann, Manfred Schell, Bernhard Sinkel, Theo Sommer, Prof. Hans Stiller, Prof. Carl-Friedrich von Weizsacker; among allied commanders in West Germany, Gen. Jean-Louis Brette, Gen. Sir Brian

Kenny, Air Marshal Sir Anthony Skingsley, Gen. Ronald Watts, Gen. John Woodmansee. I profited from a spirited conversation with Prince Louis Ferdinand. Prof. Lothar Hönnighausen and Prof. Günter Peise were kind enough to arrange meetings with their students. Among East Germans who gave me their time, I would like to thank Stefan Heym, Michael Müller, Ines and Manuel Richter, and Rolf Schneider.

I am very grateful to friends and acquaintances who read through parts of the manuscript and made invaluable comments and suggestions. I particularly benefited from the advice and constructive criticism of Prof. Michael Stürmer and Claus Duisberg. Martin Mauthner, Robert Flower, Richard Imus, Prof. Herbert Strauss and Thomas Kielinger helped greatly in matters of style, fact and content; Ernst Moritz Lipp, Holger Schmieding, Prof. Gerhard Fels, Gert Dahlmanns, and Prof. Juergen Donges gave special assistance on the German economy; Mark Walker, Thomas Roser and Keith Duxbury expertly scanned and commented upon the section on nuclear energy. Responsibility for the views expressed – as well as for any errors of fact, omission or judgement – of course rests alone with the author.

Thanks are due to my colleagues in the *Financial Times* offices in Bonn and Frankfurt. David Goodhart, Haig Simonian and Andrew Fisher came up with tips, encouragement and corrections. Patricia Naatz gave indispensable assistance in office-work and research. I thank too my brother Peter for advice on the chemical industry, and Jan Schling for digging out facts at the *F.T.* Library in London. The reference library staff of the Bundestag, and of the British and American embassies in Bonn, were supremely helpful, as were the Institute of Germanic Studies and the West German Embassy in London. I am grateful to my agent Arthur Goodhart, and to Mark Booth at Century Hutchinson, for their effort and encouragement. Rudolf Lauer and Magda and Carola Hamsher provided valuable additions to source material,all the more welcome for being unexpected.

Veronika made it possible.

David Marsh
Bad Godesberg, February 1990

1

On the Fault Line

Deutschland ist noch ein kleines Kind
Doch die Sonne ist seine Amme;
Sie säugt es nicht mit stiller Milch,
Sie säugt es mit wilder Flamme.

Germany's still a little child,
And the sun's his nursing maid;
She suckles him not on placid milk
But on wild flames unstayed.

Heinrich Heine, 1840[1]

This is not the only Germany that we shall live to see, but we have to consider that at present two or three men have that wonderful, scientific, intelligent, docile, valiant people in their grip.

Winston Churchill, 1934[2]

We are a people of brooders. There is something Faustian in us. The permanent questioning; the knowledge that we can know nothing – that is something which is in every German. We make every question more difficult.

Hans-Dietrich Genscher, 1987[3]

Germany is a place of energy, where the earth has shifted and erupted; quieter during four post-war decades, but not brought to rest. At the start of the 1990s, as the divided halves of the nation move together after the breakdown of Communism in eastern Europe, Germany has again become the epicentre of a continent in transition.

Like Siegfried, the Nibelung warrior brought down through a weak spot on his dragon armour-skin, the post-1945 Germans are strong but singularly vulnerable. They have rebuilt, but not healed, a land rent by total war. During the past forty years, the Germans have survived, laboured, prospered. In the West, at least, they have become democrats. They have perfected a system of economic and political consensus

1

which has become notoriously inflexible partly because of worries about the consequences if society ever became less organised. They have some of the best-quality homes, hospitals, restaurants and motor cars in the world. They have even started to enjoy life. The recovery has been admired and envied by the countries which won the Second World War; but the Germans have less than anyone overcome its aftermath. Success has not erased trauma; prosperity has been accompanied by fears that it could all again somehow be swept away. Now, after the crumbling of the Berlin Wall and East Germany's first democratic elections, the Germans and their neighbours are watching as the tremors rippling out from the East bring German reunification into view. The pace of change since the autumn of 1989 has been breathtaking – and, as often the case in Germany, unleashes a kaleidoscope of contradictory emotions.

Some countries over the centuries have weathered catastrophe and then regained their place in the world. Others have sunk into oblivion. Germany, in a sense, has done both. It has lost its ability to play a world role, yet has remained at the fulcrum of the international power balance. With the passing of the Cold War, nowhere has détente between the US and the Soviet Union produced a greater impact than on the two Germanys formed as a by-product of confrontation between Communism and capitalism; and nowhere are the changes under way the focus of so much hope, fear, yearning, suspicion and intrigue.

For the Germans, ending of division brings the chance of closing off Hitler's cycle of dictatorship, destruction and defeat. The cleavage of Germany was merely the provisional outcome of the 1939-45 war, reflecting the break-up of the victorious anti-Hitler coalition, and the failure of the US and Soviet Union to agree on a common peace policy for central Europe. The Third Reich left a delayed legacy: 100 miles of concrete around West Berlin, and 860 miles of wire fence across the German countryside. As the result of the shift in the superpower balance brought by Mikhail Gorbachev, these monuments have toppled; the ugly frontier across Germany and Europe has disappeared from the map.

Having absorbed democracy and prosperity from the western war victors, the Federal Republic has the opportunity to extend these benefits to the eastern part of the nation so far denied them. This is a historic chance – but it is not an unmixed blessing. The world has become used to seeing East and West Germany as junior partners of their respective alliances. Now, a reforged Germany is on the way to becoming the dominant political, economic and cultural force in Europe – bringing responsibilities and challenges which the Germans as a people are not yet ready to bear.

The path towards unity is not without pitfalls. If Gorbachev fails in his efforts to reform the Soviet system and put relations with the West on a new footing, the two German states will be the first to register the disadvantages. Lessening of East-West tension inevitably weakens the forces which have kept the Federal Republic firmly in the western camp. The paradox is acute: the shifts in international politics which have suddenly reopened Germany's national options could also undermine stability in the middle of Europe.

Partition indeed coincided with an unprecedented period of wealth and economic growth; but the Germans have not been able to throw off an air of disappointment. Over the past 40 years, the Germans have won foreign markets but not security; they have, for the first time, found friends in the world, but not trust and understanding. By dint of effort and exports, they have acquired economic power, but not the self-confidence to make full use of it.

The two German states appeared to grow apart within two separate political, economic and military blocs. Yet East and West Germany are bound together by cultural, historical and human ties which cannot be wiped out in two generations and which have, in some ways, even been strengthened by the artificiality of partition. Both Germanys have been united by their growing reluctance to accept the post-war concentration of weaponry and war risks on their soil. The willingness of the West German electorate to accept defence burdens has declined rapidly precisely because the Soviet Union is now perceived more as a partner than a threat. The Federal Republic and the German Democratic Republic are less under the control of their respective superpowers, and more free to evolve their own policies, than at any time since both states were founded in 1949. They see their vital interests less in terms of ties to West or East – more as Germans.

One factor strengthening the bond between East and West Germany has been an undertone of shared resentment that neither state is in control of the nation's ultimate destiny. The key to settlement of the post-war German Question is shared with the four victors – the US, Soviet Union, Britain and France. The war allies' residual political rights over Germany, and the heavy foreign military presence on German soil, represent the unfinished business of the Second World War – consequences which the Germans are finding increasingly irksome.

The Federal Republic is the only member of the western community with a built-in national grievance: the desire laid down in the constitution to reforge, in some ill-defined way, national unity. Other countries, above all France, fear a unified Germany. This anxiety is matched by the equal and opposite fear of how the Germans would react if they believed the West was deliberately blocking the road to reunification. The way out of the diplomatic conflict was based on subterfuge: to keep the German Question permanently open as a way of turning the provisional solution of cleavage into a lasting answer. This delicate equilibrium can no longer be maintained. As the outline of a resurgent German nation shimmers over the contours of Europe, western diplomacy towards the centre of the continent faces its stiffest test for half a century.

West Germany's basic dilemma over reunification has been unchanged since the chancellorship of Konrad Adenauer; it has now sharpened considerably. Unity cannot be reforged unless the German Democratic Republic is detached from the Soviet sphere of influence – and this can only be achieved at a price. That price – a weakening of the Federal Republic's links with the West – has always been beyond Bonn's means to pay, but now it is becoming affordable. As long as eastern Europe was Communist-ruled, and Moscow posed a clear-cut military threat, the Federal Republic had little difficulty persuading its electorate of the overwhelming benefits of western integration. The 1989 erosion of Communist hegemony east of the Elbe, as well as the Federal Republic's greatly enhanced economic power *vis-à-vis* its western partners, have undermined the foundations of that argument. The forces binding West Germany to the European Community and Nato are weakening. The West will have to accept that reunification will be impossible without a thorough restructuring of Nato which, in the most extreme case, could lead to its dissolution.

Precisely because the Federal Republic's ability to occupy a 'half way house' in Europe has increased, suspicions among its neighbours tend to increase whenever Bonn attempts to strike out on an independent course. Germany's role as the Janus of Europe has been restored. After 1945, the conflicting pressures between East and West to which Germany has been exposed throughout history were put in abeyance. Now, they are reappearing.

Germany is marked by a classic dualism. The post-war Germans have always been able to see two sides to every question. Did not capitulation on 8 May 1945 bring simultaneously destruction and salvation? The Germans' turbulent history has been both cause and effect of remarkable creativity. But their strength and defects lie very close together. Only a thin line separates idealism from escapism, pride from arrogance, discipline from servility. An ill-understood vein of emotion runs through the country – above all in relation to their own history. The Germans themselves are split between those who say that constant, wearisome preoccupation with the past is blocking the view to the future, and those who believe that critical self-examination and the hunt for old Nazi demons have not been pursued far enough. Two generations after the eclipse of Hitler, soul-searching over the Third Reich has worked its way through to the surface with a vengeance. In East and West Germany – underlined by the slogans hurled by both sides in the arguments about a revival of far-Right German nationalism – skeletons from the past are regularly disinterred as instruments of political in-fighting.

The list of paradoxes can be extended at will. Exports have given Germany wealth, but unwelcome dependence on outside events. Technological advance – the splitting of the atom, for instance, a German discovery – is seen here, more than in most countries, as both deliverance and devilry. The Germans fret more than others about the damage to their forests from car exhaust fumes, but appear to rule out one obvious remedy – driving their high-powered cars more slowly. They give priority to a society based on materialism and self-discovery, but worry when this leads to a loss of communal feeling or a sinking birth rate.

The phase of slower West German economic growth during the 1980s has been welcomed by many because it may reduce environmental damage, but adds to nervousness about whether the country can afford its generous social security and pensions systems. Membership of Nato provides protection, but also appears to increase the danger of a war on German soil. Four-power responsibility over the whole of Germany has held the nation together and simultaneously kept the two parts separated. Most paradoxically of all, only by providing evidence that they have outgrown nationalism can the Germans have a real chance of becoming a nation again.

The pattern of light and shade permeates the multi-layered structures making up the new Germany. A gauze over the German landscape filters out the fine grain of historical continuity, leaving only post-war blandness. The visitor may see the rebuilt city centres, the department stores combining solidity with glitter, and the shiny Mercedes gliding down the Autobahnen. But even wealthy Hamburg, resurrected from the bombing, has run-down areas and the social problems which go with it, to say nothing of the fading coal and steel communities of the Ruhr. Although the poor in West Germany live on higher incomes than their

5

counterparts in other European countries, pockets of relative deprivation and discontent appear to be growing. Society is showing signs of brittleness – one of the reasons for growing support for the radical parties on the far Right.

Less evident, too, are the well-equipped craft-based factories blending into industrial towns, or maybe hidden in a forest glade. They turn out precision machinery with the same efficiency and attention to detail as at the end of the last century. Despite the anti-technology slogans of Greens ecologists, the Germans have a much closer affinity to industry than the British or the French. This helps explain why the most talented people go into manufacturing, not politics. Ironically, for a country often said to 'have no history', the past runs into everyday life more in Germany than most European countries. Along with video recorder and leather sofa in an average-income living room will sit an old-style oak table, topped with a traditional posy of dried country flowers. The family may roar off on holiday to Spain or Austria in the Ford saloon. But at weekends they will decamp to their garden retreat, the *Schrebergarten**, growing runner beans and dahlias next to the railway track on the city outskirts. German customs come out at Carnival time, or after the harvest, in festive parades through the streets and squares of small towns. But they are apparent above all in the local skittles or athletics clubs, in the skat circles, in the small affairs of family life. Germany's multiple national traditions have been broken up, discredited and dispersed. People prefer the ones they are sure of, closer to home.

Certainly, in West Germany, the 1945 collapse and the fresh start under the allied occupying powers provided a hitherto unknown impulse for modernisation. The break with the past was strengthened by the need for a form of brand image to mark the difference with the East. Anti-totalitarianism and anti-Communism neatly dove-tailed into a single policy. The 'social market economy' (*soziale Marktwirtschaft*) of the first Economics Minister, Ludwig Erhard, not only symbolised an end to the *dirigisme* and cartellisation of the Weimar Republic and the Third Reich, but also firmly underscored the contrast with centralised planning in Communist East Germany.

All the same, the old ran on alongside the new. Despite the success of post-1949 parliamentary democracy, a residual authoritarian streak still colours attitudes to politics. The Germans are one of the peoples most exposed to international influences, through geography and history, and now the export culture; and yet their reactions are often incorrigibly

---

* Named after the 19th-century Leipzig doctor Daniel Gottlob Schreber.

provincial. German politicians not only have names like characters out of Grimms' fairy tales, but often act like them too. As an understandable, and necessary, correction to the post-war shame attached to German nationality, both Right- and Left-wing politicians made an effort in the 1980s to revive a spirit of patriotism. Such attempts however begged a lot of questions – for how can people identify with 'the Fatherland' when no one can be quite sure what it is and how it should be re-attained?

Continuity strides on in economics. The all-pervasive joint stock companies set up in the last 30 years of the 19th-century prospered under the Kaisers, the Weimar Republic and Hitler. In spite of war-time destruction, and post-war loss of assets in the East, they quickly found their places in the new Republic. Although the family plutocracies are no longer in control, the great corporate names of 19th-century German capitalism are marching through to the 1990s, flourishing as never before. Despite the Federal Republic's evident internationalism, the economic regulation and corporatism of the 1920s and 1930s maintain a vigorous existence beneath the rhetoric of the *soziale Marktwirtschaft.* One reason why the Germans worry about the move to a more integrated and competitive European market after 1992 is because they will have to dismantle protection for some of the less efficient parts of the economy.

Overriding support for consensus politics implies lack of faith in a less ordered society. The Germans fear that if business and labour practices were subject to less rules, life would be less predictable, less stable, and more hazardous. Desire for financial stability is bolstered by memories of the monetary disorder left by two world wars. As the single most important factor increasing post-war international respect for the Germans, the possession of a hard currency has become, in effect, both the principal instrument and one of the chief goals of overall foreign policy. The German parliamentarians of the 1950s who ceded control over the creation of money to an autonomous central bank (though not without a fight with Adenauer) recognised a weakness in the democratic process. Germany has seen more than most countries how politicians can debauch the currency.[4]

To the vexation of its allies, German dualism makes its grandest and most disturbing entrance in the field of defence. Almost any military initiative is bad news for the Federal Republic. In the 1970s, the West Germans became fearful over the Soviet preponderance of medium-range missiles aimed at western Europe. When, to reaffirm the strategic link between the US and western Europe, America proposed deploying its own medium-range weapons in West Germany, the mood swung round to anxieties that rearmament could lead to limited nuclear war on German territory. Now that the missiles have been removed as part of the US-Soviet détente, worries have risen again that Germany could become the battlefield for the conventional armies and the short-range nuclear missiles which remain.

Over the question of the foreign troops on their soil, the Germans will agonise, whatever happens. As one symbol of discontent with the post-war order, a public debate has flared up over whether the NATO military presence constrains West German sovereignty. Today's Germans do not want the troops in their neighbourhood, but they do not want them to go home either. Once the US moves to scale down its military strength in western Europe in the early 1990s, the West Germans will feel unease that they are being left unprotected – and will perhaps cast around for protection elsewhere.

In an increasingly interlocking world, the term 'sovereignty' is somewhat anachronistic. Especially in a post-1992 Europe, states will be growing accustomed to sharing power. The greatest potential discord with West Germany's allies stems from the debate about whether a unified Germany should be free of foreign troops – and possibly move away from NATO. Neutrality, although condemned by mainstream West German politicians, may prove a temptation above all for the newly-enfranchised electorate in the East. The Christian Democrat-led government in East Berlin which came to power after the March 1990 elections, however, seems to accept, like the coalition in Bonn, that a neutral German state would almost certainly destablize Europe.

Some of today's German challenges are perplexingly similar to those in the immediate post-war years. A total of 720,000 fugitives from Communism streamed into the Federal Republic in 1989, above all from the Soviet Union, Poland and East Germany in 1989 – matching in numbers (although not in the manner of their coming) the tide of refugees from the East who flooded into the fledgling Federal Republic in the early post-war years. The political parties are again indulging in endless debate over reunification and disarmament, over the clash of priorities between integration with the West, and Germany's older ties and leanings towards the East. The Berlin Wall is reduced to a ruin. But in many areas – defence and nuclear policy, immigration, attitudes towards terrorism, Berlin, the border with Poland, relations with Moscow and Washington – the Germans are still struggling with Hitler's legacies.

8

The social make-up and lifestyles of today's comfortable Germans have changed immeasurably, but the constitutional structure under which they live has in many ways stayed frozen in 1949 provisionality. Post-war Germany is no longer a 'little child', no longer an adolescent; it is now entering its fifth decade. But are not 40-year-olds, as well as teenagers, sometimes tempted to change their lives?

The forces for German unity which have burst to the surface emphasise that, in the life of a nation, four decades are but a short time. The Germans' epic voyage through history did not, after all, come to an end after the Second World War; it was only interrupted. This confirmation of national continuity buttresses the claim of the Germans to live together in one state; but it also explains the rest of Europe's qualms over the prospect. If the passing of two generations has not been long enough to cause the Germans to forget their 'Germanness', then neither has it been sufficient to erase their neighbours' memories of the outcome of the Third Reich. Because Germany's history is so much part of its present, the Germans still have a duty to prove that they have accepted and mastered the lessons of the past. Germany's task for the 1990s is to show unequivocally that unity will provide a beacon, not a blemish, on the map of Europe.

2

Consequences of Catastrophe

Will we ever be able fully to understand the monstrous experiences which were our lot during the twelve years of the Third Reich?
Friedrich Meinecke, in *Die deutsche Katastrophe*, 1946[1]

In reality this 8 May 1945 remains, for every one of us, the most tragic and questionable paradox in our history. Why? Because we were rescued and destroyed at the same time.
Theodor Heuss, 1949[2]

Anyone who closes his eyes to the past is blind to the present. Whoever refuses to remember the inhumanity is prone to risks of new infection.
Richard von Weizsäcker, 1985[3]

Horst Krüger, a large dishevelled man exuding an engaging mix of melancholy and good cheer, is an expert on the German trauma. A well-known author and essayist, he writes with particular poignance about the division of Germany. Born in 1919 in Magdeburg in what is now East Germany, he was brought up in middle-class Eichkamp, a sedate residential part of Berlin now in the British sector on the western side of the divided city. During the 1930s he watched the influence of National Socialism gradually spreading across suburbia – a fuse which exploded in mechanised fury in 1939 and was snuffed out in flames and destruction six years later.

Krüger lives now in an apartment house of faded elegance in the West End of Frankfurt. It is one of the few intact corners of the trading city on the River Main, for centuries the place of coronation of medieval German emperors. Ruined by wartime bombing, Frankfurt narrowly missed selection in 1949 as the capital of the new Federal Republic. The city has risen again to become the country's prime financial centre, a boom town dotted with banking skyscrapers and department stores. Many Frankfurt-dwellers say its soul was lost amidst the rubble, but Krüger expresses a rare affection for the city. He says that his

tree-shaded street with small shops and *Litfassäule* advertising pillars*
reminds him of Berlin. He admits that Frankfurt's rapid-sprouting
hedonistic post-war architecture gives it a perpetually half-finished look,
but adds: 'Half-solutions are typical of the Germans.'[4]

Sprawled back in a settee in his large book-lined living room, Krüger
spells out his view of his compatriots. 'The Germans are an unpolitical,
romantic people who lean towards extremes – they confuse reality and
dreams.' Adolf Hitler was 'art mixed with politics – he appeared as God,
and turned out to be the devil.' Krüger declares the building of the West
German state a success which forty years ago would have been thought
impossible. But, whether they like it or not, the Germans are carrying
with them Hitler's inheritance: the questioning, and the drama, and the
pain. 'The more years go by since the Third Reich, the more demonic it
appears – like a mystery play. The past needs therapy,' he says. The
treatment needs to last all the longer because the symptoms keep
recurring. Krüger's haunting epilogue in his 1966 autobiographical
novel *Das zerbrochene Haus (The Broken House)* still holds good: 'This
Hitler, he will stay with us – to the end of our lives.'[5]

I

Germany's past is a thick rich flood, tinged with black-red-and-gold,
flowing on irrepressibly into the present. One place to tap a sample is
Ludwigsburg, north of Stuttgart, in the prosperous state of
Baden-Württemberg. The town is the home of the sales headquarters of
the Porsche sports car company and the site of a sprawling 18th-century
palace. A short walk along the main road from the ochre-walled
Baroque pile stands a stout three-storey building, set back slightly from
the other houses and protected by a security gate. Children's swings
hang in neighbouring gardens. It turns out to be a former women's
prison, built in 1780, its gauntness now softened by a coating of pale
yellow paint. The porter, burly and amiable, is sifting through a thick
pile of letters, most of them written in Polish, which have just arrived
with the morning post. He discharges his duty with a paper-knife. Each
one is slit open neatly, imprinted with the thud of a heavy-duty date

* Concrete pillars bearing advertisements, named after the Berlin printer Ernst Litfass
who started the practice in 1854.

stamp and laid out meticulously in an out-tray, ready for the attention of his superiors upstairs.

The envelopes contain inquiries into wartime barbarities committed nearly fifty years ago in eastern Europe. It is 1988. But the letters keep arriving. This is the central office established by the West German justice authorities in 1958 to coordinate legal proceedings against Nazi criminals. It took over the job – with some delay – after the ending of Allied occupation and the return of German files from the US put responsibility for the prosecution of German war criminals into West German hands. At the peak of its activity, the Ludwigsburg bureau employed more than 120 people. The staff is now down to about forty, of whom roughly half are judges and state prosecutors.

The office has been involved in around 13,000 individual criminal investigations over three decades, leading to 800 convictions. Overall, West German prosecutors have launched investigations concerning some 91,000 persons suspected of Nazi crimes. Only around 6,000 of these cases ended in convictions. Twelve people were condemned to death and 160 given life sentences. The low level of successful prosecutions was not really surprising. During the years of economic recovery, the Federal Republic had other priorities than tracking down perpetrators of Nazi atrocities. The first chief of the Ludwigsburg bureau when it was set up in 1958, Erwin Schüle, had plenty of experience for his job. Schüle himself was a former member of the Nazi party and of the terrorist militia, the *Sturmabteilung* (SA). This uncomfortable fact forced his resignation in 1966 after it was revealed in one of the habitual 1960s Nazi exposés of the East German press.

The presence of men like Schüle in high places in administration, banking, politics and industry was nothing uncommon. At the end of the war, the Nazi party had slightly more than 8 million members.[6] Millions more were enlisted in the party's myriad associate organisations, across the gamut of German life. To survive and carry out the role allotted by the western Allies of forming a bulwark against Communism, the post-1949 Federal Republic needed politicians, bankers, administrators, journalists, diplomats, lawyers, industrialists, doctors, judges and generals. As the Cold War gradually enveloped Europe, West Germany was thrown into the breach to repel the westward spread of Soviet influence.

One inevitable consequence was that the US backed away from thorough-going denazification. If all Nazis had been barred from office – even supposing they had been identifiable – the country would not have managed to take its place in the western community so quickly. The presence of ex-Nazis near the levers of power speeded up material reconstruction, but it was to hamper greatly West Germany's efforts to throw off the spiritual yoke of the past.

Willi Dressen, a 53-year-old state attorney from Aachen, is the deputy chief of the Ludwigsburg bureau. He joined the centre unwillingly in 1967, but quickly found the work fascinating and stayed on.[7] The Ludgwigsburg centre itself was set up amid a flurry of indignation about mild sentences handed down in a notorious trial in Ulm in 1958 of men from Hitler's elite Black Guards, the *Schutzstaffel* (SS), who were deployed on 'mopping-up' campaigns of mass murder in occupied Europe. SS members accused of killing a total of 4,000 Lithuanian Jews were found guilty simply of carrying out orders. The Ulm court gave them sentences averaging two days' jail for each proven killing. The judgement that murderers in the occupied territories and concentration camps were simply 'aiding and abetting' crimes originating from the Nazi leadership set the tone for future court cases. Judges in Nazi courts, above all in the notorious *Volksgerichtshof*, the People's Court, who handed down around 32,000 death sentences between 1933 and 1945, largely escaped unscathed after the war. 'Begowned murderers', they have been called,[8] but in the eyes of the law they were mere instruments of the Nazi state, without personal responsibility.

The people of Baden-Württemberg during the 1950s were tired of hearing about Nazis and thought that the country should get on with building up its future. Ludwigsburg was at first distinctly uncomfortable about hosting the centre. During the 1960s the mayor called it a 'blemish' on the town, and neighbours forbade their children to play with the prosecutors' offspring. 'These days, though,' says Dressen, 'the people show more sensitivity.' The Ludwigsburg unit still has several thousand cases on its hands. It has been sifting through a list of 30,000 names of suspected war criminals handed over in 1986 by the United Nations, but only 'very, very few' will ever result in court action, he says. Three-quarters of the names apply to cases which have already come to court or have been otherwise resolved. Additionally, German state prosecutors no longer mount action against anyone born before 1900: 'It's not worth the effort.'

The Ludwigsburg centre commemorated its 30th anniversary in 1988 with a symposium looking back over its history. It was the occasion for self-congratulation. The Baden-Württemberg Justice Minister, Heinz Eyrich, pointed out that West Germany had called war criminals to account 'even when their actions had been tolerated, approved or ordered by a perverted state leadership'. Certainly, the Federal

13

Republic's record of prosecuting its own citizens for crimes committed during the Third Reich is laudable in comparison with Austria – but it still has plenty of blemishes. The smugness was punctured by a guest at the symposium, Professor Kazimier Kakol, director of the official Polish commission on Nazi crimes. He described West Germany's low conviction rate as 'appalling' and accused the federal authorities of lacking the political will to investigate war crimes against Polish citizens.[9]

Ludwigsburg's work will carry on into the next century. However, the centre is slowly changing its function from a place of legal investigations into a museum. It keeps around half a million documents on microfilm and 1.4 million card index entries covering names, places and specifications of police and army units involved in Nazi crimes. This is much smaller than the Berlin Document Centre, run by the US (but paid for by the Bonn government), which contains card-files on the entire Nazi membership of more than 10 million (including roughly 2 million who died or had left the party by 1945).[10] Like the Berlin Centre, Ludwigsburg is used increasingly by historians and students researching books and theses on the Third Reich. 'This is increasing from year to year,' says Dressen, pointing to a map on the wall showing more than 1,000 concentration camps – including labour camps set up as offshoots of the main sites – spread across central Europe during the Third Reich. Large German companies involved in the war effort used some of the prisons as sources of slave labour. An estimated 8 million foreign workers were employed across German territory in 1944, of whom 1.9 million were prisoners-of-war and 5.7 million civilian deportees. Around 500,000 were concentration camp prisoners.

'If we allow the past to be forgotten, we are condemned to experience it again,' Dressen says. 'It is good if as many people as possible are informed.' Norbert Gansel, one of the most active of the younger generation of Social Democrat deputies in Bonn, says people up and down Germany are examining their 'grass roots history' by looking into the past of their own towns and villages. 'They are asking, "Where were the KZs (concentration camps); where did the victims come from; where are the perpetrators?" ' he says.[11]

Desire for knowledge can suddenly arise after being suppressed for many years. The centre often deals with personal inquiries. Dressen describes how relatives of men who have just died are sometimes anxious to establish what their late husbands or fathers did during the war: 'Often there are things which they suspected during the men's lifetime, but didn't dare to ask. Documents can sometimes be found with the will which lead to questions. It is normally the daughters. A week or fourteen days after the death, they write us a letter and ask if they can come and look in our files.'

II

The gentlemen from the chemical industry were not amused. An 8½-hour West German television film shown in four peak-time instalments in late 1986 attempted to retrace a history many would rather forget: the role of big business in Hitler's war effort. The film, *Väter und Söhne (Fathers and Sons)*, starred Burt Lancaster, Julie Christie and the German actor Bruno Heck. Broadcast as well in the US, France, Italy and Austria, the DM18-million production was one of the most expensive ever made for German TV. The film combined both fact and fiction – a sometimes confusing amalgam which made it easier for its detractors to criticise. It portrayed the story of I.G. Farben, the giant German chemicals group spawned through a First World War cartel and then formally established in a 1925 merger of the nation's largest chemicals companies, led by the 'Big Three', BASF, Hoechst and Bayer. I.G. Farben reached full strength under the Third Reich, becoming a supreme example of unholy partnership between German industry and the Nazis.* The aim of the broadcast was to raise public awareness about the chemical industry's unsavoury past in the same way that the US television film *Holocaust* screened seven years earlier stirred German consciences about anti-Jewish persecution.[12]

After 1945, as part of a general bid to break up the industrial concentration of Nazi Germany, the victor powers split up I.G. Farben into its original component parts to reduce its strength. In one of the most prominent signs of West Germany's industrial rebirth, the 'Big Three' have since grown into the three largest chemical companies in the world.[13] Each now is far larger than I.G. Farben at its zenith. BASF, Hoechst and Bayer are multinational giants with total turnover in 1989 of DM133 billion – equivalent to the combined gross national product of Ireland and Portugal. In the US alone, the three companies now have combined turnover of $17 billion and employ 70,000 people. Ironically, I.G. Farben's nerve centre during the Third Reich – a monumental nine-storey, six-winged office block in the north-west of Frankfurt – today is surrounded by security fences and patrolled by American

* See Chapter 6.

15

guards. I.G. Farben occupied the building – constructed in 1929-30 – for just fifteen years, but the American army, which now uses it as a corps headquarters, has been there three times as long.* The sweeping surrealistic building, clad externally in Travertine stone, its corridors lined with marble, is still one of the best-known Frankfurt landmarks. In 1945 the Americans moved in upon the collapse of the Reich; they have stayed there ever since.

The I.G. Farben film was slammed as 'a poor effort'[14] by Hermann-Josef Strenger, today's Bayer chairman, whose father and grandfather worked for the company before him. Ronaldo Schmitz, a high-flying board member at BASF, called it an attempt to 'shake confidence'.[15] Chancellor Helmut Kohl, a politician of brawn but little finesse from the vineyard and forest region of the Palatinate in south-west Germany, was equally dismissive. Born in a suburb of Ludwigshafen, the Rhine port which has been BASF's headquarters since 1865, Kohl started his career in the 1950s as a junior official in the chemical industry, and nearly ended up joining the board of a chemicals group in the 1960s.[16] When I asked him about the I.G. Farben film at a press conference, Kohl irascibly condemned exaggerated 'snuffling around' about the Hitler era. He said that he, for one, had not watched the film.[17] West German television has shown an estimated 30,000 hours of programmes informing the population about the Third Reich in the last thirty years. For many people, Kohl included, that is more than enough.

The men of I.G. Farben were synonymous with the best and worst in Germany. The scientist Fritz Haber achieved the breakthrough allowing I.G. Farben to make both fertilisers and explosives when in 1909 he invented the synthesis of ammonia from atmospheric nitrogen. Haber's expertise during the First World War in developing poison gas used on the Western Front almost placed him on the Allied list of war criminals. A Jew who was converted to Protestantism as a young man, Haber received the Nobel Prize for chemistry in 1918. Resigning his post at the Kaiser Wilhelm Institute for Physical Chemistry after Hitler's anti-Jewish civil service legislation of April 1933,** Haber died in Basle on his way to Palestine in 1934.

The film told Haber's story through a fictional character supposed to be an amalgam between Haber and Carl Bosch, the long-time BASF chairman. It also described I.G. Farben's support for Hitler's war preparations through its manufacture in the 1930s of synthetic oil and

* See Chapter 11.
** See Chapter 10.

rubber. Although, like much of big business, the chemical combine was initially suspicious of Hitler when he became Chancellor in 1933, it ended up as a vital cog in the war machine. During the war, around 200 German companies put to work prisoners from concentration camps. I.G. Farben was one of the most assiduous practitioners of enslavement. The company built its own concentration camp to house prisoners from the Nazi death camp of Auschwitz in Silesia, and from 1941 onwards they were used to build a nearby synthetic rubber plant. More than 30,000 of I.G. Farben's slave labourers, mostly Jews, died there.[18] Following the tradition of Haber in the First World War, Germany also produced a poison gas specialist in the years leading up to the Second World War. He was Gerhard Schrader, an I.G. Farben scientist who invented the nerve gases Tabun and Sarin in 1937 and 1938.[19] They were not used in the war, on account of Hitler's fear of Allied reprisals. I.G. Farben, together with the chemical companies Degussa and Goldschmidt, owned a stake in the insecticide company Degesch which provided the cyanide gas, Zyklon B, used in the mass extermination of concentration camp prisoners at Auschwitz.[20]

In 1957, six years after I.G. Farben was broken up into twelve parts and put into liquidation, the receivers paid DM30 million to the US Conference on Jewish Material Claims against Germany in compensation for the company's treatment of Auschwitz prisoners.[21] The I.G. Farben compensation came several years after the Adenauer government decided in 1951 to pay restitution to victims of Nazism. In the years up to 1988, the Bonn Finance Ministry paid out total compensation of around DM82 billion, roughly 80 per cent of which (including an initial delivery of DM3 billion worth of goods directly to Israel) went to the Jews.[22] German restitution payments, mostly in the form of pensions to Jews living in the US and Israel, are due to continue at the rate of around DM2 billion a year until into the 21st century.

Most of the large German companies which prospered during the war economy quickly established their position in the post-war republic. In contrast to the German state, only a handful however paid compensation for their use of slave labour.[23] One of the most conspicuous was Daimler-Benz, the motor and engineering firm which was one of the chief beneficiaries of the Nazis' armaments build-up, and is today West Germany's most powerful conglomerate.* In June 1988 – forty-three years after the crumbling of Hitler's Germany – Daimler decided to make a DM20 million payment to the US Jewish Claims Conference

* See Chapter 12.

17

and other humanitarian organisations 'to ease consequences still ensuing from those times'.[24]

The I.G. Farben story on prime-time television underlines how, forty years after the war, the Third Reich has a habit of returning. For German TV, used to foreign production teams making the running in resurrecting the past, the showing was an innovation. Bernhard Sinkel, the film's Left-wing producer, told me that when he discussed selling the film to British television, he was told sarcastically, 'Only the BBC is allowed to make films about the Third Reich.'[25] In his late forties, Sinkel is very much a product of Germany's 1960s generation of anti-parent revolt. He says the film was a deliberate bid to help him come to terms with his own family's past. Sinkel's own father worked for I.G. Farben during the war. His great-uncle Fritz ter Meer was the I.G. Farben board member responsible for the company's plant at Auschwitz. Ter Meer was one of thirteen I.G. Farben executives found guilty of war crimes at one of the post-war US trials of leading industrialists at Nuremberg in 1948. He was sentenced to seven years' jail in 1948, but was given early release in 1951, at about the same time that other leading war industrialists such as Alfried Krupp and Friedrich Flick were also being freed. Like many of the I.G. Farben elite, ter Meer went on to help rebuild the 1950s chemical industry, becoming the supervisory board chairman of Bayer.

'Germany exercised its imperialism through the retort flask,' Sinkel told me. People like his great-uncle made themselves guilty by obeying the state's orders. 'The elite, the intelligentsia – what were they doing at Auschwitz? We need to learn the ability to be disobedient,' he says. Sinkel added that the experience of making the film humbled him. 'I realised in the last few years I had to stop making reprimands about my family, and try to put myself in their shoes. I loved my father, but he disappointed me terribly.'

Controversy in the late 1980s over the actual and potential use of poison gas in the Middle East revived memories of I.G. Farben. Deadly quantities of Tabun used in the Iran-Iraq war were rumoured to have stemmed from old Wehrmacht stocks of the gas stored in eastern Europe, which had made their way to the Middle East via the Soviet Union. Reminders of Zyklon B also have a way of coming to the surface. In 1988 the US government called the attention of the Bonn government to evidence that West German companies had helped Libya build a plant capable of making poison gas that might be used against Israel. After the affair was revealed in January 1989, the *New York Times* published this comment, under the headline: 'Germany Can't Ignore Auschwitz-in-the Sand':

One might think that those generation of Germans, aware of the guilt of their fathers in the gassing of millions of innocents not so long ago, would be particularly sensitive to the prospect of complicity in the murder by gas of civilians in a terrorist state today.[26]

The row over responsibility for the Libyan factory cast a shadow over US–West German relations – just one of the reasons behind a growing rift at the end of the 1980s between Washington and its most important ally on the continent. Companies from at least half a dozen countries were thought to have been involved in building the Libyan plant. Because of the Nazi past, the world media singled out the Germans for special attention. Frantically trying to overlook the fact that its own secret service, the Bundesnachrichtendienst (BND)* had also communicated its suspicions about Libya months before, the Bonn government tried foolishly to dismiss the storm as an example of anti-German press campaigning. Underlining his own emotional links to the chemical industry, Chancellor Kohl even told me that complaints in the US media reflected American irritation over German chemicals companies' world-wide dominance.[27]

Degesch, meanwhile, 70 years old in 1989, although absorbed into another company at the beginning of 1990, is still making the same basic products, used now for fumigation and rodent control.[28] Not many German enyclopaediae contain an entry for Zyklon B (now produced under another name). One that does, *Brockhaus*, gave a definition in the mid-1960s which seemed to deny the atrocities of the war. Zyklon B is used, it said, 'for the extermination of vermin, fruit tree pests, and so on', making no mention of its use for mass killing. With the passing of time, however, *Brockhaus* has become more honest. In a new edition in 1988, the encyclopaedia's entry admits that Zyklon gas was used for exterminating prisoners in concentration camps.[29]

III

In December 1987, millions of West German TV viewers received a Sunday midday shock. Werner Höfer, the 74-year-old doyen of West German television, was no longer there to host his long-running weekly

* See Chapter 16.

chat programme, *Der Internationale Frühschoppen*, broadcast from the Westdeutscher Rundfunk (WDR) studios in Cologne. For 36 years, practically without a break, Höfer had been sitting in front of the cameras with five other journalists (nearly always from foreign countries) to discuss topical events over a glass of white wine.

In a country which loves continuity, the ritual was part of a way of life. Höfer, who was well known to have been a member of the Nazi party,[30] gained a reputation after the war as a television liberal and became a senior figure at WDR, the largest public sector broadcasting network. His love for elegant phrasing could verge on verbiage, but a lot of his viewers (especially the older ones) doted on him. Some, including Höfer himself, had been wondering how and when he would eventually bow out. The end came not gracefully, but with a jolt. In December 1987 the news magazine *Der Spiegel* published a story on Höfer which underlined a new severity over the past lives of public figures. After a political flurry and a brusque demand from WDR for Hofer to clear his name, the *Frühschoppen* host resigned in bitterness just before Christmas. In a note of incongruous pique, he enjoined his former employers against any moves to commemorate either his 75th birthday or his death.

The long *Der Spiegel* story documented an article by Hofer in 1943 in a Berlin newspaper harnessed, like the rest of the press, to the Nazi propaganda machine. In it, Höfer unctuously praised the Nazis' killing of Karlrobert Kreiten, a talented young pianist who had been hanged a fortnight earlier for allegedly insulting Hitler. Höfer claimed that the passage had been written into his article without his knowledge by the Propaganda Ministry. In a smear campaign from East Germany during the 1960s, Hofer's condonation of Kreiten's hanging – one of thousands of executions of Germans accused of undermining the war effort – had already been revealed to the West. But then, public opinion seemed ummoved. Many ex-Nazis were holding far more important positions in business and politics – often, people like Höfer who had become embroiled in the movement for reasons of opportunism, cowardice or comfort. Four decades after the end of the war, however, the climate suddenly seemed a lot less forgiving. *Der Spiegel*'s barbs hit home. Höfer launched legal action (which he later lost) to recover DM100,000 damages from *Der Spiegel* for its description of him as a *Schreibtischtäter* (desk-bound criminal), and said his goodbyes, appearing close to tears, on a final TV programme which bordered on an inquisition. Quizzed about his record, he said he was 'ashamed' about his 'lack of courage' under National Socialism. His *Frühschoppen* programme, helping to give post-war viewers a broader view of politics, was an attempt to make amends, he claimed.

Höfer's show was an institution among two generations of foreign correspondents who became his regular guests. Terence Prittie, the veteran *Manchester Guardian* correspondent and author, in 1983 called it 'probably the most popular television programme' in Germany and said its success illustrated West Germany's 'growing political awareness' and a slackening of 'veneration of the *Obrigkeiten* (authorities)'.[31] Having taken part myself about half a dozen times, I had been startled by the programme's following. German people recognising me after this brief number of appearances included a policeman, several taxi-drivers, a member of the audience at a political rally, a drunken guest at a fight at a neighbour's party (most unusual in sleepy Bad Godesberg) and Prince Louis Ferdinand, the head of the German royal family. Even though I believed that Höfer should probably have bowed out several years before, I felt the manner of his departure was over-harsh, and went to see him several months afterwards at his Rhineside home, south of Cologne.

Höfer told me in October 1988 that he had received 3,000 letters, all but a handful supporting him. They included many from foreign journalists who had appeared on his programme over the years. 'If you take 1,000 German journalists who could read and write and worked under the Third Reich, there were not five who with their hearts and minds were really in favour of the system. We were waiting for the day when it would end.'[32] He saw *Frühschoppen* virtually as his life's work. What were the reasons for its extraordinary success? 'There is no other big country so interested in the rest of the world as we are – partly because we want to see if the rest of the world likes us.' Höfer recalled that he had been a prisoner-of-war for six months at the end of the war. The British occupation authorities investigated his Nazi past before he got a job in 1946 with the Nordwestdeutscher Rundfunk, the broadcasting precursor of WDR*. His career was advanced in particular by Hugh Carleton Greene, in charge of British-controlled broadcasting in north Germany. 'If I had really done such terrible things, then people who would have read the articles would have come forward then,' he said. Why the outcry over the revelations now, when they were basically known already? Höfer hinted at some form of conspiracy to get rid of him at WDR, adding bitterly: 'If I had been a war criminal, I would be in freedom now.'

* See Chapter 8.

When I asked Rudolf Augstein, founder and publisher of *Der Spiegel*, for his version of the affair, he admitted he felt sorry for Höfer and had tried to warn him. 'I knew it would destroy him inwardly.'[33] Augstein told me that on two previous occasions, incriminating stories about Höfer were kept out of his magazine. Augstein's hand was forced by the strength of feeling of younger journalists on his paper that the article should be published – even though few of the details of Höfer's propaganda work were new. Augstein said, 'People are more strict over the past because the real perpetrators are no longer with us.' Could it be that the Germans like feeling guilty? The Germans, he says, 'are a guilt culture'. Sardonically, he pinpoints the difference as compared with Germany's former allies: 'The Japanese are a face culture, bent on saving face. They would go to Auschwitz and take photos of each other.'

Hildegard Hamm-Brücher, the veteran deputy from the Free Democratic Party, also believes people are taking a tougher view of the Nazi period.[34] Born in 1921, she was a friend of Hans and Sophie Scholl, two young students who were beheaded for treason in February 1943 after mounting a solitary anti-Hitler protest at Munich University. They have since become symbols for the courage of the few who stood up vainly against totalitarianism. Warning against complacency over West Germany's democracy, Hamm-Brücher says that younger people after the war were not told the whole truth about the foundations of the new state. Denazification was extremely limited; in the first Bundestag in 1949, 57 deputies were former members of the Nazi party or related organisations, she says.

Konrad Adenauer, the dominant figure in early West German politics, Chancellor between 1949 and 1963, was notorious for choosing former Third Reich administrators as advisers, but few at the time seemed to mind.[35] One of the most striking examples of restoration of figures from the Third Reich was Adenauer's chief confidant Hans Globke, who served until his retirement in 1963 as state secretary in the Chancellery. In 1935 Globke wrote the commentary to the racist Nuremberg decrees forbidding marriage and sexual relations between Jews and non-Jews – later punishable by death – and taking away their right to vote.* Kurt Georg Kiesinger, Prime Minister of Baden-Württemberg between 1958 and 1966, and then Chancellor in Bonn in the 1966-69 Grand Coalition government, was a member of the Nazis

* See Chapter 10.

between 1933 and 1945, although he appeared not to play an active role in the party.[36] Karl Blessing, the first president between 1957 and 1969 of the independent central bank, the Bundesbank – perhaps West Germany's most respected institution – joined the Nazis in 1937 and in 1939 became a member of the circle of industrialists and businessmen grouped around Heinrich Himmler, the SS leader.[37] Blessing was not a convinced National Socialist, and his name was on the list of candidates for high economic office drawn up by the conspirators who tried to kill Hitler on 20 July 1944.[38] However, Blessing's highly ambiguous position during the Third Reich was given little attention during his twelve years as Bundesbank chief.*

The Germans described 1945 as '*Stunde Null*' – zero hour: a new start. The horrors, the lunacies, the shame before that date were deliberately – and perhaps inevitably – pushed into the background. Freed from Hitler the 'magician-manipulator',[39] the post-1945 Germans were only too willing to accept the myth that his spell alone accounted for the destruction of civilised values and the violation of human rights. As the shutters came down on the view back to the Third Reich, Germany swivelled into a new relationship with the conquerors. The defeated nation became a focus of ideological and military struggle between the US and the Soviet Union. The Germans in East and West identified themselves with their respective victor power – almost as if they had been on the same side all along.

Amid the helter-skelter of reconstruction, guilt about the Nazi state was 'swept away with the rubble', Hamm-Brücher says. Only now, after more than forty years, do the Germans have the necessary distance from events to re-examine the past; and a new period of reckoning is under way, opening up old wounds thought cauterised. She says that the Germans have faced up neither to the 'great crimes' of the Third Reich nor to the countless smaller cases of individual entanglement such as Höfer's. 'Now these cases are coming up again, and the younger generation is starting to ask: What really happened after 1945? What have you – parents and grandparents – done to free yourselves from Nazism?'

However, a great many Germans disagree with Hamm-Brücher. Helmut Kohl, aged 15 when the war ended, the first post-war Chancellor too young to have been involved in the conflict, puts forward another view which, in its own way, sums up equally well the feelings of his compatriots:

* See Chapter 6.

The Germans are extraordinarily peaceful. They have become rather sated. They are entirely normal people, just like in Britain. What do they want? They want to live in peace. They want to live in freedom. They want social justice. They want a good livelihood. They want to find happiness in life. They want to be glad. They don't want to walk around stressed, confronted from morning till evening with the burden of history. There are however people who want to persuade us that we should not be allowed to do this. There are of course people who say, 'How is it that those who produced the Nazis and lost the war are now the most important exporting country in the world?'[27]

Almost certainly, most people in West Germany today – two-thirds of whom were born after Hitler came to power – are, like Kohl, tired of apologising for the Nazis.[40] An opinion poll carried out for the centenary of Hitler's birth in April 1989 indicated that 26 per cent of present-day Germans had either a good or a neutral opinion of the Führer. Without the war and extermination of the Jews, 38 per cent thought that Hitler would have gone down in history as 'one of the great German statesmen'. This was a lower percentage than in the 1950s – but higher than the numbers registered in a similar poll in 1978.[41] On the other hand, a sizeable proportion of people, both old and young, stick to the view that it would be fatal if the skeletons of the Third Reich were ever locked away. The split is hopeless but one irony has to be noted: even those who want to escape the past somehow cannot stop talking about it.

IV

Catharsis arrived in Germany in spring 1945. In mid-March, Hitler – six weeks away from suicide on 30 April in his Berlin bunker – told his Armaments Minister Albert Speer: 'If the war is lost, the people will be lost also.'[42] The Führer's vision was considerably more apocalyptic than the proposal to 'pastoralise' Germany entertained in the short-lived plan of US Treasury Secretary Henry Morgenthau the previous autumn.[43] Hitler decreed that the country should be reduced to scorched earth. All transport, industry, communications and food-supply facilities should be destroyed in the path of the enemy. 'It is not necessary to worry about what the people will need for elemental survival. On the contrary, it is best for us to destroy even these things. For the nation has proved to be the weaker, and the future belongs solely to the stronger eastern nation. In any case only those who are inferior will remain after this struggle, for the good have already been killed.'

Hitler's demonic orders, wrote the historian Golo Mann, were the fulfilment of an innermost wish:

> *Götterdämmerung* in death and flames. Conscious or unconscious, that had been his aim; in the end, his whole unbelievable career served only to realise this dream. He wanted to wrench Germany with him into ruin; to make his funeral pyre a spectacle for the going down of the world.[44]

Disobedience had not been a feature of the Third Reich. Briefly, it flowered now. Assisted by parts of the Wehrmacht and even some local *Gauleiter*, Speer frustrated Hitler's directive of complete destruction. None the less, when at the end of the war Britain's Air Marshal Sir Arthur (later Lord) Tedder surveyed the major cities devastated by Allied bombing, he was reminded of Babylon and Carthage.[45] Alfried Krupp, the heir to the great armaments empire which had fired the German military machine in three wars since 1870, surveyed the ruins of his dynasty's home city of Essen; he thought that the rubble would take fifty years to clear.[46]

Hitler left behind 55 million dead and the destruction of the European order. In the motley documents which passed for his testament, he directed his paintings to his home town of Linz; to the German people was addressed the last command to 'observe painstakingly the race laws and oppose ruthlessly the poisoners of all nations – international Jewry'.[47] Carrying out the Führer's last orders, Hitler's SS followers burned his corpse, along with that of Eva Braun, in the garden of his Berlin bunker.[48] The flames also singed away old German illusions. New realities were forged out of the slag of war.

The Führer's heritage was to stretch far into the future – for better and for worse. The bonfire of German ambitions left two German states – one capitalist, one Communist. For both of them, the Third Reich would provide a warning signpost for the years ahead, always accompanying the journey. Paradoxically, the majority of Germans who survived the fighting and the first mean, hungry, dangerous years of occupation under the four victor powers benefited from his legacy. The Morgenthau Plan was forgotten as America concentrated efforts on shoring up the new western republic eventually born in 1949. President

Truman's adage was that 'hungry people are bad democrats'. Economic and political reconstruction went hand in hand. The country was spurred by booming world markets, the currency reform of June 1948*, American economic assistance and, above all, the energy and enterprise of the German people. The Federal Republic started along the path of the *Wirtschaftswunder*, while in Soviet-occupied East Germany, the new masters took over Nazi prisons and propaganda policies and adapted them to another form of totalitarian rule.

A document in November 1948 from the military government in the combined US-British zone spelled out the emerging realities of European economic inter-dependence which, in the 1950s, culminated in the forging of the Common Market.† The document underlined the fact that economic weakness at the centre of Europe was hurting the West. The low level of German imports was 'resulting in economic as well as political dislocations in many places'. Anticipating what would become a *Leitmotif* of US policies towards Europe, it added: 'It is no longer seriously disputed that without a healthy prosperous Germany there can be no effective European recovery.'[49]

After the mass migration set in train by the Communist takeover across eastern Europe, by 1950 the Federal Republic was home for 70 per cent of the people living in the two new German states. In 1953, in a symbolic act demonstrating that the Federal Republic had become, in international law, the successor of the German nation, Bonn took over the Third Reich's foreign debts. By 1954, exports were five times the 1949 level, and West Germany had built up a large creditor position towards its European trading partners.

Henry Wallich, who during the 1970s became a governor of the Federal Reserve Board, the US central bank, observed the transformation with mixed feelings. Wallich came from a German Jewish banking family. His father held a senior post at the Dreyfus bank which was sold in 1937-38 to the Munich banking firm Merck, Finck & Co. as part of a tide of 'Aryanisation' of Jewish businesses.** Paul Wallich, pressed by the increasing force of anti-Semitism but reluctant to face new uncertainties by emigrating to the US, committed suicide in Cologne in November 1938. His farewell note to his son – 'Things in Germany are no longer tolerable' – was written two days after the organised burning of synagogues on *Reichskristallnacht*, the Night of Broken Glass, on 9 November.[50] After succeeding in fleeing to the US,

* See Chapter 6.
† See Chapter 3.
** See Chapter 10.

26

Henry Wallich in 1955 ruminated on the reasons for the German economic revival in the columns of the *Yale University Review:*

> It is largely thanks to the East-West split that things have worked out so differently for West Germany: the rapid mutation from foe to friend, the shift of occupation policy from holding down to building up, the flow of Marshall Aid. For all this, Germany has had to pay the heavy price of partition. This is a national tragedy, and may be the cause of trouble in the future. But economically, West Germany has suffered surprisingly little from partition.[51]

Wallich ended his well-balanced account on a note of foreboding, not surprising in the light of his experiences: 'The present political and cultural vacuum in Germany compels one to consider what might fill it ... The existing condition appears unstable, and in danger of being displaced by some new enthusiasm. God help Germany and the world if it is again the wrong one.'

In fact, Germany's new enthusiasm was channelled not into politics, but into factories and workshops. Rolling up the sleeves was a way of exorcising the bad memories. Theodor Heuss, the liberal Swabian journalist who in 1949 became West Germany's first president, said in 1946: 'We are the trustees of the most infamous and fraudulent bankruptcy in history. We have practically only one chance – and that is work.'[52] From the economic point of view the loss of great territories in the East – through the separation of East and West Germany and the annexation by Poland of land east of the Oder/Neisse line – turned out to be a blessing in disguise for the fledgling Federal Republic. It lost its sprawling agrarian regions, accounting for about one-quarter of Germany's pre-war production of bread grains. However, Germany could draw on powerful manufacturing traditions laid down at the end of the 19th century. It rediscovered an export culture which had been dissipated during the Depression of the early 1930s and under the drive for autarchy of the Third Reich.

Germany turned to exports both to pay back foreign debts and also as a symbol of moral renewal. Edzard Reuter, the son of Ernst Reuter, the post-war Social Democrat mayor of West Berlin, is today chairman of the motor group Daimler-Benz. The Reuter family fled abroad in 1933 to escape the Nazis' persecution of Social Democrats. Ironically, in 1988-89 Reuter became embroiled in a political row over his company's growing armaments reach, which brought back memories of the company's role in the Third Reich.* Reflecting on the post-war

---

* See Chapter 12.

27

recovery, Reuter said in 1987: 'The motto *"exportare necesse est"* was an important way of regaining international independence and respect after the ignominy of Hitler's atrocities.'[53]

The catharsis also at last brought forth respect for democratic tolerance among a people always held to be unpolitical. In spite of periodic worries about its long-term resilience, the overall strength of West Germany's political system has been the most impressive feature of recovery. Hitler's 'last goal' had been to destroy Germany, wrote the historian Sebastian Haffner. But he achieved the opposite: 'Germany broke away from him much more quickly than hoped, and more thoroughly.' In France, he pointed out, only thirty-three years after the fall of Napoleon, a new Napoleon was elected president of the republic; in Germany, support for neo-Nazi parties has remained negligible.[54] One of the Federal Republic's most thoughtful diplomats, Karl-Günther von Hase, points out that present-day support for democracy is partly a reaction to what went before:

There would be far more dissatisfaction with the political system if we didn't have the past to remind us. We would have more calls for order and strong men. We learned the hard way the truth of Churchill's remark that democracy is the worst form of government but for all the others.[55]

V

Recovery, of course, was not the whole story. Restricted in their options and in their outlook, the Germans lost their self-confidence for good and evil alike. For two inter-linking reasons, the damage to their psyche was long-lasting. Hitler's dictatorship was overthrown not by the Germans themselves, but by foreign armies; and the price paid was dismemberment of the nation. It left bruised pride, suspicion and silence. For reasons which are only too understandable, the post-war Germans hid the experience of the Third Reich from themselves – and from their offspring.

The lack of a functioning German resistance was part of the Federal Republic's uncomfortable birthright. Belief that there was no viable resistance to Hitler led President Roosevelt and Churchill to declare in January 1943 their aim (to which Stalin quickly adhered) of forcing unconditional German surrender. Just over two years later, in April

1945, Russian and American troops advancing from East and West shook hands symbolically at Torgau on the Elbe near Leipzig. The decisiveness of the victory ruled out any post-war revival of Weimar-type legends about German defeat at the hands of 'enemies within'. There could be no 'stab in the back', for Germany's back was broken. On the other hand, had negotiations been possible with an alternative government in Berlin, peace would have come earlier, and perhaps at the Rhine and the Oder. As it was, Germany ceased to play its historical role as a buffer to the might of Russia. As Stalin said at the Potsdam conference, Germany simply ceased to exist.*

Responsibility for the ensuing division of Europe was shared among many nations, but the prime progenitor was Hitler. The Catholic Church sees partition as a penance. Cardinal Joachim Meisner, formerly Bishop of East and West Berlin, is now Archbishop of Cologne – a peculiar reminder of the way both the Catholic and Protestant Churches bridge the East-West German divide.** In a sermon in 1985 commemorating the 40th anniversary of the end of the war, he declared:

> The division of Europe, yes, of the world, and above all the division of our Fatherland ... belongs to the saddest and most tragic consequences. The wretched result of sin is always separation: the separation from God, and separation of people.[56]

Ernst Breit, the head of West Germany's Trade Union Federation (DGB), a Social Democrat who proclaims his wish for the two Germanys to come together in a single state, puts it more simply. 'What we are complaining about,' he says lugubriously, 'is the consequence of German policies.'[57]

Dispute about the consequences of the unconditional surrender objective ran through the early years of the Federal Republic. The proclaimed war aim of occupying and breaking Germany represented a further hurdle for any opponent of the Nazis who had not already been jailed or murdered. Taking up arms against Hitler risked precipitating the tearing apart of the nation. As the Wehrmacht made its retreat through eastern Europe, exposing the civil population to the Soviet Army bent on vengeance for German cruelties, the dilemma for anti-Hitler elements in the army was near-impossible, and the attempt to blow up Hitler on 20 July 1944 came when the end was already within sight.

* See Chapter 3.
** See Chapter 16.

The officer behind the assassination attempt, Colonel Claus Schenk von Stauffenberg, was promptly executed, and an estimated total of 4,980 people suspected of complicity in the plot were put to death. Only in recent years has Stauffenberg become accepted as a war hero in the Federal Republic.[58] In the early post-war years admiration for the officer's bravery was tempered by disapproval over his breaking of the army oath of allegiance to Hitler. According to an Allensbach opinion poll in 1964, only 29 per cent of the population took a favourable view of such wartime resistance by a soldier. As the passage of time brought a new perspective, the percentage rose to 60 per cent by 1985. From time to time, calls are made to proclaim 20 July as West Germany's national day, replacing the melancholy 17 June (Day of German Unity), which marks the anniversary of the uprising by East Berlin workers in 1953. But the dilemma over the historical treatment of the resistance provides one reason why the campaign for 20 July has not so far gained a following.[59]

Why was Hitler not stopped by the Germans themselves? Post-war incomprehension has lain bare the generation gap. Prince Louis Ferdinand, the grandson of William II, who was forced to abdicate at the end of the First World War, is now a benevolent old man of 80 with a taste for horse-riding and sherry. He spent most of the Second World War on a Hohenzollern family estate near Danzig. He knew some of the 20 July conspirators, but had nothing to do with the plot. The Prince has somehow gained a reputation since the war as a kind of *résistant*. When I suggested to him that, if he had really opposed Hitler, he would probably be dead, Louis – in the one angry moment during our interview – retorted that I was being 'cruel and cynical'.[60]

Just as older people living through Hitler's time have been too eager to cover up their actions or hide behind self-pity, the young generation forty years afterwards is too quick to criticise, says Manfred Rommel, the Christian Democrat mayor of Stuttgart. A well-respected liberal conservative, he is the son of the legendary Field-Marshal Erwin Rommel who was forced to commit suicide in 1944 after discovery of his opposition to Hitler.[61] Speaking in his cavernous office at Stuttgart city hall, the mayor says that the younger generation scorns as 'old donkeys' those who did nothing to impede the Nazis. But such critics are blind to the real nature of a totalitarian state. 'Under the Third Reich, critics of the system had their heads taken off. Nowadays, they appear on television,' Rommel says. The Germans are indulging in their tendency to moralise, he states. 'So many authors say the Germans have not regretted enough, have not mourned. I must say I have regretted a lot.

30

But I cannot mourn from morning to evening. One should think of tomorrow, not just yesterday.'[62]

VI

The past remains preoccupying – and not just to those old enough to have played an active part in the war. One reason why the effect has lingered is because most of the present generation of West German opinion-leaders – politicians, business leaders, journalists – are in their fifties and sixties. They lived through the war as children, when trauma takes hold. Among the seminal memories of Helmut Kohl are the 100 bombing raids on his home town of Ludwigshafen, the miraculous post-war Care packets from the US, and the suicides at Christmas 1945. Hans-Dietrich Genscher, Foreign Minister since 1974, was born near Halle in Saxony in what is now East Germany. He recalls the shock, as an 18-year-old, of seeing the Red Army take over his native region in July 1945 as US and Soviet troops moved to their agreed postwar occupation zones and American soldiers pulled out of Thuringia and Saxony.[63]

One solid company man to whom I was talking stopped, by chance, in mid-lunch bite to relate the nightmare of his experience in 1945 fleeing from the Soviet zone, as people and their possessions were trampled over by Russian military horses. A senior Bonn official takes up a great deal of time in a conversation about economic policy regaling me with memories of being driven out of German-speaking Czechoslovakia in January 1946. Reflecting that Germany cannot afford any resurgence of nationalism, he points out that initials such as SS (for instance on car number plates or to denote 'state secretary') are still banned. 'When I see American football supporters shouting, I get gooseflesh,' he says. Even on trains, conversations can turn easily to past terrors. A chance acquaintance in a buffet carriage, a 44-year-old survivor of the destruction of Dresden in 1945 – when he was one year old – insists on telling me his story. His uncle, the mayor, had been given a tip-off ahead of the murderous Anglo-American bombardment. 'We Germans would not be so concerned with the past if we had solved it,' he adds, brooding over his bottle of Bitburg beer.

The Germans have turned their backs on demagoguery; yet Hitler remains the fundamental yardstick of modern German politics. The almost pathological desire to reject the black side of life helps to explain

31

the mawkishness of many politicians' public utterances. The Third Reich has also poisoned the German language. Politicians of Left and Right regularly swap insults by declaring each other to be Nazis. Christian Democrats will tell rowdy hecklers that they are behaving like the SA;[64] Social Democrats may say that experiments in genetic engineering are a throwback to the Third Reich.[65] The Social Democrats forever like to remind the conservatives that they were the only party to vote against Hitler's Enabling Act in March 1933. Walter Wallmann, the Christian Democrat Prime Minister of Hesse, tried to get his own back in October 1989 when he declared that the Social Democrats had supported Hitler in a Reichstag foreign policy motion in May 1933, and had even sung the *Deutschlandlied* together with the Nazis. The ensuing row, in which leading Social Democrats protested that their party half a century earlier was acting under massive duress, including death threats, rumbled on for months.

The study of Nazi vocabulary has become an etymological growth industry.[66] Proof of Hitler's contorted modernising influence is that many German words misused by the Nazis – ranging from concentration camp terminology to expressions in sport and culture – are either avoided or replaced by foreign ones. I was once told by Björn Engholm, one of the brightest hopes of the younger generation of Social Democrats, that even the word *Macht* (power) should be avoided when talking about politicians taking office.[67]

One of the reasons why Helmut Kohl ran into difficulties in the early 1980s in trying to reintroduce the use of the word 'Fatherland' is because the term was despoiled by Hitler. The Third Reich has left behind linguistic traps for unwary politicians. Take, for example, Kohl's speech in 1983, comparing the style of the new Christian Democrat government with the previous thirteen years of Social Democrat rule between 1969 and 1982:

> The people who most severely denounce our modern technological civilisation are at the same time the sharpest critics of our system of values. They work their scorn on expressions like loyalty (*Treue*) and home (*Heimat*), fulfilment of duty (*Pflichterfüllung*) and Fatherland (*Vaterland*), human warmth (*menschliche Wärme*) and family (*Familie*) ... Therefore, my friends, renewing the spiritual-moral foundations of politics is so important.[68]

Shortly after Hitler came to power in 1933, he used terminology of striking similarity to lambast the previous fourteen years of democratic government under the Weimar Republic.

Starting with the family (*Familie*), extending through all expressions of honour (*Ehre*) and loyalty (*Treue*), people (*Volk*) and Fatherland (*Vaterland*), culture (*Kultur*) and business (*Wirtschaft*), up to the eternal foundations of our morality (*Moral*) and our faith (*Glaube*), nothing has been spared from this drive to negate and destroy. Fourteen years of Marxism have ruined Germany.[69]

Kohl should have been warned. One of his top advisers, Wolfgang Bergsdorf – a conservative professor who helped model the Chancellor's public relations during the 1980s – has persuasively explained that words like 'nation' or 'Fatherland' are still 'suffering from the encumbrance of National Socialism'.[70] The dilemma for West German politicians is that, if they try to preach a return to traditional virtues, they can very easily end up sounding like Nazis.

One man who blundered into a minefield over the Third Reich was Philipp Jenninger, the president or Speaker of the Bundestag – in constitutional terms, second only to the federal president.[71] Jenninger, affable, owlish and bespectacled, is a confidant of Kohl and has no pretension to brain-power. In November 1988 Jenninger, eager to establish himself as an orator, made a speech in the Bundestag to commemorate the 50th anniversary of the anti-Jewish pogrom of *Reichskristallnacht*. In a misguided attempt to 'explain' Hitler's popularity, he quoted large tracts of Nazi propaganda, distinctly failing to find the eloquence and the emotion to fit the occasion.[72] Kohl had been making an effort to repair relations with the Jews which had been damaged by his joint visit with President Reagan to SS war graves at Bitburg during Reagan's West German visit in 1985. An outcry from many deputies – not only Social Democrats – left Kohl with little choice but to ask his friend to resign, and he stepped down twenty-four hours later.[73]

The affair came a day after Kohl, showing once again the quality of his speech-writers, had given a thoughtful address on the 9 November anniversary at the West End synagogue in Frankfurt. No one accused Jenninger of sympathising with National Socialism, but his tactlessness attracted world-wide publicity and, however unfairly, supported prejudices abroad that the Germans had failed to learn from history. Perhaps the most astonishing feature of Jenninger's speech – though hardly noticed at the time – was his reference to the Weimar Republic as a 'system'. This was the contemptuous phrase used by opponents of the republic during the 1920s. It was almost as if Jenninger was showing his agreement with the many Germans sixty years ago who, in self-pity and, in the end, self-destruction, regarded the Weimar democracy as no more than an example of western corruption.

33

VII

The fear among even sober-minded people that old demons have not been securely locked away is an element behind general caution in West German economic policies – for instance, over the risks of inflation or excess government spending. The memory of the great 1920s inflation is kept alive in a variety of ways. The West German savings banks, for example, feature pictures of 500-billion Mark notes issued in 1923 in newspaper advertisements preaching the virtues of low inflation.

One of the *éminences grises* of the business world, Rudolf von Bennigsen-Foerder, the chairman of the Veba energy and chemicals group, has a strong sense of history.* He can trace his aristocratic Hanoverian family tree back to the year 1200. His forebear, Rudolf von Bennigsen, founded the National Liberal Party in 1866, which worked hand in hand with Bismarck to unite the Reich in 1871. Bennigsen-Foerder, a member of the Christian Democrats but a wily operator in dealings with all the political parties, believes that present-day politics are framed by *Angst*: 'The Germans have suffered during their history a series of monumental reverses. We have been burdened by fate to be more fearful than other people – and more concerned about our security. A young man at the age of 20 starting a job, for instance, is worried about how high his pension will be.'[74]

History also colours international relationships. Former Chancellor Helmut Schmidt, who left office in 1982, is now past 70. These days he is a successful author and co-publisher of the weekly newspaper *Die Zeit*. He speaks in his cramped offices at *Die Zeit* accompanied by spurts of snuff; with a trace of self-mockery, he says he shares the habit with Frederick the Great. Schmidt is anxious about the eventual consequences on the world economy of the enormous US balance of payments and budget deficits, and the corresponding surpluses built up by Japan and West Germany. He tells me, full of foreboding:

> The people of New York will deeply resent a situation where the two countries which started the Second World War, and lost it totally, become the greatest creditors, maybe arriving at a position where they can dictate conditions. It will go far beyond New York and the Jews of New York city.[75]

* Bennigsen-Foerder died unexpectedly in October 1989.

VIII

The key to the puzzle over the past seems to lie in German dualism. Memories of the Third Reich are a troublesome burden. But the Germans feel secure under the shadow – insurance against anything similar happening again. They appear to feel strong only if they remind themselves of their own fragility.

At the Bundestag ceremony in May 1985 to commemorate the 40th anniversary of Germany's capitulation, President Richard von Weizsäcker told present-day Germans that they were 'liable' for the past, warned sternly against rewriting history and said they had a duty to 'keep alive' memories of German crimes. Weizsäcker's address was printed in 2.5 million copies, translated into most European languages as well as Japanese and Chinese, and turned into a 245-page school textbook. The speech had an immense impact, especially on younger Germans; the president's office received 60,000 letters. In one of the signs of growing East-West German understanding, a few weeks after the breaching of the Wall in November 1989, a leading East Berlin publisher agreed to bring out in East Germany a collected version of Weizsäcker's speeches.

Weizsäcker's move to persuade his countrymen and women to confront the past is driven by strong personal motives as well as by a form of moral *raison d'état*. As a young infantryman in the Wehrmacht, Weizsäcker took part in the invasion of Poland in September 1939; his elder brother was killed there on the second day of action. His father, Ernst von Weizsäcker, was a top career diplomat in the Third Reich, serving from 1938 to 1943 as chief state secretary in the Foreign Ministry under Joachim von Ribbentrop, who was hanged after being found guilty of war crimes at Nuremberg in 1946. The elder Weizsäcker played an important part in preparing the non-aggression pact with Moscow in August 1939 under which the Soviet Union and Germany agreed to divide Poland between them – preparing the way for the Second World War.

Weizsäcker survived the rigours of the eastern front and ended the war as a captain. He helped to defend his father from charges as a war criminal at a later Nuremberg tribunal. The state secretary was imprisoned but amnestied after 18 months in jail.[76] In his 1985 speech, Weizsäcker appeared to be thinking of his father – and also perhaps of himself – when he admitted, 'There were many ways of not burdening

35

one's conscience ... When the unspeakable truth of the Holocaust became known at the end of the war, all too many of us claimed that we had not known anything about it or even suspected anything.' Weizsäcker, on the liberal wing of the Christian Democrats, regularly runs into pungent criticism from ultra-conservatives – especially some of the new far-Right parties which gained support at the end of the 1980s. They accuse the president of being over-ready, because of his family history, to apologise for the Second World War.

Weizsäcker's 1985 speech provided the background to an academic dispute on the origins of the Holocaust which burst out in a flood of newspaper articles, books and lectures in 1986. The *Historikerstreit* (Quarrel of the Historians) was in a sense a typically German dispute: nowhere else would professors have received so much attention. The debate may have been about the past, but it was an attempt to point the way towards the future. Ernst Nolte, the Right-wing historian from Berlin's Free University, sparked it off in an article in the conservative *Frankfurter Allgemeine Zeitung* (*FAZ*), arguing that the Nazis' extermination of the Jews was a reaction to the massacres practised by the Bolsheviks after the 1917 revolution. Put at its simplest, Nolte's message was that the Nazis murdered the Jews because Hitler feared that, otherwise, Soviet Communists (regarded as Jewish-supported) would murder the Germans.[77]

Nolte's postulation that the crimes against the Jews were simply 'copies' of Russian ones marked the first round of ferocious swapping of blows among rival groups of Left- and Right-wing historians. But the *Historikerstreit* spilled out far beyond academe. Nolte and his supporters were seeking to renegotiate and diminish the national mortgage of guilt. Arguing that Auschwitz had a precedent in the 'Asiatic' deeds under Bolshevism, they sought to redistribute responsibility for the evils of the Third Reich. Nolte complained that 'the past hangs over the present like an executioner's sword'; he was trying to blunt it a little. Reaction and counterreaction are bound to rumble on. Not least, the far-Right political parties seem to have gained support from Nolte-like feelings in the general population that agonising over the past has gone far enough.

Joachim Fest, the author and historian who is one of the co-publishers of the *FAZ*, came down on Nolte's side during the dispute. Fest has become Germany's master-biographer of Hitler; after spending twenty-five years delving into the Third Reich, he says there is nothing new to say on the subject. He was brought up before the war in Karlshorst, the villa-lined suburb of Berlin, now in the eastern sector of the city, which has been used continuously since May 1945 as Soviet military headquarters. Fest believes that preoccupation with the Nazis will not weaken. Suspicious of a Soviet move to split off the Federal Republic from the rest of the West, he remarks, 'I fear sometimes that anti-Americanism in Germany and isolationism in the US could play into each other's hands; the result would be terrible.'[78]

Fest says the Germans have become hopelessly beset by a yearning 'to cut themselves free from the troubles of the world'. At the beginning of the 1970s, he wrote approvingly in the final chapter of his study on Hitler that the younger German generation had at last become realists; something, he says with a grimace, he would not write today. All the while, the clouds of guilt and worry scud overhead. 'The shadow of Hitler will remain for a long time; it is not to be put aside. With the same perfectionism with which they put Europe under their heel, the Germans now wear the sackcloth,' he says. 'The Germans are enthusiastic about this role, and other countries get their advantage too. It is so well-practised. It has become a stereotype. Why should it change?'

3

The Dilemma of East and West

I never thought more about the East than during the time I was looking
for an understanding with the West.

Gustav Stresemann, 1927[1]

The part of Germany which is not occupied by Russia is an integrated
part of western Europe. If this part remains sick, it will produce the
most difficult consequences for western Europe, including for England
and France.

Konrad Adenauer, 1945[2]

The Soviet Union is interested in good security for the Federal
Republic of Gemany. If the Federal Republic were unstable, there
could be no hope of stability for Europe, and hence for the world.

Mikhail Gorbachev, 1987[3]

Germany's turbulent fate over the centuries has been guided by
philosophers, princes and popes, statesmen, storm-troopers and steel
barons. But it is the cartographers who have always had the last word.
An amorphous land in the centre of Europe, undulated and atomised by
hills and forests, it is open to the world and closed to itself. The
metaphysics of its geography have shaped its history. Germany's
frontiers are permanent only in their impermanence, an invitation and a
threat for foreign armies; its internal topography disperses ideas to the
corners and hampers the centralisation of influence.

Across 80 per cent of the terrain today covered by West Germany, the
view is limited to 1,000 metres.[4] The statistic, much regarded by
military strategists and makers of battle tanks, is also significant for
students of national psychology. Germany may have the look of a
causeway between eastern and western Europe, but the road sometimes
forks off to become a maze, and may even come to a dead end against a
wire fence unfurled with precision across the landscape. With the
dismantling of the ugly East German frontier in autumn 1989, the
barbed wire has now come down. Across what used to be the barren

38

no-man's-land of the border regions are now leaping the sparks of German unity.

Germany is the central component in the checks and balances of European power. 'Whoever holds Germany, holds Europe,' said Lenin; for Churchill, Germany was the 'keystone of Europe'. But equilibrium has been reached only seldom. Coexistence with its neighbours has brought centuries rarely punctuated by anything but deprivation and disaster. Germany's position as *das Land in der Mitte* – the land in the middle – has either forced upon it weakness and fragmentation or tempted it, with catastrophic consequences, to over-try its strength.

Seventy-four years of unity created in 1871 and destroyed in 1945 gave way to a provisional, only superficially stable, phase of German division. Partition started with a paradox. Each of the two German states set up in 1949 was needed by its sponsor superpower to act as an opposing pole to the other – one to spearhead the spread of Communism, the other to resist it. But at the same time, West Germany's constitution placed the reattainment of national unity as its highest political goal. The 1949 Basic Law, deliberately construed as provisional since it was promulgated only for the western half of the nation, sets down the objective of achieving 'in free self-determination the unity and freedom of Germany'. One set of strategic magnets kept East and West Germany apart – and another all the time was drawing them together.

Late 1980s détente between the US and the Soviet Union changed the polarity of the European force field more thoroughly than many at the time realised. America's financial difficulties and reassessment of its international priorities are inevitably weakening its strategic bonds to western Europe; the threatened break-up of the Soviet empire is clearly refocussing Moscow's attentions too. The drawing back of the super-powers, and the process of political and economic fusion now under way between the East and West German states, make it likely that Germany will emerge in the 1990s as the dominant force in central Europe. The upheavals in the East-West constellation are inevitably forcing changes in the structure of the military alliances which framed the post-war reconstruction of Europe; but changes in NATO are not going ahead fast enough to satisfy the Germans. In spite of its energy and industry over 40 years, the Federal Republic has not been able to change one salient consequence of the Second World War: the power, in terms of interna-tional law, to decide the final post-war shape of the nation rests with the US, the Soviet Union, Britain and France. None of these four has quite trusted the Germans; and the potential is now increasing for that distrust to come to the surface.

I

For four decades, the Federal Republic has maintained an astonishingly successful balancing act. It has achieved economic, political and cultural integration with the West, and has restored its East-facing options. Now, the opportunities in the East are starting to look increasingly alluring.

The strains appearing between the Federal Republic and the US are not completely new, for the relationship has never been an easy one. The US forced Germany to its knees in 1945, hoisted the western half back on to its feet, and now sometimes becomes alarmed when its forty-year-old client state shows signs of wanting to stand up to its full height. Both sides see the problems in parental terms. Robert Leicht, deputy editor of the weekly *Die Zeit*, says, 'Unlike the English or the French, we learned democracy from American soldiers smoking Lucky Strike. It's associated not just with gratitude but also with bad memories. The relationship is just as difficult as that of children to their parents. It can go on like this even when the child is 60 and the parent is 80.'[5] One senior US diplomat describes relations in the language of the consulting room:

> Germany has a history both good and bad. It is a divided country. It faces the most serious security threat of any country in the Alliance. I'm like a psychiatrist who has to see a child from a broken home with complex problems. I take time with that child, and then I have to go back to Washington to explain it to the child's parents.

At the beginning of the 1980s, during the row over stationing American Pershing II and cruise missiles in the Federal Republic, the two countries already went through serious discord. Towards the end of his tenure, Chancellor Schmidt was forced to deny from time to time that his country was turning neutralist. Relations improved at first under the centre-Right Kohl administration which took office in 1982, but drifted back towards the rocks later in the 1980s. The German and US political establishments are growing apart – a trend which developed under the presidencies of Jimmy Carter and Ronald Reagan, and is likely to continue under George Bush. American capacity to maintain the Federal Republic firmly in the western camp will decline in the 1990s, for three main reasons:

• Soviet policies are eroding traditional West German anti-Communism by offering the chance of a new cooperative structure across Europe.
• The ebbing of America's economic power, portrayed in its massive trade and budget deficits and yawning foreign debt, will weaken US ability to maintain a strong defence commitment in continental Europe.
• As reunification prospects grow, and the superpower field loses its force, support is building up in both East and West Germany for a reforged German nation to follow a course of 'equidistance' between East and West.

The Soviet Union has had to concede the intellectual and economic bankruptcy of Communism as practised by Gorbachev's predecessors. But for the moment, that increases rather than diminishes the attraction for West Germany of cooperating with Moscow. Because its own empire in the Soviet Union and eastern Europe is under strain from growing nationalism, Moscow's options for adopting an active strategy in winning over the Federal Republic are necessarily limited. None the less, sheer geography deals it intrinsically strong cards. The Federal Republic packs western Europe's most important economy on to a land only 150 miles wide; the Soviet Union stretches 5,500 miles. The distance between Bonn and the Soviet border is only 680 miles; from Bonn to the US is 3,800 miles.

Pondering the outlook for the German nation, many European observers during the 1980s believed that, even if democracy came to the fore in the GDR, East and West Germany would remain separate states. It was assumed that the relationship between the two could become similar to that between the Federal Republic and Austria. The breaching of the Wall, however, showed up the GDR's full economic plight, exposed to the economic might of the Federal Republic; economic factors are compelling forces for German unity. Whatever politicians inside and outside Germany may claim about the Federal Republic's unchanging ties to the West, pressures are likely to build up for withdrawal of all foreign armies from Germany, which could be a prelude to the Germans' departure from NATO. Pressure for unity is coming far more from the people in East Germany than from the West. But that has made it all the more difficult to resist the idea.

The lessons of history indicate that the re-emergence of a neutral German state would undermine the security and economic balance across Europe. An unwritten law among Bonn's allies is never to allow circumstances to develop under which the Federal Republic would have to make a straight choice between East and West. This will continue to be a prime task of western statecraft, but the time may be approaching when West Germany will be forced to give an answer.

41

II

Ripples across Germany can send troubling tides through Europe. For a country so long suffering the pangs of frustrated desire for unification, it is paradoxical that in the Middle Ages, under the Saxon and Hohenstaufen emperors, Germany was on the verge of establishing Europe's first nation-state. The Reich founded by Charlemagne in 800 was to continue as a more or less loose form of political organisation for more than a millennium. But the Empire was never a whole; over the centuries it functioned as a shifting tectonic plate which either overstretched Germany by conquest to well beyond its national borders, or else shrank back to cover only part of the German people within its limits. Under a combination of external attrition and internal particularism, the diffuse organisation entitled 'the Holy Roman Empire of the German Nation' went into decline. The beginning of the 16th century was the high water mark; thereafter came the deluge. The nation-states – England, France, Spain, Russia, Poland, Hungary, Sweden, the Netherlands, Denmark – crystallised out of the European crucible. Germany after the Thirty Years War (1618-48) was left stranded, an amalgam in search of the mould of nationhood.

Two great upheavals – one economic, the other spiritual – precipitated the decline. The 16th-century opening of the Cape sea route to India destroyed the trade-built prosperity of the Rhine and Hansa cities, paving the way for later economic collapse. By nailing on the door of the castle church in Wittenberg in 1517 his 95 theses attacking church indulgences, Martin Luther raised his standard for a national reformed religion. But at the same time as breaking with Catholicism, Luther bowed to the temporal power of the German princes. The agent of individual liberation prepared the ground for state authoritarianism. The Thirty Years War which started as an uprising of Bohemian nobles became a struggle for religious domination, ending as a battle for European mastery played out on German soil by Austria, Spain, France, and Sweden. The outcome, as always in Germany, was inconclusive. The Reformation, and the religious warring which ended in 1648, a century after Luther's death, failed to leave either Catholics or Protestants clearly in control. Although there is no great religious intolerance today, Germany remains the only major European country split on confessional lines. One more factor was added to German dualism.

The Thirty Years War turned Germany into a wasteland, depleting the population by a third, fixing the traditions of feudalism and barring the country from the full flowering of the great intellectual movement of the 18th century – the European Enlightenment. Under the 1648 Treaty of Westphalia, Germany was preserved in a patchwork of more than three hundred states and principalities, each one boasting virtually independent sovereignty. Germany became the marching ground for the armies of Louis XIV, the French Revolution and Napoleon. The only two German states large enough to play a decisive role in the history of Europe were rivals: Prussia and Austria. German fragmentation was upheld in the post-Napoleonic order at the Congress of Vienna in 1815, but counter-forces were at work. Prussia wrested from the Habsburgs mastery over the German Confederation and, after the victory over France in 1870-71, Bismarck was able to establish Prussian-dominated national unity. In January 1871, William I was proclaimed Deutscher Kaiser at the Palace of Versailles.

The Reich faced a battery of challenges. Internally, a struggle developed between fledgling parliamentarism, the old forces of autocracy and the new interest groups – business and organised labour – emerging from Germany's rapid industrialisation. Haunted by fears of anti-German power coalitions in Europe, Bismarck maintained a delicate array of foreign alliances devised to keep opponents off balance. After the Iron Chancellor was ousted in 1890, Wilhelmine Germany in its moody desire for aggrandisement disrupted the alliance system, and the 'nightmare of coalitions' became reality. In the First World War, conflict on several fronts became unavoidable and – even after Russia's withdrawal in 1917 – unsustainable. Defeat was all the more crushing because right up to the end in November 1918 the German population had been led unswervingly to believe in victory.

Peace brought a search for scapegoats. The Treaty of Versailles left Germany alone with its grievances and its reparations bills. It had little alternative but to try a revival of the Bismarckian alliance system – under still less propitious conditions. The Weimar Republic was a fragile half-way house, maintaining the Reich without its Emperor. Walther Rathenau, the Jewish industrialist who played a vital role in organising First World War raw material supplies, became Foreign Minister in 1922 and promptly forged *rapprochement* with the Soviet Union by signing the Treaty of Rapallo. The pact was motivated not only by political considerations, but also by industrial and military requirements* – and has become a symbol for Germany's recurring

* See Chapter 12.

43

fascination with the economic benefits of dealings with Russia. Two months afterwards, Rathenau was murdered by nationalist zealots claiming they were eliminating a traitor*.

Gustav Stresemann, Chancellor in the crisis year of 1923 – which started with French occupation of the Ruhr and ended with the Mark 'stabilised' at 4,200 billion to the dollar – also had to sustain a juggling act on several fronts. Stresemann put in train anti-inflationary measures which eventually quelled the monetary unrest, but was ousted from the Chancellorship in November 1923. However, as Foreign Minister between 1923 and 1929, he judiciously steered Germany through the European policy shoals.[6] Under the 1925 Treaty of Locarno, he secured a *modus vivendi* with the West, but also maintained eastern options with a new treaty with Moscow in 1926. That year Austen Chamberlain, the British Foreign Minister, received – together with Stresemann and their French opposite number Aristide Briand – the Nobel Peace Prize in recognition of the Locarno achievement. Anticipating language which also was to be used in the 1950s, Chamberlain made clear that Europe was playing for high stakes. He told Briand: 'We are battling with Soviet Russia for the soul of Germany ... The more difficult our relations with Russia become, the more important was it that we should attach Germany solidly to the western powers.'[7]

Amid growing cynicism and discontent with the democratic republic, the 1929 Wall Street crash allowed the Nazis to enter power through the crumbling arch of Weimar. Germany suffered disproportionately from the post-1929 Depression. Business confidence drained away in the 1931 European banking crisis. Unemployment, around 3 million at the beginning of 1930, rose to 4.4 million at the end of the year. By the end of 1931 the numbers out of work reached 5.6 million, rising to 7 million in 1932. Hitler became Chancellor on 30 January 1933. The Nazis received only 43.9 per cent of the votes in the election on 5 March 1933, but on 23 March the Reichstag in its temporary quarters of the Kroll Opera House passed the Enabling Act suspending parliamentary democracy. Germany had voted itself into dictatorship.

Economic difficulties and vain western hopes that Hitler would after all show goodwill prevented England and France from reacting firmly to German rearmament and territorial expansion. When Berlin concluded the non-aggression pact with the Soviet Union in August 1939, the way was cleared for the Wehrmacht to invade Poland on 1 September. But the alliance lasted only until June 1941. In *Mein Kampf* written in 1924

* See Chapter 10.

in the prison of Landsberg in Bavaria, Hitler had already foretold the future: 'In the very fact of an alliance with Russia lies the signal for the next war. Its result would be the end of Germany.'[8] That is what happened. By 1945, the Soviet Union had extended its arm 700 miles westwards across Europe to the centre of the Reich. For the victors, the option of maintaining Germany in its old amorphous form as a buffer in the European power balance was no longer available. The Red Army was in Berlin.

III

The Second World War cleaved Germany into two – the result not of a formal peace settlement, but of the absence of one. As the anti-Hitler coalition fell out and, after the outbreak of the Korean War in 1950, West Germany was drawn towards the western military alliance, the objective of a German peace settlement was put into abeyance. Throughout ensuing post-war decades, the victor powers masked their intentions towards Germany with a mixture of vagueness, subterfuge and bluff.

In September 1944, the US, Soviet Union and Britain drew up a protocol for post-war occupation of Germany.[9] The plan was to divide the country into three zones on the basis of its frontiers at the end of 1937, before the absorption of Austria in 1938 and Czechoslovakia in 1939. Berlin was to come under special three-power control, to be run by a joint governing authority. At the Yalta conference in February 1945, the three allies included among their objectives the 'dismemberment of Germany as they deem requisite for future peace and security'.[10] It was also agreed that Germany should pay reparations for war losses 'in kind' through future dismantling of plant and equipment. Roosevelt stated that American troops would not remain in Europe for longer than two years.[11] The French were assigned a fourth occupation zone to be carved out of the British and American sectors.

The four powers took up their final occupation zone positions in July 1945, two months after the German surrender on 8 May.[12] US, British and French troops – with some difficulty caused by Soviet obstruction – moved into their designated sections of ruined Berlin, which had been ruled for nine weeks solely by the Russians.[13] American troops who had advanced to the Elbe in April 1945 moved westwards to their prearranged positions. Soviet forces advanced between 50 and 150 miles further west of the Elbe (except in the far north) than they had reached at the end of the fighting. The zonal boundary, separating what are today East and West Germany, came into force. As Churchill foresaw in a message to President Truman in June 1945, an 'Iron Curtain' came down across Europe.[14]

In mid-July 1945, the leaders of the Big Three convened for their final war conference at Potsdam, the royal town of the Hohenzollerns and the place where Hitler opened the first Reichstag of the Third Reich in March 1933. Churchill led the British delegation at the start of the proceedings, but Labour leader Clement Attlee took over on 28 July following the Conservatives' general election defeat. France, which was determined to block the revival of any centralised German state, was not invited – a factor which later complicated efforts to arrive at a common western policy.[15] The Yalta proposal for dismembering Germany had been shelved a few months previously, when the US, Britain and Soviet Union had all come round to the view that a single German state would be easier to control – and also in a better economic position to deliver reparations, in the form of goods and equipment. However, a large slice of Germany had already been lopped off. The Russians had ceded to Poland the territories of the Soviet zone east of the Oder/Neisse line, causing Truman to remark that five countries were taking part in the occupation of Germany rather than the four set down at Yalta. Churchill's account of an exchange among the three leaders shortly after their arrival gives an apt indication of the imbroglio over Germany's future – confusion which was to persist into later decades:

> 'What,' I asked, 'is meant by Germany?'
> 'What it has become after the war,' said Stalin.
> 'The Germany of 1937,' said Mr Truman.
> Stalin said it was impossible to get away from the war. The country no longer existed. There were no definite frontiers, no frontier guards, no troops, merely four occupied zones.
> At length, we agreed to take the Germany of 1937 as a starting point. This shelved the problem, and we turned to Poland.[16]

With latent discord among the victor powers finally coming to the surface, the final communiqué from Potsdam's Cecilienhof palace was not a model of clarity. The document declared that Germany was to be treated 'as a single economic unit' during occupation, and that 'certain essential central administrative departments should be set up', although

46

'for the time being, no central German government shall be established'.[17] The principle of economic uniformity was however directly contravened by an agreement giving the Soviet Union far-reaching dismantling rights in its zone. The victors set down four overriding 'purposes of occupation':

1. The complete disarmament and demilitarisation of Germany and the elimination or control of all German industry that could be used for military production ...
2. To convince the German people that they have suffered a total military defeat and that they cannot escape responsibility for what they have brought upon themselves ...
3. To destroy the National Socialist Party and its affiliated and supervised organisations, to dissolve all Nazi institutions, to ensure that they are not revived in any form, and to prevent all Nazi and militarist activity or propaganda.
4. To prepare for the eventual reconstruction of German political life on a democratic basis and for eventual peaceful cooperation in international life by Germany.

Ironically, over the next decade, rapid progress would be made on fulfilling points 2,3 and 4 – but point 1 was superseded as Germany was remilitarised. The Potsdam communiqué also declared that transfer of German populations from Poland, Czechoslovakia and Hungary should take place in 'an orderly and humane manner'. In fact, the forced migration was not humane, but murderous. Poland's eastern annexation alone forced the exodus of between 8 and 9 million Germans. Up to 2 million may have died of starvation and ill-treatment on the way.[18] Between 1945 and 1953, around 12 million expellees and fugitives from Communism settled in the Federal Republic from the territories east of the Oder-Neisse line, other parts of eastern and central Europe and the German Democratic Republic – the largest movement of humanity in history.[19]

The Potsdam statement declared that the four victors (including France), represented by their commanders in chief, maintained 'supreme authority' over their respective occupation zone, as well as 'jointly in matters affecting Germany as a whole'. A council of foreign ministers was authorised to help prepare an eventual German peace settlement, as well as to deal with other outstanding post-war questions.[20] The leaders agreed, in nebulous language, 'The Council shall be utilised for the preparation of a peace settlement for Germany to be accepted by the Government of Germany when a Government

47

adequate for the purpose is established.' Six foreign minister conferences took place in the ensuing four years, but East-West differences over the treatment of Germany grew ever more acute and became unbridgeable after the Soviet Union attempted to usurp power over Berlin in the 1948-49 blockade. The last, futile foreign ministers conference took place in Paris on 23 May 1949, the day of the promulgation of the Basic Law of the Federal Republic of Germany. The German Democratic Republic was born in October. The victor powers ended up supervising the birth of two mirror-image states. But the Big Three plus France retained rights to determine matters affecting 'Germany as a whole', including the question of eventual reunification, and also maintained joint supreme authority over Berlin. All subsequent post-war German agreements and treaties have not affected these crucial conditions. Potsdam and its aftermath did not solve, but merely shelved, the German Question.

IV

The Germans know that their place on the map circumscribes their freedom of manoeuvre. But in the 1980s, the West German government has started to talk less about constraint and more about self-interest.

For Bismarck, a strong army was the answer to Germany's exposed position: 'The European pond is too full of pikes for Germany ever to become a carp.'[21] After Hitler, West German Chancellors voiced their warnings about the pitfalls of Germany's geography in a different fashion, dampening self-assertiveness and reassuring the rest of the world of the new aims of peace and reliability. Adenauer cautioned, 'When you have fallen from the heights as we Germans have done, you realise that it is necessary to break with what has been. We cannot live fruitfully with false illusions.'[22] Willy Brandt, Chancellor between 1969 and 1974, won the Nobel Peace Prize in 1971 for his *Ostpolitik* – normalising relations and rebuilding bridges with the countries of eastern Europe. He said on receiving the prize in Oslo: 'A good German cannot be a nationalist.'[23] Brandt, who chaired the Social Democratic Party for twenty-three years until he resigned in 1987, explained to me: ' "Nationalism" in the German language, unlike English or French, is associated with something aggressive, expansionary.'[24]

Helmut Schmidt, Chancellor between 1974 and 1982, often said that the Federal Republic must steer between two markers, Berlin and Auschwitz – meaning that it must never forget that the German nation is divided, nor what it did when it was last united. Schmidt's judgement is that history constrains Germany to turn towards western Europe, but not to lead it. 'After Hitler, Auschwitz and the Potsdam agreement, the German political class cannot be considered for (European) leadership.'[25]

During the 1980s, however, the centre-Right administration of Helmut Kohl started to relay two new messages to the West. First, the Federal Republic was no longer prepared to accept a subtle form of international discrimination on account of the Nazi past. Second, the rest of the West had to respect special German interests – in the political, military and economic spheres. Although West Germany proclaims the priority of the bond to the West, it reserves the right to look eastwards. The holes opening up in the Berlin Wall on 9 November 1989 enlarged the view to an extent which few in East or West had thought possible.

One marked consequence of superpower détente has been a fading of West Germany's support for close dependence on the US. Opinion polls show a marked increase in the number of West Germans in favour of their country taking up a policy of equidistance or neutrality between the two superpowers. According to one poll in 1988, only 23 per cent of the population favoured strong dependence on the US, as compared with 47 per cent supporting this in 1983. A total of 70 per cent preferred a policy of equidistance between the US and the Soviet Union, against 41 per cent in July 1983.[26] Nine out of ten West Germans in 1989 said that they trusted Mikhail Gorbachev – against only 58 per cent saying the same of President Bush.[27]

At the same time, German support for the European Community has been falling. A majority of Germans continues to say that their country benefited from Community membership – 55 per cent at the end of 1988 (against an average of 60 per cent for the Community as a whole). But Germans seem to fear that the 1992 single market programme could cause difficulties for protected parts of the West German economy.*[28] Additionally, worries have arisen that the expansion of the European Community towards the south will be financed largely by West German taxpayers.[29]

Karl Otto Pöhl, the president of the Bundesbank, who is playing a central role in discussions on working towards European monetary

* See Chapter 6.

union during the 1990s, observes that his compatriots are growing increasingly egoistic about the subject:

> The Germans are proud of having recovered economically after being on the floor. There is a certain aversion now against the idea of extending European integration because of the feeling that we Germans will have to pay for it. On the question of monetary union, West Germany would probably be ready to accept any ensuing loss of sovereignty. But the real fear is that other countries – the economically less efficient countries such as Italy, Portugal, Spain – would be digging into our pockets.[30]

The more hard-headed German views on Europe also reflect some cooling of enthusiasm about the ideal of a western European federation. According to regular European Community polls, 43 per cent of Germans in 1975 said they were 'very much' in favour of European union. The percentage fell to 38 per cent at the end of 1987 and 27 per cent at the end of 1988.[31] Jürgen Ruhfus, a former German ambassador to Britain and state secretary at the Foreign Ministry, who is now Bonn's envoy in Washington, says: 'During the 1950s, 1960s and 1970s we could believe in a united Europe. Now the EC has gone on the path of enlargement. It is not a coincidence that we are looking more to the East.'[32]

The ideal advanced by Mikhail Gorbachev of a 'European home', a peaceful order from the Atlantic to the Urals, has struck a particular chord in the Federal Republic. The expression is disliked by Britain and France because it appears to leave little room for the US – and therefore suggests a Europe where Russia would be the dominant power. Hans-Dietrich Genscher, Bonn's long-serving Free Democrat Foreign Minister, has no such fears. Genscher has become the principal practitioner of West German *Ostpolitik*. In 1987, he was the first senior western politician to come out strongly in favour of Gorbachev's reform policies. Born in 1927 in what is now East Germany, he started his political career in 1946 in the state-controlled East German Liberal party. He crossed to the West in 1952 after studying law at Halle and Leipzig universities, and quickly built up a career in the Bundestag in Bonn. Asked why he did not become a Communist before 1952, Genscher replies in his rasping dialect with dry Saxon humour: 'Because I happened to have read Marx and Lenin.' Now that Marxism appears to be on the retreat in Moscow, Genscher puts forward with missionary zeal the goal of spreading democratic values across the whole of Europe: 'The rule of law and respect for human rights must stand out

in the whole of the European home.'[33] The concept of a 'common European home' was agreed as part of a political declaration signed by Kohl and Gorbachev in Bonn in June 1989.

President Richard von Weizsäcker also has a vision of overcoming East-West barriers – like Genscher's, based on personal experience. 'People are again becoming aware of the old, the larger Europe. The time is ripe for an open conception that excludes no European nation,' Weizsäcker says.[34] As a young soldier in the eastern campaign against the Soviet Union, Weizsäcker took part in the 900-day siege of Leningrad in 1942 – and now wants Germany to be a force for peace. Giving a speech in the city in 1987, he said, 'I am here today to do everything in my power to spare future generations from the violence, anguish and death brought by war.' Ever with an eye for cultural detail, Weizsäcker recalled that Shostakovich's 7th 'Leningrad' symphony composed in the besieged city was given its première there in 1942 within range of German guns – in the same concert hall where Beethoven's symphonic mass *Missa Solemnis* was played for the first time in 1824.[35]

Genscher, a tireless traveller seldom out of an aeroplane, narrowly escaped death when stricken for two years with tuberculosis as a 19-year-old in Halle – a factor explaining both his restlessness and his periodically-recurring frailty of health.[36] He masterminded the FDP's switch in coalition partners in 1982 which brought down the Schmidt coalition and made Kohl Chancellor, and is West Germany's most skilled exponent at playing to several different political audiences at once. Although a great supporter of expanding western European integration, Genscher has his heart in *Mitteleuropa* – the area of central Europe roughly covering what used to be the Holy Roman Empire.[37] He pays regular annual visits to his homeland around Halle to see relatives and friends, and even sends Christmas cards carrying views of a statue on the old Halle marketplace.

Underlining the traditional friendship with Russia both before and after the 1917 revolution, Genscher chose his first ever official speech in East Germany – at Potsdam in 1988 – to call for greater East-West economic and technological cooperation, and declared: 'We want to reactivate the once so varied and fruitful bonds between Germans and Russians.'[38] A particular bond comes from West German industrial groups which had close ties with Czarist Russia 100 years ago – and are now trying to build up new business links with Gorbachev's reformists.

Genscher's central tenet is that the more firmly the Federal Republic is rooted in the West, the further it will be able to extend the bridge to the East – a policy which suggests the need for strong building materials

51

and subtle engineering. His natural instinct to look both ways at once can make him an object of suspicion in the US, Britain or France,[39] but it is not difficult to recognise in his weaving strategies the desire to steer a course through the cluster of hostile forces which have marked Germany over the centuries. He told me: 'The most important point about post-war German politics is that we have learned from history to look at our fate as part of Europe as a whole. All the problems which affect Europe come together on German soil.'[40]

Gorbachev's 'European home' will clearly be populated by nation-states. Would there be two German states or one? The question has been an agonising one for Kohl, who fiercely criticised his predecessor Schmidt for damaging ties with Washington during the dispute in 1981-82 over the deployment of American medium-range missiles. Against heavy domestic opposition, the Kohl government succeeded in pushing through deployment. Bonn was rewarded in 1987 by the conclusion of the superpowers' Intermediate Nuclear Forces (INF) agreement to eliminate all US and Soviet medium-range nuclear missiles from Europe. However, the disarmament accord brought to the surface West Germany's fundamental ambivalence over its national goals. As a result of the agreement to scrap all medium-range missiles with a range of more than 500 kilometres, the only land-based nuclear weapons left in Europe are those which, if used, would explode in a geographical area roughly delineated by what Kohl likes to call the 'Fatherland' – East and West Germany.*

Worse, Kohl came under almost immediate pressure from the US and Britain to bring in more accurate, longer range versions of the sub-500-kilometre weapons to support NATO's strategy of nuclear deterrence. These missiles would threaten directly the other half of Germany. 'I am carrying out a policy for Germany and 17 million of my countrymen live in the German Democratic Republic,' Kohl told me. 'Of course I have to reflect that the missiles would be targeted on Germans.'[41] The combination of the arrival of Gorbachev, the INF accord, Bonn's own rhetoric and the sincere wishes of many Germans to overcome the barriers dividing the nation helped bring back the German Question to the forefront of international politics – two years before the flows of fugitives from East Germany started to capture the headlines in August and September 1989.

Bonn's aspirations over national unity have increased suspicions among its allies that, at some stage, West Germany might be prepared to

* See Chapter 11.

forsake its western partners and play the national card. Kohl has been forced to underline regularly that there will be no recurrence of a *Sonderweg* (special path) between East and West.[42] When Adenauer told the Bundestag in his first government statement in September 1949 that, 'We belong to the west European world,'[43] he was speaking from a position of weakness. Adenauer's greatest fear was that, as a result of isolationism in the US, the Allies would let the economically and morally shattered western half of Germany drift into the arms of the Soviet Union. However, when Kohl declared to the Bundestag thirty-eight years later, 'There is no German *Sonderweg*!'[44] the position was different. West Germany had attained the economic power at least to consider other options, and Kohl was seeking to convince public opinion at home and abroad that there would be no independent policy to overturn the status quo. During a visit to Moscow to see Gorbachev in 1988, Kohl reaffirmed, 'We will not wander between the worlds'[45]; he repeated the formulation to President Bush in 1989. 'The Federal Republic is not for sale,' he asserted to the French newspaper *Le Monde*.[46] Again in 1990, Kohl reaffirmed his 'clear rejection of a special path'.[47] Geography and history were responsible for the feeling that the message was not completely credible; so Kohl had no choice but to keep repeating it.

Division of Germany has both maintained and threatened Europe's power balance. The Federal Republic is the most stable, prosperous and peaceful state in German history, but the constitutional goal of 'state unity' obliges it to seek to change the foundations on which this success has been built. A peculiar sense of half-yearning, half-fear stalks government policy on the subject. 'Reunification is not on the agenda at the moment – it would lead to instability and the danger of a neutralised Germany,' I was told by Wolfgang Schäuble, one of Kohl's closest advisers.* 'But,' he added in the next breath, 'this division is so unnatural.'[48]

The dilemma between East and West grew more apparent in the early summer of 1989. Defending his opposition to deployment of the new shorter-range nuclear missiles, Genscher told the Bundestag that the Germans had to build 'the main pillar in the bridge of trust' between East and West, and asserted that his 'obligation to the German people ... does not end at the border through the middle of Germany.'[49] Weizsäcker said in an address marking the Federal Republic's 40th birthday:

---

* Schäuble was apponted Interior Minister in April 1989.

> We in the West stand before an enormous test ... Under the conditions of the Cold War, it was easy to be united. Now that the world does not indicate so clearly who is for us and who is against us, it is becoming more uncomfortable.[50]

The Germans, as well as the four powers of the Second World War which maintain responsibility for an ultimate peace settlement, have always followed both overt and covert aims on reunification. Any public statements on the issue invariably contain less than the whole truth. Since 1945 the US, Britain and France have not been prepared to sign a peace treaty with either German state, since this would cement division. Neither have they been willing to accept reunification on a basis which would involve anything less than a firm German commitment to the western bloc.[51] The Soviet Union during the 1950s urged creation of a single German state embracing Moscow's version of 'democracy', i.e. Communism. Although it later switched to backing the legitimacy of East Germany as a separate sovereign state, Moscow showed no sign of wanting to sign a peace treaty with the German Democratic Republic on its own. The Soviet Union also kept alive the ideological line of a single German 'nation'.

France's position is highly delicate, proximity to Germany lending its policies still more marked ambivalence than those of the US and Britain. Having suffered three German invasions since 1870, but also relying on a strong westward-orientated Federal Republic as a buffer against the Warsaw Pact, France fears both the strength of Germany united and the frustration of Germany divided,[52] and has launched its own set of policies to try to discourage any West German drift to the East. Paris and Bonn have set up bilateral Defence and Finance Councils in an effort to harmonise policies in these fields – although it remains to be seen how effective these new bodies will be. A reunified Germany will not only damage France's defence interests. France is already in a state of palpable national anxiety about the competitive weight of the West German economy and a combined German state will be even more uncomfortable to live with.

In spring 1952, Stalin sent to the other three occupying powers notes suggesting terms for a peace treaty to achieve German reunification on a neutral basis. Could Gorbachev revert to encouraging reunification as a means of extending Russian influence in central Europe? Certainly, for a long period he tried to play down the idea and emphasised that attempts to overturn 'historically-produced' division could be 'incalculable, even dangerous'.[53] When I asked Kohl whether

Gorbachev might make a new offer of German unity in the next few years, the Chancellor brushed the idea robustly aside:

> 'I do not write futuristic novels like Orson Welles (sic). What you ask now, that is in the realm of fantasy.'
> 'You would rule it out altogether?'
> 'Of course, his [Gorbachev's] position of interest today [compared with Stalin] is quite different.'

However, Moscow has one important advantage over the three western powers: it has a lever over Berlin, as an island of foreign jurisdiction within East German territory. Encouragement of a neutral unified Germany may well form one long-term Soviet option for increasing its strategic reach in the 'European home'. Over the future of the two German states, Gorbachev in 1987 developed what seemed like a suitable long-term view: 'History should decide what will happen in 100 years.'[54] Two years later, history accelerated. In January 1990 Gorbachev was forced to admit that the principle of German unity was no longer 'in doubt.'[55] When Kohl flew 10 days later to the Kremlin, Gorbachev told him that the Germans had the 'sole right' to decide whether they wanted to live in one state.[56] The Soviet Union gave the green light to unity – but left tantalisingly open the conditions under which it would take place.

V

In April 1955, a month before West Germany joined NATO, Kurt Georg Kiesinger – chairman of the foreign affairs committee of the Bundestag and later to become Chancellor of the Grand Coalition – addressed the annual discussions of the German-English society in Königswinter. The title of the deliberations was 'In the Magnetic Field of East and West'. Kiesinger spelled out faithfully how Chancellor Adenauer's policy of western integration would provide the necessary magnetic force for reunifying the nation, which was perhaps only a few years away. The watchword, he said, was: 'Choose your friends! That is in fact something which in my opinion it is impossible to repeat too often to my compatriots. Our entire history of the last half century since Bismarck's resignation has been a failure to do so.'[57]

In the post-war decades, there was no doubt that the choice had fallen on the West. The first significant step was the setting up in 1951-52 of the European Coal and Steel Community. Economic and political links were extended when the Treaty of Rome was signed in 1957 between West Germany, France, Italy, the Netherlands, Belgium and Luxembourg. The pact was designed to guarantee the post-war ideals of peace and freedom – a *Leitmotif* continued a quarter of a century later when the Community was enlarged to include the emergent democracies of Greece, Spain and Portugal. Germany's surging capital goods industries received markets, in exchange for German help in shoring up agriculture in France. As it turned out, the Common Market proved of enormous benefit for both German farmers and German industrialists, but at growing cost to the taxpayer.

On the military front, Adenauer saw his hopes founder in the early 1950s of setting up a combined European army through the European Defence Community (EDC). The French National Assembly rejected the EDC treaty in 1954. German rearmament was unpopular in West Germany, and regarded with suspicion by some of its neighbours. But it went ahead with the setting up of the Bundeswehr – billed as an armed force of 'citizens in uniform' – when West Germany joined NATO in 1955. Bonn first in 1954 renounced the right to manufacture on its territory – although not to acquire or control – atomic, chemical and bacteriological weapons. The Bundeswehr, consisting of land, air and sea forces, had no independent general staff and would be committed to NATO in wartime. Its upper limit was set at 500,000 men (the size of the army of united Germany in 1936 after Hitler brought back conscription and reoccupied the Rhineland), a level it did not in fact reach until the 1970s.

After de Gaulle returned to power in 1958, growing divergence over defence between the US and France provided further complications. In 1963, Adenauer and de Gaulle signed the Elysée Treaty to sanctify Franco-German cooperation, although de Gaulle's anti-US campaign and veto of Britain's Common Market membership severely limited the treaty's application. France's drive towards strategic independence, culminating in its exit from the integrated command of NATO in 1966, split the Bonn government between its allegiance to the US and its wish for closer European defence ties. It also provided a further discomfort for Adenauer in his sparring with the Atlanticist Erhard, who eventually took over the Chancellorship in 1963.

Adenauer's belief in the power of western integration to block extension of Russian hegemony may have been sound in principle, but he had to run the gauntlet of powerful opposition from Kurt Schumacher, the post-war leader of the Social Democratic Party. While also suspicious of the Soviet Union, Schumacher charged that the western Allies were simply using West Germany for their own ends, and that Adenauer's western ties would block the path to reunification. Faced with these opposing pressures, Adenauer's complex balancing act was almost Bismarckian. He had to persuade his western partners that integration was the only way to stabilise the Federal Republic, and dampen suspicions about resurgent militarism. And, all along, he had to maintain that the reunification door was ajar.

Was Adenauer's advancement of reunification hopes – as Schumacher claimed – simply a cynical bluff to make western ties and rearmament palatable to the German people? Certainly, Adenauer had always favoured orientating Germany to the West to lower the influence of Prussia. His post-war policies bore all the hallmarks of his plan put forward in the 1920s (when Mayor of Cologne) of establishing a Rhineland state independent of Prussia. In the late 1940s he told a friend, anticipating words used forty years later in the Community's 1992 programme, 'In my mind the ultimate solution must be the creation of one single enormous internal market in western Europe, a unified trading area which should comprise England, France, the Low Countries and Germany.'[58]

Schumacher maintained that western integration and reunification were mutually exclusive. The SPD leader did not live to see the proof – he died in August 1952 – but he was right. Adenauer's hard-line policies towards the East, in particular the ill-fated Hallstein doctrine between 1955 and 1967 of cutting off diplomatic relations with countries which recognised East Germany, hindered his ostensible reunification goal. At the same time, the alternative objective of a western European federation also faded from view, which contributed to a general fading of the credibility of the Chancellor and of his party. It paved the way for the policy of dialogue with East Germany introduced under the Grand Coalition. In May 1967 Chancellor Kiesinger was the first Chancellor actually to reply to a letter from East Berlin – from Willi Stoph, the East German Prime Minister – rather than returning it unopened or throwing it away. *Ostpolitik* was expanded when the SPD and Brandt came to power. West Germany signed treaties with the Soviet Union and Poland (both in 1970), and Czechoslovakia (1973) on accepting the post-war borders and improving political and economic relations. In the 1972 Basic Relations Treaty, the Federal Republic conceded that East Germany, though still not a foreign country, was a separate sovereign state.

The Adenauer principle that the Federal Republic could extend links with the East bloc only from a position of western integration was adopted by all successive Bonn governments. The difference was that the administrations of Brandt, Schmidt and Kohl all implicitly took their cue from the policy of *Wandel durch Annäherung* (Change through Convergence) laid down in 1963 by Egon Bahr, Brandt's key *Ostpolitik* adviser. In a remarkably far-sighted speech, Bahr said that Bonn's rigid policy of piling up pressure on East Berlin was only hardening division. The US had come to the conclusion, he stated, that Communism could not be eliminated, merely changed; Bonn would have to do the same. Admitting it sounded like a paradox, he said that the only way to change the status quo between East and West Germany was first to accept it. In the 1960s, the Christian Democrats attacked Bahr's ideas as betrayal – then, twenty years later, proceeded to put his precepts into effect. The speech set the groundwork for what became, under the Kohl administration, a policy of financial, technological and economic help to support living conditions in East Germany.* Bahr tellingly identified the key problem of carrying out reforms in the GDR: 'Precisely because, in contrast to Poland or the Soviet Union, we are dealing with a divided people, social and economic demands spill over immediately into political and national revendications.' He added:

> It is certainly impossible for the Soviets to allow the (Soviet) zone to be wrested away to strengthen the potential of the West. The zone has to be transformed with the approval of the Soviets. If we could go that far, we would make a large step towards reunification ... Our first concern must be with human beings and with the exploration of every conceivable and defensible means of improving their situation. An improvement in material conditions in the zone must lead to a relaxation in tension.[59]

Bahr, today still one of the most influential figures in East-West German politics, was Brandt's minister in charge of negotiating the 1972 Basic Relations Treaty. Bahr's policies went through something of a U-turn in the 1980s, when he called the official reunification line 'hypocritical', and came out in favour of the two Germanys signing separate peace treaties with the Second World War victors. Along with the rest of the SDP leadership, he was considerably embarrassed by the unforeseen East German revolution of 1989. Bahr would have done better had he adhered to the philosophy of his 1963 speech: 'Reunification is not to be a once-for-all affair but a process with many stages and many pauses.'

* See Chapter 5.

VI

A mixture of agreements balancing the Federal Republic's exigencies and obligations in defence and economics provides the cement embedding it into the western community. In these two fields, the balance of West Germany's interests is now clearly moving away from the US and towards Europe. In Western efforts to control the Federal Republic's eastward tilt, France has been forced to move to the front line.

One significant success story for the Franco-German axis has been European monetary cooperation. The centrepiece is the European Monetary System, set up in 1979 under the initiative of Schmidt and French President Valéry Giscard d'Estaing. The EMS was all part of what Schmidt in later years liked to call his 'grand strategy for integrating Europe'[60]. Schmidt has also revealed that one of his unspoken reasons behind the idea was to anchor the Federal Republic more strongly to the West – another sign of continuity with Adenauer. The EMS has clearly given western Europe in general, and the Federal Republic in particular, more weight in international monetary affairs. The lowering of dependence on the US ran broadly parallel to West Germany's effort to win greater manoeuvring room in foreign policy through *Ostpolitik*.

The EMS – linking as full members West Germany, France, Italy, Spain, Belgium, Luxembourg, the Netherlands, Ireland and Denmark – enables member central banks to keep their currencies stable within set 'fluctuation bands' through coordinated economic policies and foreign exchange intervention. The aim was to provide a zone of currency stability in Europe and reduce exposure to the fluctuating dollar after the break-up in 1971-73 of the Bretton Woods system of fixed exchange rates.[61] In spite of sporadic currency unrest forcing periodic D-Mark revaluations and French franc devaluations, over the past decade the EMS has proved far more effective than expected in stabilising European currencies. The scheme has forced member countries to follow broadly similar anti-inflationary fiscal and monetary policies. This has increased West Germany's economic influence by requiring other European countries to follow the anti-inflation policies of the Bundesbank – a constraint which has sometimes irritated France and Italy. Cooperation has not spread evenly throughout the 12-member Community, since Britain has not become a full member.[62] The EMS, however, has undoubtedly helped prepare the way for the larger post-1992 move to integrate European economies.

The EMS has given West Germany vital help in enabling it to consolidate its position as the world's leading exporter.[63] West Germany has massively built up its markets in Europe since the six-nation Common Market was set up in 1958. Around 55 per cent of West Germany's exports now go to the European Community, which accounted for 70 per cent of the Federal Republic's record DM135 billion trade surplus in 1989.

The pull towards Europe through the EMS has been accompanied by a series of disagreements with the US on economic, strategic and technology issues. The 1970s saw plenty of disharmony over economics, but German Ministers would still deferentially talk of the American security guarantee over Berlin as a reason for dampening down quarrels. Today, West German politicians realise that putting the Americans in their place can be politically popular. A good way of deflecting American criticism over West Germany's flagging economic growth rate earlier in the 1980s was to dispense advice to Washington on how to cut the US budget deficit.

A traditional area for discord is over the question of controls on exports of high technology. To guard against Moscow acquiring militarily-useful expertise in areas like computers or telecommunications, the US favours tight regulations on trade with the East bloc – tougher than the Germans would wish. In 1963, the Americans forced Bonn to ban deliveries of pipeline to the Soviet Union by the Mannesmann steel group. The embargo lasted until the 1970s – a degree of German compliance which would be unthinkable today. Similar differences emerged at the beginning of the 1980s in connection with contracts with Moscow over building a Siberian gas pipeline to Europe. West Germany believes that such action by the US has been counter-productive, since it tends to spur European industry towards self-sufficiency in dealings with the Soviet Union. West German politicians argue strongly in favour of slimming controls to help Gorbachev's economic restructuring. East bloc trade makes up only just over 4 per cent of total German exports, but in coming years can add up to an important support for economic reform in eastern Europe.

The greatest potential for discord between Bonn and Washington comes over defence. The Kremlin's arms control plans are geared to encouraging removal of all nuclear weapons from German soil – a step which Washington, as well as Paris and London, believes would greatly weaken NATO defences. Already during the crisis over missiles deployment at the beginning of the 1980s, US strategists worried about a Russian plot to detach West Germany from NATO. The latest phase however will require still more careful handling. Whereas Leonid Brezhnev was using threats and expanding Moscow's nuclear arsenal, Gorbachev is promising peace and pulling weapons out.

Gorbachev's popularity is encouraging the Germans to seek some form of ill-defined 'security partnership' with Moscow. Pressure in the American congress for reductions in US troops stationed in West Germany is likely to grow during the Bush administration for both budgetary and political reasons. To offset a possible reduced US presence, France and West Germany have been investigating proposals for greater military cooperation. However, this aim is hampered by France's absence from the military structure of NATO, and also by the difficulty of finding a place for France's independent nuclear deterrent in the two sides' strategy. France has no intention of giving a formal nuclear guarantee to protect the Federal Republic with its nuclear strike forces. Instead, the two sides are placing emphasis on conventional defence. The two countries are gradually installing a joint brigade of 4,200 troops in south Germany to symbolise France's readiness to play a more active military role east of the Rhine. But this hardly looks like a convincing preparation for the day when the US may decide to make substantial withdrawals of its own troops.

According to an opinion poll given warm publicity in both Bonn and Paris, 67 per cent of West Germans considered that France was their best friend, while 54 per cent of the French held this view about the Federal Republic.[64] But France's wish to strengthen political ties reflects the established worries of French politicians and commentators about the Germans' eastwards drift. In 1965, President de Gaulle reflected: 'Germany feels a sense of anguish, sometimes rage, prompted by its own uncertainty over its limitations, its unity, its political regime, its international role. Its destiny appears all the more disquieting to the whole continent because it remains indeterminate.'[65] Mulling over the uncertainties affecting West Germany's position within NATO, a senior official at the Elysée Palace compares the Federal Republic with an unhappy schoolchild seized by doubts about his relationship with his classmates. As one European ambassador in Bonn puts it, 'The Germans accept that the French don't trust them. That is the basis on which they go into partnership.'

President Mitterrand has called for the rest of Europe to accept Germany's 'view towards the East' as a natural consequence of history and geography. 'Why should it not play a specific role in agreement with

61

its historical reality? This obligatory preoccupation is not to be confused with neutralism,' says Mitterrand.[66] As the upheaval in East Germany gathered pace at the end of 1989, Mitterrand made clear that he saw German reunification taking place primarily as the result of self-determination for the German people. 'What counts above all is the will and the determination of the people ... I am not afraid of reunification,' he said during a visit to Bonn.[67] Mitterrand also however laid down the limits of the process: 'The will of the people cannot be exercised without the agreement of the states – the German states and the states which guarantee the statute of Germany.'[68] And on a pre-Christmas visit to East Germany, he pointed to the danger of 'disequilibrium' in Europe and of the 'problems' of the four powers' armies still stationed on German soil: 'The four still have some things to say.'[69] Some of Mitterrand's advisers were more blunt. Pierre Bérégovoy, the French Finance Minister, a long-time confidant of the President, was a deportee under the Germans during the Second World War. Bérégovoy warned that the Soviet Union 'will not accept central Europe dominated by the Germans' and said, of the Germans' aspirations towards unity: 'I am one of those who experienced the effects of the great German Reich.'[70] Another senior figure in Paris, Jean-Pierre Chevènement, the Defence Minister, voiced similar concern: 'The Europeans do not want to be brought again into disequilibrium by a very large Germany.'[71]

One well-informed German in no doubt of French anxieties is Rudolf Augstein, the founder and publisher of *Der Spiegel* news magazine and West Germany's most influential journalist.* Augstein has never been a starry-eyed believer in reunification. He opposed Adenauer's policies of western integration in the 1950s because he believed, like Schumacher, that they would obstruct the goal of unity. Through *Der Spiegel's* persistent campaigning, he helped pave the way for Brandt's 1972 agreement to recognise East Germany as a separate state. Augstein told me in 1988 that the division of East and West Germany had been made 'more solid' as a result of the policies of rapprochement followed since the 1970s.[72] 'But we can put up with this ... No power in the world could hinder the Germans of the German Democratic Republic to come together with the Federal Republic if the Russians left. France would fear this the most, the concentration of power in the middle of Europe.' Speaking almost 12 months before the events of November 1989, he added: 'The people in the German Democratic Republic previously thought of themselves more as Communists; now, they see themselves as

* See Chapter 8.

Germans. If the SED (the East German Communist party) would allow them to go, there wouldn't be enough step-ladders to let them over the Wall.'

At the centre of the changing magnetic field in Europe, the forces drawing the Germans together across the Berlin Wall have been growing steadily stronger. They are now irresistible.

4

Uncertain Democracy

I am convinced that the German people can never develop a love for democracy, for the simple reason that they cannot love politics; the oft-described authoritarian state remains for the German people the most suitable political system. It is also the one for which they yearn.

Thomas Mann, 1918[1]

The political socialisation of the German is incomplete ... The democratic institutions are accepted, but they remain external, distant, ultimately irrelevant.

Ralf Dahrendorf, 1965[2]

Not a strong Germany, but an economically weak one, is a danger for democracy.

Willy Brandt, 1990[3]

The arrival of parliamentary democracy in West Germany was that most unusual event in history: a revolution imposed from outside. As Theodor Heuss pointed out in his inaugural presidential speech in 1949, 'It is the historical misfortune of the Germans that they did not fight for democracy, but that it came, as the only means of legitimising our existence, when the state had collapsed in catastrophe and war.'[4] The misfortune may be fading from memory, but it is still there. West Germany's real post-war miracle has been the establishment of confidence in the new political institutions, but because democratic roots in West Germany lie in more shallow soil than elsewhere, confidence is a fragile plant. 'We Germans remain an endangered people, needing political orientation,' said Helmut Schmidt in his farewell speech in the Bundestag in 1986[5]. Democracy still cannot be taken completely for granted – even when the West Germans are in the process of extending it eastwards.

I

Uwe Barschel appeared the best possible advertisement for West Germany's modern parliamentary system. Competent and coolly handsome, the Christian Democrat Prime Minister of Schleswig Holstein, Germany's northernmost state, took office in 1982 at the age of only 38. When I met him on an early spring day in Kiel in 1987, he was at the crest of his career.[6] A successful lawyer, married to a Bismarck, moving easily among industrial barons and smooth-talking technocrats, Barschel combined the whiff of old Protestant money with youthful drive and ambition. His aim was to turn his small farming state perched between the Baltic and the North Sea into a window on the world. Compared with heavily centralised countries like Britain, West Germany's federal system gives regional politicians a great deal of scope – and Barschel was determined to use it to the full.

Barschel entered local politics at the age of 16 and by the time he was 25, he was vice-chairman of the state's Christian Democrat party organisation. At 27, he was a deputy of the *Land* (state) parliament. Now, Barschel was grooming himself for the national stage in Bonn. During an hour-long conversation in his office in the red-brick government headquarters, he spelled out his hopes. Schleswig Holstein was no longer predominantly a farming community, he explained; the way forward lay in microelectronics, the chemical industry, precision engineering. Barschel had been to Tokyo in 1985, and his Industry Minister was currently in China. A Japanese company had agreed to build telecopier equipment at the town of Neumünster, providing 120 jobs. He was negotiating personally with a cluster of multinational corporations to bring a big European Community electronics project to the northern state. Microchips, environmental technology, nuclear energy – the future was open.

Uwe Barschel's own future was closing in fast. Two months later, flying back north after a meeting in Bonn with Chancellor Kohl, his private aeroplane crashed on a night landing at a small airport near his home. His pilot was killed, but Barschel crawled out of the wreckage, badly injured. His health and state of mind clearly under strain, he was quickly back behind his desk, anxious to hurry on with the planning – and the intrigue.

Schleswig Holstein is a farming state which received a strong influx of refugees from the East after 1945. Protestant by faith, it is conservative by temperament and by instinct. The Christian Democrats had ruled Schleswig Holstein, as if by fiat, since 1950. The party had practically taken over the state by packing the civil service and judiciary with political appointees. But as the crucial September 1987 *Land* election approached, the party was growing nervous, for the opposition Social Democratic Party was gaining ground fast in the polls. A particular threat stemmed from its pipe-smoking local leader Björn Engholm, a thoughtful *protégé* of Willy Brandt, who had served in a junior post as Bonn Education Minister in 1981-82.

Already, at the beginning of the year, Barschel had started to plot a Byzantine 'dirty tricks' campaign against Engholm, which intensified in the months leading up to the election. A detective agency was hired to inquire into Engholm's sex life; anonymous letters were sent claiming that the candidate had evaded taxes; rumours were spread that Engholm suffered from Aids and that the SPD favoured legalising sex with children. The Barschel aide organising the campaign was a journalist named Reiner Pfeiffer with an unsavoury reputation for political manoeuvring. He developed a grudge against Barschel. Claiming that conscience prevented him from carrying out the Prime Minister's scheming, Pfeiffer leaked the undercover operation to *Der Spiegel*, which undertook to pay him compensation for his inevitable loss of a job.

The story came out on election day in September 1987. This was too late to make much difference to the outcome – a stalemate between the Social Democrats and the Barschel-led coalition – but the news stirred up a hornets' nest in the days afterwards. Barschel at first strongly denied the allegations, but was forced to resign at the end of September as his Christian Democrat friends made it clear they regarded him as a liability. A parliamentary inquiry meanwhile started work in Kiel. In the weeks afterwards, the investigation quickly showed that Pfeiffer's almost unbelievable allegations were true.

After a short holiday in the Canary Islands, Barschel was due to fly back to Kiel to appear at the inquiry, but he never arrived. The ex-Prime Minister made an unscheduled stop in Geneva on the way back and on 11 October was found dead, fully clothed, in a water-filled bath in Room 317 of the luxury Beau Rivage hotel. He was first thought to have suffered a heart attack, but the hypothesis changed to suicide after the autopsy showed Barschel had taken a massive dose of sleeping tablets and tranquillisers.[7] His family spread the story that he had been murdered – a claim which, like Barschel's earlier protestation, lacked credibility.

Barschel's body was discovered in Geneva by a journalist from the illustrated magazine *Stern* who had travelled to Switzerland to try to interview him. Before informing the police, he had time to read through notes left by Barschel in his bedroom and to take photos of the one-time political golden boy ghoulishly propped up in the bathtub. The picture later appeared on the front page of a special edition of the magazine. Pleased to have stolen a march on its arch rival *Der Spiegel, Stern* crowed over its competitors with a self-congratulatory editorial: 'The truth comes first!'

Barschel's bizarre death left behind an emotional tangle. Because of the widely-felt need to underpin democracy, the Federal Republic mounts a superficial show of demanding high standards of personal behaviour from its politicians, but the holders of office have to fall a long way from grace before they are sanctioned with resignation. Unlike in Britain or the US, politicians are not forced out of office over sexual peccadillos. Although popular newspapers give plenty of space to the amorous adventures of sports stars, the press does not write about ministers' extra-marital affairs; nor do financial misdemeanours normally represent a permanent political millstone. If Barschel had simply infringed a code of personal honour, probably he would have been forgiven or, perhaps, never exposed. His crime, however, was to have transgressed in a particularly flagrant manner the highest prescript of German political order (and the one most demonstrably suspended during the Third Reich): that the state must be a *Rechtsstaat*, based on law.

Pastors at Protestant churches in Hamburg and Schleswig Holstein added extra prayers for reconciliation to their Sunday services. 'The terrible events surrounding Uwe Barschel have cut our Republic to the quick,' pietistically declared Philipp Jenninger, the Speaker of the Bundestag, soon after Barschel's corpse was discovered. 'Our democracy is experiencing one of its most difficult crises of credibility in its history.'[8] Just over a year later, Jenninger himself was forced to resign amid uproar over his insensitive Bundestag speech about Hitler and the Jews.*

The following month, in November 1987, two policemen were shot dead by militant demonstrators in Frankfurt. It was the first time in the history of the Federal Republic that policemen had been killed during a demonstration. Politicians fretted about the stability of West German democracy. Alfred Dregger, the veteran Christian Democrat Right-winger, reminded the Bundestag that the Weimar Republic had gone

---

* See Chapter 2.

67

down beneath street fighting between Nazi and Communist paramilitary organisations. 'We must not allow this to be repeated.'[9] Richard Stücklen, the 71-year-old Bavarian conservative, and the only member of the Bundestag to have sat as a deputy continuously since the republic's foundation in 1949, told me that Barschel's acts had 'damaged the standing of our democracy'. Recalling the crimes of Nazism, he noted lugubriously that, 'When political morality declines, we know where the journey leads.'[10] Sixty-five per cent of the population, according to one opinion poll, thought that politics was a 'dirty business'.[11]

Two years later, another shock to the political system, the murder by terrorists in November 1989 of Alfred Herrhausen, the chief executive of the Deutsche Bank*, sparked off, on the whole, rather less soul-searching; but renewed references to the Weimar Republic were inevitable. Just two days before his armoured Mercedes was blown up by a powerful bomb in the sleek suburb of Bad Homburg outside Frankfurt, Herrhausen, West Germany's most powerful business mogul, spoke of German reunification as 'desirable and inevitable'.[12] At an emotional funeral service a week later in Frankfurt's rebuilt Gothic cathedral, Helmut Kohl, who had built up a close relationship with the murdered banker, called Herrhausen 'a German patriot' who had served his Fatherland.[13] In a reference to the violence of the 1920s, he declared: 'The second German democracy must not suffocate on satiety, intellectual laziness and moral indifference.' Contrasting West Germany's 'freedom and prosperity' with the 'enemies of the republic' who had killed a long list of Germany's top businessmen, Kohl asked in near-despair: 'What is wrong with the Germans in the Federal Republic?'

Just as the Herrhausen assassination underlined the perils of confronting the symbolic figures at the helm of the German economy, the Barschel drama focussed attention on the growing isolation from the realities of life of the new post-war breed of professional politicians. Barschel's whole adult life had been in politics. Engholm, who left school early and became a printer's compositor before going to university on a trade union grant, at least had gained an insight into another side of life. Speeding through the Schleswig Holstein countryside several months afterwards, during the campaign for the re-run state elections in May 1988, Engholm told me that at one point he had thought of quitting politics over the Barschel affair. However, he decided against because, had he done so, 'The Christian Democrats would have been proven right.'[14] He went on to win a crushing victory in

* See Chapter 6.

the new poll and today sits in the Kiel government building with a secure Social Democrat majority.

Engholm at least claims that politics does not dominate his life. He remains, along with Oskar Lafontaine, the Prime Minister of the Saarland, the SPD's principal hope for new dynamism in the 1990s. Both combine pragmatic politics with rare rhetorical fire. Engholm says his prime wish is to play the piano well, and brushes aside the idea of returning to a government post in Bonn. He has a penchant for collecting art, and has promised himself and his artist wife to retire from active politics before he is 60. If Engholm sticks to this resolution, he has a maximum of ten years to bring the Social Democrats fortune in the North – and perhaps beyond.

II

The Barschel affair put in the shade the scandal which previously ranked as the most murky in the Federal Republic's history, centring on illegal political payments by the Flick industrial group. The Flick affair is a story of Byzantine relationships between members of Germany's political and corporate oligarchy – and provides an insight into the continuity of German business dealings before and after 1945.

At the beginning of the 1980s the Flick company was one of West Germany's largest industrial concerns, with holdings spreading from steel and chemicals to paper factories and motor cars. Revelations of the company's complex role in financing political parties through clandestine transfers came out in the press in 1981-82 – above all, as a result of reporting by *Der Spiegel*. The magazine was also responsible in 1982 for divulging the third great German scandal of the 1980s, over the trade union-owned Neue Heimat housing concern, which badly rocked public confidence in the union movement.* The Flick affair dragged on for six years and reached its climax with a long-running trial in 1986-87, when two of West Germany's best-known politicians – former Economics Ministers Otto Graf Lambsdorff and Hans Friderichs (both from the Free Democratic Party) – were charged with corruption.

Flick was at the centre of a cluster of corporations which for years had illicitly channelled large sums to political parties – above all the

* See Chapter 9.

Christian Democrats and the Free Democrats, but also including the Social Democratic Party. By making under-the-table payments, mainly routed through anonymously-named 'front' organisations billed as charitable foundations, the companies defrauded considerable amounts in tax – and also put themselves in a position of potential influence over politicians. The most important tax shelter association, the quaintly-named *Staatsbürgerliche Vereinigung* based in Cologne, was believed to have funnelled DM200 million to all the main parties, from the 1950s onwards. The illegal payments saga led to a flurry of judicial investigations and court action, with some court cases continuing still in 1989.

The Flick payments – estimated at around DM25 million between 1969 and 1980 – hit the headlines for two reasons. The first reflected the history during the 1920s and 1930s of the Flick group's legendary founder, Friedrich Flick. The second related to one of post-war Germany's most sensational business transactions – the deal in 1975 under which Flick's son and heir, Friedrich Karl Flick, sold a 29 per cent stake in motor group Daimler-Benz to the Deutsche Bank, West Germany's largest and most powerful banking group.

Friedrich Flick amassed a steel and coal empire during the Weimar period and became a prime source of funds for the republic's jousting political parties. Although at first transferring cash primarily to the bourgeois parties, Flick was a notable financier of the Nazis during the 1930s, and later joined the party.[15]. Flick's humble birth – he was the son of a rural timber dealer – distinguished him from the other Ruhr industrialists embroiled with the Third Reich. Like many other magnates, Flick profited greatly from the war economy, and his group was one of the most notorious employers of slave labour. Flick was given a seven-year jail sentence at Nuremberg in 1947. Released ahead of time in 1950, he was forced to sell his iron and steel interests – a move which proved highly fortuitous. He reinvested the proceeds judiciously in a string of industrial investments, and became one of the richest men in post-war Germany – the supreme example of an ex-Nazi businessman making a fortune from the *Wirtschaftswunder*.* Flick's most notable shareholding, acquired in the mid-1950s, was a 39 per cent stake in Daimler-Benz – passed on to his heirs when he died in 1972.

Flick's third son, Friedrich Karl Flick, left in control of the conglomerate, decided to restructure its rambling shareholdings. For DM2 billion, he sold all but 10 per cent of the Daimler-Benz participation to the Deutsche Bank in a move coordinated with the Bonn

* See Chapter 6.

government to stop the Shah of Iran buying the stake.[16] The younger Flick invested the proceeds of the DM2 billion sale in a variety of industrial ventures and, at the same time, maintained his father's practice of disbursing funds to the main political parties. The Free Democrats were among the principal beneficiaries of Flick largesse. In the 1986 trial of Lambsdorff and Friderichs, the state prosecutor's case was that the Flick group had bribed the government to grant a tax exemption on the profits of the sale. Although the most serious charges were dismissed, Lambsdorff and Friderichs were found guilty of evading taxes by accepting illegal donations, and were fined heavily. They were not the only casualties. Helmut Kohl faced an investigation from the Bonn public prosecutor at the beginning of 1986 into accusations that he lied to a parliamentary panel investigating the saga. At one stage, it even looked possible that the Chancellor might resign over the affair – but the turbulence died down after a few months.

Lambsdorff, a descendant of the Prussian aristocracy, an admirer of Bismarck and a great-nephew of a Foreign Minister of Czarist Russia, is one of the survivors of German politics. He went on to become the Free Democrats' chairman in 1988. A bogeyman for the Left because of his role in prompting the Free Democrats to desert the coalition with the Social Democrats in 1982, Lambsdorff declares pugnaciously that he has trumped his opponents who wanted the Flick trial to break his career.[17] The affair however certainly damaged Lambsdorff's stature, and also had a deeper effect. Since all the main parties acquiesced in the convoluted system of illegal payments uncovered during the investigations, the Flick affair damaged the reputation of German politics – and heightened the potential for protest voting.

The saga had an ironic postscript. Friedrich Karl Flick grew tired of the years of bad publicity over the scandal, and resolved to retire from the headlines. He sold the entire DM10 billion-turnover family company in 1985 – and, again, it was the Deutsche Bank which handled the deal. It bought the conglomerate from the frustrated heir for DM6 billion and then resold it in pieces to earn DM1 billion profit. Friedrich Karl Flick, ranked as the fourth richest person in West Germany, with wealth estimated at $2.4 billion,[18] today lives in well-guarded seclusion. The Deutsche Bank, however – its twin silver and glass towers glittering above the Frankfurt skyline – is as visible as ever. Not for the first time in its 120-year history, the bank showed that, whatever the political convulsions, it normally finishes up on the winning side.

III

The combined effect of the 1980s scandals was to contribute to an increase in disenchantment with politics. The mood needs to be put into international perspective: the Germans still seem much more satisfied with their democratic system than people in other European countries.[19] But at the end of the 1980s, West Germany started to experience fragmentation of the popular vote and a strong move away from the established parties to an extent not seen since the first election in 1949. The main political parties and the people who run them appeared increasingly lack-lustre and out of touch with ordinary voters. At the same time, the checks and balances of West Germany's decentralised political system, so much admired in the early post-war years, started to look less like a recipe for stability and more like a source of inflexibility.

Part of this is a sign that West Germany is reaching political maturity. No industrialised country is completely satisfied with its method of democracy, but the Germans have been less inclined to show disgruntlement than electorates in other countries because memories of totalitarianism have been still relatively fresh. The fall in the electoral turn-out in the late 1980s reflects, on the surface, a natural move towards politics becoming less slavish and more routine. The 84 per cent turn-out in the 1987 general election, though the lowest since the first poll in 1949 and down heavily from the figures of around 90 per cent during the 1970s, was nevertheless still much higher than in most of West Germany's neighbours[20]. On the other hand, West Germany cannot readily be compared with other countries with longer democratic traditions. The confusion and bitterness surrounding the breakdown of Schmidt's Social Democrat-led coalition in 1981-82 and the failure of Chancellor Kohl to live up to his promise to provide 'spiritual and moral renewal' have added to the pall of disillusionment. West German parliamentarism may simply have been going through growing pains; or is it something more worrying?

The revival of the ultra-Right is the most potentially disturbing development. This is especially so since it has come during a period of slow but steady economic upturn. Ultra-Right parties have picked up support in response to frustration with the established parties, disappointment over unemployment, housing and the European Community, worries over immigration* and dissatisfaction with the consequences of German partition. The conservative appeal of Franz Josef Strauss, the long-time leader of the Christian Social Union – the

* See Chapter 15.

Bavarian sister-party of the Christian Democrats – prevented many far Right voters from transferring their allegiance to extremist parties. Although condemned in the 1980s to play a maverick role in German politics, Strauss was one of the country's few genuine orators. His death in 1988 robbed the mainstream conservative parties of a lightning conductor for protest votes. By setting free forces on the Right previously integrated into the established conservative groupings, Strauss's death is likely to reshape the political landscape in the 1990s.

The increased following of the far Right represents the counterpart to the splitting of votes on the Left caused by the rise in popularity of the Greens ecology party.* The Greens, born out of the peace movement at the end of the 1970s, favour radical measures on disarmament and the environment. They won representation in the Bundestag for the first time in 1983 and, despite periodic bouts of in-fighting, now look an established part of politics. The inability of the two large parties – the Christian Democrats and the Social Democrats – to meet the aspirations of a growing number of fringe voters marks a significant change. The Christian Democratic Union (set up in 1945, partly from the residues of the old Catholic Centre Party), and the Social Democrats, formed in the 1860s, are the two *Volksparteien* (people's or 'catch-all' parties). They attempt to cover a wide spectrum of allegiances and opinions, but these days their appeal is fading. The groups on the far Right jostling for protest votes remain much less important in numerical terms than the *Front National* in France. But politicians' constant repetition of the memories of the Weimar Republic underlines that West Germany is handicapped by history: it cannot face extremism with equanimity.

Certainly, the Federal Republic has proven that it is not simply a fair-weather democracy. At no time since 1949 has the electorate chosen a government supporting anything less than wholehearted integration with the West. Parties of the extreme Right or Left have consistently failed to attain a parliamentary foothold. In all but four years[21] since its foundation, the Federal Republic has been run by centrist coalitions. If one electoral *Leitmotif* had to be selected to sum up the post-war era, it would be 'No experiments', Adenauer's campaign slogan in the 1957 general election. This powered the Christian Democrats (in league with the Christian Social Union) to an absolute voting majority – the only time a party has scored more than 50 per cent of the votes.

Over forty years, the electorate's underlying conservatism has not

* See Chapter 14

impeded acceptance of necessary reforms. Although voters have not been inclined directly to dispatch sitting governments from office, the coalition arithmetic has generally changed in line with the mood of the people. The most obvious example was the gaining of power by the Social Democrats in 1969 after the three-year interregnum of the Grand Coalition.

Because of residual memories of the consequences of the post-1929 Depression, occasional heart-fluttering has come from fears that democracy could crumble in the wake of a severe economic downturn. The first post-war recession in 1966-67 – when average unemployment in the course of a year almost tripled to 459,000 from 161,000 – provided particular grounds for unease. The pooling of forces of the Christian and Social Democrats during Kiesinger's Grand Coalition gave a powerful stimulus to the far Right. Above all it boosted the National Democratic Party (NPD), a grouping propounding nationalistic views similar to the initial policies of Hitler (although it purports not to be neo-Nazi).

At about the time in 1966-68 when the NPD was gaining seats in several *Land* parliaments, John Le Carré wrote his book *A Small Town in Germany*. He came up with a plot which, at the time, seemed believable; it centred on the messianic figure of Karfeld, an industrial chemist with a plant outside Essen, who wanted to swap links with the West for a 'trade alliance' with the Soviet Union. Karfeld led massive anti-government demonstrations with slogans like: 'The West has discarded us – Germany can look East without shame. End the Coca-Cola culture now.'[22] In the Le Carré book, the Federal Republic looked set to tumble like Weimar. Real life proved different. The far-Right NPD narrowly failed to gain a place in the Bundestag in the 1969 elections, and during the 1970s faded away almost as quickly as it had risen. By splitting votes on the Right, the NPD dampened the score of the Christian Democrats in the 1969 elections and paved the way for the Social Democrats to head their first post-war government. Student radicalism of the 1960s, the politically-inspired terrorism of the 1970s, the rise in unemployment to above 2 million, together with the massive and frequently violent protests against nuclear energy throughout the 1980s: West Germany appeared to take all this in its stride. But commentators still ponder whether basic democratic deficiencies linger beneath the impressive mantle of gross national product – and the renewed pull of Right-wing extremists has nourished the doubts. Like so much in post-war Germany, anxiety is a natural accompaniment to stability – indeed, perhaps a condition for it.

IV

Paradoxically, one of the reasons for successful adaptation to parliamentarism may have been Germany's lack of firm political roots. By 1949, the Germans were ready as never before for a new attempt at parliamentary democracy. Geography played a part in this. The western portion of the country fated for democracy was, by happy coincidence, the part best equipped for the new experience. In the Reichstag elections of November 1932, only in today's Federal Republic – in contrast to the area of today's GDR or the eastern territories – did the parties of the Weimar Republic record a higher score (43.4 per cent) than the anti-democratic Right. 'The historical conditions for parliamentary democracy were evidently better in the western states and provinces than in middle and eastern Germany,' according to sociologist Ralf Dahrendorf.[23]

In the past, distaste for upsetting established patterns had always dampened appetite for change. The Social Democrats in 1919 proclaimed '*Rot ist richtig, aber Ordnung muss sein!*' (Red is right, but we must have order!). The Germans' proclivity for elevating discipline to the highest of the virtues – a characteristic which, although less acute, has certainly not died out in intervening years – was summed up in Stalin's memory of his visit to Leipzig in 1907 as a young man, when he came with 200 German Communists to attend an international conference.

> Their train arrived punctually at the station, but there was no official to collect their tickets. All the German Communists therefore waited docilely for two hours to get off the platform. So none of them were able to attend the meeting.[24]

After the collapse of the Third Reich, discipline was channelled into the extraordinary feat of rebuilding – and the Germans became model democrats. The foundations were provided by the 1949 *Grundgesetz* (Basic Law), a judicious effort to learn from the past which was drawn up in 1948-49 by the Parliamentary Council under the chairmanship of Adenauer. This grouped the Landtag representatives from the state parliaments which had already been set up by the allies in the western zone. In giving priority (in the first 19 articles) to an inalienable charter of human rights, the Law combined the better features of Weimar and the abortive Frankfurt constitution of 1848-49, and at last linked Germany to the mainstream of the western Enlightenment.

Marking a symbolic break with the misuse of state power under the Nazis, the Basic Law chiselled away at – but did not eliminate – the philosophy of authoritarianism. Hitler bequeathed to the West Germans the difficult task of finding the right balance between the twin necessities of disobedience and respect towards the state.* By increasing the powers of the Chancellor and limiting those of the president – who henceforth became a kind of neutral state spokesman rather than a kingmaker – the 1949 constitution laid the foundations for cabinet government. The instability and the 'over-democratisation' of the Weimar years were to be avoided. The Bundestag could vote the Chancellor out of office only if simultaneously it could elect his successor with a majority of its members. The Basic Law laid down that 'the people' were the repository of all state authority (Article 20), but, to codify the way this was to be channelled, the parties were specifically enshrined (in Article 21) as the agents of political decision-making.

Voting arrangements encouraged consensus politics based on coalition governments. The electoral system of proportional representation was buttressed by the rule preventing parties winning less than 5 per cent of votes from gaining seats in the Bundestag. This has hindered the formation of large parliamentary majorities, while at the same time hampering the emergence of the splinter groupings which plagued Weimar. Although the conservative parties gained between 44 and 50 per cent of the votes in every general election since 1953, they were able to rule without a coalition partner for only one short period under Adenauer, and for thirteen years (between 1969 and 1982) were consigned to the Opposition. Compare this with Britain's 'first past the post' majority voting system. Margaret Thatcher's Conservatives succeeded in winning large majorities in the House of Commons in the three general elections since 1979 – with an average share of the votes of only 42.7 per cent. Kohl, whose mind is constantly searching for a well-loved anecdote, often regales visitors from England (including on one occasion the Duke of Edinburgh) with the tale of how he won 48.6 per cent of the votes in the 1976 election – and still finished up as leader of the Opposition.

For three decades through to the early 1980s, the CDU/CSU, Social Democrats and Free Democrats formed three competing blocs in a stable political landscape. The liberal Free Democrats functioned as a semi-automatic regulator between the two *Volksparteien*; switching coalitions twice, the Free Democrats have been partners in governments in Bonn for all but seven years since the Republic's foundation. The

* See Chapter 7.

76

Greens' Bundestag entry in 1983, together with the renewed strength of the far-Right, has now made the interaction between the parties much more complex and difficult to analyse. The CDU and the SPD have been trying to spread their appeal simultaneously towards the centre ground to attract a growing mass of floating voters, and towards their flanks to avoid losing votes to the radical fringes.[25] Rising volatility of personal voting patterns has been accompanied by a blurring of distinctions between the parties. The mainstream parties' attempt to stretch their policies over an ever-wider span of potential voters has inevitably diminished their credibility. Opinion polls in 1988-89 indicated that the CDU/CSU and the SPD each could count on less than 40 per cent of the votes, compared with the 90 per cent which the two blocs normally shared in general elections over the past thirty years. In a proportional voting system, the importance of the extra 10 per cent accruing to the radical parties is magnified considerably. The *de facto* five-party system in the 1990s looks likely to be more polarised – and less stable. Memories of Weimar may return anew – especially in view of the fragmentation of the vote observed in the March 1990 East German elections. The new enfranchisement of the East German electorate – a population which previously participated in democracy only through West German radio and TV – may add to overall German political volatility.

If one aim of the West German constitution was to avoid the excessive number of parties participating in Weimar parliaments, the other was to curb centralisation. A crucial role stemmed from the federal system – reflecting both Germany's decentralised political traditions and also the overriding post-war American aim of imposing a framework of political checks and balances. In drawing up federal state boundaries after 1945, a prime objective of the occupying powers was to scour Prussia and its centralising influences from the map, and also to prevent a concentration of economic might in the industrial heartland of the Ruhr. Although the ancient kingdom of Bavaria remained intact, other states such as North Rhine Westphalia or Lower Saxony were totally new creations. An additional safeguard against concentration of power comes from the judiciary. The Federal Constitutional Court in Karlsruhe has responsibility for ensuring that the Basic Law is observed, and more particularly for ruling on the constitutional spheres of the federal government and the *Länder*.

Sizeable administrative powers were devolved to the *Land* governments. With the principal exceptions of foreign and defence policies, most federal laws are executed by the *Länder*. Although Bonn remains the centre of political decision-making, the *Länder* retain strong influence over legislation. Roughly half of all federal laws require the consent of the Bundesrat, the second administrative chamber, in which all the *Länder* except West Berlin have voting power. The Bundesrat enjoys an absolute veto over measures which would seriously affect the financial or administrative interests of the *Länder* (such as tax laws), and must also approve amendments to the constitution.

Political devolution has also been aided by financial arrangements. The three levels of government – central, regional and local – divide up revenue from the three most productive taxes: income, corporation and value added tax. Additionally, the *Gemeinden* (municipalities) are empowered to raise some local taxes independently. A system of equalisation payments between the *Bund* and the *Länder* shares out payments among the better and less well-off regions. The share of all tax revenues flowing outside the central government has been increasing steadily over the years, with the *Länder* and municipalities now taking up roughly half of all revenues, as against only 45 per cent in 1971.

The federal system has proved extraordinarily adept at meeting several objectives at once. It has married self-governing Germanic traditions with the need to avoid both undue concentration and exaggerated fragmentation of power. The Empire after 1648 had more than 300 territories; the German Confederation in 1815 was reduced to 39 states, ranging from the two great powers of Austria and Prussia to tiny principalities; the Second Empire forged in 1871 had 25 states and one administered territory (the so-called Reichsland, comprising Alsace and Lorraine). The Weimar Republic had 25 constituents; occupied Germany under the four powers was cut down to 18 units (four *Länder* each for the Americans, British and French, five for the Soviet Union, plus Berlin.) When the Federal Republic was formed in 1949, it had 11 states. Since then the Saar, after the war under French control, has acceded to the republic, while three states have merged. West Germany now counts 10 *Länder* plus West Berlin, which has special status.[26] Three centuries of trial and error at last produced regional administrative units of manageable size. The revival of the East German *Länder* as part of the reunification process shows that Germany has well understood the benefits of federalism.

The states have made full use of their extra policy-making tools. During his long period as Bavaria's dominant politician, Franz Josef Strauss, for instance, used his influence to turn the state from a backward agricultural region to a world leader in aerospace and computers. Lothar Späth, the cigar-puffing Christian Democrat Baden Württemberg Prime

Minister, has gained personal popularity by building up his state's expertise in high technology. 'Competition between the *Länder* produces dynamism,' he told me crisply.[27] Späth has sealed friendship with Edzard Reuter, the chairman of Stuttgart-based Daimler-Benz, and is on convivial terms with pragmatic Social Democrats such as Oskar Lafontaine. Späth has based his appeal on canny economic management and clever public relations – as well as avoidance of ministerial responsibility in the federal government during a difficult phase for the Christian Democrats.

Self-government in the *Länder* has provided an important support for democracy, enabling people to identify with local policies and personalities. The rise in popularity of federalism over the years has been impressive. According to a long-running Allensbach survey, in 1952 60 per cent of respondents said they favoured 'centralism' and only 17 per cent 'federalism'. By 1960, 41 per cent of the population called themselves federalists and 25 per cent centralists, and by 1988 the percentage favouring federalism had soared to 71 per cent, against only 8 per cent in favour of centralised government.[28] The growing support for federalism helps explain why the West Germans have grown more critical about perceived 'centrist' interference from the European Commission in Brussels.

However, decentralisation of administrative, legislative and financial authority to the *Länder* has gone much further than the fathers of the 1949 constitution intended. Rivalry among individual *Länder* has damaged the policy-making cohesion of central government – a reminder of traditional German particularism. The federal states resorted to near-blackmail to push through their special economic interests in the 1990 tax reform proposals which were voted through in 1988. Lothar Späth, for instance, threatened to block passage of the tax bill in the Bundesrat unless the government maintained tax concessions for Daimler-Benz workers buying their own cars.

A more serious warning signal for West German democracy comes from the untrammelled growth of the party bureaucracies. The parties are invested by the constitution with the task of representing the people, but this aim has become increasingly frustrated by a growing distance between the parties and the electorate, and by the tendency for the governing party to confuse its interests with those of the state. During the past twenty years, the top echelons of the civil service and of the broadcasting corporations* have become increasingly politicised. Unlike the position in Britain, a spoils system has grown up in government under which new administrations make sweeping changes among top civil

---

* See Chapter 8.

servants. As an indication of the difficulty in holding on to grass roots support, membership of the main parties, which boomed during the 1970s, dropped sharply towards the end of the 1980s. The Christian Democrats lost around 30,000 members since the 1983 high point of 734,000; the Social Democrats at 920,000 fell nearly 10,000 from their mid-1970s peak; and the Free Democrats dropped to about 67,000 members, down from 80,000 at the beginning of the decade. The only party to show an increase was the Greens – with about 42,000 members.

Politics should be a natural play of conflicting interests, but the lingering vestiges of German authoritarianism tend to give unfair weight to the party in power. Ambivalence is even expressed in the language: the post-war democracy is often referred to as a 'state order' by both Left and Right.[29] The leader of the opposition in West Germany has a greatly inferior status to that of the head of government, whereas in Britain the two posts – in sheer protocol terms – are equivalent. Richard von Weizsäcker has pointed out that some ordinary Germans see 'the business of opposition as downright disreputable'.[30] At election meetings or on other occasions where ordinary people come into contact with *die Prominenz* (a word for which there is no complete translation – and which is used as much in East as in West Germany), the man in the street tends to treat Ministers with the respect accorded elsewhere to royalty. Counting all the *Land* governments, there are well over a hundred Ministers, and countless state secretaries, all with the trappings of power: chauffeur-driven BMWs or Mercedes, and security men with walkie-talkies. Illogically, their large numbers seem to increase rather than lower their importance. A television journalist acquaintance once told me how he had been reprimanded by an elderly viewer for having interviewed too brusquely Joschka Fischer, the Green Environment Minister in the state government of Hesse up to 1987. Although the viewer was a conservative and by no means a Greens' sympathiser, he told the interviewer fiercely: 'That was no way to treat a Minister.'

V

Lack of proper contact between politicians and the people is accentuated by the peculiar status of the capital. Bonn was chosen as the capital in 1949 rather than Frankfurt above all in accordance with Adenauer's wishes.[31] For almost a quarter of a century it was officially regarded as a 'provisional' choice, to be superseded eventually by Berlin upon German reunification. John Le Carré wrote in the 1960s: 'The very choice of Bonn as the waiting house for Berlin has long been an anomaly; now it is an abuse';[32] and he was right. Bonn gave up its 'provisional' status only in 1973, after the signing of the Basic Relations Treaty between East and West Germany. Cocooned in their caucus meetings, most of the deputies who stream to Bonn during the weeks when the Bundestag is sitting have never made much effort to get to know the town; and the town remains largely indifferent to the parliamentarians. Although most deputies try to spend as much time as possible in their constituencies, the inevitable focus on Bonn cramps their horizons. Helmut Schmidt says, 'I would have chosen Frankfurt. You need a place where politicians can talk to intellectuals at night.'[33] Friedhelm Kemna, editor of the main Bonn newspaper, the *General-Anzeiger*, says that if the capital were transported overnight, either to Berlin or to the Lüneburg Heath, most local people would probably not miss it.[34]

Bonn still has a certain Rhineside charm and much of the administrative machinery retains a trace of provisionality. The Finance, Economics, Labour and Interior Ministries were all formerly army barracks; as was the Defence Ministry before it moved to its present hill-top site outside the town. Part of the army quarters taken over by the Finance Ministry were previously used as stables for imperial cavalry and officials in the Ministry's monetary and credit department – who sit closest to the former stables – say that on hot days a distinctly horsy smell permeates their office walls. The Foreign Ministry, a building of small windows and endless corridors, was earmarked as a hospital. Embassies and ambassadors' residences still bear the hallmarks of the occupation years. The US embassy was built in the early 1950s as a temporary prefabricated construction deemed to have a life expectancy of twenty-five years; in the event that the capital moved to Berlin, it was thought that this building too would be used as a hospital.

Bonn is being given a face-lift with a DM3 billion construction programme to provide a new Bundestag, re-site Ministries and construct hotels, conference centres and museums by the early 1990s. According to Hans Daniels, the mayor, the idea is to give Bonn a more representative character without detracting from its small-town homeliness. 'This is a capital without triumphal arches,' he says.[35] Although officially Bonn is 'provisional' no more, he admits that many people still find it difficult to accept. 'Bonn is capital of the Federal Republic, but not of the whole of Germany. There is a lack of symbolic

identification when the concepts of state and nation do not overlap.'
Ironically, just as the building boom reached a peak at the beginning of
1990, Bonn started to look provisional again as calls grew for Berlin to
be renamed the capital of a united Germany. The economic
consequences for Bonn in the event of the capital's migration to Berlin
would clearly be severe; Daniels launched a campaign to 'share' the
functions of the capital with Berlin, arguing that this would make clear
the contrast with the centralised pre-war Reich.[36] Among the many
reunification supporters who believe that Bonn should be preserved as
the capital, Thomas Kielinger, the editor of the Bonn-based weekly
Rheinischer Merkur, insists that a move back to Berlin would deprive
Germany of 'necessary understatement'.[37] Although Berlin would bring
cultural *Glanz*, relocating the capital there would not only disturb the
balance of power with the *Länder*; it could also, he adds, ominously,
bring the temptation for Germany again to 'show its muscles'.

Bonn is only too well aware of its lack of appeal. Few Germans have
any desire to visit the place unless they are politicians, functionaries or
industrial lobbyists. To counter the indifference, the Federal Press
Office every year spends DM17 million ferrying 70,000 citizens to Bonn
and providing them with board and lodging for three days. The
'popularisation' programme accounts for 20 per cent of all hotel
bookings in the town.

The make-up of the Bundestag gives a hint of its insularity. More than
half the deputies are officials of various kinds. They are led by the state
functionaries or *Beamten*, members of an institution which forms one of
the lasting legacies of Prussia, including government officials, judges,
teachers, professors, policemen, and post and railway workers. Only a
third of deputies are drawn from industry, agriculture and the professions
– a category which has fallen in recent years.[38] Most parliamentary
debates tend to be set-piece rituals, without spontaneity. Kemna of the
General-Anzeiger, pointing out that the themes and the politicians were
much more interesting in the republic's early decades, looks back wist-
fully to the Bundestag's pioneering days. 'Then, the galleries were full of
people. Now, one can scarcely look at it, it is so boring.' The veteran FDP
deputy Hildegard Hamm-Brücher, a protagonist of parliamentary
reform, points out that the Bonn parliament sits much less often in full
sessions than its counterparts in other countries, and that speaking
arrangements are unnecessarily bureaucratic. Deputies have considerably fewer opportunities to aim questions at ministers. She also recommends opening Bundestag committee proceedings to the public, as is the
case with the parliaments in Britain and the US.[39]

Politics is in urgent need of outside blood. According to Kurt Biedenkopf, a former CDU secretary-general – who made headlines in 1990 by taking up a part-time professorship at Leipzig university – 'West German politicians have become a specific breed depending on politics not just for prestige and influence, but also for income.' He says that politicians' lack of experience of other walks of life restricts their ability to make decisions and cleave through vested interests: 'They are not very risk-happy, they are very careful.'[40] Industrialists are often openly scornful at the lack of economic policy expertise among politicians of both Right and Left. The arrival of Chancellor Kohl's government in 1982 was initially enthusiastically welcomed in industrial and banking circles, but, during the next few years, relations between the Christian Democrats and the business community cooled.*

One area where industry and politics have been forced apart is in the field of political donations. The Flick scandal, and the stream of criminal investigations in its wake, made companies extremely wary about extending largesse to political parties in their former manner. The overall loser, ironically, has been the taxpayer. Once companies stopped the practice of evading taxes by illicit contributions, the parties faced a drop in revenues and were unable to boost membership fees sufficiently to cover costs.

Under a package of measures decided in 1983 to put political funding on a more stable footing, the parties have greatly increased their demands on state coffers. During the five years between 1983 and 1987, the five parties represented in the Bundestag drew on public funding of nearly DM1 billion, covering more than one-third of their outlays.[41] Additionally, the well-equipped party foundations, which provide research, travel and other back-up facilities for the politicians, also rely on funding from taxpayers. The government pays out funds to reimburse the parties for their election expenses according to a sliding formula depending on the proportion of votes they gather. For example, in the 1987 general election, the parties were able to divide up a state jackpot of DM225 million.[42] In the first East German election in March 1990, East German parties received large-scale financial and material help from 'sister' parties in the West; indirectly, roughly one third of the cash involved came from the West German tax-payer.

The only individual corporation to continue to make regular party donations of more than DM100,000 is the Deutsche Bank, which has contributed more than DM30 million to political parties since the early

* See Chapters 6,9.

1960s.[43] Other businesses channel funds via industry associations, but have held back from donating by name as the result of a law requiring the names of larger contributors to be published. The fall in parties' dependence on large donations from industry and banking is certainly welcome; the experience of the Weimar Republic was that parties which became dependent on finance from industry quickly found themselves open to various forms of blackmail.[44] But the trend towards exaggerated reliance on public funding is also unhealthy. The parties have established for themselves a central role in West German society; but the role has outgrown their resources. Unless they can find some way of establishing broader support, they risk becoming mere appendages of the state.

VI

One of the necessary curiosities of West German politics is that radical parties on the Left and Right are listed in an annual report by the security services. The *Bundesamt für Verfassungsschutz* (literally, the Federal Office for the Protection of the Constitution) keeps an eye on the parties to check if they represent a threat to democracy. The BfV, under the jurisdiction of the Interior Ministry, has its headquarters in Cologne and maintains a web of semi-autonomous offshoots under the jurisdiction of the *Länder*. It is also West Germany's counter-espionage agency; like political extremists, spies are considered to endanger internal stability.

Parties ruled by the Constitutional Court to be 'anti-constitutional' (*verfassungswidrig*) are banned altogether, while those considered to be 'a threat to the constitution' (*verfassungsfeindlich*) are kept under surveillance. Members of the listed parties who work for the public sector (in the army, civil service, post office, railways and so on) are kept under individual scrutiny and are liable to dismissal if their political activity is deemed to be undermining the state. In 1988, the *Verfassungsschutz* listed 225 Right-wing and 2,095 Left-wing extremists (most of them Communists) in the public service.

Pride of place in the annual BfV report has always been enjoyed by the Communist Party (DKP) – but this seems likely to change in future. The BfV in 1988 recorded membership of 35,000 while the party claimed nearly 50,000. The DKP was re-established in 1968 after its forerunner, the KPD, was banned in 1956 as anti-constitutional. Sitting in his cramped office in Düsseldorf, Herbert Mies – a cheerful, dishevelled man in a burgundy pullover, DKP chairman since 1973 – told me at the end of 1988 that the DKP was not an enemy of the Republic. The danger that it could be dissolved like its predecessor still hung over the party 'like a sword of Damocles'.[45] Mies's words had a prophetic ring; just over a year later, the party began to dissolve as a result of the collapse of Communism in East Germany.

The DKP, traditionally the most Moscow-orientated of western European Communist parties, had already been suffering a severe internal split as the result of a battle between pro-Gorbachev reformists and party hardliners. A DKP-backed 'peace list' in 1987 gained only 0.5 per cent of the votes, less than the 0.6 per cent scored by the far Right National Democratic Party (NPD). Only once – between 1949 and 1953 – did the Communists send deputies to the Bundestag. 'We used to have the monopoly of peace efforts,' Mies told me ruefully, admitting that West Germany's better understanding with Moscow has diminished the party's novelty value and cut support from industry workers. Although Mies denies receiving illicit monies – 'Ask the auditors,' he protested – the security services claim that the party relied on DM65 million a year sent by clandestine channels from East Germany. Following the fall of the Communist leadership in East Berlin in December 1989, the funds were cut off. Mies's job was reduced to supervising the sacking of DKP employees, closing offices (including the party headquarters) and preparing the party for gradual receivership.

On the opposite side of the spectrum, but also in the *verfassungsfeindlich* category comes West Germany's most bizarre extreme Right party, the German People's Union (DVU). It is run by Gerhard Frey, a Bavarian publisher considering himself a patriot who is standing up for Germany's best interests. Hence mention of the *Verfassungsschutz* tends to make his glinting eyes bulge with anger. Frey, in his mid-fifties, a bulky, puffy-faced man, has his headquarters in a well-guarded villa in a Munich suburb. When I went to see him, a large Alsatian dog was patrolling the snow-covered garden.[46] Frey – referred to always as 'Doctor' by his staff and followers – has been on the circuit for a long time. In 1965, the Israeli journalist Amos Elon described attending one of his meetings in a Munich beer cellar.

He uses short, lucidly formulated sentences. Words spring lightly and rapidly out of his small mouth; he pauses regularly for applause. His standard phrase begins, 'I say ...' 'I tell you, friends ...' and in a soft, intimate tone of voice he announces 'outrages', terrible affronts 'kept secret' by the government. Then abruptly his voice rises; hysterically – either genuine or intended – he screeches: 'I fear the wages of history ... I tremble ... I am troubled that our policies come not from national interests but from blackmail by National Jewry.'[47]

The style has not greatly changed. While waiting to be received in Frey's large book-lined office, I notice that a bust of Hitler's deputy Rudolf Hess stands on the mantelpiece in the ante-room. Hess died in Spandau prison in 1987, apparently after committing suicide, but it has become an article of faith among extreme Right-wingers to claim he was murdered by the Allies. I leaf through some of Frey's publications; he produces three far-Right weekly newspapers for which he claims a circulation of 160,000. The largest of them, the *National Zeitung*, serves up a regular diet of anti-Jewish propaganda and claims that the Germans are still being victimised by the war victors.[48] Its large red and black lettering is a feature of every railway station news kiosk, doling out lurid conspiracy theories. 'Plan for extermination of the Germans,' was one headline in November 1987. 'How Kohl's reunification plan is being sabotaged' was the message in January 1990.

Contact with the press over the years has made Frey cautious. He greets me by the sofa with a tape-recorder turning ostentatiously to record our interview, just in case I feel like misquoting him. Two young men, one of whom appears to be his son, are in reverent attendance. Frey tells me that the DVU movement, formed in 1971, has 16,000 members, while the election-fighting arm of the organisation – the so-called 'D List' – is 6,000-strong. (The *Verfassungsschutz* is more cautious, but presumably well informed. It puts the DVU membership at more than 12,000.) After a period of rivalry between the two, the DVU now collaborates with the National Democratic Party (NPD) and won a seat in the Bremen city parliament in 1987. Frey has enlisted the help of David Irving, the British author and Nazi researcher, who has gained notoriety for his thesis that mass murder of the Jews was carried out without Hitler's orders or knowledge.[49]

Irving appears regularly at Frey rallies, elaborating among other things on the Hess 'murder'. He was engaged by Frey in 1988 to comb through Nazi party files at the US-run Berlin Document Centre in West Berlin to glean material on the Nazi past of prominent Germans.[50] Irving told me he sympathised with Frey's attempt to clear up 'hypocrisy'. He was offered DM1,000 per name for the material, but no money changed hands because he was barred from access to the US centre.[51]

86

For the 1989 European parliamentary elections, Frey built up a war chest of more than DM12 million. He receives contributions primarily from small businesses which feel 'betrayed' by the European Community, and says that he and the NPD together ask for the support of all those who feel 'cast out' of society – unemployed steelworkers, for instance. He rambles a little through some well-rehearsed themes – the bombing of Dresden, the Nuremberg war tribunal and the killing of the Indians by the Americans. 'Is it dangerous to love one's country?' he asks with a flourish. Frey spells out plans for reunifying Germany as a neutral state 'in peace and freedom'. He talks about the importance of linking up with Austria and breathes a last note of discontent about the consequences of the war: 'Our guilt complex is stretched too far.'

For the far-Right, the death of Strauss was a piece of good news. Sitting in his dank-looking party headquarters in a Stuttgart side street, thick-set NPD chairman Martin Mussgnug says that party rallies have been better attended since Strauss disappeared from the scene. Mussgnug is a 52-year-old lawyer employing, he says, eight people in his practice.[52] There is a small photo of an Alsatian pinned to the wall, and black-red-and-gold election posters are hung up everywhere; apart from that, it all appears highly reasonable. Mussgnug, NPD chairman since 1971, gives an impression of forced joviality. He says he is no Nazi: 'People who give Nazi salutes at our rallies are thrown out.' He also rejects any idea of anti-Semitism: 'Anyone who smears Jewish cemeteries with swastikas belongs in a mental asylum or in prison.' The NPD likes to keep its distance from a cluster of much more extremist parties with far more overtly Nazi overtones. These are led by the Free German Workers party – a 500-strong movement frequently raided by the police which specialises in attacks on foreigners and rallies lauding Hitler.

This, it seems, is not Mussgnug's line. He pleads for a return to Germany's traditional role as a broker between East and West, and says there are far too many foreigners living in Germany. 'They are perfectly at liberty to form their own identity but not on German soil.' He condemns Germany's looking back at the past, the ritual commemoration of gloomy anniversaries. 'We are looking at our crimes all the time. It's as if you keep reminding someone of all the sins he committed in his youth. This leads to defiance.' Mussgnug has reason to be grateful for West Germany's new democratic largesse. As a result of the law on party financing, the NPD received DM1.4 million from the government after scoring 0.6 per cent in the 1987 general elections. Mussgnug says the NPD has more than 10,000 members (the BfV puts the figure at 6,400), compared with 18,000 at its peak in the end-1960s. He has been

heartened by the number of 18-28-year-olds joining the NPD who find 'lack of perspective' among political parties. 'Our strength is in the younger generation,' he adds – not an enticing prospect.

The third, and most popular, force on the far Right stems from the Munich-based Republicans, a party formed in 1983 which is bidding to carve out a permanent presence in both East and West Germany. The Republicans for several years were not thought extreme enough to warrant the attention of the *Verfassungsschutz*, but several Social Democrat-run *Land* arms of the security service decided by the beginning of 1990 to bring the party under observation. Previously regarded as of no more than nuisance value, the Republicans recorded their most notable success in the June 1989 European elections, gaining 7.1 per cent of the votes – the best score by a far-Right party in a country-wide election since the Federal Republic was founded. Its chairman and founder is Franz Schönhuber, in his mid-sixties, a member of the Waffen SS during the war who afterwards became one of Bavaria's leading television journalists. Stocky, combative and persuasively tongued, Schönhuber firmly denies being a Nazi and points out that he used to be married to a Jewess. He says he expresses ordinary Germans' resentment about the division of Germany. 'My service is to articulate relentlessly the uneasiness of the Germans,' he told me.[53] 'It is a very German feeling. The Germans tend towards neuroses.' He has one daughter, living in the US, he explains chattily: she does not think much of the Germans. Schönhuber's rallies tend to be somewhat depressing affairs, in which he lambasts West Germany's fading work ethic and family spirit. Adding to the surrealism, he is a great supporter of Margaret Thatcher and rarely misses an opportunity to tell meetings of his support for the BBC and 'British democracy'. He describes as 'hate-filled' many of the younger German generation (especially those on the Left who dog the Republicans with persistent counter-protests), and likes to say that in the 1930s they would have been Nazis.

Schönhuber likes to show that he has a serious side, but also admits to a penchant for beer-hall demagoguery. 'There are two Schönhubers,' he told me in his party headquarters in an unprepossessing Munich apartment block. The front door of his office, strewn with campaign literature and staffed with amiable old ladies, has been freshly strengthened with a massive security lock and steel plating in case of attack. 'I can talk to you here, calmly and quietly. But I can also take the arena.' One of Schönhuber's catch-phrases is that he 'does not have to like' Heinz Galinski, the head of the West German Jewish Council; he balances this by calling the Third Reich 'criminal'. 'Losing the war has a

price. But I don't want to say it would have been better if we had won. Then we would have had a European slave state. And the Germans would be the slave-drivers.' Schönhuber is confident of expanding his 18,000-strong party to beyond the 30,000 level. A lot of his members, he claims, are soldiers, policemen and civil servants. In spite of being regularly denied access by East German border guards accusing him of 'fascism', Schönhuber has made a particular effort to build up a following in East Germany. He claims, 'It is part of normality to have a Right-wing party' and declares he is sticking up for the patriotic virtues which Kohl has failed to implement.

Like many other Right-wingers (along with some SPD supporters), Schönhuber thinks increased integration with western Europe bars the way to German reunification and declares, 'The European Community weakens Germany; it is strong only when Germany bleeds.' Pointing to controversy about rising numbers of refugees from the Third World as well as émigrés from eastern Europe, he proclaims, 'We are importing civil war. The anger of the people has reached such a pitch that we could have real hatred of foreigners.'

Schönhuber's party has three main weaknesses. As he admits himself, the Republicans are a one-man band which relies above all on protest votes; efforts to 'intellectualise' the party have failed. It has been damaged by unsavoury cases of violence and extremism among regional party organisations such as in Berlin; one section of the North Rhine Westphalia Republicans distinguished itself in October 1989 by presenting fraudulent papers at a local election. Above all, Schönhuber has been caught off guard – like nearly everyone else – by the prospect of reunification. The party wants to break down barriers with the East; yet it draws much of its support from voters who fear their jobs and homes may be at risk from émigrés leaving eastern Europe for a better life in West Germany. As Germany moves towards unity, Schönhuber will lose a considerable number of scapegoats: he will no longer be able to blame the western allies, the European Community or Wall Street for thwarting Germany's national ambitions.

Schönhuber prides himself on his support in the inner cities, and says: 'Generally speaking, we are the party of the poorer people.' Like the other far-Right groups, the Republicans reach out for the frustrated, disappointed voters who feel they have somehow missed the band-wagon. In spite of all its wealth, there are many such people in West Germany. It is both a strength and a weakness of German democracy that the renewed rise of the far Right parties makes almost everyone feel vaguely guilty – even the people who vote for them.

5

The German Jigsaw

The Germans, like the Jews, allow themselves to be oppressed, but not wiped out. Though discouraged, they stay strongly united, even when it is given to them no longer to possess a Fatherland.

Johann Wolfgang von Goethe, 1807[1]

History teaches that Hitlers come and go, but the German people and the German state remain.

Russian posters on the walls of Berlin in 1945
quoting a 1942 speech by Joseph Stalin[2]

If Germany becomes a united state, Europe will speak German.

Wolfgang Berghofer,
mayor of Dresden, 1989[3]

After the 1945 catastrophe, did Germany cease to exist? The New York *Random House Dictionary of the English Language* defines Germany as 'a former country in central Europe, having Berlin as its capital.'[4] Similarly, the *Great Soviet Encyclopaedia* says of Germany, 'A state in Europe which existed up to the end of World War II'[5] Diplomatic opinion has been more exact. Choosing his words carefully, Sir Julian Bullard, the then British ambassador to West Germany, stated in 1986: 'In the absence of a peace settlement, the British view of the legal position – I repeat, the legal position – is that Germany within its 1937 borders has continued to exist as a state.'[6]

When they were established in 1949, both East and West Germany lay claim to representing a better Germany. Yet each knew all along that it was only a part. The two states arose from the same birth defect. Each started its life denouncing the other as illegitimate; each demanded the right to represent the whole German people; each pledged to restore unity one day (though the official position on reunification in East Germany was to go through a variety of ideological fluctuations). Each state made the same orderly German success of economic recovery, under very different conditions. In many ways, the two states grew apart over 40 years, yet – as the events of autumn 1989 brought home to all the world – the human strands between them have proved tough and enduring.

One sizeable and obvious difference reflects migration. Today, population density in the Federal Republic is more than 60 per cent higher than the East; it was only 18 per cent higher in 1950.[7] Over the forty years' of the German Democratic Republic's existence since 1949, 3.65 million people fled to the West. The emigration total represents more than one-fifth of East Germany's 1949 population – a statistic starkly expressing the failure of Communism to win over German minds. Most of them – 2.69 million – departed before the building of the Berlin Wall in August 1961. During the 27 years up to the end of 1988, another 616,000 crossed the border, often braving death. All previous statistics were put in the shade in 1989. In a tidal wave which accelerated with the opening of Hungary's border to the West in September and led in November to the breaching of the Berlin Wall, 344,000 East Germans washed through to the Federal Republic – an exodus which made history. Alone in the first few weeks of 1990, a further 100,000 came across.

Understanding and practising East-West German diplomacy has always required an essential modicum of schizophrenia. Linked inextricably by history, East and West Germany are bound together by common concern about curbing the latest destabilising flows of fugitives seeking a better life in the West. Voices calling for reunification are growing in strength, above all in the East, and were amplified by the result of the March 1990 elections; but reassembling the German jigsaw will be a complicated task. United in their disunity, East and West Germany are the leaf in Goethe's poem on the Gingko-Biloba tree:

> *Ist es Ein lebendig Wesen,*
> *Das sich in sich selbst getrennt?*
> *Sind es zwei, die sich erlesen,*
> *Dass man sie als Eines kennt?*

> *Solche Frage zu erwidern*
> *Fand ich wohl den rechten Sinn:*
> *Fühlst du nicht an meinen Liedern,*
> *Dass ich Eins und doppelt bin?*

91

(Is it but one being single/Which as same itself divides?/Are there two which choose to mingle/So that one each other hides?/As the answer to such a question/I have found a sense that's true/Is it not my song's suggestion/That I'm one but also two?)

I

Helmut Kohl is no orator; but on 19 December 1989 he gave the speech of a lifetime – his, and Germany's. On only the third official visit to East Germany by a West German Chancellor[8], in the late afternoon dusk Kohl waded through a crowd of 100,000 East Germans in the centre of Dresden, the capital of Saxony. With the grandest of its Baroque edifices restored, but much else in dilapidation and decay, the city termed by Goethe 'the balcony of Europe' was transformed for a day to the capital of German dreams.

Surrounded by a battering-ram force of aides and security officials, Kohl struggled to deposit a wreath before the weed-strewn rubble of the Church of our Lady, destroyed in the Anglo-American bombing annihilation of February 1945. Ponderous, silhouetted against this most poignant of German ruins, he mounted the improvised podium. Only a few hours earlier local workmen put the finishing touches to the open-air platform. They accepted with good-humour the instructions of two top officials in Kohl's entourage[9]. The workers appeared to acknowledge that, in future, orders were more likely to come from the Bonn Chancellery than from the beleaguered Communists in East Berlin.

Flanked by an accompanying bevy of Bonn Ministers (some of whom admitted afterwards, with typical German pathos, that they could not restrain their tears), Kohl spoke powerfully from a few pages of hand-scrawled notes. For once, there was no carefully-crafted text from his speech-writers. Many of his phrases – for instance, his oft-repeated observation that the end of the century was not far off – he had practised many times before. Here, they sounded like a message of triumph rather than banality. Kohl spoke from the heart – and his words hit home. But how could Kohl, how could anyone fail, in front of a vast and rapturous throng, chanting for German unity and holding aloft in the glare of the TV floodlights a swirling forest of black-red-and-gold flags?

'Dear friends, dear compatriots,' the Chancellor boomed out, 'We don't want to tell anyone what to do. We will respect what you decide for the future of the country.' Back came the answer, erupting from a thousand throats: '*Deutschland! Deutschland!*' Kohl intoned his intention, agreed earlier in the day with Hans Modrow, the East German Prime Minister, to sign a formal treaty to establish 'confederal structures' between the two Germanys. For his audience – many of whom must have lived through the bombing night 45 years ago – this did not go far enough: '*Einheit! Einheit!*' they thundered back. Voice close to breaking, Kohl proclaimed his goal: 'If the hour of history allows ... the unity of the nation!' The response welled up again, seeming to engulf the Chancellor in a sea of jubilation: '*Deutschland! Deutschland!*'.

With many ordinary East Germans' desire for reunification increased by latest revelations of their country's economic plight, Kohl was aware that passions needed to be cooled. A few hours earlier, the small, goatee-bearded figure of Hans Klein, Kohl's Information Minister, strode into the crowds besieging the hard-currency Bellvue Hotel, where the Chancellor was conferring with Modrow, to plead for patience. When I spoke to one of the factory workers in the crush and told him I was from England, the boiler-suited Dresdener raised immediately Margaret Thatcher's well-publicised aversion to reunification and called out: 'Tell your Lady that we want unity – and we want it straight away!'

At the *Frauenkirche*, Kohl appealed for 'common sense and moderation' on the road to 'the German home'. Referring to Germany's neighbours in East and West, he warned: 'Many are watching us with anxiety as we go our way, and some also with fear.' To the throng the Chancellor brought Christmas tidings of 'solidarity ... togetherness ... peace'. He closed his 20-minute oration with words which, if voiced a few months' earlier in a public place in East Germany, would have resulted in the utterer being arrested and confined at the pleasure of the secret police: 'God bless our German Fatherland!'

The previous night, 12 hours before Kohl's aircraft touched down at Dresden airport, black-red-and-gold had already been much in evidence as flag-waving Dresdeners marched for German unity through the city centre. In a further gesture of defiance against the waning forces of Communism in East Berlin, some of them also brandished the green and white banner of Saxony. The old state had been officially abolished in 1952 along with the other East German *Länder* – but, as elsewhere in Germany, loyalty to century-long traditions dies hard. On an earlier, private visit to Dresden in summer 1988, Kohl had already been given an enthusiastic reception in the streets, and besieged with messages from discontented citizens seeking to emigrate.[10] The December 1989 trip confirmed Kohl's belief that German unity was now a live issue in the East as well as the West. Determined to press home the point to doubters who had claimed that most East Germans were lukewarm over merging with the West, a truculent Kohl said afterwards: 'Many people thought they could say how many [East Germans] were for reunification, and how many were against. As soon as I arrived, on the steps of the aircraft, I knew it was quite different.'[11] But were the Dresdeners looking for unity not so much as a vision of one nation, more as an escape route from the drudgery and sheer hopelessness of life under Communism?

On the Dresden *Altmarkt*, the town authorities had assembled, in line with time-honoured German practice, a Christmas market to provide a distraction from the greyness of daily life. For the children, actors in animal costumes related tales from Grimm, and plump Dresden women queued for roasted almonds at 5 Marks a packet; the decorative fir trees looked distinctly more sickly than their plump counterparts on show at West German Christmas fairs. During the afternoon, I asked passers-by on the *Altmarkt* for their views about the two Germanys' future; only two people out of 10 had any qualms about reunification, but most put preoccupations over the economy well ahead of unity.[12] 'The first priority is economic help. Otherwise the place will be empty,' said Klaus Liebe, a young man holding a baby. Another young Dresdener, Johannes Nawratir, scotched worries about a 'sell-out' of the East German economy to the all-powerful West. 'If you have been living here for 40 years, you are not concerned about being taken over. We have been sold out already – we can only go uphill,' he said.

Heinz Hennid, a pensioner complaining that his retirement income was only 440 Marks a month (a fraction of the sum he would receive in the West) said: 'Without help, the state is *kaputt*.' Expressing enthusiasm about a unified state, he said East Germany needed 'a market economy, competition, and the law of supply and demand.' Ines Schlager, a young mother wheeling a fat baby with a pink woolly hat, opined that reunification would be 'very good – but we have to recover first.' One elderly lady – significantly, the only person who did not want to give me her name – said she was opposed to unity. She talked of the danger of Right-wing extremists. 'I have lived through the war,' she added darkly. Frank Rehwein, a young father with a three-year-old child, said it was 'a good thing' that Kohl was coming. He was enthusiastic about the West. 'In West Germany, it's like a dream ... In the next five years, we will grow together.'

In a spacious and airy flat not far from Dresden's railway station, Ines

Richter, an attractive young doctor employed in the city's medical service, ponders the advantages and drawbacks of the West's magnetic pull. Her husband, Manuel, is a physicist who had difficulties advancing his career because of his refusal to toe the Communist party line; they have two young sons, Cornelius and Claudius. Ines says she wants to stay in Dresden with her family and friends, her home and her job. 'Leaving is not the way to solve the problem.'[13] She observes the bonds of unity between the East and West Germans – 'Stronger here maybe than in the West'. But, on two short visits to the West, she has not liked the 'superficiality' and 'over-abundance' of life in the Federal Republic.

Although she is still on maternity leave, Ines knows from colleagues the effects of the autumn's emigration wave. She says that 100 doctors and 700 nurses – around 10 per cent of Dresden's hospital personnel – have left since summer 1989.[14] Local volunteers, and nurses from the Soviet Union, have been brought into the hospitals. 'The doctors go, but the patients remain.' The imbalance has increased further as a result of an apparent rise in sufferers from depressive illness. Ines says that lack of motivation of East German workers is the result of the Government's 'endless lying'. 'Perhaps if there is more honesty, people will work more.' She adds: 'I sometimes think it would be easier to start again from nothing than to make something out of this economy. The *Schlamperei* (slovenliness) is unbelievable.'

This view finds confirmation from Andreas Schwenke, a young Dresden man on his way back with his parents from one of the regular Monday evening anti-Communist demonstrations. We talk seated at a dingy yellow-clothed table in a beer cellar.[15] Because of 'staff shortages', no one comes to serve any beer. Andreas complains of 'bureaucracy' and 'corruption' in the state-owned factory where he helps maintain the city's trams and buses. Although workers put in 8¾ hours a day, slackness and inefficiency is such that they work effectively only four hours, he confides. His mother, Waltraud, a florist, who is facing a busy period making arrangements for graveyards, opines: 'There are far more urgent problems than reunification.' His father, Bernd, also a factory worker, chimes in: 'We are proud of our *Heimat* (home) here in Dresden.' The future, he says, would be better if Saxony could become independent again. Like many in Saxony, Andreas sees West Germany as a provider of aid and ideas for East Germany – but not as a substitute. Asked about prospects for unity, Andreas says, 'First we must have free elections. And then the people must decide.'

II

Erich Honecker, the East German leader, in 1981 spelled out his vision of how German partition would end: 'If today certain people in the West talk big about Greater Germany, and behave as if the reunification of the two German states lay closer to their hearts than their wallets do, then what we would like to say to them is this: Be careful! One day, socialism will knock on your door too, and when the day comes for the workers to start the socialist transformation of the Federal Republic of Germany, then the question of unity of the two states will be posed in completely new terms.'[16] That was one of the few occasions when Honecker suggested that East Germany might have any other future than as a sovereign independent state. Ironically, when the time came in October 1989 for Honecker to depart in ignominy, socialism was in disorderly retreat all over eastern Europe; capitalism was not simply knocking on East Germany's door but preparing to sweep in. An ailing 77-year-old, Honecker was under pressure, from East Germany's most widespread street protests since the June 1953 uprising. Increasingly losing sympathy in Moscow because of his refusal to follow Mikhail Gorbachev's reform drive, Honecker was virtually friendless after the collapse of Communist power in Poland and Hungary. But he was still preaching an unchanged message of surreal defiance. Launching into a long-winded eulogy in East Berlin's Palace of the Republic to commemorate the 40th anniversary of the East German state, Honecker's voice was thinner and shriller than usual, betraying the aftermath of a gall bladder operation in August. In the defensive tones with which East Germany's leaders habitually describe their country, Honecker summed up the post-war battle for survival:

> Nothing, absolutely nothing, was given to us or fell into our lap. Additionally, here we had not only more rubble to clear away than west of the Elbe, but also the stones which had been placed in our way from over there.[17]

Honecker hit out with barely concealed paranoia at 'the internationally coordinated campaign of defamation' against East Germany and claimed that his country was a 'breakwater against neo-Nazism and chauvinism'. He declared that the socialist tide was rolling on: 'Always forwards, never backwards ... We will find an answer to all the questions ... Ours is the better world.'

Gorbachev, who had arrived in East Berlin earlier in the day for the birthday ceremony, spoke after Honecker. Gorbachev had a difficult task; he had to steer between the Scylla of propping up a regime which refused to countenance *glasnost* and *perestroika*, and the Charybdis of destabilising a state which was a pivot in the post-war order. Gorbachev's dilemma was in fact very similar to the one perpetually faced by the Bonn government, which has characteristically been intent on stabilising East Germany in the short term while seeking, longer term, to undermine it.

In his address, Gorbachev spelled out the familiar message that the West should recognise the 'realities' of the division of Europe, and stressed that East Berlin could solve its own problems. Later that evening, Honecker and Gorbachev stood side by side on a plinth on the main East Berlin thoroughfare Unter den Linden as thousands of members of the Communist party youth section, the Free German Youth, marched by in an extraordinary torchlit birthday parade. At one point the two leaders joined hands to hold up together a bunch of bedraggled carnations. Many of the normally well-drilled youth marchers, instead of following instructions to cry out salutations to 'Comrade Honecker', were chanting 'Gorby, Gorby'. From my vantage point just below the stand where Honecker and Gorbachev were waving to the crowd, I could see that emotions were running high; some of the girl paraders, their eyes bright like in a Leni Riefenstahl film, seemed almost hysterical.

The next day, in a private tête-à-tête with Honecker, Gorbachev gave a strong hint of impatience with the East German leader's obduracy over reforms, warning him: 'Those who arrive late are punished by life itself.'[18] Far greater pressure however was building up on the streets – on a day designed as a national celebration of the state's foundation on 7 October 1949. Honecker claimed later, perhaps truthfully, not to have been aware of the scale of the country's discontent. Sealed off in the Politburo's walled living compound at Wandlitz north of Berlin, Honecker kept in touch with East German life only through his own propaganda machine.[19]

After delivering his message, Gorbachev flew back to Moscow in the afternoon. Only hours afterwards, pro-reform demonstrators clashed with East German security forces in East Berlin, Dresden, Leipzig, Magdeburg, Potsdam and several other cities. That evening in Dresden, where protests had started at the beginning of the week over the government's closure of the nearby Czech border, I watched columns of young people marching determinedly through the city centre. It was the fifth successive night of unrest – a fact virtually unknown in West Germany, in view of the ban on foreign reporters travelling outside East Berlin. The marchers shouted 'Gorby, Gorby', and called the name of New Forum, the new amorphous opposition movement. And, in contrast to earlier protesters seeking an escape route to the West, they chanted insistently: 'We are staying here.' Blocking the way to the city's besieged railway station, a truncheon-swinging East German policeman told me: 'The people's festival is over'; all around him stood phalanxes of nervous-looking riot police and soldiers. Water hoses were laid ready to repel demonstrators; the barking of police Alsatians echoed into the night. Local people spoke nervously of rumours that the police and soldiers had been issued with live ammunition. Michael Müller, pastor at the Church of the Cross in the city centre, one of the churchmen trying to mediate over the crisis, told me that officers were threatening young conscripts with five years' jail in a military prison unless they obeyed orders to club demonstrators. 'The police have become more brutal every evening. The police and security services in this country have great power,' he explained helplessly.[20]

Gorbachev's elliptic warning to Honecker was also a signal that, in any eventual security crackdown, Moscow would not support the East German leadership. A crucial Monday night demonstration in Leipzig on 9 October went off without violence. Above all, as the result of mediation by local party officials, in which the conductor of the Leipzig Gewandhaus orchestra, Kurt Masur, played an important part, East German police and troops held back from quelling the protests by force. The refusal of Soviet forces to back up East German repression appears to have been one reason why Leipzig that night did not witness scenes similar to the bloodbath in Peking's Tiananmen Square in June.[21]

As the momentum for democratic change rose, Honecker was ousted at a Politburo meeting on 18 October. His successor was Egon Krenz, a 52-year-old former leader of the Free German Youth who had been a member of the Politburo for six years. Krenz was supremely ill-adapted to winning the population's confidence; during the summer he had congratulated the Peking leadership on the massacre which ended the student protests. Wolf Biermann, the exiled East German poet-singer, called Krenz 'the most miserable of all candidates'[22]; a view which was echoed by East German émigrés in the West whom I interviewed the day after his nomination. 'Krenz is not well-liked. He is rumoured to be an alcoholic. He is not credible – he is just trying to hold on to power,' said Andrea Hofmann, a single mother with a three-year-old son who admitted she was missing her friends from home.[23] 'He is another tough

Stalinist,' said Cornelia Grätz, a singer and percussion player from East Berlin, living in a temporary hostel in a Bonn suburb while waiting to move with her husband to a permanent address. 'He is talking about the SED [the Communist party] keeping leadership. The people don't want that. They will continue to go on the streets.'

This is just what happened. More than half a million people descended on the streets of East Berlin at the beginning of November to demand reforms; 400,000 turned out in Leipzig. As thousands more émigrés gushed out to West Germany via Czechoslovakia, officials in Bonn reckoned glumly that East Germany could lose a further 1 million citizens unless the leadership established confidence. In what was clearly a panic move, Krenz decided on 9 November to release the pressure by ending emigration restrictions; there followed the mass scenes of rejoicing at the Brandenburg Gate. Only 10 months earlier, Honecker declared sanctimoniously that the Wall would remain in place 'for 50 and even 100 years' if necessary to protect East Germany from 'robbers' and 'those ready to disturb stability and peace in Europe.'[24] Now, however, the Berlin Wall was being dismantled not, as the Communists had hoped, at a time when East Germany had drawn level with the West, but when its defects had never been more sorely exposed before the eyes of the world.

Two nights afterwards, at 2 o'clock in the morning, I watched from the eastern side as a squad of East German soldiers punched fresh holes in the Wall. They were opening a new crossing point at the Potsdamer Platz, the historic heart of old Berlin, closed off for nearly three decades. The noise of their pneumatic drills attracted a large crowd on the western side, shouting and letting off fireworks. With something approaching pride, a young *Volkspolizist* gave me details of the opening ceremony due to take place at 8 o'clock, to be presided over by the mayors of East and West Berlin. Another officer guarding the demolition work told me the Wall was no older than he, and as a result he had no great emotional attachment to it. 'It is an experiment,' he said. An astonishing admission from a representative of the land which had 'all the answers', he added: 'I don't know which system is better – the capitalist or the socialist one.'[25]

A few days afterwards, I travelled to Schwarzenberg, a small mining and metalworking town, etched by tradition and grime, buried in the Erzgebirge forests in southern East Germany. The town occupies its own modest part in German history. In an oversight after the German capitulation in May 1945, the area around Schwarzenberg was initially left unoccupied by both American and Soviet troops. The omission left a power vacuum which was filled for six short and highly provisional weeks by a council set up by Communists and anti-fascists to rule Schwarzenberg as an independent state. Paul Korb, a former metalworker now aged 85, is the only surviving member of the council. Korb, a small crinkly-faced man who has been a member of the Communist party since 1920, was put in charge of police activities – including the rounding up of local Nazi bigwigs. But the council's idea of running an enclave based on a mix 'Socialism and democracy' was soon dashed when the Russians took control in June 1945.[26] Talking to me in the well-heated sitting room of his warren-like house, bought by his grandfather (a carpenter) in 1863, Korb told a tale of dashed illusions.[27] He said he was 'proud' of his minor role in helping build up post-war East Germany. One of the legacies of the provisional government is that Schwarzenberg has no street named after Lenin, he pointed out. He wants to draw a veil, however, over recent events. 'The leadership [in East Berlin] has neglected a most fundamental rule. It has lost contact with the masses, and failed to realise the feelings built up in the population.' Korb said uncompromisingly that the Socialist Unity Party would go into opposition after the free elections planned for 1990.

For anyone seeking the answer to the future of East German Communism, what better place to visit than Karl-Marx-Stadt? Chemnitz, as the town was formerly called, has been a textile centre for 400 years. In the last century, it became one of the pivots of Saxony's manufacturing revolution. The town was renamed after the father of Communism at a singularly inappropriate moment – in May 1953, just a month before Russian tanks put down the short-lived workers' uprising. The outskirts of Chemnitz seem to have changed little since the end of the war: blackened apartment blocks, piles of rubble on the streets, closed shops, old people tottering along in the sunshine. In the rebuilt centre rise modern Socialist blocks. A girl in the city bookshop has pinned up over the cash register a statement from Marx appealing for the proletariat to show 'courage' and 'dignity'. The aim is to remind her compatriots, she tells me, not to be blinded by the new-found possibilities of travelling westwards.[27]

From Karl-Marx-Stadt's new state-owned meat factory (close by is the charmingly-named Hotel am Schlachthof – Abattoir Hotel) stem messages of another sort. It is a crumbling red-brick complex dating from the turn of the century, and looking its age; hens peck in the yard for animal leftovers. The Kombinat director, Harlieb Haas-Zens, is a man in a neat green suit with a Communist party lapel button. With apparent conviction, but only limited plausibility, he mutters words of

100

hope for new Socialist methods of running the company: '*Mehr Flexibilität ist dringend notwendig.*' (More flexibility is urgently required)[28]. The doorkeeper, a white-coated man with fingers like sausages, is more forthcoming. As he ushers me out of the building, we pass a works' sign in honour of East Germany's 40th anniversary. It is a convoluted birthday panegyric from Erich Honecker acclaiming the achievements of the Socialist Unity Party – an elaborate paean of delusion:

> The guarantee of our successes, both in the past and in the future, is leadership through the party, sure of its objective, working hand in hand with the masses and carried by their trust, a political-ideological and organisational activity of mobilisation which is renewed every day, and which represents, in line with our 70 years' experience of partnership, the decisive lever to achieve, with the support of the masses of the people, the high but none the less real goals of the people's economic plan.

The doorkeeper clearly needs to tell someone – even a complete stranger – that he disagrees. As we walk past, he explodes: 'The criminals! They have fooled us for 40 years! They must all go! And we want to be called Chemnitz again!'

More is changing in East Germany than simply names of towns. The driving force behind unification is frustration and fury at 40 wasted years.

III

Only two years earlier, Honecker was basking in emotions of a very different kind. In September 1987, on the first ever trip to West Germany by an East German head of state, the red carpet was laid out for him. It was proof, in the eyes of the world, that Bonn was at last treating the German Democratic Republic as a separate sovereign entity. When Honecker's visit was first mooted, in 1984, Chancellor Kohl was to have received him in the spa town of Bad Kreuznach to avoid according the East German top protocol status. Now Honecker was here in the federal capital itself, from which Chancellor Kiesinger two decades earlier derided the East German state as a passing 'phenomenon', soon to be swallowed up in reunification. In 1961, Erich Honecker was responsible for building the Berlin Wall when he was

Politburo member responsible for national security. Honecker was born in the Saarland, on the western fringes of today's Federal Republic. Now he was back in the west of Germany for the first time since the end of the 1940s; it was the climax of a long haul towards recognition.

In the ceremony of welcome at the squat black Bonn Chancellery building, the Bundeskanzleramt, a grey-uniformed Bundeswehr band – instruments glinting in the wan Rhineland sunshine – played successively the anthems of the Communist and capitalist states. The bird-like Honecker and the lumbering Kohl stood stiffly to attention. The first to ring out was East Germany's *Auferstanden aus den Ruinen* (Risen from the Ruins), sounding like a rumbustious Christmas carol.[29] Then followed the martial beauty of West Germany's *Deutschlandlied* (Song of the Germans).

Sixteen almost identical East and West German black-red-and-gold flags fluttered overhead, the former distinguishable from the latter through the addition of a slightly incongruous hammer and compasses. Anxious to keep alive the idea of a single German nation, West German officials stressed carefully that the melodies were simply 'hymns' rather than 'national anthems'. When the music stopped, functionaries and Ministers from the East and West German delegations merged seamlessly together, Germans among Germans, ready to get down to the business of talking about cross-border subsidies and pollution of the River Elbe.

A touch of ambivalence hung in the air. The text of the East German national hymn approved in 1949, written by the well-known Communist author Johannes Becher, contains a reference to unity of East and West as one German Fatherland. That reflected the policy of the first post-war East German Communists, including Walter Ulbricht, Honecker's predecessor whom he displaced as party leader in 1971. At the beginning of the 1970s, however, East Berlin switched its ideology towards emphasising differences rather than unity with West Germany. The Fatherland suddenly became limited to East Germany only – and the words to the hymn were no longer sung. In line with the new policy of *Abgrenzung* or 'fencing off', East Germany revised its constitution in 1974, striking out reference to the 'German nation'. The German Democratic Republic was newly defined as 'a socialist state of the worker and the farmer'. The words of the hymn automatically fell out of favour. After the ceremony at the Bundeskanzleramt, I asked an official from Honecker's delegation if he could tell me the words of his country's national anthem; he smiled, looked sheepish and replied that they were not available.

Honecker's September journey was a pilgrimage; it was also a time of emotion and contradiction. The trip had been discussed for several years and postponed on several occasions – mainly because the Soviet Union wanted to pick the right moment for Honecker to visit the West. In autumn 1987, with the superpowers on the verge of signing the agreement on scrapping medium-range nuclear weapons in Europe, the time was at last propitious. Jailed for nearly ten years during the Third Reich for anti-Nazi agitation, Honecker spent his imprisonment for the most part in the infamous Brandenburg jail used still by the Communist East German state to lock up political prisoners.[30] In response to massive pressure from its own people to be allowed to make visits to the West, East Germany had over the last year relaxed its rules on letting its citizens out for short, authorised journeys. Ex-Chancellor Helmut Schmidt, who had paved the way for the visit by travelling to see Honecker in East Germany in 1981, in a newspaper article in July 1987 hailed the leader of the second German state as 'one of our brothers'.[31]

In the West German capital, Honecker was given a subdued but friendly welcome. There were no crowds in the streets; but then, in small-town Bonn, there seldom are. At an official banquet in honour of the visitor, Kohl gave Honecker a dutiful lecture over the shooting of escapees trying to flee across the fortified border. Kohl said the German people were 'suffering from separation'. Honecker responded by telling the Chancellor that Communism and capitalism were like 'fire and water'.[32] It was clear that the two leaders got on well together, though both were compelled to play certain predictable parts. Kohl, who knows no foreign languages, was visibly pleased to be greeting a visiting state dignitary who also spoke German. Dieter Schröder, editor of the *Süddeutsche Zeitung*, who was present at the banquet, gave me an insight several months later into the conversation between Saarlander Honecker and Kohl from the nearby Palatinate. 'They talked about people they knew in common – the head of a youth hostel, and so on. For Kohl, this sort of connection is very important,' said Schröder. Kohl, says Schröder, 'is not a German nationalist, but he has all-German emotions. The people over there [in East Germany], they mean more to him than the French or the English.'[33]

Two days later in the Ruhr steel town of Essen, Honecker was fêted at a meeting with top West German captains of industry eager to extend trade links across the divide. The venue was the Villa Hügel, the 19th-century ancestral mansion of the Krupp steel and armaments empire, a company which had been one of Honecker's chief ideological targets during his Communist resistance years in the 1930s. Recalling his action in Essen in the early 1930s, when as a young Communist agitator he distributed leaflets against the Nazis, Honecker wrote in his autobiography: 'For me, Essen was not the town of the Krupps, but of the battling working class.'[34] During his return to the city in 1987, however, he saw only the bosses.

On the fourth day of his trip, Honecker moved on to the birthplace of Karl Marx in Trier. I was able to slip past the security cordon and mingle with the functionaries showing him around the house where Marx was born, now turned into a museum. Gazing inconsequentially at the exhibits, Honecker looked quite pleased to have someone to talk to. When I told him I was from England, he pointed out that Marx was buried in London and intoned reedily, 'A world without Marx is inconceivable.' Honecker also travelled down to Munich at the express invitation of the Bavarian premier, Franz Josef Strauss. The East German visitor placed a wreath at the site of the concentration camp at Dachau north of Munich, where the Nazis first imprisoned communists and Social Democrats before turning their attention to the Jews. The perimeter concrete wall and watch-towers bore a grim resemblance to Honecker's own construction across Berlin. Afterwards the mood lightened as the cavalcade swept on to the Baroque centre of Munich, exchanges of speeches and a festive lunch with Strauss. In 1963 Honecker had called Strauss a 'militarist' who wanted to march through the Brandenburg gate to reconquer East Berlin. However, the two struck up an incongruous friendship during the 1980s, and had even gone hunting together on the Politburo's estate in the Schorfheide, north of Berlin – the same area in which Hermann Göring, Hitler's Reichsmarshal, had maintained a hunting park. In 1983 Strauss was responsible for persuading the East Germans to dismantle shooting devices at the border in exchange for hard-currency credits. As he and Honecker swapped jokes and anecdotes over lunch, cameraderie filled the air.

Honecker's sentimental high noon was his return to his family home at Wiebelskirchen, part of the town of Neunkirchen in the run-down iron and steel area of the Saar. His widowed sister Gertrud lives there still, into her seventies but sprightly and blonde-tinted, presumably under the careful eye of both East and West German intelligence agencies. A few months earlier Gertrud had told me over the fence of her neat garden by the Catholic church that she did not have much news from Erich because he was *schreibfaul* (a lazy letter writer). She hoped her brother's visit would 'bring people together'.[35]

When Erich arrived in his big hired Stuttgart Mercedes, he first laid a wreath at the grave of his parents set high up in the hillside, with views of the disused collieries. Below, the crowds stood six deep in the narrow streets. Gertrud's green-painted two-storey house built by his grandfather was ringed by jostling cameramen. Cries of 'Erich, Erich' rang out from local Communists, heavily outnumbering the demonstrators with banners calling for demolition of the Berlin Wall. Hans Thul, a member of the Wiebelskirchen Catholic community which laid on a tent, refreshments and choral singing for the occasion, told me, 'Honecker is homesick and has been allowed to come home. Now the ordinary people in East Berlin who want to come to the West should also be allowed out too.'

At a reception in the evening at the Neunkirchen town hall, Honecker, clearly moved by the welcome, added a few impromptu lines to his set speech. Speaking as an 'old Neunkirchener', he said he looked forward 'to the day when the border will no longer separate us but unite us'. It was a tantalising hint of how his heart-strings were tugging him across the ideological rift, back towards the 'other Germans'. Were 'fire and water' really so incompatible after all?

IV

'Where and what is the Fatherland?' There has never been just one answer. When the Allensbach institute asked West Germans to define the 'German nation' in 1986, 37 per cent said the Federal Republic, 35 per cent the Federal Republic and the German Democratic Republic together, 12 per cent the Federal Republic, GDR and the former eastern territories, and 11 per cent replied 'all German-speaking areas'. Perhaps the most honest response came from the 5 per cent who said the question was impossible to answer.[36]

The poet Ernst Moritz Arndt gave the matter some reflection in 1813:

> *Was ist des Deutschen Vaterland*
> *Ist's Preussenland? Ist's Schwabenland?*
> *Ist's wo am Rhein die Rebe blüht?*
> *Ist's wo am Belt die Möwe zieht?'*
> *O nein! nein! nein!*
> *Sein Vaterland muss grösser sein*
> *Das ganze Deutschland soll es sein!*
> *O Gott vom Himmel, sieh darin*
> *Und gib uns rechten deutschen Mut*

105

Dass wir es lieben treu und gut!
Das muss es sein!
Das ganze Deutschland soll es sein!

(What is the German's Fatherland/Is it the land of Prussia? Is it the land of Swabia?/Is it on the Rhine, where the vine grows?/Is it on the Belt, where the seagull hovers?/O no! no! no!/His Fatherland must be bigger/The whole of Germany it must be!/O God in heaven, grant us this/And give us good German strength/That we should love our land with all our hearts/That it must be!/The whole of Germany it must be!)

This was tantalising but hardly satisfactory. Another answer came three decades later with the *Deutschlandlied*. This was written in 1841 by August Heinrich Hoffmann, a German professor from Breslau in Silesia, while staying on the rocky island of Heligoland in the North Sea. Heligoland was owned by the British at the time, later to be given over to the Germans in exchange for Zanzibar. Up to then the professor's compositions had rarely extended beyond children's ditties. Hoffmann composed three verses, the first of which was fated to reverberate around the world:

Deutschland, Deutschland über alles
Über alles in der Welt
Wenn es stets zu Schutz und Trutze
Brüderlich zusammenhält!
Von der Maas bis an die Memel
Von der Etsch bis an den Belt
Deutschland, Deutschland über alles
Über alles in der Welt!

(Germany, Germany, above all things/Above all things in the world/If in defence and offence/We like brothers together hold/From the rivers Meuse and Niemen/From the Adige to the Belt/Germany, Germany, above all things/Above all things in the world.)

Hoffmann's patriotic composition showed unparalleled adaptability. Played to the music of Haydn, the song echoed out frequently in the years leading to the attempted nationalist revolution of 1848. It was revived in the 1890s, and was sung by troops marching to their deaths in Flanders in the First World War. It was intoned by the parliament of the Weimar Republic in 1919. The song was proclaimed the national anthem by President Friedrich Ebert in 1922. After 1933, the Nazis chorused it in combination with the *Horst Wessel* marching song and the Hitler salute. When the Third Reich collapsed, the Allied Control Commission included the *Deutschlandlied* in the list of banned Nazi songs.

In the early years of the Federal Republic, Schiller's 'Ode to Joy' rang out to Beethoven's music at international football matches and other sporting occasions. The first president, Theodor Heuss, tried setting to music a 'Hymn to Germany' composed by a poet friend, Rudolf Alexander Schröder, but it was not a success. Adenauer's wish to bring back the *Deutschlandlied* won the day and in May 1952, Hoffmann's work was again declared the national anthem. The decision is still the subject of some controversy, as it was never turned into a formal law.[37] Adenauer decreed that on state occasions, only the third verse should be sung:

> *Einigkeit und Recht und Freiheit*
> *Für das deutsche Vaterland!*
> *Danach lasst uns alle streben*
> *Brüderlich mit Herz und Hand!*
> *Einigkeit und Recht und Freiheit*
> *Sind des Glückes Unterpfand;*
> *Blüh im Glanze dieses Glückes*
> *Blühe Deutsches Vaterland.*

(Unity and right and freedom/For the German Fatherland!/And for this let us all strive/Like two brothers hand in hand./Unity and right and freedom/Are good luck's security;/Thrive in the glow of this good fortune/Thrive, O German Fatherland!)

The first verse acquired its overtones of martial nationalism in Imperial Germany and, later, under the Third Reich. In Hoffmann's day, the three rivers and a strait mentioned in his first verse constituted an ambitious but defensible choice for the borders of a future German nation. The Meuse, which rises in Burgundy, flows on its way to the North Sea through North Limburg. Today this is part of Holland, but when the professor wrote his song it belonged to the German Confederation. The Niemen, flowing into the Baltic, formed the border between East Prussia and Lithuania; the last 60 miles of the river ran through German territory. Today the area is part of the Soviet Union.

The Adige empties into the Adriatic, the second longest river in Italy after the Po; it rises in the Alpine mountains and runs through South Tirol. In 1841 this was part of Austria, also a member of the German

Confederation (until 1866). The Belt was the northernmost sea frontier of the Duchy of Schleswig, which in Hoffmann's time belonged to Denmark.

During the Germans' quest for *Lebensraum* in the first half of the 20th century, ironically, these waterways came to lie ever further outside the shrinking space on the map allotted to Germany. By the time Adenauer and Heuss discussed the matter in 1952, the experience of the Third Reich had made the first verse unusable, but had given the third one a new meaning. Heuss admitted that he had erred in wanting to fashion a completely new national anthem; he wrote to Adenauer: 'I have underestimated the forces of tradition.'[38]

Tradition was also apparent in the East German anthem selected in 1949. Becher's text, to a melody composed by Hanns Eisler, reflected the German Democratic Republic's objective to one day represent all the German people in a Socialist state. The first verse went as follows:

> *Auferstanden aus Ruinen*
> *Und der Zukunft zugewandt*
> *Lass uns dir zum Guten dienen,*
> *Deutschland, einig Vaterland*
> *Alte Not gilt es zu zwingen,*
> *Und wir zwingen sie vereint*
> *Denn es muss uns doch gelingen,*
> *Dass die Sonne schön wie nie*
> *Über Deutschland scheint.*

(Risen from the Ruins/Turned to the future/Let us serve you for good/Germany, our Fatherland/Old troubles must be overcome/And united we shall overcome them/For we must yet succeed/That the sun bright as never before/Shines over Germany)

The East German reference to 'Fatherland' explains why – up to the building of the Berlin Wall in August 1961 – it was possible for the Communist leadership to make polemical speeches matching almost word for word West Germany's own appeals for reunification. For instance, in 1960 Walter Ulbricht called solemnly on the US government to give 'the West German population the right to free self-determination, for lives in peace and security, freedom and democracy'. He added:

But what is happening in West Germany in the year 1960? The Bonn government has quite clearly given up on any kind of peaceful reunification. It is getting ready for war and, in the case that this should not succeed, the perpetuation of division. Commentators and philosophers are being mobilised to prove that reunification of Germany in democracy and freedom is neither necessary nor desirable.[39]

With 'East' substituted for 'West Germany' and 'East Berlin' instead of 'Bonn', Ulbricht's speech could quite possibly have stemmed from a West German Christian Democrat rather than an East German Communist. Just over a year afterwards the Wall went up across the former capital of the Reich, damming the streams of fugitives who had been flowing into West Germany at a rate of nearly 20,000 a month. The way was laid down for East German *Abgrenzung*. Erected under the pretence that the West was preparing a military expedition against the East, the Wall and the fortifications across the inner-German border cut down emigration, but did not end it. Compared with the average of 220,000 a year crossing from East to West Germany between 1949 and 1961, the numbers between 1961 and 1988 fell ten-fold to an average of 22,500. In 1988, the trend rose as 40,000 East Germans left the country by legal or illegal means (roughly 30,000 after gaining approval, and another 10,000 illicitly, mainly by absconding from authorised trips). Even before the tidal wave of 1989, the constant pressure for emigration depressingly underlined how little had changed in East Germany over a quarter of a century.

East Germany argued that the Wall was to keep the West Germans out rather than the East Germans in. Claiming that the West was preparing military and economic action to win back East Germany, in his autobiography published in 1980 Honecker asked readers to suspend credulity as he gave this preposterous justification for the building of the Wall:

> Could we remain inactive, when in the heart of Europe a situation had arisen which, with scarcely concealed mobilisation and enhanced war hysteria on the western side, resembled the eve of the Second World War? ... Would the people of the German Democratic Republic, would the peace-loving peoples of Europe and the world have forgiven us if we had encouraged the aggressors by doing nothing? At the end of the Second World War, we had sworn to make every effort that war would never again stem from German soil. It was our will to redeem this obligation under all circumstances.[40]

Construction of the Wall stabilised the East German economy. The wave of immigrants had also threatened to swamp West Germany's capacity to absorb them and, for this reason, the building of the Wall was not unwelcome to the Adenauer government. The three western Allies lost the position in the eastern sector of Berlin given to them by four-power supreme authority over the city, but consolidated their presence in the western sectors. The Wall, however, sounded the death knell for East Germany's efforts to pretend that the Communist state was the repository of German liberties. As long as the Berlin Wall remained, Communism in the East would be seen by all the world as a failure.

V

One small change triggered by the 1989 upheavals in East Berlin concerned East Germany's national anthem. Dietmar Keller, the new Culture Minister, quickly spoke out in favour of singing the hymn 'with our old text' – including the phrase 'Germany one Fatherland'.[41] In autumn demonstrations across the country, the East German population showed that they had not forgotten the words. If *Wir sind das Volk* (We are the people) was the early slogan of the revolution in October, by the end of the year it was superseded by *Deutschland einig Vaterland*, scrawled on placards, waved on flags, and chanted into the frosty air. Behind the Fatherland banners, however, lie divergent opinions, in both East and West, over whether reunification is really a good idea.

Because neither is a nation, East and West Germany have always shared a similar identity problem. The Federal Republic could use catchwords like 'Freedom' to sum up the values of its post-war system. Slogans like 'western integration' or even 'USA' were previously of assistance, but have lost their attraction. As a form of ersatz nationalism, Left-wing West German intellectuals such as Jürgen Habermas coined the term *Verfassungspatriotismus* (patriotism of the constitution) to declare the primacy of allegiance to the democratic and humane principles of the 1949 Basic Law. But since even the constitution is deemed provisional pending its application to the whole of Germany, this begged rather than solved the national question.

In East Germany, the choice of identity badge was still more difficult. Other east European countries ruled by Communists after 1945 – Hungary, Poland, Czechoslovakia – are nations; not the GDR. The East Germans did not succeed even in inventing a suitable adjective to describe 'East German' (*DDR-deutsch* is not satisfactory). The

Communist leadership's rediscovery of Luther and Frederick the Great as past national heroes, together with the partial rehabilitation of Bismarck, highlighted the search for reliable symbolism. Firm identity could be sought only through Marxism and unrelenting opposition to the 'imperialist' republic in the West; Ulbricht and Honecker always knew that, when either started to crumble, the very foundations of the state would weaken too. The clearest exposition of this principle came from Otto Reinhold, a Communist party ideologist, two months before the Wall was broken through:

> The German Democratic Republic is only conceivable as an anti-fascist, socialist state, as a socialist alternative to the Federal Republic.... What right of existence should a capitalist East Germany have next to a capitalist Federal Republic? Naturally, none.[42]

East Germans, more readily than their counterparts in the West, have always pointed out that reunification would not be reached without deep-seated changes in NATO and the Warsaw Pact. There has been an undertone in many statements from East Berlin that, however ugly, East Germany has been the keystone in the post-war European mosaic. The implication for Germany's neighbours is that, if the stone slipped or (by reunification) were removed altogether, the European power balance would inevitably be disturbed.

Stefan Heym, the veteran East German novelist, has earned considerable royalties from sales of his books in the West criticising East Germany's past Stalinist rigidity. A Jew born in Chemnitz, he fled the Third Reich in 1933, joined the US army, and took part in the 1944 Normandy D-Day landings. He clings still to the idea of making socialism 'attractive' in East Germany, but admitted when I saw him in August 1989: 'The more you wait to tackle the changes, the more difficult it will be.'[43] Heym played a part in rallying support of artistic and cultural figures for the 1989 protests. Once Honecker was swept away, Heym however realised there was a risk that the pendulum might swing too far in the other direction. He was one of the main signatories of a somewhat desperate petition launched in November 1989 by East German intellectuals warning of the risks that their country could be simply 'absorbed' in a 'sell-out' to the West.[44]

Focussing on foreign fears of a united Germany, Heym claims that East Germany has to continue to exist to safeguard European stability. With an intensity born of his own past traumas, Heym emphasised the dangers of unity – 'because of [Germany's] economic strength, and

111

because of possible nationalistic tendencies.' He admitted that 'historical trends' were making for some form of *rapprochement* between the two Germanys, but added: 'Changes will have to be made in East and West Germany before they can become one.' Asked what would be the prime condition, he replied, 'They [the two German states] should stop being prime pawns on the side of their respective superpowers.' Heym's own reply appeared to make him reflective; for this condition is already on the way towards being fulfilled.

Similar views are held by Egon Krenz. Speaking in an interview in his office in the Communist party's massive East Berlin headquarters, a fortnight after the opening of the Wall – and only 10 days before he was himself forced to resign, at the beginning of December, as party leader – Krenz underlined: 'For the near future, I see the necessity for two independent German states.'[45] Asked if a confederation could become feasible in coming years, he saw this as a possibility if NATO and the Warsaw Pact were to be dissolved. 'The question of reunification is not on the agenda at the moment ... But, concerning the building of a European home, I say we will have to wait and see how the German Question develops.'

Jens Reich, a macrobiologist, is one of the founders of New Forum. Like Heym, he has spoken out hopefully of establishing 'a Socialist system which is acceptable to everyone.' He told me that there was no reason why reunification should be inevitable once East Germany renounced Stalinism:

> I don't believe that this country has no right of existence. I think this country is viable. There is a long historical tradition – the states of Saxony, Brandenburg, Mecklenburg could form a corpus together and survive as many such units have done in the past. It's 19th-century thinking to say there's no alternative to Greater Germany. Greater Germany existed for just 74 years. Mecklenburg, Saxony – they go back 1,000 years.[46]

Many East German intellectuals indeed dreamed of drawing on Germany's multiple federal traditions, reviving the East German *Länder*, and maintaining a reformed East German state as some form of anti-capitalist utopia. But, with the same number of people – 16m – as West Germany's most populous *Land*, North-Rhine Westphalia (and with a considerably lower gross national product) East Germany would have little chance of prospering on its own. Several months before the autumn unrest, Hans-Otto Furian, a spokesman for the East German Protestant Church, outlined to me East Germany's underlying survival problem:

There is a fundamental difference from the Poles and Hungarians. They are people with an unbroken national consciousness. In the German Democratic Republic, there is hardly any. The people feel themselves as Germans living in this part of Germany. The German Democratic Republic is a creation of the Cold War. What will become of it when the Cold War flags and confrontation is eased?[47]

By 1990, the answer was clear, even to the Communists. The German Democratic Republic had finally run out of time.

VI

Most West Germans have thought a great deal less about reunification than in the East; the subject has simply not been pressing. In previous years, the bulk of the population came to regard the prospect of unity as fascinating, but intrinsically infeasible. During the 1950s and 1960s, opinion polls indicated that between 30 and 50 per cent of West Germans believed that reunification was the most important challenge facing the Federal Republic – a figure which in later years fell to only around 1 per cent. Throughout the 1980s, between 70 and 80 per cent of the population still said they supported reunification in principle. Only a small minority – less than 10 per cent – however believed reunification would be practicable in coming years.[48]

Even after 40 years of separation, the human links are surprisingly strong. Around one-third of people in the Federal Republic are estimated to have relatives in East Germany, while in the GDR, about half the population is thought to have relatives in the West.[49] Even before the complete lifting of travel restrictions in November 1989, East Berlin allowed around 5 million individual East German visits to West Germany in each of the years 1987 and 1988, with more than 1 million people of under pensionable age allowed to make temporary trips. In previous years, younger people were hardly allowed to leave at all. Most East German homes watch West German TV – which played an important part in triggering the events of autumn 1989. Even before the crumbling of the Wall, West Germans sent roughly 75 million letters a years to East Germany – more than to the rest of Europe combined.[50]

A moralistic note often creeps into conversations about East Germany with ordinary people. One Bonn office worker without any family links to the East told me she felt somehow responsible for the people

113

unfortunate enough to live on the wrong side when Germany was divided. A 50-year-old middle-level executive speaking over dinner at a management seminar said, 'It is part of our culture. I want to be able to go to Dresden if I feel like it.' Younger people, however, have seemed to believe increasingly that the East has after all become a foreign country. Among a group of students I quizzed at Münster Polytechnic, Charlotte Cirkel said she had 'no emotional links' with the GDR; Axel Brumm said, 'They are slowly drifting away from us.' Barbara Tömp replied that she had been to Leipzig three years ago – 'They have nothing in common with us but the language.' Their lively business studies professor is Günter Peise, in his mid-fifties, born in Leipzig, who crossed to the West after the war. He summed up his complex thoughts:

I have experienced the pain of division. We were deprived of part of the nation. That left the people with a wound. The emotional links become less now as the family ties die away. My son says I'm slightly mad to talk about it! We speak the same language as the people in the East, but we use it differently. We have different living standards. We can't proclaim that we will make Europe more stable through reunification. On the contrary: being divided is the price we pay for more stability.[51]

The pathos of partition has been immeasurably increased by the rhetoric expended on it by West German politicians. In the fifteen major Bundestag policy speeches made by West German Chancellors since 1949 setting out government programmes, only one failed to make a restatement – in some form – of the 'unity of the nation'. The sole exception was the inaugural address by Chancellor Schmidt in 1974. The coolness was hardly surprising; Schmidt had just taken over from Brandt, who had been forced to resign after the discovery of an East Berlin spy in the Chancellery.*

The doggedness has a touch of relentlessness: West German policy statements have a habit of repeating slogans. Before November 1989, no West German Chancellor had any intention of making the achievement of 'unity' a part of operational policy. In 1949 Adenauer looked to the day when 'nothing (would) stand in the way of reunification with our brothers and sisters in the Eastern Zone and Berlin.'[52] Eight years later, he repeated: 'Without the reunification of Germany, the peace of Europe and the world is not secured.'[53] In 1965 Chancellor Erhard complained that a democratic all-German state had been hindered

* See Chapter 16.

solely because 'the Soviet Union has not wanted the reunification in freedom of the German people.'[54]

Brandt in 1969 brought a change of vocabulary by renouncing the aim of 'reunification', but declared still 'the unity of the nation' and the Germans' 'right to self-determination'.[55] Schmidt in 1976 said 'the border in the middle of Germany hurts us'[56]; and repeated, less forthrightly, in 1980, 'We want to keep awake consciousness of the unity of the German nation.'[57] Kohl declared in 1982 that the 'wall, barbed wire and orders to shoot are not and cannot be the last word between East and West.'[58] In 1987 he affirmed: 'Our goal remains: freedom and unity for all Germans.'[59]

In line with the pattern set by Brandt, in the first seven years of his Chancellorship Kohl made no attempt to re-introduce the word *Wiedervereinigung* (reunification), last used by a Chancellor in the 1960s. Kohl had no clear idea on how reunification could actually take place, as my conversation with him in February 1989 showed.[60]

Q. What should reunification look like? Why don't you use the word reunification? Does not the word *Wiedervereinigung* sound a bit anachronistic?
A. No, not at all, when I say 'Unity of the Nation' that is the same. Under *Wiedervereinigung*, one understood something else, the attachment of the GDR to the Federal Republic.
Q. Isn't that the idea?
A. The idea – the vision – is that we want the political unity of Europe ...
Q. But I repeat my question. What should unity look like?
A. The difference is that you are a prophet, and I am only the Chancellor.

Kohl at last gave a clearer idea of the way forward in November 1989, in his 10-point statement on German unity proposing 'confederal structures' between the two states as a stepping stone towards a German federation.[61] Kohl's previous caution reflected his belief that reunification was simply not on the agenda; he told a press conference in Moscow in 1988 that he did not think he would live to see it.[62] The November 1989 fall of the Wall opened up the road to national unity; but neither West Germany – nor its allies – had anything approaching a route map.

VII

Between 1986 and 1989, I asked a number of influential West Germans for their views on reunification. Their answers underline the general surprise caused by the East German revolution.

Willy Brandt:
'I have long been against the "re-" in "reunification", because that suggests that we could produce something again like the Bismarck Reich, or the Weimar Republic. That is illusory. But if the division of Europe, as I hope, in the next decades gives way to a process of growing together, then there will be a position where the two parts of Germany will have a closer relationship than other states. Some might call this a confederation – but I will leave the form open.[63]

Joachim Fest, co-publisher, *Frankfurter Allgemeine Zeitung*:
'I do not believe in reunification, but I often go to East Germany. When I come back, I have been turned into a passionate supporter of reunification. I see the hate and discontent of the people there towards the regime. We cannot simply say that they have had bad luck and give them up. It need not be a reunited Germany, but it must be a system which allows human rights.'[64]

Ernst Breit, chairman, German Trade Union Federation:
'It would be desirable that it [reunification] should come, so that sisters, brothers, children and their parents could visit each other. We would like normal conditions and what we have is not normal. It would be normal to be in one state.'[65]

Werner Holzer, editor, *Frankfurter Rundschau*:
'We gave up reunification as a solution thirty years ago. It will not happen in this way. We should give up the Sunday speechifying. Whether we like the political system in the GDR or not, we need a normal working relationship with them.'[66]

Manfred Rommel, Mayor of Stuttgart:
'Fatherland? In my youth, it was so misused. The Fatherland for me starts in Stuttgart. Politically, the links are far stronger with France, England, Holland, than with the government in East Germany. We cannot be indifferent to the fate of the people there. But the idea of

116

reunification is completely hopeless.'[67]

Karl Otto Pöhl, Bundesbank president:
'As a historical development, I would hope that the East bloc over time would dissolve itself, and that the system would become democratised, so that people, goods, capital could pass over the borders in freedom, and that the frontier between East and West Germany would become basically like the one with, say, Belgium. It could take time – perhaps fifty years – for such a system to develop. But, if events happened in this way, we would not need to forge a unitary German state, which would certainly alter the balance of power in Europe, not so much from the military as from the economic point of view.'[68]

Philipp Jenninger, former president of the Bundestag:
'I believe that, although one must dream, the dream must be realistic. One could imagine that, through a gradual process of contacts and meetings, of economic, technological and cultural cooperation, of setting up joint committees in certain areas, we could work our way to what could become a loose confederation between the two states. There are many possible ways forward, and the word "unity" covers a wide band of meaning.'[69]

Daniel Cohn-Bendit ('Dany The Red'), Green magazine editor, former student agitator:
'I can see the Germanys moving together as a cultural unit. I can think of the two German states becoming like West Germany and Austria. I can think of East Germany joining the European Community in the year 2000 as part of a federation of *Mitteleuropa*. But I reject the word reunification.'[70]

Bishop Martin Kruse, chairman of Protestant Church Council:
'What becomes of all this will be left to history and the hand of God. I am neither a prophet nor a politician, but I believe that we are growing together, not apart.'[71]

Edzard Reuter, chairman of Daimler-Benz:
'If this experiment of Gorbachev succeeds – for which we can only pray – this could reduce many problems in the centre of Europe. No one thinks of reunification of the German state – it's a question of lowering the border between East and West Germany.'[72]

Helmut Schmidt:
'The German nation, like the Polish or Hungarian, is 1,000 years old. A couple of generations does not interfere with these fundamental identities. I would say that at some stage over the next century, the East and West Germans will live under one roof. I express myself ambiguously – I have not used the word "reunification" for thirty years.'[73]

West Germany was evidently unprepared for the national challenges confronting it after November 1989. In the highly-charged aftermath, many West German politicians and commentators who had previously shown little interest in unity suddenly elevated it to the peak of their preoccupations. Both Left and Right issued warnings against real and imagined efforts by the western allies to block Germany's ambitions to recreate a national state. These ambitions were indeed legitimate; but the West German body politic had previously proved singularly inept in explaining them to the rest of the world, and the rest of the world had been highly reluctant to understand them.[74]

The Federal Republic has won the opportunity of reforging unity as a direct result of its perseverence and success over four decades. In 1990, after all the waiting, German voices started to grow both impatient and fearful – just when the prize was drawing within reach.

6

The Rise and Fall of the Economic Miracle

In disconsolate despair, the masses of our German people in their millions, pursued by economic disaster, gazed into a grey and empty future ... It is a mistake to believe that any Government unaided can achieve the miracle of a restoration ... For there can be no miracle – whether it comes from above or without – which gives to man anything which he has not himself earned.

Adolf Hitler, 1934[1]

That which has taken place in Germany these past six years was anything other than a miracle. It was merely the result of honest endeavour of a whole people, who again had the chance of applying human initiative, human liberty and human energies.

Ludwig Erhard, 1954[2]

The German engine has lost steam quite considerably. The virtues which characterised the first post-war period – courage to liberalise and to accept full competition, a firm belief in the free market model – are still accepted as basic principles, but often neglected in practice.

Wilfried Guth, supervisory board chairman of the Deutsche Bank, 1987[3]

Germany's economy has traced a zig-zag passage across a stormy century. The trail has frequently changed tack, but it has kept reverting to the same basic direction. Germany was a latecomer to both nationhood and industrialisation; but during the vicissitudes in the years between German unification in 1871 and dismemberment after 1945, the prowess and influence of German industry have provided great continuity. For most of the post-war period, West Germany's economic performance has been widely admired abroad. During the 1980s, the German economic model lost its shine. As the country starts to tackle

119

the unexpected challenge of reunification, Germany's economic attention is likely to be distracted away from western markets towards the task of rebuilding the East.

Both during and since the *Wirtschaftswunder* in the 1950s and 1960s, the economy's success has contributed substantially to the stability and affluence of Europe. The Federal Republic, the third largest industrial economy after the US and Japan, makes up about one quarter of western Europe's output. Post-war achievement has stemmed above all from internationalisation of the economy. West Germany's exports have exceeded imports every year since 1951.[4] During the second half of the 1980s, the trade surplus reached unprecedented proportions. The Federal Republic became the world's largest exporter[5], and the second biggest creditor after Japan.[6]

The country is still Europe's economic powerhouse. Now that unity is approaching, Germany's economic dominance, over the medium term, will increase; but the process of absorbing East Germany – with an economic size of roughly one-eighth of the Federal Republic's (equivalent to that of the state of Hesse) – will take time and capital, energy and effort. West Germany's gross national product per head is roughly 40 per cent higher than in Britain;[7] a united Germany's overall wealth however will be automatically reduced by the absorption of a state where living standards and productivity are only half that in West Germany.

The average industrial worker earns about 20 per cent more than in Britain, and over the whole year works about one-sixth fewer hours.[8] West Germany is much more strongly geared to manufacturing industry than its neighbours. The overall output of West German industry is only a little less than that of Britain and France combined.[9] However, the engines of the domestic economy are turning more slowly, and parts of the machinery need overhauling. After the post-war dash for recovery, economic growth started to sag during the 1970s and, in the 1980s, despite faster-than-expected expansion at the end of the decade, dropped comprehensively below the average of the industrialised world. The huge trade surpluses of the 1980s have been a reflection of relatively low growth; West German industry has been bursting out abroad, breaking through the limits of the relatively confined home market.

With material needs increasingly satisfied and the rapid post-war population increase going into reverse, West Germany's risk-taking spirit has subsided. The new markets beckoning in the East will provide fresh incentives. But, over large stretches of the economy, hunger for economic growth has given way to desire for comfort, security and defence of the status quo. Objectives such as improved leisure, cuts in working hours and protection of the environment have come to the fore.* The 1990s may see a recovery of entrepreneurial activity as the 'baby-boom' generation of the 1960s starts to play a role in economic affairs. Youth is likely to play a special role in the economic reconstruction of East Germany. Although West Germany lags behind the US and Britain in fostering an 'enterprise culture', the creation of new businesses by younger people has shown an improvement in recent years.[10] But the breed of free-wheeling post-war entrepreneurs appears to have died out. There are no obvious successors to businessmen such as Max Grundig, who assembled a radio and electrical products empire, or Heinz Nixdorf, who built up the country's biggest home-grown computer group. Both men are now dead; and both groups have been taken over by multi-nationals – Grundig by Philips of the Netherlands, and Nixdorf (in early 1990) by Siemens.

In the 1990s, one crucial question will be whether the unification process, combined with large population shifts between East and West Germany, triggers a rise in the birth rate. German unity is likely to provide an expansionary fillip. But forecasts of a new economic miracle may be premature. The process of welding on to the Federal Republic a part of Germany which has been run on totalitarian lines for near 60 years will bring considerable social and economic problems – difficulties which have so far been under-estimated. In view of the need for a large transfer of resources towards the East, German exports are likely to taper off – a welcome development for the world economy. German industrial companies are in the long term likely to extend further their international reach. Buoyed by the sudden expansion of their home base, profiting from strong traditional links with pre-war industrial areas of East Germany, West Germany's largest corporations look set to become Europe's leading multinationals during the 1990s. Well used to holding course through political turbulence, Daimler-Benz, Siemens and Volkswagen are the new ambassadors of German power.

* See Chapter 14.

I

The curtain has come down conclusively on the miracle. The growth spurt of 4 per cent in 1989 represented the first year since 1979 that economic growth in West Germany out-performed the average of the Organisation of Economic Cooperation and Development (OECD).*[11] The number out of work has remained above 2 million since 1983. The unemployment rate in West Germany rose by 120 per cent between 1979 and 1989 – a greater percentage rise than in any other OECD country except Iceland, Greece and Ireland. During the 1990s, unemployment is likely to drop as a result of the demographically-induced fall in the number of people of working age.** But the numbers out of work in East Germany – which has previously enjoyed notionally full employment – are likely to rise sharply as it moves towards a market-orientated economy.

During the 1980s, West Germany showed world-beating performances in only two areas: bringing down inflation (to an average between 1985 and 1989 of 1.2 per cent and registering ever-growing trade surpluses – averaging during this period DM103 billion per year.[12] The surpluses reflected not only continued growth in exports but also cuts in the value of imports, due to falling prices for oil and raw materials. Additionally, between 1987 and 1989, exports to the European Community were boosted by the under-valuation of the D-Mark within the European Monetary System,† which gave German exports a significant competitive advantage. After the Second World War, the fledgling Federal Republic was forced to export to earn dollars to pay back foreign debts and to finance reconstruction. Forty years on, the export surplus is a reflection of the specialisation, efficiency and product quality of West German companies, but it also illustrates how the dash has gone out of the domestic economy. Annual economic growth between 1980 and 1989 averaged only 1.9 per cent a year, down from 8 per cent in the 1950s, 4.5 per cent in the 1960s and 2.7 per cent in the 1970s. By contrast, Japan's growth rate was 4.2 per cent during the 1980s, while Britain has grown at 2.2 per cent, the US at 2.7 per cent and France at 2.0 per cent.[13]

The slowdown in growth raises some tantalising questions. Economic dynamism after the war under Ludwig Erhard, Economics Minister

---

* The 24-member organisation of industrialised countries.
** See Chapter 15.
† See Chapter 3.

between 1949 and 1963, was practicable only at a time of exceptional effort to rebuild a shattered country. In some ways, similar conditions now prevail in East Germany. Now, however, there is a ready-made alternative; the existence next door of the rebuilt economy of the Federal Republic may, paradoxically, make the challenge more difficult to master. Liberal economics in Germany has fallen from favour. It may take a while for the pendulum to swing back again.

Erhard, chosen by the Americans as economics director in the joint US-British occupation zone, was responsible for lifting a range of controls on prices, wages and supplies in 1948. This was announced on the day of the currency reform which saw the birth of the Deutsche Mark. A staunch opponent of the monopoly capitalism and cartels of the Weimar Republic and the Third Reich, Erhard resisted calls for state intervention despite high unemployment and the electorate's initial doubts about Germany's economic future.[14] Helped by expanding markets abroad, the psychological effect of Marshall Aid funds, an influx of cheap labour from the East and sheer hard work, Erhard's 'social market economy' laid the foundations for the 'miracle'.[15]

Erhard also played a central part in the establishment in 1957 of the statutorily-autonomous central bank, the Bundesbank. Adopting the fight against inflation and defence of the currency as its highest precept, the central bank is the pillar of West Germany's economic well-being.[16]*

The rotund cigar-puffing Erhard, with his motto *Wohlstand für Alle* (Prosperity for All), has passed into popular West German mythology – even though he made a poor Chancellor when he eventually took over from Adenauer. There was nothing magical about Erhard's formula; if external circumstances had not been favourable, his policies would not have worked nearly as quickly, or as well.

Erhard brought in a commitment to market economics, but the state maintained a strong role to organise welfare and secure social harmony. The social dimension was reinforced during the 1960s as part of a general move towards a more collectivist approach on the economy. This was supported both on the Right by the Christian Democrat and Christian Social parties, which dominated the first two decades of West German politics, and on the Left by the Social Democrats, who took part in the Grand Coalition in 1966 and headed the government in 1969. West Germany's Right-wing parties are not Tories in the English sense; they are not natural supporters of *laissez-faire* or even of big

* See Chapter 8.

business. Inheriting part of their policies from the pre-war Centre party, they have taken up social policy traditions rooted in Catholic teachings of communal responsibility for the disadvantaged.[17] Since German economic thought has always been an amorphous blend of different philosophies, neither pure liberalism nor central planning has ever been established economic doctrine. The Third Reich maintained centralised controls, for instance in the price and wage freeze imposed in 1936. But Nazi Germany also practised a form of hybrid economy in which private business, under growing state influence, became increasingly entangled with totalitarian government.

The beginning of the 1980s saw a brief revival of liberal economic principles, but by the end of the decade market-orientated economics was again on the defensive. Subsidies, totalling more than DM120 billion a year, counting all kinds of aid, rose during the 1980s. Large areas of the economy – agriculture, housing, coal-mining, telecommunications, the service sector and parts of heavy industry such as shipbuilding – remain highly regulated. A senior OECD official says bluntly: 'For a country which professes economic liberalism, German subsidies are a scandal.' Gerhard Fels, director of the Institut der deutschen Wirtschaft, an economic research think-tank linked to the Federation of German Industry (BDI), says, 'Germany has always been the classical land of cartels and collectivism, from the time of the Kaisers onwards. After the Erhard period, we have now become corporatists again.'[18]

Memories of the economic difficulties of 1980-82, when for the first time West Germany simultaneously faced a weak currency, rising inflation and recession, contributed to unadventurousness in government policies during the 1980s. The episode, which was caused by the combination of a modest reflationary package in 1978 and the international oil price rise in 1979, helped bring down the Schmidt government. Since then, the economic policy slogan has been 'safety first'. Despite the obvious competitiveness of its export industry, West Germany is making heavy weather of facing up to a more complex and challenging international economic environment. The post-1992 plan for the single market in the European Community is regarded with suspicion by wide sections of the population, because it will upset protective arrangements benefiting less robust parts of the economy. Otto Schlecht, the veteran state secretary at the Economics Ministry in Bonn, who used to work with Erhard during the 1950s, points to the irony. During the Erhard era, he states, in the fledgling years of the European Common Market, the Federal Republic used to be suspicious of ideas from Brussels because they encouraged bureaucratic

124

'planification'. Now, he says, through the 1992 programme, Brussels is providing a stimulus for economic liberalisation which would not otherwise come from within West Germany.[19]

II

As late as the 1960s, one in five West Germans was a refugee. Nowadays, in stark contrast to the flexibility shown by their émigré compatriots from the East, West Germans have had enough of moving. Even settling in a different area to look for a job, for instance, is a task which few people today would face with equanimity. The average German house owner stays in occupation for twenty-eight years.[20] Helmut Kohl explains the mood with a personal anecdote. His wife Hannelore, three years his junior, was brought up in Leipzig in what is now East Germany. She lived through the horrific last two years of the war in the provincial town of Döbeln, helping as an 11-year-old to separate dead and wounded soldiers arriving at the station from the eastern front. After Germany's capitulation, her family fled before the advancing Red Army to the western sector, finally arriving near Kohl's home town of Ludwigshafen in 1946. Her first home in the West was a 15-square-metre washing-cellar. Kohl related his wife's experiences in a speech in 1987 in which he pointed out how psychology left over from the war was hampering mobility:

> People are finding again the sense of being at home. This can be as important as improving material conditions. After the war, 13 million people lost their hearth and home. My wife had to move house 13 times as a child. Now, at last, people want to put down roots.[21]

At the same time, emphasis has shifted from earning wealth to enjoying it – and spreading it around the population through redistributive taxation and a generous pension system. Corporate tax levels in the Federal Republic are among the highest in the industrialised world,[22] while working hours are around the lowest.[23] Although the number of strikes in West Germany remains very low by international standards[24], social peace has its price: labour costs have risen sharply. This is the result less of high wage settlements, more of the rising contributions made by employers to the country's comprehensive social security system.[25] As one result of higher industrial costs, corporations' profit expectations in Germany have diminished, and capital investment has fallen sharply from the peak levels at the end of the 1960s.[26]

The consensus-based system of economic management is also coming under strain.* The collaborative network welding together employers and employee representatives owes its strength partly to the desire for harmony left by memories of the disruption of two world wars. Well-organised consensus has been a crucial factor steadying West German society. Cooperation between both sides of industry provides the means to keep down labour disputes and to handle activities like industrial training, a system which is the envy of Germany's competitors. The occupational training scheme, the origins of which date back to Germany's medieval guilds and craft associations, provides jobs and experience for about 1.8 million apprentices. It not only maintains low youth unemployment, but also is a crucial factor ensuring the insistence on quality which is a cornerstone of West German industry.

Yet the consensus system has also provided interest groups with near-veto power to block change. The ability of the trade unions to play a constructive role in the capitalist system has been called into question during the 1980s, partly as a result of the unions' Neue Heimat housing group disaster.** Additionally, the strength of private and public lobbying appears to have increased. About 1,300 associations of various kinds are accredited to make representations to the Bonn government. In contrast to centralised countries like Britain or France, strategic economic decisions on taxes and government spending frequently become bogged down in contorted political wrangling.

The roots of consensus stretch far back into Germany's past. The basis of the West German system of collective bargaining, under which employers and trade unions negotiate working conditions and pay settlements on an industry-wide basis, dates back to 1918.[27] 'Co-determination' (*Mitbestimmung*), giving workers' spokesmen seats along with shareholder representatives on companies' supervisory boards, was introduced in the coal and steel industries under British military occupation in 1947. It was extended throughout other large and medium-sized companies in the 1950s, and expanded further under a law in 1976 covering all companies employing more than 2,000 people. Co-determination allows the unions a share in corporate decision-making. The supervisory board appoints members of the management board, which is in charge of day-to-day operations, and meets between two and four times a year to control the performance of the management board. However, *Mitbestimmung* also makes unions partly responsible for the performance of their companies

* See Chapter 9.
** See Chapters 4,9.

– and so imposes an element of discipline.

Other elements of the consensus system – for instance, the sizeable control of the banks over industry – have roots in the era of rapid industrialisation at the end of the 19th century. Additionally, the panoply of strict norms and standards governing trades and professions is a characteristic also reaching back to the medieval guilds – bodies which, because of Germany's late industrial start, continued their lives into modern times. As late as 1840, a law in Saxony solemnly enacted that each village might have one tailor, shoemaker, white-bread baker, butcher, smith, saddler, harness-maker, carpenter, glazier, rope-maker and cooper.[28]

Despite the acknowledged need for economic and social reforms to cope with challenges in the 1990s, the Federal Republic has failed to put into effect growth-boosting deregulation practised in the US, Britain and Japan. The Christian Democrat-led administration in 1982 promised Erhard-like efforts to free market forces. It made some cuts in personal and company taxes by achieving better control of government spending, but in many areas intervention and economic rigidities have remained. Although some privatisation measures went ahead, other attempts to sell off public shareholdings in industry have been blocked by opposition from *Land* governments.[29] During the 1980s, the institutions which exert a corporatist hold over the West German economy – big business, banks, the unions and employers' associations – did not relax their grip.

Karl Schiller, Social Democrat Economics Minister between 1966 and 1972 (and Finance Minister too in 1971-72), has played a more important role in shaping post-war economic policy-making than anyone except Erhard. Through his 'concerted action' meetings with trade unions and neo-Keynesian measures to overcome the 1967 recession, Schiller brought in additional instruments to steer the economy. He resigned in 1972 when he failed to persuade Chancellor Brandt of the need for tough anti-inflation action. Schiller, now well into his seventies but retaining the boyish air of a perpetual *enfant terrible*, lives with his fourth wife in a woodland villa outside Hamburg. He told me that today's Bonn governments face greater policy complexities than in his day:

> The splitting up of public opinion into interest groups is much stronger than it was twenty years ago. Economic policy is made much more difficult because at every step someone will get up and protest. Because of its links to business organisations and farmers, one of the problems of a Christian Democrat-led government is that they are much more involved with such interest groups ... The Christian Democrats no longer seem to be the party of Ludwig Erhard.[30]

127

III

Exports are at the root of German economic power. Per head of the population, the country sells four times as much abroad as the US and more than twice as much as Japan. During the 1980s, companies have stepped up the search for exports as a shortfall in demand and investment in West Germany coincided with prolonged economic buoyancy abroad. Germany these days exerts domination peacefully, through its great engineering, automobile, chemicals and electrical companies.

The *Mittelstand* – small and medium-sized businesses scattered around the country, often family-owned and occupying specialist niches in the engineering or machinery sectors – also plays a considerable export role. Between them, these companies account for half of economic output and make up two-thirds of employment in private industry. They are also on the whole much more flexible and adaptable than big business.

Export expansion has brought wealth, but also exposes the country to external economic shocks. Exports at the end of the 1980s accounted for about one-third of gross national product, twice the level in the 1950s, and up from just over 20 per cent at the end of the 1970s.[31] The country's specialisation in investment goods such as cars, machinery and industrial equipment allows it to profit disproportionately from world economic buoyancy of the sort seen during the second half of the 1980s. But if a period of international economic downturn or currency unrest should return during the 1990s, the Federal Republic would also suffer more than less export-oriented countries.

Partly to try to protect themselves from capricious export cycles, leading West German corporations have been building up production abroad through a wave of takeovers and acquisitions, above all in the US. The 1980s – a decade of faltering domestic thrust – has been the time when West German business moved fully on to the international stage. Between 1986 and 1988, West German companies channelled a massive DM55 billion abroad, with DM18 billion going to other countries in the European Community, and no less than DM26 billion flowing to the US. West German companies have recovered with a vengeance their post-war lag in building up investments abroad. By the end of 1987, capital investment abroad exceeded the assets of foreign companies in West Germany by DM40 billion.[32]

The Big Three chemical groups have led the way with a sizeable increase in their US operations, most spectacularly through Hoechst's

1988 purchase of the Celanese chemical company. Siemens has taken over American companies in areas like telephone exchanges and automobile electronics. Bertelsmann, the music and publishing concern, now among the world's biggest media groups, has acquired the Doubleday publishers and the music business of RCA. Many lesser-known specialist companies have also expanded into the US, ranging from Heidelberger Druckmaschinen, the world's largest printing machinery company, to Hugo Boss, the fast-growing clothing group. None the less, reticence about foreign expansion has not been entirely dissipated. Siemens – the Federal Republic's second biggest company after Daimler-Benz – adopts caution as one of the lessons of history. The First World War cost Siemens 40 per cent of its assets, mainly through the loss of overseas factories and businesses. At the end of the 1939-45 war, the company lost 80 per cent of its assets and suffered wholesale dismantling of its nerve centre at Siemensstadt in Berlin.[33] Siemens admits that lingering memories abroad of past German aggression mean it has to 'tread carefully' in making hostile takeover bids for foreign companies.[34] In efforts to reinforce its foreign presence, Siemens conceals its might behind a partner; in the 1989 takeover bid for Britain's Plessey electronics concern, Siemens was careful to link up with the General Electric Company.

The symbol of economic power is the Deutsche Mark. The West German currency is now the pivot of the European Monetary System (EMS),* and has also become the world's second most important reserve currency after the dollar. Through the EMS, the Bundesbank effectively sets the monetary policies for the other countries which are members of the scheme. The special status of the D-Mark has extended West Germany's economic influence, but the anti-inflation philosophy which buttresses the currency also underlines a streak of German vulnerability. Monetary union with the East brings risks as well as opportunities.

Post-war monetary stability has served a series of interlocking aims. The Deutsche Mark's potency has allowed West Germany to amass wealth at home and regain weight in its economic dealings abroad. In comparison with the inconvertible East German currency, the D-Mark's international importance highlights the success of capitalism over communism in the two German states. Most of all, though, sound money is insurance against upheaval. The message of history is that monetary laxity stores up its own revenge. The experiences of 1923 and

* See Chapter 3.

1948 have been enough to drive home to the Germans that, as John Maynard Keynes put it:

> There is no subtler, no surer way of overturning the existing basis of society than to debauch the currency. The process engages all the hidden forces of economic law on the side of destruction, and does it in a manner which not one man in a million is able to diagnose.[35]

During the First World War, and again between 1933 and 1945, the debt of the Reich government rose roughly thirty-fold each time.[36] Hitler's boast in 1942 that, 'The German Reichsmark must be made unassailable and must become the most stable currency in the world'[37] served only to underline the Führer's ignorance of economics. In both the First and the Second World Wars, government borrowing was funded by the printing press rather than through taxation: the Germans counted on the debts being repaid through conquered territory and reparations from the vanquished. Each time, the gamble misfired. Since the debts and the money supply soared far beyond Germany's redemption capacity, crumbling of the currency was inevitable.

In the first years of the Weimar Republic, the debt and note issue reached astronomical levels and by the end of 1923, 497 billion billion Marks were in circulation. A total of 1,783 presses were running night and day to print them. The cost of living index was 1,250 billion times the level in 1913,[38] and the Mark was stabilised against the dollar at one-1,000 billionth of its value at the start of the war.[39] A penny postage stamp cost as much as a villa had done a few years earlier. The suicide rate – which in the Weimar Republic of 1923 was roughly the same as that of the Federal Republic in the 1980s – started to climb, although it did not reach a peak until the Third Reich.[40] 'Instead of taxing the rich, Germany paid her way and paid off all the costs of the war by destroying the savings of the poor and middle classes,' wrote A.J.P. Taylor.

> The saving, investing middle class, everywhere the pillar of stability and respectability, was in any case newer in Germany than in France or England – it was now utterly destroyed ... The former *rentiers*, who had lost their all, ceased to impose a brake; they became resentful of the republic, to whom they attributed their disaster; violent and irresponsible; and ready to follow the first demagogic saviour not blatantly from the industrial working class.[41]

The Führer's own monetary legacy was executed on 20 June 1948, when the occupying powers replaced the Reichsmark by the D-Mark, exchanged in the three western zones at a rate of 6.5 for every 100 old marks.[42] Compared with 1923, the ruin was held within limits, but the wiping out of 93.5 per cent of savings was one more consequence of the catastrophe of the Third Reich. Moreover, by setting up a different currency regime in the West as compared with the Russian zone, the birth of the Deutsche Mark marked one more step towards national division. The Russian blockade of Berlin started on 24 June, triggering the Allied airlift to the city – and starting the countdown to the establishment of a separate Federal Republic in May 1949.

The post-war central bank system showed both differences from and continuity with the past. Both the president of the directorate of the Bank deutscher Länder, Wilhelm Vocke, and the first head of the Bundesbank, Karl Blessing (a member of the Nazi party), were members of the directorate of the Reichsbank before 1939. Led by president Hjalmar Schacht, the directorate addressed a now celebrated memorandum to Hitler in January 1939 warning against inflationary state expenditure, and most of the Reichsbank directors were subsequently dismissed.[43] The Bank deutscher Länder was set up on federal lines in accordance with the American desire to end centralisation of the economy. The statutory independence of the Bundesbank when it was established in 1957 was not, strictly speaking, breaking new ground. The Reichsbank itself was formally independent of the government between 1922 and 1937 – although this was a result of conditions imposed by First World War victors in a vain bid to assure reparations payments.[44] Also there was no shortage of attempts during the 1950s to exert government influence on the central bank.[45] These have continued to the present day, with conflict between the Bundesbank and Bonn centring on the search to find the right balance between policies fighting inflation and sustaining growth.[46]

The Bundesbank's power does not lie simply in its formal independence, but in the stature of its top officials – and in the knowledge that the Germans have learned the lessons of past monetary recklessness. Karl Otto Pöhl, the central bank's president since 1980, says that the Bundesbank's main weapon is the confidence it enjoys in public opinion.* In fact, since German commitment to sound money is virtually a substitute for patriotism, inveighing against the Bundesbank is practically taboo. These days the only public figure to carry on a crusade against the central bank is ex-Chancellor Schmidt – but it is a lonely battle.[47]

* See Chapter 9.

IV

Some German businessmen, bankers and economists may seek inspir-
ation from the direction of Margaret Thatcher's Britain. Although it is
incontestable that the West German economy has problem areas, they are
nothing like acute enough to justify the kind of radical treatment
Thatcher applied to moribund Britain at the end of the 1970s.
Additionally, there is almost universal agreement that Thatcherite
policies in West Germany simply would not work. Hans Tietmeyer,
long-serving state secretary at the Finance Ministry, who moved to the
Bundesbank at the beginning of 1990*, told me that Thatcherism would
be inappropriate because of 'past traumas'. German society must not be
stretched too far. A member of the Christian Democrats, who none the
less proved his skills in working under the Social Democrats in the 1970s,
Tietmeyer admits that, in the thirst for consensus policies, 'spontaneity
and pioneer spirit' may disappear. But he believes that German society
would not be able to weather the sort of hardship and social conflict which
Thatcher's policies brought to Britain in the early 1980s.[48]

Wolfgang Kartte, the long-serving president of the Federal Cartel
Office in West Berlin, says the Germans draw their basic conservatism
from a mixture of 'history, tradition, bitter experiences, folk-character and
Angst. German public opinion demands security, not experiments.'
Kartte, a jovial man with a fondness for irreverent quips, is charged with
supervising the country's anti-trust laws introduced in 1957 to counter the
cartels and concentration of the Weimar Republic and the Nazi period.
He fought his biggest battle in 1989 against the merger of Daimler-Benz
and Messerschmitt-Bölkow-Blohm to form the country's largest defence
group.** His battered-looking office building, near the Tempelhof air-
field where Allied aircraft landed during the Berlin blockade of 1948-49,
formerly housed the Third Reich's Air Transport Ministry. Conversations in his office are interrupted every half-hour by the insistent tones of a
cuckoo clock on the wall. Kartte looks into the German psyche – and
observes barriers in the way of more adventurous economic policies.

> Of course, we are all waiting for more deregulation, more privatisation – but
> then you come up against the demand for security. People are afraid to say
> that the state should make a complete exit, because the state is the good

* See Chapter 9.
** See Chapter 12.

father, it has to do everything ... The search for harmony is good. But if you make harmony your first priority, you can lead neither a company nor a state. We are in the process of structural change – coping with new markets, new products, falling birth rates, worries about the health and pensions systems. A bit of innovation would be very good. It cannot only be done through consensus.[49]

Kartte's view, however, is not a popular one. When I asked Hans-Jochen Vogel, leader of the opposition Social Democrats, about growing German economic rigidities, he disputed that anything much was wrong and then said: 'We could ask people to put up with a lot if we as a country were poor. But in comparison with the 1950s, we are as rich as kings.'[50]

Over forty years, the transformation has indeed been remarkable – comparable with the four hectic industrial decades between 1870 and 1910. The once war-shattered country is now channelling billions of dollars across the Atlantic to finance huge American budget and trade deficits. The Germans who queued up to receive DM40 a head in the June 1948 currency reform now own DM2,400 billion in savings – an average of DM91,000 per family household compared with a mere DM1,600 in 1950. Average family income from interest and dividends amounts to DM4,000 a year – against only DM70 in 1950.[51] One of the melancholic themes running through German history, however, is that good times do not last. While they savour their economic accomplishments, the Germans may be distracted from preparing for the 1990s. Partly in an attempt to propel the government to take a more pro-business line, corporate leaders such as Tyll Necker, head of the Federation of German Industry, warn about 'growth defeatism'. He told me: 'We are thinking too much about our prosperity and not enough of our future.'[52]*

Martin Bangemann, the former Bonn Economics Minister,** likes to quote lines from Thomas Mann's novel *Buddenbrooks* – the story of a well-to-do north German family caught in genteel decline – to illustrate what might be happening to the West German economy.

I know that the outward, visible and tangible signs and symbols of happiness and achievement often only appear when in reality everything is already starting to go downhill again. The outer signs take time to arrive – like the light of a star which shines most brightly when it is on the way to being extinguished, or maybe has already gone out.[53]

* See Chapter 9.
** Bangemann left the Government at the end of 1988 to join the European Commission.

The German tendency towards agonising may have given an important stimulus to post-war industry. Eberhard von Koerber – a former BMW manager who is now chairman of the West German subsidiary of Switzerland's Brown Boveri engineering group* – has brought in widespread rationalisation and trimmed the workforce to improve efficiency at the ninety-year-old company. But he also admits that, because of high German manufacturing costs, his group is focusing new investments elsewhere in the European Community rather than in Germany. Koerber points to the advantages of German sobriety:

> We Germans are always complaining how terrible the world is. The Americans announce that things are bright, when in reality they are not flourishing at all. Our attitude is positive because it avoids arrogance and complacency. People are kept on their toes if they always think there is a disaster round the corner. You know that there's a way of avoiding it, provided you do your duty and work hard.[54]

West Germany at the end of the 1980s would like simply to relax and enjoy the fruits of economic achievement. Instead, it is facing, with very little time for preparation, the challenge of remaking a nation out of two different economic systems.

V

The industrial bridge between the two Germanys is likely to be quickly rebuilt. The foundations have not been erased by four decades of separation – for they go back 100 years. In the golden age of industrial growth before the First World War, England set the pace. Germany was late in following, but caught up in a breathless rush. By 1870, 60 per cent of the population of England and Wales lived in towns, and two-thirds of its railways had been built. The town-dwelling proportion of Germany's population rose from only 36 per cent in 1871 to 60 per cent by 1910.[55] During this period, the overall population increased more than 50 per cent (from 41 million to 65 million), the railway

---

* Now merged with ASEA of Sweden.

network tripled, coal production rose six times and iron and steel output went up eightfold.

In the 1840s, Germany lagged behind not only Britain but also Belgium and France in terms of coal production. But cutting of internal tariffs, national unity in 1871, the growth of the railways and a series of inventions in steel, electricals and chemicals gave the impetus to an industrial drive which changed the face of Germany and, ultimately, that of Europe. By 1910 Germany's iron and steel output and its railway system were each about 60 per cent larger than Britain's.[56] Although Britain remained the richer country, between 1883 and 1913 Germany's production of manufactures grew at 4.2 per cent a year, twice the rate of Britain.[57]

The first phase of European industrialisation was in textiles, coal, iron-founding, railways and shipbuilding, when most key inventions were British. In the second stage towards the end of the 19th century, growth focused on steel, chemicals, electricity, optical goods and the internal combustion engine, and many of the breakthroughs were German. Germany moved ahead of Britain in industrial training and technical education as well as in social legislation. Acts covering sickness, accident and old age and invalidity insurance were passed in 1883, 1884 and 1888 respectively.

Wary of Germany's growing industrial strength, England tried to ward off German export competition, but the effort was singularly counter-productive. The British government in 1887 passed a law obliging imports to be labelled with the country of manufacture; this was at the behest of Sheffield cutlers who had been losing business to imported German products. Far from repelling buyers, the 'Made in Germany' tag soon became a mark of quality. Between 1880 and 1913, the British share of world markets for manufactures fell from 38 to 27 per cent, whereas the German share rose from 17 to 22 per cent. In 1987, the Germans celebrated the centenary of the act with a certain smugness. West Germany's share of hugely expanded world exports of manufactured goods in 1987 was 15 per cent, while Britain's had fallen to a mere 6 per cent.

Growth of a modern banking and financial system from the 1870s onwards coincided with the creation of the leading joint stock companies. In no country was the alliance between banking and industry closer. The Deutsche and Dresdner Banks, set up in 1870 and 1872 respectively, played a leading role. Johann Jakob Schuster, one of the leading board members of the Dresdner Bank before the First World War, commented in 1908, 'In Germany our banks are largely responsible for the development of the Empire.'[58] A series of banking mergers in the crisis years of 1929-31 led to the crystallisation of the Deutsche and Dresdner Banks and the Commerzbank as the three dominant pillars of the financial sector – a structure which was to continue into the post-1945 era.

At the end of the Second World War, all the Big Three banks suffered huge asset losses through bomb devastation and the confiscation of holdings in the East. A financial investigation team from the US occupation authorities – after examining in 1945-46 the banks' role in Germany's pillage of Europe – recommended that both the Deutsche and Dresdner Banks be liquidated. The proposal went unheeded; but in accordance with overall American ideas on decentralisation, the three banks were split up in 1947-48 into small institutions allocated to each of the original eleven states in the western occupied zones.[59] After the birth of the Federal Republic, the banks were allowed to re-establish themselves from 1952 onwards. The banks were regrouped into single institutions in 1957 – and applied themselves to the task of rebuilding their power.

Germany's other great corporations showed similar capability for survival. Eight of the top ten industrial corporations in West Germany today were founded in the 19th century. Siemens was set up in 1847, BASF in 1865, Bayer and Hoechst in 1863 and Thyssen in 1871. Motor giant Daimler-Benz is the product of a merger in 1926 between Daimler and Benz, formed in 1890 and 1883 respectively. The electrical group Robert Bosch was established in 1886, while Rheinisch-Westfälisches Elektrizitätswerk (RWE), the country's largest utility, was founded in 1898. Even the two 'newcomers' in the top ten, Volkswagen and the Veba energy and chemicals conglomerate, are more than fifty years old, incorporated in 1938 and 1929 respectively. Each of West Germany's largest companies is thus older than the East German state – a factor explaining why Germany's great corporations will be at home when they set up business again in the East.

In the list of West Germany's top twenty companies, five more – BMW (1916) and Opel (1862) in vehicles, and Mannesmann (1890), Maschinenfabrik Augsburg-Nürnberg (1908) and Krupp (1811) in steel and engineering – were founded before the end of the First World War. By contrast, only one of the present top ten British companies was established in the 19th century: Unilever in 1894. (The General Electric Company was formed in 1900.) In the US, four of the top ten – Exxon and Mobil (both 1882), American Telephone and Telegraph (1885) and General Electric (1892) – owe their origins to the last century. Taking

136

the top twenty corporations in the three countries, ten US and six British companies were established before the end of the First World War – against thirteen in Germany.

Germany's dominant corporate structure therefore has a considerably greater element of tradition than either Britain or the US, two countries which have benefited from incomparably greater political stability. Family plutocracies ruled over several of the largest German concerns up until the Second World War, but several of their members afterwards ended up in Allied jails. The families have now left the scene. Today's largest corporations are for the most part multinational companies run by professional managers and owned by a wide spread of shareholders. But the family names live on – a strong force for continuity in a country otherwise marked by upheaval.

Continuity is evident in links with East Germany. Alone in the mechanical engineering sector, around 400 West German companies were set up after the war by businessmen who had fled from the East. The heart of the East German chemical industry at Leuna and Buna was set up by the I.G. Farben companies. BMW used to produce pre-war cars in Eisenach, in Thuringia, beneath the celebrated Wartburg castle – on the same site used after 1945 to manufacture East Germany's Wartburg models. Siemens, which will play an enormous role in building up East Germany's communications, energy and transport sectors, had at least 10 big plants on the territory of the German Democratic Republic; Krupp also had several plants, the largest in Magdeburg; Mannesmann ran three – in Berlin, Bitterfeld and Eberswalde.

Daimler-Benz possessed an aero-engine factory south of Berlin dismantled by the Soviet Union; its subsidiary AEG owned a large network of locomotive, cable and electrical plants in East Germany. Veba – which, like Siemens, previously had its headquarters in Berlin – has already been the most active West German company doing business with East Germany, with annual two-way business of DM1.5 billion. Veba is now going back to its roots by preparing to extend activities in chemicals and electricity generation in the old Prussian provinces in the north of East Germany. Volkswagen owns Audi, which was established in Zwickau (in Saxony) at the beginning of the century – the place where East Germany produces the puffing two-stroke Trabant cars. Carl Hahn, VW's chairman, was born in the Saxon industrial city of Chemnitz – and has already ensured that VW will be setting foot there through a joint venture to produce modern cars for the new East German market. At the beginning of 1990, Hahn referred to the reopening of eastern markets as 'an unimaginable gift of fate'.[60]

The final decades of the last century also saw the birth of the powerful industrial associations which were to make their mark in history. In the depression which followed the overheated boom of the early 1870s, groups of German iron, steel and textile concerns lobbied successfully for protection. The *Kartell*, a German institution which has entered the English language, was born in the years 1880 to 1910. Agreements among industrial producers to check competition through price-fixing and market barriers were nothing new; they were set up first in England, and also proliferated in the 19th-century French iron, steel and chemical trades. But in Germany, according to one expert, 'such agreements were more ingeniously elaborate, far more general, and more frankly accepted as part of a rational economic organisation of society than among any other people'.[61]

Starting in the metallurgical and coal industries, by the end of the century about 275 cartels were active, in practically every sector. German companies also played a leading role in promoting various international cartels during this period. At the hub were the greatest names of industry. The Rhine-Westphalian Coal Syndicate, formed in 1893, was merged with the cartels for coke and briquettes in 1903. After a crisis in the electrical industry in 1900, AEG and Siemens merged with rival groups to forge two dominant poles, and in 1908 agreed to collaborate with each other. The Steel Union was formed in 1904 by combining four separate steel trade cartels. By 1911, the Steel Union contained thirty steel-works, mainly in the West but including two in Silesia. The Krupp group was only one unit in a great organisation. In 1904, two chemical cartels were formed out of Agfa, BASF and Bayer on the one hand, Cassella and Hoechst on the other. These companies, together with three others, pooled forces in 1916 to work together in the dyes sector. A cryptic observer of capitalist society in Germany and the US, Vladimir Ilyich Lenin, wrote pointedly that year, 'The statement that cartels can abolish crises is a fable spread by bourgeois economists.'[62]

VI

Concentration entered a new phase after the First World War; the number of cartels grew to around 1,500 in 1925, and 2,200 in 1933, before falling back slightly during the Third Reich. In 1907, roughly 25 per cent of industrial production was estimated to be cartellised. During the Third Reich, according to estimates for 1935 to 1938, between 46 and 50 per cent of industrial production was controlled by cartels.[63]

I.G. Farben* was formed in 1925 through a merger of the already cartellised chemical groups and became the largest company in Europe, surpassed worldwide only by General Motors, US Steel and Standard Oil of New Jersey. United Steel Works (Vereinigte Stahlwerke), formed in 1926 from the merger of three concerns, immediately became the second largest steel firm in the world behind US Steel. Severe business difficulties for the motor industry led to the 1926 merger between Daimler and Benz, masterminded by the Deutsche Bank. The plan nurtured by Emil von Stauss, the dominant Deutsche Bank board member during the 1920s, to form a giant automobile trust linking companies such as BMW, Adler, NSU and Magirus to compete with Opel however never came to fruition.**

The growth of the cartels was accompanied by increasing intrigue as the Weimar political landscape clouded. In contrast to the support given to the Nazis by small capitalists and local entrepreneurs, big business in general had strong misgivings about Hitler before he became Chancellor. Walther Funk, the successor to Hjalmar Schacht as president of the Reichsbank and as Economics Minister, stated at the Nuremberg trials that at the beginning of the 1930s the greater part of industry's political funds was still going to the bourgeois parties.[64] However, like the German people as a whole, once the Führer was in power, industry followed his beckoning.[65] Among heavy industry, the main support for the Nazis came from the Rhine and Westphalian coal and steel producers. They were led by Emil Kirdorf, the so-called 'Bismarck of Coal' who played a prominent role in forming the 1890s Rhine-Westphalian Coal Syndicate; Fritz Thyssen, the heir during the 1920s to the Thyssen steel empire, who merged his company into United Steel in 1926 after the death of his father August; and Albert Vögler, managing director of United Steel. Big business turned out to profit mightily from the Third Reich's war economy, but it played less of a part in Hitler's coming to power than frequently believed.

Hitler had a revolutionary's dislike for large-scale capitalism, but possessed an unfailing instinct for bending it to his purposes. He prefaced his address at the Industry Club in Düsseldorf in January 1932 (which was arranged by Fritz Thyssen) with the remark that the Nazis

* See Chapter 2.
** See Chapter 12.

were widely regarded as 'hostile to business'.[66] It was his most important encounter with the leaders of big business before he took power. Hitler's speeches were peppered with warnings that individualistic profit had to submit before the needs of society as a whole.[67] A prime reason for the dictator's success in dealings with Germany's corporate leaders was that they were perpetually unsure of his true motives and intentions towards them.

Already in the 1920s, Hitler railed publicly against the rise of business interests in Imperial Germany, arguing against free trade and excessive urbanisation. He declared that the ascendancy of joint stock companies damaged the position of smaller enterprises and marked a 'sign of economic decay'.[68] Hitler, however, never sided with the outright anti-capitalist Left wing of the Nazis calling for nationalisation of big business. Hitler's decision in March 1933 to recall Schacht, a stern defender of capitalist values, to the Reichsbank was a message to industry that there would be no wild experiments. Early in the Third Reich, Hitler explained: 'What need have we to socialise banks and factories? We socialise human beings.'[69]

With his mind unschooled in any form of economic thought, Hitler believed that economics was merely a matter of will-power. 'Inflation is lack of discipline ... I'll see to it that prices remain stable. That's what I have my storm-troopers for,' he told a confidant during his quest for the chancellorship.[70] In a speech in 1939, he claimed: 'We have fashioned a new economic system and its basis is that capital is workpower.'[71] Later, he expressed himself with still more brutal simplicity:

> Inflation is not caused by increasing the fiduciary circulation. It begins on the day when the purchaser is obliged to pay, for the same goods, a higher sum than that asked the day before. At that point, one must intervene. Even to Schacht I had to begin by explaining this elementary truth: that the essential cause of the stability of our currency was to be sought for in our concentration camps. The currency remains stable when the speculators are put under lock and key.[72]

Heavy industry became increasingly enmeshed with the Third Reich. I.G. Farben received a state subsidy as early as December 1933 to develop synthetic fuels at its Leuna plant, and the Nazis also harnessed the conglomerate's expertise in production of synthetic rubber, light metals and explosives.[73] Increasing regulation, centralisation and cartellisation accompanied the ploughing of funds into the armaments, raw materials and motor sectors. Efforts to offset the effect of potential

140

war blockades had exceptional priority. Some agrarian experiments carried out in the Federal Republic today on turning crops to industrial use are based on work pioneered during the Third Reich.[74]

Economic stimulus brought down unemployment and by 1936 made Germany the first country to emerge from the Great Depression. A lot of companies – particularly those involved in exports – did not do well out of Hitler, but big business as a whole reaped its reward in profits and dividends. The eventual degree of involvement with the totalitarian state was striking. Advertisements from large and small companies – ranging from Daimler-Benz, AEG and Siemens to local chocolate makers – filled half the 170-page official programme for the Nazis' 1936 Nuremberg rally. In the 1940s the war economy provided not only markets for the combines' production, but cheap and expendable labour from the concentration camps as well.

Industry magnates tempted to underestimate Hitler's fanatical will met humiliating disillusionment. Carl Bosch, the I.G. Farben chairman, interceded in vain with Hitler in summer 1933 on behalf of Jewish scientists. Bosch was shown the door after Hitler told him that the Reich, if needed, would get along for 100 years without physics or chemistry.[75]

Gustav Krupp von Bohlen und Halbach, who married the Krupp heiress Bertha in 1906 and ran the Essen steel concern between 1909 and 1943, also had his brushes with the Nazis. The Krupp chief had not concealed his dislike of Hitler before he took power, but the elderly Krupp von Bohlen later became one of the Führer's favourite war industrialists and in 1940 was personally awarded the Nazis' gold badge of honour on his 70th birthday.[76] The Krupp company had forged with William II one of history's most notorious armaments alliances during the First World War. Now the Essen steel concern became the Third Reich's chief weapons supplier – just as Krupp guns supplied by Alfred Krupp, 'the Cannon King', had powered Prussia to victory over France in 1870.

After two of his sons died in the fighting and the Gestapo imprisoned his sister-in-law and her husband, Gustav Krupp lost his mind. He handed the company over to his son, Alfried, who went on trial in one of the post-war American tribunals at Nuremberg and was jailed on charges of plundering occupied territories and using slave labour from concentration camps. Alfried, a member of the SS as well as of the Nazi party, was freed in 1951* and moved to re-cast the concern's steel

* See Chapter 12.

fortunes with the assistance of slogans like 'Children not Cannon'. The Krupp heir selected Berthold Beitz, only 31 when the war ended, as chief executive; during the war Beitz had shown unusual self-confidence in administering Polish oil fields for the German army, helping rescue thousands of Poles and Jews from the Holocaust. Beitz used his contacts in East and West to rebuild Krupp's name and, after Alfried Krupp died in 1967, took over the reins completely.

Fritz Thyssen meanwhile tried to promote Hitler's interests in the Ruhr, but soon lost the dictator's favour. In 1934 Hitler brushed aside Thyssen's complaints about this ingratitude: 'I never made you any promises. I've nothing to thank you for.'[77] On the eve of war in 1939, Thyssen fled abroad and denounced the regime; his property was expropriated and, after he was turned over to the Nazis by France's Vichy regime, he found himself in a German concentration camp.[78] His widow presided over the company's early post-war fortunes, but the Thyssens – like the Siemens and the Krupps – now no longer play a role in the concerns which bear the family names.

VII

If the great German corporations have managed to retain their influence, another lasting German legacy has come from rules and controls. According to the Kiel Economic Institute, the most active defender of free-market principles among the country's five top economic research establishments, only about half the West German economy is free of state regulation and subsidy. 'The Germans are for order in everything,' Juergen Donges, the institute's vice-president,* told me.[79] Subsidies are popular. Partly because of memories of how the coal industry kept Germany's lights burning in the years after the war, 78 per cent of the population said they favoured state aid for coal in a 1987 survey.[80] Lack of interest in the marketplace is illustrated by the feebleness of Anglo-Saxon-type consumer associations to protect consumer rights. As a general rule, Germans tend to distrust cheaper products on the grounds that they may be of lower quality.

The main justification for the country's panoply of product rules stems from the requirements of safety and quality. There are around

---

* Donges moved in 1989 to the University of Cologne.

26,300 DIN (German Industrial Standard) norms in operation, and a further 45,000 technical rules governing the way in which products have to be made. Exporters to the German market have to face bureaucratic procedures to gain access for their products. The story circulates of a Belgian manufacturer of draught beer pumps who had to fill in a form thirty-five times before the beer-pump testing bureau in Frankfurt could begin its approvals process. Annoying though the technical standards might be for exporters to Germany, they will be an important advantage in efforts to fuse together the East and West German industrial systems. An identical approach to norms – as well as shared roots in vital areas like industrial legislation, training and the role of the trade unions – provide great common ground between East and West Germany. Jürgen Schwericke, the head of a committee at the Bayer chemicals group studying plans for East German investment, points to 'the common language, mentality, history.'[81] Schwericke – who was himself born in Potsdam – told me meaningfully in January 1990, 'Political convergence will take place very fast.'

One striking example of economic continuity is the law setting the regulatory basis of the West German electricity industry. This goes back to 1935, and has its roots in the Weimar Republic. It lays down the obligation for utilities to provide near-absolute security of supply. This is one of the reasons behind present over-capacity and minimal competition in the West German grid network. Protectionism in the electricity system also explains why France has had little success in selling its cheap nuclear-generated power across the Rhine into the West German market.

Strict regulation of the transport sector – one of the areas where the Federal Republic faces difficulties in adapting to the European Community's 1992 plans – also dates from the 1930s. High road tariffs, levied to protect the pre-war railways, form a growing impediment to flexible movement of freight. A government decree of 1931, still in use, specifies the precise number of haulage companies to be licensed and curtails competition between them by fixing overall tariffs. On the waterways, charges for moving goods around within West Germany are often a multiple of those for shipment to or from a foreign port. German gravel companies seeking to move their products on Rhine barges have found one way to escape the high charges laid down under German regulations: they consign their cargoes to the French side of the river, so that they can move under lower French tariffs.

A more recent set of rules covers retail hours. At the beginning of the century, shops were allowed to stay open between 7 o'clock in the morning and 9 o'clock at night. However, under a law introduced in 1956 to regulate competition and give workers settled hours, shops are obliged to close at 6.30 in the evenings and at 2 o'clock in the afternoon on all Saturdays except the first in the month. The legislation meets criticism from the public, but is staunchly defended by retail workers' unions as well as some of the big store groups. The government changed the law in 1989 to bring in so-called 'service evenings' to allow shops to open later once a week, but even this modest move attracted protests and warning strikes from unions. One question seldom asked is why High Street stores need the government to tell them when they should open and close.

VIII

West Germany's economic structure is ponderous, but reliable. This is most apparent on the financial markets, which remain relatively underdeveloped – and where the banks rule uncontested. In spite of the country's very large pool of savings, relatively little private wealth is directed into shares. According to a 1987 survey, only 6 per cent of West Germans invest in equities, against 20 per cent in the US, 16 per cent in Japan, 15 per cent in Britain and 11 per cent in France.[82]

With an eye on competition from London as 1992 approaches, West Germany is trying to improve the functioning of the financial sector. Banks are expanding into areas like insurance, and barriers have been broken down between regional stock exchanges, where Frankfurt competes with Düsseldorf, Hamburg, Munich and Berlin. None the less, the lack of a single financial business centre is a clear drawback for business life. West Germany's financial fragmentation also helps to explain why very few of the country's business journalists write well about the interrelation between industry, politics and economics.

The provincialism of the financial markets not only makes life easier for the largest industrial corporations but also increases the attractions of their well-protected relationships with the banks, which both own and trade shares in the big concerns and have representatives on their supervisory boards. The banks amass power over industry not only through direct participations, but also by controlling blocks of shares held for customers in their security trading departments. Big German industrial groups have historically relied more on banks for loans and equity capital than in countries like the US and Britain with large stock markets. The banks' strong position helps shield companies from unwanted takeover bids, thus enabling industry to look at business and product cycles on a long-term basis. The twin presence of representatives of banks and the trade unions on company supervisory boards brings stability, but a number of cases have arisen in recent years where supervisory boards have proven insufficiently alert and incisive to cope with difficulties. Krupp, in which the Iranian government took a 25 per cent stake in 1974, has failed – in contrast to Thyssen – to diversify sufficiently out of steel. The company has weathered a succession of financial strains, calling on the Deutsche Bank for help on more than one occasion. In a rescue of another of Germany's oldest established industrial names, in 1988 Deutsche took over the Klöckner trading company, after it suffered sharp losses in oil trading. The mishap wiped out the Klöckner family capital in the company – and brought another industrial shareholding into the portfolio of the Deutsche Bank, before it was sold in 1989 to the Viag industrial conglomerate.

Alfred Herrhausen, chief executive of the Deutsche Bank before his murder in November 1989,* never tried to hide that he relished his position as West Germany's most powerful business chief. With tragic irony, his assassination coincided with a period of intensive preparations for the bank's return to its roots on East German territory. With customary self-assurance, Herrhausen remarked less than a month before his death that Deutsche Bank had counted up 30 former branches in East Germany;[83] with 10 days left to live, he remarked:

> Germany, a reunified Germany, will be an enormous, strong economic force … and when you as a bank are strongly positioned within this country, then I think you are destined to play a major role in global banking.[84]

Deutsche Bank has had plenty of practice in defending itself from criticism about its concentration of might. 'It is wrong to say we aren't powerful,' Herrhausen liked to say, adding, 'We should use our power responsibly.'[85]

Deutsche Bank's battery of controlling shareholdings range from 28 per cent of Daimler-Benz to 35 per cent of the Holzmann construction company and 25 per cent of retail concerns Karstadt and Horten. Deutsche Bank representatives occupy around 400 supervisory board seats throught West German industry. These include most competing power generation, retailing, steel, chemicals, industrial gas, sugar, oil,

* See Chapter 4.

145

cement, electrical engineering and computer sectors. Herrhausen himself was supervisory board chairman of Daimler-Benz and sat on the boards of a clutch of other blue-chip companies. The Daimler-Benz link is part of the bank's tradition: since the 1926 merger which established the motor group, a Deutsche representative has sat in the dominant supervisory board position without a break.

Herrhausen's power on the German corporate scene has been matched by only one other post-war figure – Hermann Josef Abs, the grand old man of German banking who helped to rebuild Deutsche Bank as chief executive after the war. Now well into his eighties, and cutting the refined figure of a country squire, Abs has shown a remarkable capacity to operate under both dictatorship and democracy. He entered the Deutsche Bank management board at the beginning of 1938 aged only 36, and has been going strong ever since. A man of prickly vanity, he is still today the bank's honorary chairman, and revered as one of the dynamos behind the post-war boom. During the Third Reich, he was at the centre of Germany's financial machinery. In an armchair on the veranda of his parents' villa in Bonn, Abs looks back today at the recovery years and says in clipped English, 'Erhard was the right man for the Ministry of Economics at that time. He couldn't survive now.'[86] Speaking more than a year before the upheaval in East Germany, Abs took the view that Bonn was still only a provisional solution as Germany's capital: 'The local people say that Bonn [as the capital] will pass over.'

A confidant of Schacht of the Reichsbank, Abs represented Germany at pre-war negotiations to freeze the banks' foreign debts. He was placed in charge of Deutsche Bank's foreign operations and became the most prominent board member at a time when the bank's writ ran across the occupied and plundered countries of Europe. Abs was closely involved with the domestic war economy, sitting on more than forty supervisory boards during 1941-42. He was no friend of the Nazis, but has never tried to pretend that he stood up against the Third Reich. He says: 'A man who has not been imprisoned or hanged or shot by the Nazis cannot claim to have opposed Hitler.'

Abs was interned briefly by the British at the end of the war, then quickly made himself indispensable again. In 1948 he organised the setting up of the Kreditanstalt für Wiederaufbau, the corporation which supervised the channelling of Marshall Aid into industry, housing and commerce. He became a close adviser to Adenauer and won status and influence abroad as the country's premier financial diplomat. Abs headed the German delegation which in 1952-53 successfully renegotiated Germany's DM14 billion of outstanding foreign debts. Appointed Deutsche Bank's chief executive after the bank was re-established in 1957, he collected twenty-four supervisory board posts throughout industry – so many that in 1965 a law was passed limiting bankers' board appointments. Abs likes to say that the measure improved his health and gave him more time for playing the organ. In his political manoeuvring, Abs by no means encountered only success. Reflecting his closeness to industry, which feared the consequences of a strong D-Mark on German exports, Abs twice tried to use his influence with the Christian Democrats to ward off D-Mark revaluations in the 1960s. Each time, however, he failed; revaluation went ahead.[87]

Abs praises the post-war consensus structure. Worker co-determination and single-industry trade unions introduced in the British occupation zone were important instruments for social peace. The establishment of trade unions with sole responsibility across a whole company was 'a wonderful thing the British didn't do in their own country', he says. With a banker's eye for the smooth working of labour markets, he stresses how the refugees streaming in from the East kept down wages. 'We had 12 or 14 million expellees and refugees. They were very hard working. In the years prior to 1948, people didn't want to work for ridiculously low wages. They were often replaced by refugees.'

'The tremendous situation of emergency was essential for recovery,' comments Abs, but when he turns to today's comfortable Germans disdain creeps into his voice. 'We are going through a phase of inflexibility – they own apartments, little houses. They all have a little piece of ground, close to their families.' Abs scolds his countrymen for travelling around the world too much. 'They want to work less, have more free time,' he sniffs. 'They spend more than DM40 billion a year abroad. They fly off – they don't know what to do – so they send postcards.'

The miracle is over – and the Germans want to go on holiday. Instead, they are off on an uncertain journey to unity.

7

Rich and Bothered

In an empire which has been divided for centuries, where Germans have fought against Germans, nearly always under foreign influence, there can be no great love of one's country; and the love of glory can hardly flourish in a land without a centre, without a capital and without society.

Germaine de Staël, 1813[1]

The German has a strong tendency towards discontent. Who of us knows a contented fellow-countryman? I know many Frenchmen who are content with their fate and their experiences ... Their great ambition is to retire as a pensioner until the end of their lives. Compare them with the German – whose ambition is not fixed on a pension to be enjoyed after fifty years. His ambition knows no boundaries.

Otto von Bismarck, 1878[2]

It is well known that prosperity has its dark side.

Ludwig Erhard, 1961[3]

According to an international opinion survey published in 1987, only 10 per cent of West Germans describe themselves as 'very happy', compared with an average of 21 per cent for other European countries and a score of 33 per cent for Americans. The Germans are also most negative about their personal well-being. Only 14 per cent classify their health as 'very good', against a European average of 22 per cent, and 40 per cent in the US.[4] The conclusion to be drawn is not that the Germans are naturally more doleful than other people; rather that they are more given to pondering upon the definition and the meaning of happiness. The Germans are aware of the world – and frustrated about its defects. Seeking high standards, they are impatient if these are not met. In today's Germany, material needs are sated; wealth and leisure provide time and opportunity to dwell on life's imperfections.

I

The German state railway is one of the few surviving national institutions. It provides the best way to see Germany's rivers and forests, to peer into fairgrounds, car scrapyards and the back windows of apartment houses. The railway also gives insights into complexities not visible from the road. Watching the way people get on and off trains reveals national traits. In Germany, passengers move nervously towards the door ready to descend about ten minutes before the locomotive stops. They fear that life will somehow run out of control, leaving them stranded.

The German railway age started in 1835. There may soon be a chance that anniversaries will be celebrated together, rather than separately, in two German states. The first line linked Nuremberg and Fürth, today in West Germany; the first trunk service was between Leipzig and Dresden, now in the East. Incongruously, the state railway of the German Democratic Republic retained the name of the pre-war company, the Reichsbahn, set up in 1920 – almost as if the Empire were still waiting in the shunting yard. West Germany's Bundesbahn is richer and smarter-looking than its East German sister, and provides it with discreet subsidies through the complex accounting arrangements covering East-West German travel. East-West German communality shows up on railway platforms. The loudspeaker announcements on East German railway stations *'Bitte einsteigen, Türen schliessen. Der Zug fährt ab'* ('Please climb aboard and close the doors. The train is departing') use not only the same words, but have also the same intonation, as the voices heard in the West. (The main diference is that the instructions in the East have always appeared to have a more authoritarian ring, but even this may now be changing). The Bundesbahn dispenses largesse to travellers from East Germany. Because they are assumed to be hard up, they do not have to pay the standard DM6 supplements on express trains.[5]

East and West Germany have rival model railway companies. Märklin, the market-leader, founded in 1859, has its headquarters in the Swabian town of Göppingen in Baden-Württemberg. It regards itself as considerably superior to its East German counterpart, Piko, based in Sonneberg, the Thuringian centre of the East German toy industry. Germany is the spiritual home of European miniature railways, accounting for about half the continent's model train buffs. Reflecting

149

the fall in the birth-rate, Märklin is pitching its sophisticated and expensive products increasingly towards adults. Even a modest Märklin train set can cost around DM600.

Speaking like a psychoanalyst, Wolfgang Huch – Märklin's quietly decisive managing director – told me that grown-ups are turning to his company's products not only because of growing leisure but also because of the rising pressures of everyday life. 'A model railway can be directed – it is a way of recovering from a world outside which is not so easy to control.'[6] Märklin offers imperial railway trains stretching back to the 1840s. West German railway enthusiasts are traditionalists; next to the soft-porn magazines in station bookstalls can be found copies of pre-1945 Reichsbahn timetables.

The Bundesbahn itself is a mixture of ancient and modern, combining plushness, pride and functionality. It costs the West German taxpayer DM14 billion a year, including contributions to retirement pay for the railways' 260,000 pensioners; plainly it believes it deserves every penny. Large West German stations are crammed with delicatessen stores (shops on railway stations are virtually the only ones allowed to stay open until after 6.30 in the evening), and efficient-looking railway police roam the precincts looking for drunks. Computerised ticket terminals – described as 'user-friendly travel systems' – are being installed for the 1990s. The maroon Inter-City coaches exude aristocratic solidity, their corridors controlled by blue-coated *Schaffner* (conductors) with the air of medieval majordomos. The Bundesbahn consumes 3 million rolls of toilet paper a year in its well-disinfected lavatory compartments. The gliding restaurant cars are a pleasure to patronise; they dispense 1 million breakfasts, 170,000 steaks and 180,000 hotpot soups a year. You can choose muesli with hot milk if you like. The meals arrive on china crockery, not plastic. One of the best lunches in Europe is *Sauerbraten* served on the spectacular stretch of the Rhine between Koblenz and Mainz.

There are 11,000 *Schaffner*, all state functionaries, or *Beamte*, a species bequeathed by Prussia. One pleasant surprise is that they are friendly and not at all imperial. Most *Schaffner* are male – their girth, age and sense of importance increasing in proportion to the size and speed of the trains entrusted to them. Until a few years ago, the head conductor used to wear a red breast sash to denote authority – another Prussian tradition. The band is now worn discreetly around the arm in what the Bundesbahn says is more 'pragmatic' fashion. West Germany does not yet seem ready for conductors from Turkey. Being *Beamte*, *Schaffner* have to be of German nationality although one or two foreigners have crept in as naturalised German citizens. In the largest Bundesbahn operating region, Lower Saxony, there is said to be one Italian among 1,300 conductors; in Cologne, a solitary Pakistani has been admitted to the ranks of 1,100. By contrast, 50 per cent of the service staff in the restaurant carriages and sleeping compartments are from abroad, mainly from Yugoslavia. It is plainly a different class of job.

Conductors have an elaborate, set-piece way of asking for tickets, like a question from a multiple-choice examination. '*Noch jemand zugestiegen?*' ('Has anyone got on?') they intone. Late-coming passengers can pay fares to the conductor *en route* for a small extra charge. The *Schaffner* will not protest he has no change; he will not even sigh. It is an absolutely routine service – a praiseworthy mark of flexibility. Railway conversation also follows a ritual. Passengers sitting opposite each other wish each other good day and remain wordless for two hours. But they are enjoined by custom to say '*Auf Wiedersehen*' when they get out at the station; if you simply rise and leave without saying goodbye, people will think you are most unfriendly.

One hallmark of the Bundesbahn is that there are always a lot of active old ladies on board with felt hats and bags full of salami sandwiches. The conductors will carry out their suitcases, normally without being asked. The more seasoned and self-confident *Schaffner* are apt to pass the time of day and even tell jokes. Some proudly speak English to American tourists. Over the tannoy, the Bundesbahn broadcasts messages of welcome after each main station, and sometimes music. Once – another sign of open-mindedness – I heard them play the 'Dambusters' March' on the way to the Ruhr valley. Since 1985, the Bundesbahn has prevailed upon its *Schaffner* to serve drinks and snacks to First Class passengers. Reiner Gohlke, an enthusiastic former IBM computer executive who has been the Bundesbahn's chairman since 1982, says that persuading *Beamte* to serve coffee was one of his greatest achievements. 'That was an unbelievable sensation,' he says.[7] They are shown how to do it in modern training centres equipped with video cameras. On a salary of DM450,000 a year, Gohlke earns nearly half as much again as the federal Chancellor, who gets around DM350,000. (A board member in a top German company earns more than DM1 million.) A tousle-haired ox of a man perpetually in shirt-sleeves, Gohlke says he knew nothing about trains when he took on the job; he always used to travel by car. Now, he says, driving along the Autobahn makes him '*kaputt*'.

151

II

The motorways show *Wanderlust* in action; they are clogged with gleaming cascades of metal, flashing their headlights at sub-80 mph dawdlers. The airports are lined with sun-seekers; the West Germans have become the world's greatest tourists – a sign of restlessness. As anyone who has ever heard East Berliners comparing the prices of holidays in Leningrad, Havana and the Romanian Black Sea coast will confirm, the love of travel is shared by the East Germans too – one of the reasons for their discontent at having had a long wire fence as a border with the West.

West Germany has 30 million cars, crammed into a country the size of the US state of Oregon. The automobile is part of the German soul. Some of the drivers are simply on their way to work. Many people drive 20 or 30 miles from their village to the factory or office. In a large economy with no single business centre, executives are constantly on the move. But the lion's share of drivers are off spending their increased allocations of leisure. The West Germans make 90 million holiday journeys a year, about half of them abroad.[8] The Germans' travel enthusiasm is an expression of national character, befitting a people whose borders have never been fixed. The English have always been shopkeepers; the Germans are given to roaming. Goethe believed that, *Die beste Bildung findet ein gescheiter Mensch auf Reisen.* (For a man of intelligence, travel gives the best education.) According to the 19th-century poet Gustav Freytag, 'The German love for wandering ultimately expresses the search for an ideal country.'

Needless to say, the Germans are still looking – and they go ever further afield. In English, to 'star-gaze' is to day-dream; 'starry-eyed' means naïve, gullible. For the Germans, the *Sternstunde* is the hour of destiny. It is possible not only to reach for the stars but also to bring them down to earth (*die Sterne vom Himmel holen*). Footloose knights accomplished the conquest of eastern Europe. As part of the medieval guild system, apprentices used to journey for a year – the *Wanderjahr* – to gain experience before settling down in a trade. Although legends of rovers and dreamers form part of every nation's folklore, traditional German songs and fairy tales feature excessive numbers of wandering carpenters and journeymen, princes and tailors. Hänschen, the subject of a popular child's ditty, is a small boy who leaves his mother to strive for adventure out in the world. There is a deep-held view that individual destiny can only be found far from familiar surroundings. *Heimweh* – 'homesickness' – can be rendered into English (although *Heim* is not easy to define). But *Fernweh* – 'longing for beyond' – cannot be translated.

One of the tales collated by the Grimm brothers in the 19th century begins:

A tailor had a son who was so very small that he gave him the name of Thumbling. The little mite was, however, courageous, and said to his father: 'Father, I must go out into the world.'[9]

On his first stop, Thumbling worked for a master-tailor, but complained about the food: 'Too many potatoes, too little meat.' Today's German tourists are also demanding in their quest; *Schnitzel* and *Schwarzwälder-Kirschtorte* have been exported to five continents. The Germans have enlarged their geographical horizons, but many are un-Teutonically timid. 'Safety first' is the motto – an attitude of mind which also extends to East Germany, where the authorities have followed a policy of brightening up crumbling motorway and railway bridges with advertisements for state-sponsored insurance schemes. The Bonn government sends out a free twelve-page brochure for holidaymakers (modernistically entitled '*Tips für Globetrotter*'), which contains helpful suggestions for warding off everything from sunburn to Aids. The leaflet contains instructions on hanging mosquito nets; it recommends travellers to avoid Asian crab cocktails, and counsels them to take with them disinfectant, a spare pair of glasses and a litre of boiled water containing salt and glucose. Insurance companies also provide policies to cover the cost of flying sick patients home from holiday in ambulance jets. If you fall seriously ill in Las Palmas and need to be flown back to Hamburg, the advertisements claim, the flight could cost DM35,000 unless you are insured. Having a holiday spoiled is bad enough; ruining your bank balance into the bargain would be a tragedy.

Travel is partly a means of escaping drudgery. Surprisingly, for a country with such a reputation for industriousness, the Germans do not appear to enjoy working. Elisabeth Noelle-Neumann, the doyenne of the country's opinion-pollsters, has discovered this – and has also found that by comparison with other countries her compatriots are rather depressed. She puts this down to Germany's traumatic history.

153

Noelle-Neumann, slim and over 70, runs the Allensbach opinion research institute which she founded with her late husband Erich Peter Neumann in 1947. She has no professional interest in castigating her compatriots. She is a confidante of Helmut Kohl, who is always lecturing the press for excessive gloom. None the less, Noelle-Neumann grits her teeth and writes:

> The Germans are vulnerable, because they have already been wounded ... The Germans stand out in such a peculiar way from their European neighbours, and above all from the Americans, because the Germans lack warmth, enterprise, joy of life. But the characteristic of falling from one extreme to another, which always was thought of as typically German, is still there.[10]

According to polls conducted in 11 countries, the West Germans appear exceptionally dissatisfied with their jobs. Only 15 per cent said they were very proud of their work, as against 83 per cent in the US, 79 per cent in Britain, 71 per cent in Ireland and 42 per cent in Spain. (However, in France the score was even lower – only 13 per cent.) The Germans need to rest at weekends far more than people in other countries – work seems to wear them out. Noelle-Neumann herself has had a chequered career, working (with her husband) under the Third Reich on the newspaper *Das Reich* run by propaganda chief Joseph Goebbels; she told me she was no supporter of the Nazis and was thrown off the paper in 1943.[11] She says she set up the research institute partly to provide an 'early warning', monitoring tendencies which could lead to the return of dictatorship. Now, ironically, she believes that German society is traumatised by Hitler. Born in Berlin, Noelle-Neumann laments that Bonn is a poor substitute. But the Germans do not complain about not having a capital. 'They are so introverted,' she observes.

The Germans have a reputation for scepticism. The English expression 'count your blessings' – 'look on the bright side' – has no equivalent in German and, if it did, would be thought of as unspeakably naïve. If you ask a German, 'How are you?' the question will not be treated as a polite formality but more often than not will elicit a full medical history. There has often been a good reason for painting a description of circumstances in the most dreary possible colours. Modern research into the Thirty Years' War has revealed that the population and material losses, though still horrific, were much smaller than made out at the time. Anxious to claim maximum damages, some districts reported more villages destroyed than were known to have existed.[12]

The Germans can be relied upon to tell a morbid tale or expound a gloomy prediction with a smile on their faces. 'That's not being pessimistic; that's realism,' they will tell you. Taxi-drivers in big cities like Berlin or Cologne often delight in telling stories about road deaths: 'There goes another one on the way to the cemetery,' is frequently heard as a remark of scorn for some minor driving error. One taxi driver in Mönchengladbach, the home of the British Army of the Rhine, launched unasked into an outlandish lavatorial allegory to exemplify the West Germans' lack of patriotism. 'In Germany, you could put the national flag in the street and people would pee on it; everyone would just be embarrassed. In England, a person doing that with the Union Jack would be lynched.'

Noelle-Neumann's international survey seems to bear out the taxi driver's comment. The polls showed that only 21 per cent of West Germans said they were 'very proud' of their country, compared with 79 per cent in the US, 66 per cent in Ireland, 55 per cent in Britain, 49 per cent in Spain, 41 per cent in Italy and 33 per cent in France. Only 35 per cent of West Germans said they would be willing to go to war for their country, against 69 per cent in the US and 62 per cent in Britain. That the age of militarism in Germany is dead* was confirmed when a Post Office *Beamte*, advising on a new telephone in our Bad Godesberg home, apologised that the handset was dark green: 'Is it not too military-looking?' he asked.

III

The Germans are fascinated by authority – but are also suspicious of it. The abuses of the Third Reich have left a mistrust of state power – especially for those born after the war. When respondents were asked whether they believed, in general, that more respect for authority was desirable in coming years, 84 per cent in the US replied 'Yes.' The numbers were 85 per cent in Ireland, 73 per cent in Britain, 76 per cent in Spain, 64 per cent in Italy, and 56 per cent in France; but in the Federal Republic, only 44 per cent agreed. None the less, a certain reverence for authority appears built into German genes, apparent, of course, above all in the GDR. I have always been struck by the number

* See Chapter 11.

of normal, even moderately Left-wing young Germans who involuntarily bow their heads upon being introduced to someone – simply (I suppose) because their parents have brought them up to behave in that way. The Germans fear society without order and organisation; and so defer to older instruments of guidance. This is the reason for an extraordinary slavishness to deep-seated principles of hierarchy, and to rules and regulations in general.

Public signs check any tendency to spontaneous behaviour. *Parken auf eigene Gefahr!* (Parking at your own risk!), they warn. Traditionally fixed to every fence around building sites (in both East and West Germany) is the admonition: *Eltern haften für Ihre Kinder* (Parents are liable for their children) – as if children would want to climb through the barbed wire. News of winning lottery numbers on East and West German radio and television is always accompanied by a careful waiver that the broadcasting company can accept no responsibility for errors. This is presumably to guard against the Germans' feared litigiousness. At the beginning of 1990, a perfectly healthy seven-year-old Munich child launched a lawsuit against the Bavarian government. His parents claimed that he had suffered exposure to radioactivity by playing outside after the Chernobyl nuclear accident in 1986. I once watched an irate would-be passenger, frustrated by some administrative hold-up from boarding an airliner with his elderly mother at Berlin's Tegel airport, proclaiming for all to hear how he would seek redress: *'Verklagen, Mutter! Verklagen!'* ('Sue, mother! Sue!').

Respect for titles is much lower than it used to be, but lingers still. A *Herr Doktor* or *Herr Professor* still has status; forging of academic qualifications, though risky if discovered, can bring employees rich rewards. Food-processing companies – following the lead of the old-established Dr Oetker concern, which makes everything from soup to baking powder – rely on the Doktor marque to add solidity. One of Germany's leading chains of sex shops is called Dr Müller's, presumably to assure clients that all its products have been scientifically tested. A German doctor carries more weight than a policeman, who does not have the natural authority still enjoyed – despite periodic revelations about corruption – by his British opposite number.

In a small town, a German police chief will be a local *notable*. But German policemen in general, often seen only in their patrol cars or behind riot shields, are mere anonymous tools of the state. Security around public buildings which might be terrorist targets, both in Bonn and in other cities, is often very lax – refreshing in a way, but also vaguely disconcerting. Young policemen on guard, nervously fingering their automatic rifles, are sufficiently conscious of hierarchy that they will allow past almost anyone in a suit carrying a briefcase, so long as you remember to look stern and stare them in the eye. The German police do not want to stir up reminders of totalitarianism. When Erich Honecker, the East German leader, visited Bonn in September 1987, I was surprised to be able to approach his car – a vast Mercedes with a Stuttgart number plate, hired out by Daimler-Benz for such occasions – without being challenged. When I mentioned to a West German security official how free and easy it all appeared, he pointed out reasonably enough, 'We are not a police state.'

Nevertheless such liberalism is not always on display. A jungle of rules hedges in everything from the keeping of brothels to the hours when bread may be baked, or when inhabitants of blocks of flats may take baths. Some rules may be thoroughly sensible, but they can also stop people from thinking. If you go against the code and traverse a German road when the pedestrian lights are red, you may well inadvertently lure into danger a swarm of old ladies waiting at the kerb. Believing that the lights have changed, they will cross blindly with you and may not be nimble enough to avoid the approaching columns of heavy limousines.

The saleslady in a bread shop where I wanted to change a loaf bought a few minutes earlier told me that she would be happy to replace it with another. Unfortunately though, she went on, an official decree on food and grocery vending prevented her from exchanging goods once they had left the shop. Bus drivers are not permitted to pick up passengers unless they are standing precisely at the bus-stop, in case the bus company is sued by people who stumble as they climb aboard. Caretakers, drivers, supervisors of football pitches or gym clubs and other people in minor positions of responsibility are often of kindly demeanour; but they will advance complicated excuses about 'lack of insurance cover' or 'opening regulations' as a reason for not carrying out simple requests. I once asked a taxi driver to sound his horn to signal to a colleague spotted in another car. He told me that, if it was simply up to him, he would be pleased to do so, but compliance could cost him a DM20 fine in view of the constraints on unauthorised hooting.

Aversion to authority applies in particular to parental relationships. If the generation gap is especially large in West Germany, this is partly a delayed effect of the guilt and soul-searching since the Second World War. 'A new generation normally grows up through being told things by their parents,' says Christian Meier, professor of history at Munich university. 'But after the war, a whole generation of parents remained silent – both to themselves, and to their offspring.'[13]

The international survey revealed that only 48 per cent of Germans agreed that children should love and respect their parents, regardless of their merits and faults. This compared with 69 per cent who agreed with this in the US, and an average of 63 per cent in the rest of Europe. Only 18 per cent of Germans more than 18 years old said they had very close ties to their parents when they were children. This compared with percentages of 37 per cent in Britain, 45 per cent in Italy and 34 per cent in France. Asked whether they had the same views on morality as their parents, only 49 per cent of West Germans replied 'Yes,' against 84 per cent in the US and 76 per cent in Britain.

The gulf between the generations occasionally explodes in the outbreaks of urban terrorism which have sporadically shaken society since the late 1960s, and in the ferocious massed demonstrations around nuclear power plants which have become a German speciality of the 1980s. German young people at football grounds or in bars and restaurants on the whole appear considerably better-behaved than British ones. When they do go on the rampage – for instance, the occasional inner-city riot in the Kreuzberg area of West Berlin – German youth displays not mindless hooliganism but impressive organisation. Without the discipline of the hundreds of thousands of young people surging peacefully through the streets of East Germany, the autumn 1989 revolution might have led to a spiral of violence.

What of the liberated spirits of the 1968 anti-parent student revolt? Twenty years later, the most depressing feature of the 1968 age-group is the extent of their resignation. One of the reasons is that society itself has not changed in the intervening years. Instead, the rebels have conformed and adapted to demands of a materialistic way of life – and they feel guilty about it. German psychologists have labelled the '1968ers', born at the end of the war or in the early post-war years, as 'the sad generation'. They are particularly prone to psychic disorder, suffering in their late thirties and early forties from symptoms such as excessive tiredness, low self-confidence and diffuse feelings of discontent. This is also blamed on inability to form strong emotional links with parents who were tainted in some way with the defeat of the war. Christiane Behrendsen, a Frankfurt psychoanalyst, points to the paradox: 'How is it possible that the rebellious post-war generation, in spite of its ability to fight for autonomy, should be weighed down with self-hindering symptoms of weakness, *Angst* and difficulties in making contacts?' She has classified them as suffering from 'revolutionary neurosis'.[14]

Today's under-25s are less idealistic and more hard-headed than

158

their 1968 forebears – partly because the opportunities for changing the world have become more limited. Protest rallies – for instance, against the International Monetary Fund and World Bank meetings in West Berlin in September 1988 – remain isolated affairs. Like their opposite numbers in other western countries, German students are now quite conservative in character. Suffering from overcrowding of courses in many German universities, they are primarily worried about jobs and money, and much less likely to take up arms in support of a far-off cause.

Daniel Cohn-Bendit, 'Dany the Red', born in south-west France in 1945 as the son of a Berlin Jewish doctor, was one of the leaders of the 1968 student unrest in the *boulevards* of Paris – and quickly became famous on German streets too. He is now a campaigner for the German Greens and runs an 'alternative' magazine *Pflasterstrand* in Frankfurt. Talking over a mug of coffee in the café beneath his offices, Cohn-Bendit has kept his wit and his mop of red hair; but he points to the way society has lowered its horizons over two decades: 'The 1968 generation had a false idealism. The world was there to be conquered. Now there is more pessimism about basic positions. The great revolutionary movement has given way to everyday pragmatism. There is a difference if you have to worry about the future. Then, we thought it didn't exist.'[15]

IV

Germans have high expectations, but are not gullible; therefore, they are prone to be more easily disappointed. They have formidable powers of self-analysis, and are more adept than most people at spotting the gap between the desirable and the attainable. *Angst* is really just a form of psychological insurance policy, as Freud explained:

> The individual will have made an important advance in his capacity for self-preservation if he can foresee and expect a traumatic situation instead of simply waiting for it to happen ... Anxiety is therefore on the one hand an expectation of a trauma, and on the other a repetition of it in a mitigated form[16].

Fear is something the Germans have to live with. It is estimated that roughly one quarter of adults in the Federal Republic will suffer from psychic illness at least once in their lives.[17] But worries have shifted away from material questions towards other preoccupations. Living standards have boomed during the 1980s – even though more than one in twenty of the population (3.1 million people) rely on social security, double the number in 1965. The Germans also worry less about war than they used to; but opinion polls show an increase in the perceived threat from various types of disaster. 'Yes, the cliché of the Germans' *Angst* vagabondising from one subject to another is actually true!' one journalist from *Stern* magazine told me exultantly. *Stern* specialises in ecological scare stories – and Allensbach records that the number of people worried about water and air pollution rose from 57 per cent of the population in 1979 to 73 per cent in 1987.* In 1979, 60 per cent were worried abut unspecified threats to health, a percentage which rose to 72 per cent in 1987. By contrast, the Germans were less worried about crime, where the percentage fell slightly to 54 per cent from 57 per cent. Aids, however, has become a particular source of concern – 30 per cent of West Germans, apparently, are worried that the disease will strike either them personally or someone close to them.

Exaggerated worries about ecological damage may be partly the fault of the media. Here is one example of *Stern*'s paranoid style, an editorial dealing with the massive oil spill off the Alaskan coast in April 1989, allegedly caused by the ship-master's drunkenness:

> There are many other drunken captains on space ship Earth, and they are driving us tottering towards the year 2000. The ship is half-sunk, but fully lit. Unswerving, the string-band is playing the *Song of the Titanic*. Ship's doctors, smiling, are constantly treating our allergies with new ointments, there are fresh mushrooms from Chernobyl and Three Mile Island in the kitchen, the life-boats are made of tropical wood and the engines are powered with nuclear-generated electricity. Everything is normal.[18]

Whatever the reason, fear over the *Umwelt* (environment) runs as a form of epidemic, and seems to be passed on to children. According to one survey in 1989, 75 per cent of children between 8 and 12 were worried about all the trees dying.[19]

VI

Is there a 'German look'? The small band of individualistic entrepreneurs who run the country's clutch of successful fashion and

* See Chapter 14.

design companies are responsible for a new German image abroad. In an area which is no longer a monopoly of the French or the Italians, German fashion houses during the 1980s have built up an international reputation for cool and expensive style. Attention to quality has been the main factor behind the rapid growth of companies like Hugo Boss, Escada, Jil Sander, Wolfgang Joop and Mondi. Their classically tailored wares can be seen on shoulders and hips from Turin to Tokyo.

Jil Sander, a pert ex-model and fashion journalist based in Hamburg, has broadened her company's product range to include accessories for both men and women, as well as spectacles and perfume. Sander, an attractive blonde, in her early 40s but looking younger, who has now brought her company to the stock market, prides herself on having started the 1980s German design surge. Boss, based in the hills of Baden-Württemberg, has enterprisingly placed its products on popular US television shows like *Miami Vice*, while Munich-based Escada has also gained an international foothold through highly colourful women's clothing. However, the designers admit difficulties in forging a German fashion identity. Revealingly enough, Boss was bought up by a Japanese group at the end of 1989. Wolfgang Joop, from Hamburg, points out ironically that the Nazis were 'stylistically perfect'. He says, 'We have an unbelievable design problem because the last German style was too powerful.'[20] Fashion figures also complain that the country does not take the subject seriously enough. According to Klaus Steilmann, who runs Europe's biggest ready-to-wear women's fashion group from an unimposing industrial estate in the heart of the Ruhr industry belt, Germany's staid newspapers and politicians do not care enough about fashion. 'We need to get public opinion makers interested in the fashion lifestyle, then we can build up new creators.'[21]

Leisure and prosperity have been of clear benefit to the sports sub-culture. Two of the richest young people in West Germany are tennis stars. The Germans take their pleasures seriously, and it is not a complete coincidence that Boris Becker and Steffi Graf both come from hard-working Baden-Württemberg. Parents' willingness to send their children to an expensive local tennis club has become a form of neighbourhood status symbol in the last ten years. But if a dedicated and perfectionistic approach to training can bring players to the top, satisfying fans' demands well enough to stay there can be difficult. The Germans do not give their heroes an easy time.

Becker, who won the men's singles at Wimbledon for the first time in 1985 at the age of 17, now lives in Monaco, where he is glad to get away from photographers investigating his love-life. He is rumoured to have earned as much as $10 million in his peak year in 1986, when he won Wimbledon for the second time. The impossibility of keeping up the momentum eroded Becker's *Wunderkind* image. The Bavarian-based Puma sports shoe and clothing company cancelled a promotion contract with Becker in 1988 in view of his fading performance and the company's own financial difficulties. After Becker won Wimbledon again in 1989 his star waxed once more; a new multi-million sponsoring agreement was signed with an American tennis raquet company. But by then, Becker did not really have to worry about money.

Steffi Graf, living at home in Brühl under the watchful eye of her father-manager Peter, is made of more wholesome stuff than Becker. She became No.1 in the women's world ratings in 1987 at the age of 18, and seems to think that tennis is more important than boy-friends. Relaxed enough off court, she is concentrated and unsmiling in her victories. While the fashion houses' models portray the fresh yacht club look, Steffi, like the machine tools industry, personifies power and precision. The Germans are proud of her. So far, this heroine has not fallen from grace.

VI

There are just 10 Germans in *Fortune* magazine's list of the 130 wealthiest people in the world, and only one or two with glitter.[22] 'We lack the chic charity set you have in America,' laments Werner Rudi, the somewhat flashy-looking former editor of the country's best-selling daily, *Bild*. He concedes that a lot of spicy German news has to come from abroad – 'the likes of Rambo or Joan Collins' – because of the lack of home-grown material. He casts envious eyes at Britain: 'The British royal family is like a dream – it's Dallas, only it's true.'[23]

Top of the German wealth league is Johanna Quandt, the widow of industrial magnate Herbert Quandt. Johanna and her family own 70 per cent of car-maker BMW, and are reputed to be worth $3.6 billion. They lead discreet lives. Herbert's step-mother later married Joseph Goebbels and died with him in the Berlin bunker in May 1945 – but, this detail aside, nothing about his life appeared over-exciting. Konrad Henkel, the grandson (now in his 70s) of the founder of the Henkel chemical company – famous as the maker of Persil – has a fortune of $2.7 billion and throws parties at his villa home near Düsseldorf. Next in

162

the list, Erivan Karl Haub ($2.6 billion), is the owner of the Tengelmann supermarket and drug-store chain. Haub spends most of his time in the US; Friedrich Karl Flick ($2.4 billion) mainly stays in hiding.* The only real candidate for *Bild*'s attentions is Prince Johannes von Thurn und Taxis – valued, at $2.5 billion. In 1490 the Prince's ancestors established a European mail service which provided the family with a continental postal monopoly until the 19th century. The Prince is a playboy-turned-ageing husband now in his sixties. In 1980, to the delight of the gossip-columnists and the fashion photographers, he married a young countess, Gloria, who rides motor-cycles around Bavaria and wears outrageous dresses. Franz Josef Strauss died in 1988 at the start of a hunting expedition at the Prince's estate in Regensburg. At the funeral on a dour October day in Munich, Gloria sent a flutter through the waiting crowds by waving as she left the service in the cathedral.

The head of the House of Hohenzollern also enjoys the eye of the public – at least, the older people who still care for such things. Louis Ferdinand Viktor Edward Albert Michael Hubert, Prince of Prussia and the grandson of William II, is an avuncular 80-year-old with a look of well-worn gentility. He parries questions about his finances, murmuring, 'We are not exactly poor' – but he is not on the *Fortune* list. If the royal family is still held in some esteem, 'that is because we are completely harmless,' Louis Ferdinand chuckled when I visited him in the Prussian dynasty's ancestral home, the neo-Gothic Hohenzollern castle south of Stuttgart.[24] The Hohenzollerns lost virtually all their lands in the East after the Second World War. Louis does not think he will get the estates back again, but none the less is a fan of Mikhail Gorbachev. 'I hope Gorbachev turns from a Saul into Paul,' he observes. Louis' wife and maternal grandmother were both Russian, and he would like Gorbachev to pave the way for cooperation with Germany reminiscent of pre-1914 links with Czarist Russia. 'A free regime and a market economy in Russia would be an enormous blessing for the world.'

The Hohenzollerns are descended from a line of medieval counts from the southern uplands of Swabia. With the establishment of the kingdom of Prussia in 1701, the royal house rose to domination over Germany from the bare plains wrested from the Slavs east of the River Elbe. The Prussians built their power on frugality, discipline and devotion to the service of war. Now their main monument is this tower-strewn Swabian pile, teeming with day trippers and echoing to the

* See Chapters 4,6

strains of charity violin concerts on summer evenings. The castle chapel contains the coffins of Louis' ancestors Frederick William I and Frederick the Great, formally at Potsdam, which were buried in a Thuringian salt-mine during the war and recovered by American soldiers in 1945. A high-class refugee, Louis fled westwards after the war and settled in a village outside Bremen; he comes down to Swabia during the summer months.

As he ushered me into the castle's modest public restaurant for a lunch of *consommé*, trout and wine, elderly visitors at nearby tables burst into spontaneous applause. The restaurant manageress welcomed the Prince as 'Imperial Highness' – which he admits is a courtesy title only – and kissed him affectionately on both cheeks. The Prince gets on well with Helmut Kohl – partly because Kohl also calls him 'Imperial Highness'. He dislikes Helmut Schmidt, who has undiplomatically brought up the subject of early support for Hitler from some members of the Hohenzollern family. Louis Ferdinand's favourite Social Democrat politician is Willy Brandt, who as governing mayor of West Berlin in 1965 allowed him to use the city's Charlottenburg palace for his eldest daughter's wedding celebrations. Louis maintains his claim to the throne, but says this could be realised only after reunification of East and West Germany – something he told me in 1988 he would not live to see. The pages of illustrated magazines are full of the tame exploits of Louis' well-behaved children, but the Germans are quite happy to maintain the Hohenzollerns as no more than inoffensive curiosities. In 1976, Allensbach discovered that only 7 per cent of the population wanted a restoration of the monarchy.[25] Thereafter, it considered the subject insufficiently interesting to be worth polling further.

VII

The Germans have plenty of humour, but go in for organised burlesque rather than spontaneous levity. Leaning to *Schadenfreude*, the Germans like to home in on a target; they seldom have enough self-confidence to laugh at themselves, something which comes naturally – perhaps, too naturally – to the English. Rolf Breitenstein, a diplomat with an unusual sideline as a satirical author, explains how serious and humorous activities are generally well-compartmentalised.[26] 'Sense of humour' in the English sense – meaning something one has all the time – cannot be accurately translated. Joke-making is a ritual associated with drinking, relaxing, enjoying oneself – in other words, not a part of ordinary life. Hans-Dietrich Genscher, the Foreign Minister, for whom Breitenstein writes speeches, can – in the right company – be a lively and entertaining late-night raconteur of jokes; but he eschews any question of lightheartedness in his official pronouncements, thinking it would be out of place. Helmut Schmidt, on the other hand, insisted that his speech-writers inject a note of humour at the bottom of the second page to keep the audience's attention.

The Germans present a specialised form of jocosity at set-piece celebrations such as a firm's outing, a birthday party, a church festival or the annual occasion of Carnival. Johannes Gross, the author, describes the fun: 'You have to call *"Prost"* to your neighbour. Anyone who says *"Prost"* enough times has humour.'[27] It is a convoluted phenomenon. Gross writes:

> Among Germans, a German must have humour, and most of them do indeed have it, but it is humour of a kind which does not exclude the suggestion that the Germans do not have any after all.

At Carnival, grown men and women occupy themselves for weeks by dressing-up in colourful parodies of military uniforms. They elect princes and princesses, and swap elaborate in-jokes about local politics at institutionalised *Karnevalsitzungen* (meetings of the Carnival association). The carnival season culminates in four or five days of mass merrymaking and parades. Then, on Ash Wednesday, the town switches back like clockwork to sober normality. There is a similar set pattern about birthdays. Offices close for the day for the boss's celebrations; the Bonn government press office publishes statements nearly every day on effusive birthday telegrams sent by the Chancellor to obscure octogenarians. Newspapers devote eulogistic columns to elderly personalities celebrating 'round' birthdays. As soon as they become 60, they rate a mention every five years. Showing such slavishness spreads to both sides of the border, birthday practices played a central part in the Federal Republic's most spectacular spy scandal. Günter Guillaume, the 'spy in the Chancellery' whose unmasking in 1974 caused the resignation of Chancellor Willy Brandt, was uncovered by West German counter-intelligence partly as a result of coded birthday messages sent by his masters in East Berlin.[28]

Alfred Biolek, a popular TV entertainment presenter, notes that the basic obstacle to German humour is German perfectionism. 'The

Germans always want to do things best,' says Biolek.[29] 'There is no land in the world which is as good at organising nude bathing beaches; in Hamburg, at the height of the sexual revolution a few years ago, you could see sex shows which you wouldn't see in Paris.' How can you laugh at your own cooking, asks Biolek, if you want to have the best restaurants in the world? However, Biolek is breaking new ground by launching an English-style 'Spitting Image' puppet show on German television, with sixty effigies of politicians and public figures. There are no taboos, says Biolek, not even the pope; but he admits that there will be no puppet of Hitler. He adds that the show is much tamer than in England – and that he is facing difficulties in finding scriptwriters of sufficient wit. Indeed, when the show went on the air in 1989 it was lamentable.

Television is the shop window for the manifold varieties of German drollery. Farce and slapstick have a certain relentlessness and chat shows suffer from stiffness, but TV relays Bavarian, Cologne or Berlin humour to audiences extending well beyond regional borders. Family-run comedy-theatre groups established by elderly stars like Heidi Kabel in Hamburg or Willi Millowitsch in Cologne have become post-war institutions, with millions of ardent fans. German television excels in political cabaret, often broadcast two or three times a week. One drawback of East-West German *rapprochement* is that the East Berlin theatre cabaret, Distel, celebrated for its jibes against the former regime, will almost certainly wither; televised, Distel would lose its sting.

Although irony hardly intrudes into daily conversation, the Germans use it to savage effect from the stage. Munich-based Dieter Hildebrandt, born in 1927 in Silesia, is the country's best-known exponent of this art. Hildebrandt formed his *Münchner Lach-und Schiessgesellschaft* sketch group (Munich laughing and shooting association) in 1956. One of his long-time rivals, from Berlin, was the *Berliner Stachelschweine* group (The Porcupines). Hildebrandt has been emulated by many – among the talented younger performers following in his wake is the bitingly funny Swabian, Mathias Richling. Hildebrandt has kept up his television satire crusade for thirty years, spitting venom at post-war hypocrisy. 'A few thousand convinced Nazis kept millions of German resistance-fighters living in fear,' he likes to say of the Third Reich.[30] Reserving his gall above all for the Right-wing parties, he is an intrepid opponent of nuclear energy and had regular tussles with conservative-leaning television management, but has never been kept off the air for too long. His denigrators sometimes accuse him of lacking patriotism; but what they fail to see is that Hildebrandt's pitilessness about his country is also a form of devotion.

8

Politics and the Media

As, in the military sphere, the aircraft has now become a combat weapon, so the press has become a similar weapon in the sphere of thought. We have frequently found ourselves compelled to reverse the engine and to change, in the course of a couple of days, the whole trend of imparted news ... Such agility would have been quite impossible if we had not had firmly in our grasp that extraordinary instrument of power which we call the press.

Adolf Hitler, 1942[1]

Probably in all parties there are short-sighted people who want control for their party over broadcasting.

Hugh Carleton Greene, director general,
Nordwestdeutscher Rundfunk, 1948[2]

The organisation of the state is an important thing. We have to keep it in order: we must criticise it.

Werner Holzer, editor *Frankfurter Rundschau*, 1988[3]

Journalism in West Germany both profits from and labours under the experience of the Third Reich. After twelve years of total information control, press and broadcasting were rebuilt after the war according to a design laid down by the western occupying powers, on foundations left over from the Weimar Republic and the Nazis. These disparate roots allowed the flowering of a media sector which became a valuable accompaniment to the new democracy, but where the old bad habits would still sometimes break through again.

In sharp contrast to East Germany, where the Nazis' centralised management of information and propaganda was continued by the Communists, the Federal Republic acquired press freedom along the road to political and economic recovery. The deliberate decentralisation of the media – an Allied attempt to construct a rampart against totalitarianism – added to the regional diversity which is one of the

167

country's strengths. All the same, if the West German relationship between politics and the media is usually complex, one reason is that, as a result of history, neither side is completely sure where it stands.

There is indeed a healthy watchfulness over the danger of state encroachment. But, to escape control of the state in broadcasting, something almost as bad has crept up in its place: the dead hand of the political parties. Because of the lack of a tradition of journalistic independence, there is an unspoken fear that broadcasting has to be controlled by party bureaucracies. Otherwise, the argument goes, it would almost inevitably become corrupted by outside influence and develop into that greatest of German fears – 'a danger to democracy'. To maintain a show of pluralism, the parties of Right and Left have divided up the power of television to establish competing pools of political bias within broadcasting.

The political and media establishments find it difficult to co-exist in a natural state of antagonism; one side nearly always tends to overreact to real or perceived hostility from the other. Criticism of the party in power is still sometimes regarded as an attack on the state. The media do not enjoy the almost instinctive self-confidence of the Anglo-American kind. Journalists in West Germany are under less professional pressure to bring out news than in the US and Britain, and are often expected to adopt some form of political cause.

As a result, there tends to be more moral skirmishing than straightforward reporting. To give an example of the moralising which would be highly incongruous in Anglo-Saxon countries, Klaus Liedtke, one of the editors of the popular illustrated magazine *Stern*, which takes a strident Left-leaning stand on most issues, told me, 'We need to recognise guilt, draw lessons from it and grow stronger as a result.'[4] He was bracketing together *Stern*'s attempts to learn from the notorious affair of the forged 'Hitler diaries' in 1983[5], and the overriding need of the German people not to forget the consequences of the Third Reich.

Journalists – and probably their audiences as well – believe that their role is to tell the public not only what is going on but also what to think. In a survey of British and German journalistic attitudes, 63 per cent of German journalists termed as a necessary skill the ability to write an article so that readers could see how to interpret a certain event. Only 37 per cent of their British counterparts agreed with this standpoint, believing that a journalist's job lay above all in providing facts.[6]

West German journalists know that they are important but unloved. Because he thinks the title 'journalist' sounds somewhat lowly, a veteran of the profession likes to call himself a *Publizist* (publicist) or *Redakteur* (editor). A regular survey by the Allensbach institute reveals that the profession is held in regard by only about 17 per cent of the population, while the respect ratings of doctors, priests and university professors are far higher.[7]

There is a general German cultural bias in favour of the teacher rather than the reporter. Showing the priority given to dissemination of opinion rather than unearthing of news, even the quality *überregionale* (national) papers rely on news agencies for a sizeable portion of the basic reporting of domestic affairs. Their senior writers concentrate on editorials or background articles. Similarly, one of the main features of nightly TV news programmes is the commentary of a chosen journalist – normally earnest and balding – on the events of the day. This might look like fulfilment of Article 5 of the 1949 Basic Law, which sets down with well-meant verbosity that:

> Everyone shall have the right freely to express and disseminate his opinion by speech, writing and pictures, and freely to inform himself from generally accessible sources. Freedom of the press and freedom of reporting by means of broadcasts and films are guaranteed. There shall be no censorship.

But the views of the broadcaster in question may well be coloured by his ties to a particular political party. This, and practices like it, make for television which is both erratic and dull. Erratic, because – even less than in the press – there is no tradition in TV for objective investigative journalism; dull, because television journalists are on the whole extraordinarily tame when interviewing anyone in authority. West German journalists generally seem incapable of interrupting a politician in full flow. Of course, they are waiting for the verb to come at the end of the long German sentence – but also they know their place. Above all, journalists are normally far too mindful of their subservience to insist that the politician should answer the question.

In the newspaper world, direct party influence seems to have fallen during the past decade, but much of the press is none the less exposed to the ever-present danger of German corporatism. Journalists normally stay far too long in their specialist areas, becoming over-acquainted with – and, sometimes mere mouthpieces for – their contacts in politics or business. The twin worlds of politics and journalism both seem remarkably narrow-minded. West Germany is of course not the only country where politicians and journalists can live in unhealthy symbiosis, but the tendency is accentuated by the country's lack of a proper capital. The best West German journalists are found in Hamburg, Munich and

169

Frankfurt. With some honourable exceptions, Bonn closets together politicians and journalists in an infertile hothouse with windows covered over to stop the light getting in.

Some of the rigidities are being broken down by a younger and more critical generation of journalists who have worked their way through to the top. But new battles for influence are opening up. The press is facing a squeeze on advertising revenues and readership as a result of the deregulation of the electronic media, where private TV channels bringing in a new approach to both entertainment and current affairs are starting to compete with the established networks. Confronted by these new challenges, both the quality and sensationalist press – of which West Germany provides some of the best and worst examples in the world – are wondering how to react. The media landscape offers a study in contrasts. Its diversity is its strength; any move to more uniformity would be a loss.

I

The heaviest cross-fire in sniping between press and politics is focused on an ugly 12-storey block in the centre of rebuilt Hamburg. *Der Spiegel*, the largest news magazine in Europe, is West Germany's most influential publication. It has grown up with the Federal Republic, and even helped to shape it. The magazine was founded in January 1947 after the British occupation authorities in Hanover handed a provisional publication licence to three young men given a clean sheet by the denazification tribunal. One of them, a pale-faced 23-year-old with a spell behind him on the Eastern front, quickly installed himself as publisher and editor. In a school essay doubting whether Hitler would win the war, Rudolf Augstein had already shown a hint of the trenchancy which would trouble two generations of post-war politicians.

Today Augstein is the country's best-known journalist, still at the helm of *Der Spiegel*, still non-conformist, sprawling in his vast beige-carpeted office at the top of the Hamburg tower block. He likes to call himself a 'positive cynic'. Behind the enigmatic gold-rimmed spectacles is still a hint of the enthusiasm of a cub reporter – combined with the rasping truculence of a press magnate. *Der Spiegel*'s malevolent intelligence and appetite for exposing scandals, hitting above all (but certainly not always) the conservative parties, have turned the magazine into an institution and made Augstein a multi-millionaire. He disclaims taking the side of any one party but likes to say that, when in doubt, 'I come down on the side of the Left.' Although past his 66th birthday, and clearly not in the best of health, he does not look ready for retirement just yet. The upsurge of German unity fever in the winter of 1989/90 gave Augstein new zest. He told me that his pro-unity articles had provoked some argument with members of staff. 'But the more the people see that unity is going to come, the less controversial these editorials have been.'[8]

Der Spiegel was originally set up with the aim of copying America's *Time* magazine. I ask Augstein why his publication is virtually the only one in West Germany carrying out investigative journalism. 'Because I was at the top from the beginning until today,' he answers. 'We do not have fluctuating proprietors, fluctuating obligations. The only thing we have to look at is advertising and circulation. If we face risks over court action, we do not have to worry about money.' Augstein admitted anxiety about sales dipping to around 950,000 in 1988, but in 1989 circulation recovered to just over 1 million – a rise which partly reflected reader interest in the dramatic events in East Germany. Augstein has rejected the idea of producing a separate edition for the East German market, but is pressing ahead with plans to spend as much as DM10 million on establishing *Der Spiegel*'s presence in East Germany. Medium-term sales prospects there are put at around 50,000 copies. Much depends on whether East Germany quickly adopts a hard currency. The magazine, in which Augstein still has a personal shareholding of just under 25 per cent, has annual sales of around DM350 million. One of Augstein's chief preoccupations is with *Der Spiegel*'s capital structure. Tensions have been rising over business development plans between the proprietor and *Der Spiegel*'s staff, who own 50 per cent of the capital through a holding company set up in 1973; in order to regain the upper hand, there is even a prospect that Augstein might want to buy back control of the magazine.

As well as a reputation for exposing humbug and impropriety, it also has well-informed specialist sections in areas like science, economics and the arts. *Der Spiegel* writes its own style of inventive radical-chic German, and is regularly assailed for murdering the language. It mixes news and opinion in a way which, Augstein recognises whimsically, was forbidden by the British. The magazine's chief faults are that it often exaggerates, that its feature stories are often unwieldily long, and that its anti-establishment slant can obscure the facts.

What does he think about West Germany's political stability?

'Parliamentary democracy here has stood the test. It does have a tendency though to become routine more quickly than elsewhere, and also to become corrupted more easily. Perhaps that has something to do with a land of Catholic traditions.' Augstein himself is a Catholic from a Rhineland family, brought up in Hanover surrounded by Protestant Northerners. He raised a theological storm in 1972 with a book claiming that the person of Jesus Christ as portrayed in the Bible never existed. I asked him if he could be corrupted himself. His laconic reply was:

> One can corrupt any person if the price is high enough – and it doesn't always have to be money. If I had been offered a daily paper in 1953, then I could have been corrupted. But my advantage has been that I have always had more money than I needed.

In his early days Augstein enjoyed himself sniping at the British occupation authorities: 'I was against the English. Without being against the English, you couldn't be against the Germans.' But he admits with a grin that he owes the early development of *Der Spiegel* to 'the English idea of press freedom'. Under General Lucius Clay, the military commander of the American occupation zone, 'nothing would have come of it [the magazine]. The same would have been true of the French, let alone the Russians.'

Augstein was the first notable post-war journalist to make the acquaintance of Konrad Adenauer, portraying him in an October 1948 issue as the man most likely to be president of what Augstein prophesied would become 'the new American-inspired West German state'. *Der Spiegel* kept up a pungent campaign during the 1950s against the first federal Chancellor's policies of western integration and rearmament, foreseeing correctly that this would close the door on German reunification. 'It was important to fire away after the war with this careless youthful impertinence,' says Augstein. 'It also encouraged some others.'

Less in keeping with his radical image, he also made a little-known contribution to forestalling the introduction of a new national hymn in the early 1950s, persuading President Heuss against the idea after they had sung the uninspiring new melody together in his office. He calls himself a 'patriot'. When I ask him what significance the word 'Fatherland' has for him, Augstein refers ironically to the diminution of Germany's eastern territories after the First World War. 'When I was small, I used to look at the map to see how much they had taken away from us.'

172

He is an enthusiastic backer of the reforms in the Soviet Union and pulled off a coup in October 1988 by travelling to Moscow to interview Mikhail Gorbachev. In December 1988 he gave DM1 million to an appeal fund for victims of the Armenian earthquake. He has no great faith in the American military presence: 'The Americans have a double book-keeping system. One is for Germany and the rest of Europe, the other for the US. At a time of war, the US would have priority.'

Augstein's hour of pain and glory came in October 1962, an episode marking a watershed in the relationship between the West German press and politics. *Der Spiegel* had already spotlighted a number of questionable actions by Franz Josef Strauss, the Defence Minister. It followed this up with a detailed report on the position of the Bundeswehr within NATO, claiming that Strauss's preoccupation with tactical nuclear weapons had lowered the army's operational readiness. On the pretext of a leak of defence secrets, police raided *Der Spiegel*'s offices and arrested several editors; Augstein gave himself up to the police and was kept in jail for fourteen weeks before court action was dropped. It was disclosed that Strauss himself asked Spanish police through the German embassy in Madrid to arrest the article's author, Conrad Ahlers (later to become government spokesman under Chancellor Brandt), while he was on holiday. Adenauer accused *Der Spiegel* in parliament of 'committing treason to earn money'. After attempting a cover-up, Strauss was forced to resign. The affair exposed the growing autocracy of Adenauer's rule and finally ended his stubborn attempts to stay in power; he was forced to retire as Chancellor in 1963. Augstein believes that, compared with 1962, West Germany has become a more democratic country. 'A similar affair, in which the Justice Minister could be circumvented [by actions of his government colleagues] wouldn't be possible today.' Both Adenauer and Strauss are dead; Augstein relished them as opponents, and had the pleasure of penning their obituaries in his magazine. Chancellor Kohl is plainly not in the same league. 'I wanted to topple Adenauer and Strauss. As for Kohl, he provides his own contribution. It would be senseless to attack Kohl himself,' Augstein says.

Augstein has been a member of the Free Democratic Party (FDP) since the 1950s; for two months in 1972-73 he was a Bundestag deputy. He says his 'most important political friend' is Hans-Dietrich Genscher, the FDP Foreign Minister, but points out that the magazine criticised him for the manner in which he deserted the Schmidt coalition in 1982. He denies that *Der Spiegel* attacks only the Right. In recent years disclosures have damaged the Social Democratic Party too, notably in the 1982 Neue Heimat scandal.* 'If Schmidt were still Chancellor and we found out fourteen days before the election that he was thoroughly corrupt, we would bring out the story, even if it meant he would lose.' But Augstein adds, 'The CDU has more weak points. It is remarkable how religious hypocrisy can lead to the same problem in politics too.'

Der Spiegel's most bizarre scoop stemmed from its revelations in September 1987 of the political smear campaign conducted by Uwe Barschel, the Christian Democrat state premier in Schleswig Holstein.** Barschel was found dead in a Geneva hotel a month afterwards, after committing suicide through a drugs overdose. Augstein says he was 'shocked' when Barschel claimed *Der Spiegel*'s story was false: 'We didn't think anyone could lie so well.' In New York on the Sunday of the death, 'I was shaken,' Augstein says sardonically. It was first thought – erroneously – that Barschel had shot himself. 'I said, "That will be very bad for *Der Spiegel*. The word of honour, man of honour – he has acted like a cavalier of the old school." ' I ask Augstein if he felt responsible for the suicide. 'Not at all.' Barschel's life had been purely politics; if he had lived, says Augstein, he would not have been able to face the consequences: 'He would have had to face all the court cases. Maybe he would not have gone to prison, but to a rest home.'

As far as the future, Augstein believes that 'Bonn does not have too many years left. By 1995, the capital will be back in Berlin, with a unified parliament and one head of state. It is not very sensible – but the pressure is too strong.'

II

Der Spiegel was just one of the success stories in the Federal Republic's formative newspaper years. The western occupying powers soon realised that democracy would only function if the press was put back into German hands. The first paper produced by Germans under Allied control was printed in Aachen while the war was still continuing. After the Americans took the city in October 1944, the four-page *Aachener Nachrichten*, with a circulation of 19,000, was published in January 1945

* See Chapter 9.
** See Chapter 4.

by an unemployed printer, Hans Holland, with the help of a team of US press officers. In an unusual example of war-time *lèse-majesté*, the American journalists used the paper to criticise the US occupation forces for installing ex-Nazis in the new town council. The report sparked a row and more than two dozen former Nazis were subsequently dismissed – but the newspaper was not allowed to report the purge it had prompted.[9]

The *Aachener Nachrichten* was the only German-produced paper on occupied territory when the war ended; but by 1949, a total of 149 newspapers were being produced in the US, British and French zones under licensing policies brought in to re-launch the German press. The Americans put candidates for licences through an elaborate screening process to check their characters and war records. But since so many journalists had joined the National Socialist party during the Third Reich, it was never practicable to bring in a wholesale ban on installing former Nazis as publishers or editors. The licensing policy in the Russian sector, meanwhile, quickly gave priority to Communist party papers. From the end of 1947, in an adaptation of the policies of the Nazis, the newspapers in the eastern zone were progressively 'synchronised' under central Communist control.

In the western sectors, the 'licensed press' enjoyed a monopoly in many regions, and their publishers soon became rich. This state of affairs changed when, with the birth of the Federal Republic in 1949, the Allies lifted the licensing regulations and allowed a newspaper free-for-all. The number of newspapers rose to nearly 500 by the end of the year, with another 80 added in 1950. The new titles mainly represented re-launches of traditional pre-war papers, but the existing 'licensed press' generally proved stronger. West Germany's main quality newspapers today all had their origins in the licensing period.

The *Frankfurter Rundschau* was the first post-war licensed paper, founded in August 1945. Today it is the main Left-leaning daily paper, with a circulation of about 194,000. In the American sector the birth of the *Rundschau* was followed by the *Süddeutsche Zeitung* in Munich and the *Frankfurter Allgemeine Zeitung* (which grew out of the *Mainzer Allgemeine Zeitung* in November 1949). The liberal *Süddeutsche* has a circulation of 380,000; the conservative *FAZ* 360,000. *Die Welt*, first published in Hamburg in April 1946 and now with a circulation of 222,000, was originally modelled on *The Times*. It was the mouthpiece of the British occupation authorities, aimed at countering propaganda from the Soviet zone. The British also authorised the start-up of the Hamburg weekly *Die Zeit* in 1946. It has grown into the country's foremost liberal intellectual

175

newspaper with a circulation of around 495,000.[10] The figures are for the fourth quarter of 1989 – a period when the tide of media interest in events in East Germany increased sales across all the West German press.

Today, the only major daily national newspaper set up after 1949 is *Bild*, launched in 1952. It was the brainchild of Axel Springer, a Hamburg publisher who had made his name under licensing by founding in 1946 the best-selling radio magazine *Hör Zu!* With its daily diet of screaming headlines, pin-ups and snappily-written trivia, genuine scoops and outrageous falsehoods, *Bild* became an indispensable part of the *Wunder* years. Springer bought *Die Welt* in 1953, turning it into a staider middle-brow accompaniment to the *Bild*'s mass-circulation raucousness. From the solid base established by the two papers, Springer steadily expanded his empire in newspapers, periodicals and publishing.

Although in the early 1950s he leant more to the Social Democrats, Springer later swung his papers round firmly to the Christian Democrat government in Bonn, uncompromisingly opposing Communism and taking a firm line on law and order. In the polarised 1960s, he heightened his papers' invective against the East German government after the building of the Berlin Wall in 1961. Springer's radicalism in turn attracted the fire of the Left, and the proprietor of *Bild* was a prime bogeyman for the anti-establishment students who spilled over into the streets in 1968. Radicals connected to the Baader-Meinhof urban terrorist group launched a series of attacks on Springer property, the most serious of which was a bomb which exploded at Springer's Hamburg offices in May 1972, injuring seventeen people.

In 1977, *Bild* suffered a notable public relations setback when Left-wing writer Günter Wallraff pulled off a coup by working for *Bild* in its Hanover office for three months under a false name. He subsequently described the newspaper's tragi-comic manipulation of readers and its own journalists in a best-selling book.[11] An opinion poll in 1981 showed that 41 per cent of *Bild* readers had a negative view of the paper. The growth of Springer's power was part of a general process of press concentration. Although the number of newspapers did not fall significantly, many lost their independence when publishers were taken over by conglomerates like Springer or joined together in groups to bring out different regional versions of basically the same product. In 1954, there were 624 newspaper publishers, and although the total number of newspapers was 1,500, only 225 were papers with a distinct editorial identity. In 1987, 375 publishing groups produced

1,260 newspapers, of which only 121 were distinctly separate products.[12]

Overall circulation of daily, weekly and Sunday newspapers stagnated during the 1980s as economic growth slowed down. In 1988 it totalled 25.8 million copies, not much more than the figure of 25 million ten years earlier. *Bild*'s circulation has fallen back during the 1980s from a peak of more than 5 million to a level of around 4.3 million. Although the Springer group's total share of the daily newspaper market has remained at around 28 per cent[13], the Right-wing publishing empire at the end of the 1980s appeared a lot less threatening. After Axel Springer's death in 1985, 49 per cent of the empire was sold off to the public in a successful stock market flotation, but the group went through an uneasy period of internal squabbling. It also faced several business setbacks, including the costly failure of a brash new weekly magazine venture and circulation problems at *Die Welt* as well as *Bild*.

One reason for the drop in the Springer group's fortunes was that, with the Christian Democrats back in power in the 1980s, *Bild* had much more difficulty in selecting targets for its political attacks. During the 1970s Peter Boenisch, its shoot-from-the hip editor, could fire away with relish at the 'Red Commandos' in the SPD government for allegedly showing laxity against terrorists, raising taxes or proposing speed limits on the Autobahnen. As the Kohl government quickly slipped into the doldrums, however, *Bild* had to tame its style.

Boenisch provided an apt symbol for the disappointment of the Right. The punchy *Bild* columnist, who moved later to become editor of *Die Welt*, was called to Bonn as chief government spokesman in 1983. This sparked a heated attack from Nobel prize winner Heinrich Böll, an old *Bild* sparring partner. In the 1970s, he centred one of his most famous novels around a young housekeeper, Katharina Blum, caught up in the muckraking sensationalism of a daily newspaper modelled on *Bild*.[14] Böll wrote a book criticising the appointment of Boenisch, pointing out that when he had called *Bild* 'chickenfeed' in previous years, this was an insult to chickens.[15] Boenisch proved disappointingly lightweight in the demanding job as chief of the government's information department; he failed to get on with Kohl, and stepped down ignominiously in 1985 amid a minor scandal over his tax affairs. His successor, Friedhelm Ost – a TV journalist specialising in economics – also failed to bring sparkle to the spokesman's job, although he stayed four years in the post. According to Rudolf Strauch, a veteran Bonn correspondent who is now editor of the *Hannoversche Allgemeine Zeitung*, Ost was 'weak and flat' and one of the poorest performers in the spokesman's job since the 1950s.[16]

Ost was replaced in 1989 by Hans Klein, a smooth-talking Christian Social Union deputy who moved into a new job as Information Minister – but also quickly ran into difficulties in marketing Helmut Kohl. Ost, meanwhile, found a new temporary role in helping to organise the East German conservative parties' campaign publicity for the March 1990 elections.

With the Springer concern entering the doldrums, the main running in the media stakes has been taken up by the Bertelsmann group, which with a turnover of DM11.5 billion is roughly four times the size of Springer. Bertelsmann owns Gruner und Jahr, which publishes *Stern*, and also has a growing clutch of European magazine interests. Based in the unfashionable Westphalian town of Gütersloh, it has been moving into cable and satellite television by taking a stake in the new private TV network RTL-Plus. Springer has been active in the new media sector too, with a 15 per cent stake in the competitor channel, Sat-1, and has been trying to build up foreign activities through new operations in Spain, Austria and Hungary. None the less, the increasingly international Bertelsmann has made Springer look distinctly provincial.

The key to restoring dynamism to Springer's newspapers appears to be youth. At *Bild* a new 37-year-old editor, Werner Rudi, was appointed in 1988 to try to stop the rot. Rudi was ejected in 1989 and his editorship passed, on a joint basis, to two other relative youngsters, Hans Hermann Tiedje, 40, and Peter Bartels, 46. At *Die Welt*, Manfred Schell took over as editor in 1985 at the age of 40 and has since presided over a modest circulation recovery. All the newcomers speak in un-Springer-like tones of the need for 'renewal'. They favour more emphasis on environmental matters – and they have also been instrumental in toning down the Springer papers' unremitting hostility to the German Democratic Republic.

Rudi dresses casually in jeans and a turquoise shirt unbuttoned at the neck; he has longish black hair and would not look out of place in a minor pop group. Talking intently in his sofa-strewn office in Hamburg, Rudi confides that he wants to give *Bild* 'a revitalising injection' and says he is afraid that the paper's readership is getting too old.[17] After previous spells as a sports and general reporter, he won his spurs at Springer editing the group's motor paper *AutoBild*. When I asked him about *Bild*'s reputation for making up stories, he denied that *Bild* has told outright lies, but admitted that the paper has a 'credibility gap'. Rudi pledges more checking of stories in future: 'simplification' of news is legitimate, but the truth should not be changed, he said. On the crest of the German *Umwelt* wave, Rudi showed enthusiasm about ecology,

178

warming to the idea of running stories on what kind of environmentally-safe food and washing powder people should buy, and how shoppers should use baskets rather than plastic bags. 'The environment begins in the kitchen,' he told me. One Rudi brainwave was a summer campaign in which readers were asked to 'adopt' at DM1,000 each North Sea seals dying in polluted coastal waters.

Tiedje, one of the paper's two new joint editors, admits his good fortune in being able to devote *Bild* not to seals but to the all-consuming theme of German unity. A lanky political journalist with tie awry and impatient swathes of black hair falling over his glasses, he says he is 'very proud' to be steering *Bild* through such a dramatic time.[18] Tiedje and Bartels – 'I am the brains, he is the belly', says Tiedje – regard Rudi as something of a lightweight. However, they took over Rudi's DM15,000 worth of cream-coloured Italian leather sofas in the Hamburg editorial suite. 'Rudi is a man of good taste,' explains Tiedje. He takes a less evangelistic view than Rudi on the need to check stories, although Tiedje admits that errors have a 'pedagogic value'. *Bild* scored two notable scoops during the East German revolution by correctly forecasting Erich Honecker's resignation as party chief and his temporary imprisonment. These compensated for its equally exclusive story a few months earlier suggesting that Honecker was dead.

Bild's front page has been adorned with patriotic black-red-and-gold practically every day since the breaching of the Berlin Wall. Tiedje points out that this has helped a recovery in sales – up to 4.3 to 4.4 million in the first quarter of 1990 – and declares that *Bild* is standing up for Axel Springer's most important guiding principles: 'Freedom and unity'. Anyone who thinks that Berlin will not be the future capital 'is not all there,' he says.

With the concentration on German unity, Tiedje, who has a curious penchant for anatomical language, expounds: 'We feel we are reaching our readers' hearts and bellies and navels.' In autumn 1989 *Bild* gathered DM700,000 from readers to help accommodate and feed would-be émigrés camped out in front of the West German embassy in Budapest. During the last six months, the Springer group has received around 100,000 letters – mostly from *Bild* readers – about the East German upheaval. *Bild* has led campaigns to find jobs for East German settlers and told its readers not to buy cheap goods in East German shops. Lately, it has run a crusade to extend the D-Mark to the East. 'We are here to make things happen,' insists Mr Tiedje. 'People are now making the politics; it's no longer politics influencing people.' He has great belief in *Bild*'s power. 'If *Bild* says that Mister Marsh is the

179

Number 1 subject of the day – then you are the Number 1 subject.'
He lambasts the Bundesbank for its caution over a united Mark,
and suggests that the Bundesbank's billions of D-Marks of profits
from 'currency speculation' could be spread out among 16m East
Germans.

Tiedje explains that *Bild*'s demand for higher taxes on West Germans
to aid East German reconstruction can be unpopular with some 'people
(in the West) sitting on their fat arses … We have pockets full of money
– the poor fellows over there have nothing.' He adds: 'This has nothing
to do with nationalism – it's just that the people over there have been
taken for a ride for 40 years.' *Bild* – like many other big West German
papers – is already investigating possibilities for printing in East
Germany. 'The people (in East Germany) want *Bild*. It has a wide
reputation – they think it's on their side.'

Die Welt has its headquarters in a squat office block on the street
between Bonn and Bad Godesberg. Before 1949, it was a tree-lined
country road; today the street is a traffic-clogged freeway lined with
embassies, odd-shaped ministry buildings, lobbyists' organisations,
party headquarters and petrol stations. The paper moved to Bonn from
Hamburg in 1974, and is still the only national newspaper with its
headquarters in the capital. Schell urges more dynamism from his
reporters, and stresses the need for 'self-discipline' to prevent
journalists getting too close to politics.[19] He criticises the Bonn press
habit of attending too many manipulative 'confidential' gatherings with
politicians. 'We have to inform people. We are here for the readers,' he
says.

Although clearly conservative, *Die Welt* takes the Christian Democrats
to task in its editorials rather more than in the old days. Schell says he
leans towards the CDU but is not a party member, and stresses that *Die
Welt*'s deputy editor supports the Social Democrats. He says the
conservatives did not pay sufficient attention to the environment in the
past, and talks with pride of how the paper confronted the government
by calling for anti-pollution catalytic converters in cars. Schell told me at
the end of 1988 that he was dissatisfied with the long-standing Springer
practice of placing hostile quotation marks around the initials 'DDR'
whenever referring to the German Democratic Republic. Springer
insisted on this punctuation during the years of the Cold War to show
his scepticism about the second 'D' for 'democratic'. 'I am in favour of
abolishing this,' states Schell. 'The time to have abolished this was in
1972' (when the two German states signed the Basic Relations Treaty).
Dropping the quotation marks was also necessary for the Springer

papers' correspondents to gain full accredited status in East Berlin. The Springer group duly decided a symbolic change in punctuation in August 1989 – just three months before the Berlin Wall came down. *Bild*'s Tiedje admitted the irony, but added loyally: 'If Axel Springer had been alive, this is a formula he would have accepted.'

Small-town Bonn's place at the hub of West German political life is a substantial drawback for the German press. The concentration of journalists and politicians in a town lacking city culture and contact with business and industry breeds complacency and parochial clubbiness.[20] Although information circulates freely in Bonn, the quality of journalism seldom rises above the mediocre. On account of easy living and working conditions, generous tax breaks (a 35 per cent income-tax allowance for members of the Bonn press conference association – although this was ended in 1990), and the exaggerated status they enjoy within their own news organisations, German journalists in Bonn are invariably highly immobile. The senior correspondents usually move away only when they retire or win a foreign posting – or if they are promoted to become editor or deputy editor at their head offices. In summer 1988, the bureau chiefs of the major newspapers and broadcasting groups had been in Bonn for an average of sixteen years; their average age was 55.[21] Immobility creates staleness among the older journalists and frustration among younger ones waiting for their chance in the pecking order.

There is no shortage of criticism about this state of affairs. Wolfgang Herles, who became head of the Bonn studio of Zweites Deutsches Fernsehen (ZDF – the second nationwide TV channel) in 1987 at the age of 37, says that being relatively young and a newcomer to Bonn is an advantage. 'One rule is not to stay here too long. Your curiosity falls, you start to speak the same language as the politicians. In this space ship Bonn, you need to be mobile – or else you get space sickness.'[22]

Klaus Bölling, a veteran TV journalist who became press spokesman for Chancellor Schmidt, and later was the Social Democrat government's mission chief in East Berlin, calls the closeness of links between politicians and journalists in Bonn 'a form of clandestine corruption'.[23] Born in Potsdam and living today in West Berlin, Bölling recalls the strength of journalism in Berlin during the Weimar Republic. Today the only *überregionale* national newspaper produced from Berlin is the *Tageszeitung*, a Left-wing 'alternative' paper disrespectful of the establishment and modelled on France's *Libération*, which has built up a circulation of just over 50,000.

Bölling says that the press connivance with the politicians leads to a 'united front' barring outsiders – the consumers of the media – from

181

access to the real news. Although during his time as Schmidt's press chief he himself was often accused of misusing his close contacts with SPD-leaning papers (especially *Der Spiegel*), he says now: 'Journalists in Bonn come together with politicians daily, it's all in the family. They think they are part of the executive branch. This leads to a shortening of the necessary critical distance. Journalists and politicians should be adversaries, not partners.' Others make the same point about Bonn's narrow-mindedness. Friedhelm Kemna, editor of the main Bonn newspaper, the *General-Anzeiger*, says, 'The published opinions from Bonn are very small minded. Part of Bonn's fate is provincialism.' Underlining the great priority given to domestic politics, Kemna adds, 'The only time that Bonn journalists look beyond their sphere is when they go abroad on an official visit with the Chancellor.'[24] Theo Sommer, editor since 1973 of *Die Zeit* in Hamburg, says, 'In Bonn it is difficult to stay aloof. There are only a few who rise above the incest.'[25] Thomas Kielinger, editor of the Bonn-based liberal-conservative weekly *Rheinischer Merkur*, is, however, mounting a campaign for Bonn to remain a 'media centre' in spite of the pressure building up for the capital to move back to Berlin. Kielinger says that the amplitude of the German unity drama has suddenly made the German press a great deal less petty and provincial; he sees East Germany, in journalistic terms, as 'a new frontier'.[26]

The German media in general – both newspapers and broadcasting – have risen to the new challenges of reporting from the East; but there is still a strong touch of unadventurousness. At the height of the anti-Honecker demonstrations in early October 1989, the *FAZ* carried a story from one of its correspondents in East Berlin explaining how the East German Foreign Ministry had recommended journalists not to travel to Leipzig or Dresden. Even though the *FAZ* calls itself as the '*Zeitung füer Deutschland*', the simple expedient of simply sending a correspondent there on the train seems not to have crossed the newspaper's mind. In spite of strong interest in West Germany in the tide of revolution across eastern Europe, all the main newspapers relied on news agency coverage for their stories on the bloody events in Romania over Christmas 1989, sending in their correspondents only later. The *FAZ*, which prides itself on its attention to eastern European affairs, used news agency stories from Romania every day between 23 and 29 December – reflecting an apparent mixture of journalistic timidity and Christmas holiday sluggishness.

Large parts of Bonn journalistic life are conducted according to time-honoured rituals. After 1949, as a mark of new openness following

182

the controls of the Nazi Propaganda Ministry, the journalists reverted to the old Weimar tradition under which they themselves invited government spokesmen to regular press conferences. Since the birth of the Federal Republic, such conferences have been religiously held on Mondays, Wednesdays and Fridays, a system which does give correspondents a good impression of the 'news of the day' by listening to questions from their colleagues. Nevertheless the rituals seldom yield much more than set-piece news items, and often the ministry spokesmen and -women are little better informed than the journalists. The three-times-weekly pattern provides one of the reasons for the herd-like nature of the Bonn press corps. Journalists on the whole are remarkably reluctant to go after innovative 'scoops'. They seldom have time for lunch. For most of their news pages, German newspapers have very early mid-afternoon deadlines, so a lot of writing has to be accomplished before 3 o'clock.

Tradition rules in other areas too. A peculiarly Germanic system of numbered codes from 1 to 3 to denote the degree of confidentiality of press briefings dates from Weimar; there is no German word for 'on' or 'off the record'. The Presseclub, an institution set up in 1952 for German journalists only, is also still going strong; it was founded to give Adenauer and his Ministers the opportunity for informal contacts with the domestic press away from surveillance by the occupying powers. Boasting more than a hundred members and an over-priced restaurant partly subsidised by the government, it is still the main forum for such gatherings.[27] Following the pattern of the informal 'teatime conversations' established in the 1950s between Adenauer and chosen journalists, Bonn journalists have also established over the years around a dozen 'circles' or clubs to swap gossip and information with political guests. Quixotically labelled 'confidential', such sessions only very rarely give rise to genuine news – but since the objective is conviviality rather than information, that does not matter too much.

III

Like the main newspapers, the West German broadcasting system owes its origins to Allied decisions made in the period of flux between 1945 and 1949. The federal structure of broadcasting stems directly from the regional networks set up in the western occupation zones. During the

Weimar Republic, radio stations were under the control of the Post Office, which owned transmitters and collected licence fees. Centralised control eased the job of the Nazis in taking over the radio networks after 1933. After 1945, the aim of decentralising broadcasting was therefore a key part of establishing democratic checks and balances.

The Americans set up four broadcasting organisations in their sector, Radio Frankfurt, Radio Stuttgart, Radio München and Radio Bremen. The British and the French established central organisations: Nordwestdeutscher Rundfunk (NWDR) in Hamburg, with branches in Cologne and Berlin, and Südwestfunk in Baden-Baden, the headquarters of the French military government. In 1948-49, the western Allies transferred legal power over broadcasting not to the central government – which did not exist at the time – but to the *Länder*. The primacy of the *Länder* over broadcasting has continued ever since – an important prop for decentralisation, but a factor which nonetheless gives broadcasting an unavoidable touch of provincialism.

The public service networks inherited from the occupation authorities became Hessischer Rundfunk, Süddeutscher Rundfunk and Bayerischer Rundfunk in the American-occupied south; otherwise the names were left unchanged. NWDR was spit up into Westdeutscher Rundfunk (WDR) and Norddeutscher Rundfunk (NDR) in 1955. The organisations were guaranteed freedom from government or parliamentary influence. Legislation was passed by the *Land* governments setting down goals of freedom, justice, truth and international understanding. The Broadcasting Councils set up to oversee the corporations and their directors-general were supposed to represent the public rather than political interests. That sounded good in theory but in practice – as Hugh Carleton Greene warned in his 1948 speech – the politicians soon decided that television was too important to be left to the broadcasters.

Believing that the regional networks were mainly in the hands of the Social Democrats, Adenauer attempted to set up a second TV channel as a government network in competition with ARD, the established TV network. But the government was beaten by the Federal Constitutional Court in 1961, which ruled that broadcasting fell – as the Allies intended – under the authority of the *Länder* and not Bonn. The new channel, ZDF, thus started to operate in 1963 as a *Land*-controlled station based in Mainz, the aim being that the new network should come under control of 'public interest groups' rather than the political parties. But the politicians once more – as with the ARD stations – quickly gained the upper hand, and seats on the governing ZDF council were carved up between the main parties.

Broadcasting today has become entangled with party politicking for two basic reasons. First, up to the 1970s, rising programme costs were met by spreading the burden over a greater number of TV-set owners. But the saturated market for sets subsequently made steady increases in licence fees necessary, and these could be decided only with the approval of *Land* parliaments. Second, politicians discovered that television was supplanting the press as the main medium for influencing the electorate. The average West German spends about two hours a day watching television, but only thirty minutes reading a newspaper.[28]

The long arm of the party bureaucracies has reached out into broadcasting in a variety of ways. The individual Broadcasting Councils in charge of the nine regional networks[29] have come progressively under the influence of the political parties, with the Christian Democrats in the majority in most cases. The myriad groups and corporations, such as sports and religious associations, the Church, and industry federations, brought on to broadcasting councils to maintain pluralism, in many cases have proved to be simply party appendages. Most director-generalships have become outright political posts, with the CDU controlling the majority of places, sometimes balanced by the award of deputy positions to the SPD.[30] Most perniciously, administrative and journalistic jobs throughout the networks are granted on the basis of individuals' political allegiance. The broadcasting stations have become giant coalitions under which politicians dispense patronage through the infamous *Proporz* (proportional) appointments system – and where the original goal of safeguarding the public interest has become almost totally obscured.

A critical observer of the relationship between politics and the media is Karl-Günther von Hase, chief government spokesman for five years under Chancellors Adenauer, Erhard and Kiesinger. He later became a state secretary in the Defence Ministry, ambassador to Britain (1970-77) and director general of ZDF (1977-82). Now in his seventies, Hase sees the *Proporz* system in broadcasting as inflicting 'cancerous damage', adding, 'The only way to counter it is through quality.' He says he is a liberal conservative although not a CDU member, and points out: 'Journalists are politicised in a way which is not the case in other European countries.' This he terms as similar to the spread of political influence over the German civil service: 'In England it is almost an insult to ask a civil servant if he has a particular political tendency. He is a servant of the crown. Here, it [party allegiance] has become the norm.'[31]

Many newspaper journalists are contemptuous about the servility of interviewers on TV. One of the most subservient is Reinhard Appel, a long-time ZDF man who for years has run a programme during which journalists toss tame questions to politicians. 'He used to invite journalists along to give questions to the politicians' answers,' says Sommer of *Die Zeit*.[25] 'On TV, German journalists are too bloody soft,' comments Werner Holzer, veteran editor of the *Frankfurter Rundschau*. 'German politicians think tough questions are unfriendliness.'[32]

Timid treatment of politicians on TV has also come under fire from within the networks themselves. Klaus Bresser, who took over from Appel as ZDF editor-in-chief in spring 1988 at the age of 51, caused an outcry even before starting his new job, when he accused two prominent TV journalists of the Bavarian broadcasting service of helping to 'destroy television' through pandering to the Right-wing Christian Social Union. Bresser has tried to speed up ZDF's reaction to news, changing schedules to bring in special evening programmes to cover events during the day like the Ramstein air show disaster or drama in the Soviet Union and East Germany. He sees his task as helping to achieve 'a widening of journalistic sovereignty'.[33] Bresser says his well-publicised remarks about the need for 'distance' between politicians and journalists earned him a lot of support from colleagues. 'I didn't really say anything new,' he adds. 'The fact that it produced such a reaction was a sign that there is something wrong with the relationship.'

9

The Barons of Consensus

We believe that the welfare of each individual depends on the welfare of all ... Germany's misfortune will be ended only when each individual sees the well-being of the whole of society as the best guarantee for his own personal good.

> Joseph Goebbels, 1932[1]

The history of the Germans is a history of extremes. It contains everything except moderation ... The normal person, not particularly bad, not particularly good; healthy, sane, moderate – he has never set his stamp on German history.

> A.J.P. Taylor, 1944[2]

It is always easy to call for strong men. But we should not underestimate the difficulties faced by politicians.

> Karl Otto Pöhl, 1988[3]

In West Germany, the application of economic and political power is a highly organised business. Germany's history of particularism and strife has left the post-war state with a built-in dread of internal conflict. Decision-making can find legitimacy only through maximum consultation, a process which aims to weld together for the common good government, business, trade unions and other segments of society.

The process has proved its worth for thirty years, but during the 1980s, reflecting the faltering of economic growth which started during the previous decade, it has been working less smoothly. Hamstrung by the abrupt increase in unemployment, relations between government, labour and employers have grown more brittle than in the 1960s and 1970s. Consensus has not broken up – but it has become less cosy. Can a country which makes harmony its first priority come up with the right answers to the social and economic challenges of the 1990s? East Germany has practised its own peculiar system of centrally-enforced consensus; how quickly will West Germany's economic and social

187

arrangements now take over? The system draws its strength from an element of weakness: the fear of the disruption which would ensue if it were ever replaced by anything else. A radical new approach to economic and political management would not be possible without a crisis. And that is just what the consensus system aims to avoid.

I

One of Germany's landmarks is a three-winged 13-storey office block shaped like a giant gravestone on the north-west outskirts of Frankfurt. This is the headquarters of the Bundesbank, the statutorily independent central bank which watches over the country's monetary policies with anti-inflationary vigilance. Karl Otto Pöhl, the president since 1980, defines his institution's place within the consensus system: 'The Bundesbank is part of the German system of checks and balances. It is a form of a state within the state, which runs according to its own system of consensus, providing an economic policy counterweight to the government.'[4] The Bundesbank is supposed to be untouched by vested interests, but as a collegiate body interwoven into West Germany's corporatist society, it can hardly avoid being drawn into the political fray. West Germany's economic weight and the international status of the D-Mark make the Bundesbank one of the most influential monetary authorities in the world, but it is also among the least well understood. The head of the Bundesbank has his hands on the levers of economic power, but he does not rule alone. The president must be not simply an economic technocrat, but also a consummate politician. Like everyone else, he has to steer through the shoals of the consensus system. The complexities seem to grow with each passing year. Pöhl's greatest challenge is now upon him: helping to extend eastwards the benefits of stable money which the West Germans have carefully built up over 40 years.

Pöhl has no shortage of experience in weathering the vicissitudes of economic policy-making, both at home and on the international financial circuit. A squat Napoleonic figure, he took over the job at the comparatively young age of 50 and now ranks as the world's most senior central banker. An incisive, open-minded and surprisingly sensitive man, he hides a melancholy streak beneath his *bon viveur* charm. Whatever the state of the dollar, Pöhl is always tanned. He delights in telling jokes, sometimes of decidedly un-bankerly taste. He has been known to preface his speeches abroad – when he speaks English – with witticisms combining economics with sex. But he would not do this at home; it would be thought 'unserious'. He does not suffer fools gladly and in private Pöhl can deliver merciless judgements on Ministers, officials and bankers who cross his path. But, in the Bundesbank's complicated political environment, success comes only with subtlety and he has to be a master at diplomatic in-fighting. His second eight-year term at the Bundesbank started in 1988, so Pöhl looks set to stay at the monetary controls until well into the 1990s. Characteristically, he is appalled at the idea of becoming some kind of elder statesman.

Born in Hanover in 1929, Pöhl has been a member of the Social Democratic Party (SPD) since 1948, but no longer plays any role in the party. He lives overlooking the hills outside Frankfurt with his wife and two youngest children. An economic journalist during the 1960s, Pöhl worked on the weekly *Wirtschaftswoche* before joining the German Banking Association and then serving as a key economic official in Bonn. Between 1972 and 1977, he was state secretary at the Finance Ministry under the governments of Willy Brandt and Helmut Schmidt. When the latter was Finance Minister before becoming Chancellor in 1974, Pöhl served fifteen vital months as Schmidt's right-hand man, helping surmount the international currency storms which led to the break-up of the Bretton Woods system of fixed exchange rates in March 1973. Pöhl is not the first economic journalist to become head of the German central bank. Walther Funk, president of the Reichsbank between 1939 and 1945, jailed for life in 1946 at the Nuremberg war crimes tribunal, was economic editor of a conservative Berlin financial paper during the 1920s.[5]

Asked about the Bundesbank's power, Pöhl likes to quote Stalin's saying: 'How many divisions has the Pope?' He says that the central bank's greatest strength lies in public support for monetary stability. In contrast to many German politicians, he is highly efficient in transmitting his message to the media. His journalistic experience gives him regard for the press – and also makes him unusually wary about being quoted with an intemperate remark. In the early years after he joined the Bundesbank in 1977 as its deputy under the previous president, Otmar Emminger, Pöhl was on the defensive, smarting under suspicions that he was 'Schmidt's man' and also that he was a little too young for the post. He now carries the appropriate air of central banking gravitas, but his natural irreverence can still break through. Pöhl plainly enjoys the intellectual challenge and the public status of his job. He is believed to earn more than DM500,000 a year. But the hierarchy-conscious German banking world – the stuffiness of formal receptions with the convoys of chauffeur-driven Mercedes outside – can also frustrate him. Sometimes, it is almost as if he had a sneaking desire to be back on the journalist's beat.

Pöhl has to play a delicate game of juggling power and influence on both the external and internal fronts. The Bundesbank faces a recurring dilemma: it comes under contradictory pressures whichever way the D-Mark moves. If the currency is strong, the government, industrialists and trade unionists start to worry about damage to the export-dependent economy. If, on the other hand, the D-Mark weakens, alarm soon rises – spurred by the Bundesbank's own success in preaching to the Germans the virtues of monetary stability – about the danger of imported inflation. Relations between the Bundesbank and the Finance Ministry in Bonn are always highly sensitive. Pöhl was appointed both as vice-president in 1977 and as president in 1980 by Chancellor Schmidt. But, ironically, his ties with Bonn during the 1980s were more harmonious under the Kohl government than with the Social Democrat-led coalition which collapsed in 1982.

Pöhl is a little saddened that his relationship with Schmidt has soured. Schmidt blamed the Bundesbank for tightening its credit policy to protect the D-Mark during the difficult recession years of 1981-82, and so indirectly contributing to the fall of his government.[6] The former Chancellor bears a strong grudge against the central bank, and these days refers to his one-time deputy as a mere 'technician'.[7] However, Pöhl also had his brushes with Gerhard Stoltenberg, Finance Minister for 6½ years under Kohl.* Pöhl has been a regular, if discreet, critic of Kohl's administration for not taking a sufficiently adventurous line on cutting taxes to speed economic growth. He also regards the general orientation of economic policies in Bonn as somewhat provincial. Although Stoltenberg supported Pöhl's reappointment for his second term which started in 1988, the relationship between the two men suffered in 1987-88 over Bonn's policies on supporting the dollar, where Pöhl felt the Bundesbank was being brow-beaten into a commitment to prop up the US currency through intervention on the foreign exchanges. The Bundesbank in 1988 opposed Bonn's levying of a withholding tax on savings and investments. The central bank blamed the tax for weakening the D-Mark, and it was later removed. Pöhl and his central bank colleagues were irritated when Bonn agreed at the

* Stoltenberg was appointed Defence Minister in April 1989.

beginning of 1988 – without sufficient consultation with the Bundesbank – to set up a joint council with France to coordinate financial and economic policies. Pöhl sits on the council, which meets every three months, alternately in Germany and France; but, in view of perpetual French belief that Germany takes too rigid an anti-inflationary line, he is sceptical as to whether the new body will add to monetary harmony between the two countries.

New reasons for friction between Bonn and Frankfurt came to the surface during 1989 when Kohl, under pressure from the French, agreed to start preparations for European monetary union much more quickly than the Bundesbank would have liked. The upheaval in East Germany, and growing pressure to extend the D-Mark east of the Elbe to dampen emigration of discontented East Germans, provided still greater potential for discord. In February 1990, Pöhl was caught unawares by Kohl's sudden U-turn in favour of speedy monetary union with the East. Sporting his favourite red tie, Pöhl appeared before the press in Bonn to underline that the Bundesbank would support the plan – but simultaneously outlined a long list of reservations. Pöhl described the proposals as 'cryptic' – a favourite way of expressing that they had not been properly thought through. Asked about lack of consultation by Kohl, Pöhl replied laconically: 'I always advise the politicians to consult the Bundesbank first.'[8]

Ironically, the Social Democratic Party had already been mounting a campaign for German monetary union. Reflecting the withering of his SPD links, Pöhl found no great difficulty in disagreeing. In 1988 he passed the milestone of forty years' adherence to the SPD without ceremony. Normally, in anniversary-conscious Germany, this would have been cause for celebration, but none of Pöhl's erstwhile comrades even noticed. Pöhl has always been on the moderate wing of the SPD, and says he joined the party mainly as a reaction against the Nazis. 'Just after the war, the bitterness against the conservatives was very strong. This was the main reason why I joined the SPD in 1948. I was not particularly Left-wing, certainly not on the economic front, but the conservatives were linked to the Nazis, and the SPD represented the only party which had voted against Hitler's enabling law in 1933. The SPD had never had a chance to establish itself as a party of government – I felt that the SPD needed one day to have the chance of ruling itself.' The real spirit of post-war consensus was established, says Pöhl, with the Grand Coalition between the Christian Democrats and Social Democrats in 1966. This led to Willy Brandt's government in 1969 – 'an event of historic significance'.

191

One factor making Pöhl's life more complicated than often realised is that he is not fully master in his own house. The Bundesbank establishes a policy consensus in a particularly complex way. In recent years, the central bank and its top officials have become more enmeshed in German party-politicking. Although the Bundesbank's formal independence has not been touched, increased politicisation has diminished its internal cohesiveness and *esprit de corps* – and appears to have lowered its weight in administering policy advice to Bonn. Pöhl sometimes gives the impression of having to devote so much attention to tactics – in both the domestic and the international arenas – that he has little time for strategy. Karl Schiller, the former SPD Economics Minister, an experienced hand in watching tussles between Bonn and the Bundesbank, comments succinctly: 'The Bundesbank's influence on the Government appears to have grown weaker. It carries out its stability policy – and that is all.'[9]

Pöhl's closest working colleagues are fellow members of the directorate, chosen by the government on the basis of both competence and political allegiance.[10] As a form of balance for Pöhl's membership of the SPD, his deputy, Helmut Schlesinger – formerly the central bank's chief economist – is a conservative who takes a more orthodox line on monetary policy than Pöhl. In contrast to his austere reputation, Schlesinger is an affable man and an acute observer of the German scene. The two form a complementary tandem, and have improved their partnership since the early days of Pöhl's tenure. To maintain his influence at the core of the Bundesbank, and reduce the number of external appointees, the president tries to keep the directorate as small as possible. In 1989, there were seven members, although ideally, Pöhl would prefer six. The appointment of Hans Tietmeyer, former state secretary at the Finance Ministry, to the Bundesbank's directorate at the beginning of 1990 has subtly changed the balance of power within the central bank.[11] Tietmeyer, a dour Westphalian celebrated for his negotiating skills, stamina and attention to detail, brings a good deal of international experience to the job; Pöhl sees him as a rival. Tietmeyer is likely to take over from Schlesinger as vice president in 1992. Although he protests that his main ambition is simply to serve the central bank well, Tietmeyer is well-placed to become the next Bundesbank chief after Pöhl's second eight-year term expires at the end of 1995.

The central bank's supreme policy-making council is an even more cumbersome body than the directorate. The Council meets fortnightly, every other Thursday, to discuss major questions of credit policy. Its moves on altering German interest rates reverberate around the foreign exchange markets of the world within a few minutes. Decisions are taken by vote; and the chairman has the same vote as everyone else. The council, currently 18-strong, groups the seven Bundesbank directors together with eleven presidents of the central banks of the individual federal states, most of whom are political appointees from the *Länder*. Reflecting the bloated branch systems run by the federal central banks, the Bundesbank has 15,700 staff – only 2,800 of whom work in the Frankfurt headquarters.

Pöhl sometimes has to struggle to fight his brief against council members who may have little regard for international complexities. However he has tried to handle the council with more *finesse* than the peppery and egocentric Emminger, who used to stir enmity by lecturing his fellow board members.[12] One seasoned member of the council says of Pöhl: 'He is masterful at the meetings – extremely capable of steering compromises.' According to Hans Apel, the former Social Democrat Finance Minister, who knows him from his Bonn days, Pöhl deploys his skill in manoeuvring: 'Pöhl is not a fighter.'[13] If Pöhl wants to be sure of winning the council's support, he knows that he must prepare his ground with Schlesinger first: a case backed by the two of them will nearly always be accepted by the *Länder* representatives.

Pöhl's time as state secretary in Bonn, when he sat as the state's representative on supervisory boards of companies like Volkswagen, gave him plenty of insight into the consensus system. He sees clear justification for it, even if he is unusually critical about certain features:

> The advantages are clear enough. Association of unions and management is of great value in assuring social peace, for instance in enabling job cuts to be carried out in an atmosphere of harmony. On the other hand, there is a certain intellectual corruption about the way that unions are brought into supervisory boards and given privileges. The costs are enormous – a purely capitalistic set-up would certainly be more efficient. But I don't say that such a capitalistic system would necessarily be better; in our society, I believe the consensus system is the one which is appropriate. We are a rich society, and we are willing to pay a certain price for social peace. The problem of course is that this system benefits only the people who are in it – the unemployed, for instance, are not.

Reflecting on the economic rigidities which can creep into labour relations, he says: 'I am not sure if the tariff agreements negotiated between unions and employers are of benefit for the employed – they are certainly not for those out of work.' Pöhl marvels at the discipline shown by the trade unions over the scandal revolving around the Neue Heimat housing group owned by the Trade Union Federation (DGB). Irregularities at the top of the concern came to light in 1982, and a steadily unfolding tale of corruption and mismanagement came to a climax with the group's financial collapse in 1986. Losses have been estimated at as much as DM4 billion. 'The Neue Heimat affair swallowed up the equivalent of several years of (DGB) members' contributions. There should have been a revolution! In fact, the unions' membership more or less accepted it,' he says.

Pöhl does have his doubts about whether harmony in German society will continue: 'I believe we will have more conflicts in future. This is partly because the importance of the fringe political groups seems to be increasing. Politics in general has suffered from the poor image of the politicians, from scandals such as the Flick affair.' Pöhl's most taxing battle with the politicians will come in the event that the German capital moves back to Berlin. The Bundesbank's statutes state that the central bank is sited only provisionally in Frankfurt, and would move back to the old Prussian capital if the government were to return to Berlin. Pöhl likes to keep a sceptical distance from the politicians; as reunification gets under way, the Bundesbank may well start a campaign to remain in Frankfurt.

II

The politicians are finding that establishing consensus is more difficult. When I asked Helmut Kohl what he most regretted after 6½ years as Chancellor, he replied:

> In these six years, I wouldn't have carried out differently any of the main policy decisions. What I would have done totally differently would have been the tackling of the question of improving the acceptance of our policies. That is the real problem of a modern democracy – not just a German problem – that too few people can look beyond their own special situations.[14]

In the art of winning people for his cause, Kohl will go down in the Federal Republic's political history as a remarkably poor communicator. He owed his climb to the peak of politics not to authority or brilliance, but to expert party management and instinctive skill in eliminating rivals. However, his capacity for maintaining accord, either within or outside the Christian Democratic Union, wore dangerously thin towards the end of the 1980s. As one Bonn ambassador puts it: 'He's good at presiding over a committee as long as it's in agreement. But if it's in disagreement, he doesn't have any better idea than to send people out of the room and ask them to sort it out.'

Like Helmut Schmidt, Kohl regards most of the media with hostility mixed with contempt. But, unlike Schmidt, he has not developed a capacity for using press and broadcasting to his advantage. Kohl's personality comes across best in small, informal groups, when his love for homely anecdotes can appear engaging; but before larger audiences, when confronted with intellectuals or when unsure of his ground, he is stiff and ill-at-ease. He is a bad listener. If he really wants to be, Kohl can be brusquely decisive; but, most often, his thick Palatinate dialect rambles uncontrollably through a jungle of inconsequential subordinate clauses. He would do better simply to stop talking. Kohl's rhetorical weaknesses are exposed most cruelly on television and in parliament – although, towards the end of 1989, he made what seemed like a deliberate effort to polish his TV manner. Kohl's meandering style also shows up in private exchanges. His conversations with Margaret Thatcher during the 1980s attained legendary quality. In spite of their common allegiance to the Right, Kohl's verbosity irritates Thatcher. 'She likes to come to the point; with Kohl, it is all preamble,' says one diplomat. All the same, in the records of talks between the two, Thatcher is usually down as speaking longer. Kohl's wordiness causes a special problem when, as in conversation with the British Prime Minister, his remarks have to be translated. The hearer therefore needs to listen to the flow of speech twice over. During earlier trips to London when Kohl was Opposition leader, his interpreter became so used to set conversational speeches that he would translate well-loved Kohl phrases which, on occasions, he did not actually use.

Despite his long period as Chancellor, which should have boosted his self-assuredness, Kohl can be remarkably thin-skinned. He also has a habit of drawing attention to his own weak spots. Treated for years as a buffoon in *Der Spiegel*, he pretends not to read it. In fact, Kohl's aides admit that he orders his press officials to comb through each issue. The Chancellor sometimes even rings up at the weekend Eduard Ackermann, his chief media adviser, to ask what is in the latest copy. In conversation, Kohl often tells people that they should not listen to what is said about him in 'Left-wing publications' – a heavy hint that he is indeed fretting about the magazine's latest barbs. Rudolf Augstein, *Der Spiegel*'s publisher, used to know Kohl fairly well during the 1970s when he was leader of the Opposition. 'Now he doesn't talk to me. That is not something I miss,' Augstein says.[15] Kohl also feels on the defensive with *Die Zeit*, co-published by Helmut Schmidt. Theo Sommer, the editor, says of Kohl:

> He hates me. He sees me as a henchman of Helmut Schmidt. He feels I despise him. He is very thin-skinned. In fact, I have a more realistic assessment of him than many of my colleagues – he's not a man to articulate ideas, but he can solve problems. When eating and drinking, he can be much more convivial than Schmidt. If he were not so dull, heavy-set, unspiritual, he would be a very good companion for an evening.[16]

Schmidt now says he regrets not having left office a year earlier instead of staying through to the bitter end of his sinking coalition in October 1982. Since leaving the Chancellery, he has become a very wealthy man through his writing and conference activities.[17] It hardly seems likely that Kohl will be a prolific author, but he says: 'I could easily imagine not having political office. I like to read a lot. I am one of the main users of the Bundestag library. As a young man I was good at sport – football, mountain-hikes. I would not be afraid to have more time on my hands.'

III

The chairman of the German Trade Union Federation (DGB) is a former post office functionary with a liking for caravan holidays. When delivering a speech, he can move an audience into a trance, mastering the difficult art of speaking without apparently moving his lips. Ernst Breit, at the top of the German trade union movement since 1982, is the first to admit that he is not very exciting. 'Quiet, hesitant, no charisma – that's completely accurate,' he agrees, sitting behind a table drinking coffee in his low-key headquarters in an office complex on the outskirts of Düsseldorf. When I ask him what his main strengths are, he replies, 'Accuracy and reliability. These are the attributes we required in the last few years. I doubt whether we really wanted people simply to be good at making speeches.'[18]

A member of the Social Democratic Party, Breit has the job of marshalling the voice of labour in Europe's biggest economy. He runs an organisation grouping seventeen big union federations with a total of

7.8 million members. His task is behind-the-scenes coordination: bargaining with management is a matter for the individual unions. The DGB, established in 1949, is the largest – but not the only – central union organisation.[19] After running the postal workers' federation for ten years, Breit took on the DGB job with the prime task of rebuilding shattered union confidence after the Neue Heimat scandal. Seven years later, he has achieved fair success in binding the wounds and stemming a decline in membership. He can even afford to relax slightly. For all his public impassiveness, in private he displays surprising warmth and a touch of self-irony. He is the kind of man who chuckles – not often, but enough – rather than laughs.

Breit's studied moderation should not be mistaken for lack of toughness. He likes to set out his principles with a certain mix of primness and pedantry, like a village schoolmaster from his native Rickelshof in Schleswig Holstein, where he was born in 1924. Steadfastness was certainly required after the Neue Heimat affair, which plunged the trade unions into deep internal in-fighting and brought a slump in popularity. Breit admits, 'There is no doubt that this cost us sympathy, trust and approval. It's hard to say whether we have recovered.' He notes that, whenever the government needs a stick to beat the unions, the Neue Heimat scandal comes up with distressing regularity. Nevertheless he unequivocally praises *Der Spiegel* for exposing the affair: 'It was doing its democratic duty. If *Der Spiegel* did not exist, we would have to invent it.'

Earning a relatively modest DM160,000 a year, Breit has been in charge of the DGB's fortunes at a time when the nature of consensus has been shifting. The change of government in 1982, stagnation of unemployment at high levels, and the structural problems assailing heavy industry have all had something to do with the change. The unions have started to re-think their role and their responsibilities as partners of capitalism. Post-war legislation brought union representatives on to companies' supervisory boards through *Mitbestimmung** and gave them a clear stake in prosperity. But when the numbers out of work started to climb at the end of the 1970s, the unions found that they had effectively surrendered independence. Where they could once have fought redundancies, they became partly responsible for them. The process has made it harder for union leaders to maintain control over their membership, and increased the danger of individual unions going their own way. Breit has needed all his powers of persuasion to maintain

* See Chapter 6.

DGB unity during the last few years.

The Neue Heimat affair and its aftermath have taken trade union self-questioning a step further. To finance the losses, the DGB was forced to dispose of the 'family jewels' – selling both the trade union bank, Bank für Gemeinwirtschaft, and its insurance company Volksfürsorge.[20] These asset sales had great symbolic as well as financial importance. A unique, highly visible link between the unions and the market economy was severed. Breit recognises that the withdrawal marks a watershed. The unions now believe that their role as shareholders in private-sector institutions 'is not optimal'. During a period of crisis – as in the housing market difficulties which undermined Neue Heimat – unions become drawn into a conflict of interest between commercial imperatives and obligations to their members, he explains. 'In difficult times, unions are over-extended.'

In a similar way, the unions' relationship with the government has become less comfortable. Although Kohl and Breit have continued the ritual of formal meetings to maintain a show of bi-partisan togetherness, Breit has not forgiven Kohl's energetic criticism earlier in the 1980s of the unions' campaigns for shorter working hours, charging that this broke the rule that the government keeps out of wage conflicts not involving public employees. (By law, these are a matter for employers and employees' representatives.) The unions were also vexed by the government's action to try to tighten up anti-strike legislation. 'We are not condemned to consensus,' Breit maintains. 'It can only be supported if one is able to have conflicts. People have to know that the unions have teeth.' All the same, Breit is careful to spell out that this should not spill over into confrontation; he publicly rebuked Kohl after the Chancellor suggested in autumn 1988 that the unions were showing 'enmity' to the government. The DGB chief told me he was genuinely shocked. 'I believe that is inappropriate. Look at where enmity got us in the Weimar republic. You can call us opponents of the government – but not enemies.'

West German trade unions pick their conflicts with care. Strikes are comparatively rare, but when they do take place they are meticulously organised and well-financed. Normally, in recent years at least, they end in union success. The last major labour showdown came in 1984 when the giant metal- and engineering-workers union, I.G. Metall, mounted a seven-week strike and forced through cuts in working hours from 40 to 38.5 a week, most notably in the pace-making car sector. While keeping its wage claims moderate, I.G. Metall later won agreement for a 37-hour week, paving the way for working-hour cuts in other industrial sectors.

The ultimate goal is a 35-hour week in the 1990s. Breit says the shorter working hours campaign is the best means of creating jobs; that it was 'absurd' of the Chancellor to try to stop the tide. Without success in pushing through cuts in hours, Breit reckons that German unemployment – steady at around 2.25 million in recent years – would be between 200,000 and 400,000 higher.

In jousting with the Government, the DGB is squarely on the side of the Social Democrats. But Breit warns that the SPD can no longer make 'big promises' about cutting unemployment. He is sceptical about the SPD's main hope for the Chancellorship in the 1990s, Saarland Prime Minister Oskar Lafontaine. In 1988 Lafontaine tried to court the middle-class vote by calling for reductions in working hours to be accompanied by proportional wage cuts. Trade unions immediately accused Lafontaine of furthering the policies of employers and betraying workers' interests. Breit believes that the Saar politician's thesis would dampen demand by reducing spending power – and suspects that publicity-conscious Lafontaine is simply trying to increase his profile.

Whatever the challenges facing the German consensus system, Breit wholeheartedly rejects the radical alternative offered by Thatcherite Britain. 'We don't want Mrs Thatcher's recipes. We have quite a different structure, another way of expressing our differences,' he says. Breit points out that the West German coal industry has achieved labour reductions on the basis of negotiations between unions and management, without the eruptions of the British coal-miners' strike in 1984-85. Britain, he says, is moving to a 'two-thirds society', where one third of the population is more or less excluded from prosperity and social advance. 'That is just what we do not want here.' German trade unionists' misgivings about the move to a more harmonised European Community stem, in part, from fears that elements of German social policy such as *Mitbestimmung* could be watered down. 'People are more sceptical, more sober about Europe,' Breit admits. 'Europe will bring chances – for workers, and for the unemployed.' But, pointing to the risks that German jobs could 'emigrate' to lower-cost countries, he adds: 'When the chances will come, and in which country, are questions which are still open.'

Breit detects a trend in West Germany towards a less cohesive society – and is worried about the possible consequences. He dismisses talk about economic rigidities as mainly propaganda from employers trying to force down industrial costs. 'We are not stiff and inflexible,' he claims. Recalling that his father used to cycle to work two miles a day, Breit says that today's workers think nothing of travelling thirty miles in their cars to get to their jobs. West German stability has been built on greater equality of income and wealth distribution than in Britain or France – but Breit now sees society becoming less egalitarian. He criticises the Kohl Government's reforms of tax and social security as placing disproportionate burdens on the worse-off. 'In cutting costs in health care, the Government should have done more to trim the drugs industry, hospital spending and doctors' costs. It shouldn't just unload the burden on to patients – they are the most vulnerable people.'

High unemployment, Breit concedes, has not up to now had much impact on West German politics. But, referring to increasing fragmentation of the popular vote and the rise of Right-wing radical parties, he says, 'I now think this is beginning to have an effect.' Long-term unemployment is clearly putting strains on society. 'People feel unsecure – they start to look for scapegoats. Unemployment is not just a very bad factor for individuals. It also has political implications. Hitler would never have got so many votes if the number of people out of work had not been so high.'

IV

Tyll Necker is an industrial spokesman who is a little worried that the consensus system has worked rather too well – and that the Germans are becoming too comfortable. Necker, the talkative owner of an agricultural machinery company in Schleswig Holstein, has been since 1987 chairman of the Federation of German Industry (BDI), grouping 80,000 companies from around the country. Born in 1930 in the suburb of Köpenick in what is now East Berlin, he moved to north Germany after the war. Like Breit, he took over his organisation at a testing time; the BDI's reputation suffered from the fall-out over the Flick political payments scandal during the 1980s and its president in 1977, Daimler-Benz board member Hanns Martin Schleyer, was murdered by terrorists in 1977. To protect him from potential terrorist attacks, Necker travels in an armoured limouisine with two bodyguards – although he tells his aides he would dearly like to give them the slip. When his term finishes at the end of 1990, he will probably go back to driving a Volkswagen.

Necker is anxious not to exaggerate his criticism of the country's economic system. Businessmen's well-broadcast complaints about high labour costs or details of the *Mitbestimmung* laws are regularly blamed by trade unionists like Ernst Breit for frightening away foreign investment. Necker, a breezy man with an expressive turn of phrase, says however that West Germany has failed to use the favourable conditions of the 1980s to put the economy into tip-top shape for the 1990s. He also played a high-profile role after the East German revolution in seeking to persuade the East Berlin authorities to import West German-style *soziale Markt-wirtschaft*.

Speaking at the federation's headquarters overlooking the Rhine in Cologne, he points out that the Federal Republic has profited from the international upswing during the 1980s. 'But the sun will not shine for ever.' Underlining Germany's dependence on exports, he says, 'If the international economy weakens, we will have a situation where demand for our capital goods weakens. That is the vulnerability of the Federal Republic. We should repair the roof in time – during the good weather.'[21] Some of Necker's plea for corporation tax cuts and more growth-boosting deregulation can be discounted as part of the BDI's normal lobbying. Industry as a whole showed sizeable increases in profits towards the end of the 1980s, and the German trade surplus has been going from strength to strength. The BDI's members do not have a down-and-out look; and Germany as a whole appears far from being uncompetitive. Necker however points to a long-term change in attitudes which could be storing up future industrial problems. 'If you look at the success of cooperation between management and unions since the war, we have saved ourselves many strikes. We work together in companies better than the international average. But difficulties arise when structures are formed which are difficult to alter. It's like having a 15-year election period when necessary corrections are not possible.'

Necker points to sluggish capital investment in the last few years to underline that companies are losing their appetite for risk. He complains about union rigidities preventing companies from laying off workers when times get tough, and about corporate tax rates twice the level in Britain. Working-hours cuts have continued, to a level well below that of most competitor countries. But he has little hope of any early change towards a more pro-business climate. In Britain, he says, Mrs Thatcher has carried out a revolution. 'But because of our proportional voting system, it is much more difficult to carry out a revolution like that here from above to below.' Additionally, like Breit, Necker reflects on the British coal-miners' strike and says that such a breakdown of consensus would be neither desirable nor possible in Germany. 'England is an older democracy,' he smiles, and turns to a sailing analogy. 'It can afford more violent

201

manoeuvres than we can here.'

Necker declares that he does not waste his time going to representational cocktail parties, but says that the chances for getting the BDI's views across to a wide spectrum of opinion are 'greater than before'. Being a practical company man himself helps him broadcast his message, he says. 'There's a multiplicity of ways of influencing people. You have to get to know people, influence them, argue with them.' Necker is not a member of a political party; he is close to the Christian Democrats – but this does not stop him, like other industrialists, from criticising the drift of the CDU under Kohl during the 1980s. There is no shortage of contacts between politics and industry. But German businessmen have started to complain that – whatever the party – politicians no longer speak their kind of language. Necker points out the small number of entrepreneurs who go into politics.* 'Politics has never had a very high reputation here,' he says. 'The best people go into more respected jobs.'

One of the most celebrated holders of political office to quit the parliamentary scene for industry is Manfred Lahnstein, now a board member of the Bertelsmann publishing and entertainment conglomerate. Lahnstein, a former state secretary at the Finance Ministry and head of the Chancellor's Office under Helmut Schmidt, served as Finance Minister for five hectic months in 1982 at the end of the Social Democratic coalition.[22] He says that, after the SPD lost power, he went into business to earn more money.[23] Lahnstein believes the gap in understanding between politics and industry is wider than it was during the early post-war period. As a member of Schmidt's inner cabinet, Lahnstein says he found the sporadic 'informal chats' between the Chancellor and his favourite circle of leading industrialists too stiff to allow a genuine exchange of views. He says that Bonn is much too geared towards meeting directors of large corporations rather than representatives of the small and medium-sized companies which form the real backbone of German industry. He concludes: 'Politics and business circles are without real contacts.'

Similar complaints about the poverty of dialogue with politicians are heard from other industrialists. West Germany's lack of a proper capital adds to the difficulties; Necker did not set foot in Bonn until he was 43. Ronaldo Schmitz, finance director of BASF, says, 'Bonn is a purely political capital. It is not a place for dialogue with industry. Industry meets politics more or less only when it is asking for favours. In

* See Chapter 4

England, when the ICI board meets, it will sometimes invite a politician for an informal discussion. This does not happen here.'[24] A year before he died, Rudolf Bennigsen-Foerder, the chairman of Veba, himself a member of the Christian Democrats, delivered the most cutting comment of all. 'Neither the Christian Democrats nor the Social Democrats understands anything about money, but at least the SPD is aware of this,' he said.[25]

Despite the industrialists' complaints, consensus has worked well for Germany as an economic spring-board and a social safety-net. As it starts to bridge the East-West divide, Germany is unlikely to find a better method to stay on an even keel.

10

Germany and the Jews

What then shall we Christians do with this rejected, damned race of Jews ... We must prayerfully and reverentially practise a merciful severity, that we may save some from the flames and the embers.... I will give my true advice: their synagogues and schools should be set alight, and what will not burn should be covered over and buried with earth, so that no man will ever again see a stone or a slag.

Martin Luther, 1543[1]

To practise his existence as a parasite, the Jew must deny his inner nature.... Yes, it can even go so far that a large part of the host people seriously believe that the Jew is really a Frenchman or Englishman, a German or Italian.

Adolf Hitler, 1925[2]

Jews are thought to be either the chosen people, or the *Untermenschen*. It is not accepted that we are normal like everyone else.

Charlotte Knobloch, president of the
Munich Jewish Community, 1988[3]

The story of German Jewry tells not only of genocide but also of genius, now gone. After persecution, exile and murder under the Nazis, the Jews in the post-war Federal Republic, in inevitably small numbers, have built up a new life. They are cloistered by worries about the past and shrouded by new taboos. Few Germans today realise the contribution of the Jews to their own culture, in particular the Jews' role in the growth of modern Germany between 1871 and 1933. Though absent, crucially, from the top strata of the army and the civil service, during this period they were increasingly assimilated. Believing they were no longer outsiders, many Jews were fatally unaware of their vulnerability. The Jews *belonged* to the nation which, under the Third Reich, turned round to seek their destruction.

Hitler's supreme legacy was to divide and suppress the identity of the

Germans – and to forge a new one for the Jews. Almost certainly Israel would not have been established in 1948 but for discovery, as the Second World War ended, of the extent of German atrocities in the extermination camps.

Post-war West Germany has made conspicuous efforts to ease the pain of the past, building close political ties with the Jewish state and paying more than DM60 billion in compensation funds to the survivors.* East Germany, claiming itself to represent Hitler's victims, has never attempted to make amends for Nazi crimes, but in 1988 announced willingness to make a symbolic indemnification payment to Jews living in the US. The change of policy is aimed above all at winning American support during a period of East-West détente – but it amounts also to a form of avowal of shared responsibility.

German Jews brought a sense of non-conformity to the centre of society. Germany is poorer now – the unpredictability is gone. In both parts of the divided nation anti-semitism is proscribed by law, representatives of the Jewish communities have regular meetings with government leaders and – at least in West Germany – films, books and discussion on the lessons of the Holocaust increase from year to year. But the effects of Nazism are pernicious and long lasting. The Jews in Germany are now a race apart.

I

The 19th-century Jewish cemetery in Schönhauser Allee in the Prenzlauer Berg district of East Berlin is not on any list of tourist attractions, but it is a recommended objective for any visitor to the eastern part of the city. The 22,800 graves packed over 12 acres by an underground railway station mark a memorial to the most dynamic period in German Jewish history. It was a glittering, ominous preface to the dark times which lay ahead, when even a rough grave would be a luxury.

In Schönhauser Allee lie the German Jewish *notables* from the last century. About 160 largely-forgotten German Jewish bankers are buried here; the number of gold Mark millionaires runs into the hundreds. The most restlessly brilliant representatives of German Jewry died in foreign

* See Chapter 2.

lands: Karl Marx, Albert Einstein – and Heinrich Heine, the German patriot, whose alert wit was suspected by serious-minded Germans as lack of depth or sincerity, yet who could write in 1824, 'At heart I love everything German more than anything else in the world.'[4] By contrast, in the Prenzlauer Berg graveyard are the Jews who believed they were secure at home in the capital of Prussia. They were conspicuous and successful during Germany's late transition from a rural to an industrial economy. They made a name for themselves in finance, business, medicine, the law, journalism, publishing and the arts. They also made enemies.

Here are the headstones of the parliamentarians Eduard Lasker and Ludwig Bamberger; Bismarck's banker Gerson von Bleichröder; composer and Berlin opera director Giacomo Meyerbeer; Josef Mendelssohn, one of the founders of the Mendelssohn bank, once the most important private bank in the country, whose business was later 'Aryanised' by the Deutsche Bank during the Third Reich; Max Liebermann, the painter; and Leopold Ullstein, the publisher.[5] Ullstein's company was also forced into 'Aryan' hands after the Nazis came to power, taken into possession in 1935 by a banking consortium. After the war, the Ullstein heirs sold the group – including the *Berliner Morgenpost* newspaper founded by Ullstein in 1898 – to the publishing empire of Axel Springer. Today the Springer concern's headquarters, towering commandingly above the western side of the Berlin wall, remit funds to East Berlin to pay for the upkeep of the Ullstein grave.[6]

At Schönhauser Allee there are also many humble headstones, some from more recent decades. Among the rows of worn Silesian granite tombstones is the last resting place of a Jewish girl hit during an Allied bombing attack during the Second World War. Wearing the yellow star marking her race, she was not allowed into the air-raid shelter.

When the cemetery was opened in 1827, Jews were still at the fringes of society. The rabbi officiating at the ceremony was reprimanded by the police for preaching in German, in a manner said to be 'imitating Christian traditions'. By the time burial space started to run out at the end of the century, the Jews had made a spectacular advance; but their emergence from the ghettos was not to everyone's liking.

The Berlin stock market crash of 1873, a reaction to an overheated boom in speculative railway stocks issued by the Jewish entrepreneur Bethel Henry Strousberg, wiped out many small investors' savings. They blamed their misfortunes on the greed of Jewish financiers. Not for the first time in German history, suspicion of a Jewish conspiracy spread around the country. The term 'anti-Semitism' – coined in

France during the 1850s – came into widespread circulation for the first time in Germany in the late 1870s.[7] Later, amid disintegration of the heady hopes of Imperial Germany, anti-Semitic resentment was to return with unbelievable virulence.

No German Jew trod the tightrope so precariously as Walther Rathenau, the eldest son of Emil Rathenau, founder of the AEG electrical company. Walther Rathenau headed the AEG supervisory board between 1912 and 1921, building it into one of the world's leading electrical concerns. For eight months after the First World War broke out, he played a vital role at the head of the raw material allocation section of the War Ministry, where he attracted the suspicion of both the military and his fellow industrialists. He was well aware of the enmity, writing in 1916, 'The more Jews fall in this war, the more persistently will their opponents prove that they were all sitting behind the front lines practising usury. The hate will multiply two- and three-fold.'[8]

Rathenau once admitted that he could not free himself from 'an uneasy feeling of encirclement and abandonment'. After the war, during the uneasy years of the Weimar Republic, he again found himself in the crossfire, attacked from the Left for his attachment to capitalism, from the Right for allegedly betraying Germany's interests. He became Foreign Minister in 1922, and soon was the target of Right-wing 'patriots' swearing to avenge the indignities of the lost war. Rathenau had a premonition he would be murdered. In June 1922, two months after his signature of the Rapallo Treaty with Russia,* he was killed by three young terrorists who ambushed his open carriage with pistols and a grenade while he was driving to the Foreign Office in the Königsallee. He was laid to rest in the family grave in the Wuhlheide cemetery in the Schöneweide district of what is now East Berlin, close to the Red Army-controlled suburb of Karlshorst where German capitulation was signed on the night of 8 May 1945.

Rathenau remains a permanent symbol of the threatened ambivalence which German Jews cannot escape – even in death, and even in authoritarian East Berlin, where anti-Semitism is deemed a characteristic of fascism. A few weeks before my visit to the Schönhauser Allee cemetery in spring 1988, a large number of graves had been desecrated by vandals from a local school. Their trial was well publicised by the East German media. Of course, the Communists blame this form of wrongdoing on a revival of Nazi tendencies in West Germany, transmitted to the East via western television.

* See Chapter 3.

East Berlin boasts the biggest Jewish cemetery in Germany – a 100-acre site at Weissensee to the north-east of the city. It was built up from the end of the 1870s onwards on ground which then lay well outside the city boundaries. This is Berlin's cemetery belt. Today the suburb, its people bustling amid the East Berlin grey, has more than half a dozen graveyards. The wealthiest Jews chose the distinction of the Schönhauser Allee, but Weissensee too is not short of well-off occupants. Some of their sepulchres are grandiose, bordering on *parvenu*.

Around 115,000 tombs are dotted among the trees, many overgrown; only about 1,000 are regularly maintained. Many places left for inscription on family tombs are empty, a reminder of how death came prematurely and elsewhere. Here lies a memorial, erected in 1927, for the 12,000 Jewish soldiers who died fighting for the Kaiser in the First World War. Near the cemetery entrance is the tomb over the remains of Herbert Baum, a Jewish Communist resistance fighter tortured to death by the Gestapo in 1942. The memorial was erected in 1949, testimony to the anti-fascist credentials of the East Berlin city fathers.

One Weissensee grave bears the name of the Tietz family, another victim of 'Aryanisation'. Tietz lives on today in High Streets all over West Germany, but very few shoppers know that the Hertie department store group – with a turnover of around DM6 billion, one of the country's leading retailing concerns – is the acronym for the Jewish founder of the company, Hermann Tietz. He set up his first store in 1882 in Gera, in what is now the German Democratic Republic. His descendants built up the group to what was said in the early 1930s to be the largest family-owned retailing concern in Europe. Boycott of Jewish department stores, together with the economic crisis, cut turnover by half from 1930 to 1933. The company was rebaptised 'Hertie' and taken over by the banks. With the family capital lost, chairman Georg Tietz was forced to quit the firm. He emigrated with his family, reaching the US in 1941 via Hungary, Yugoslavia, Liechtenstein and Cuba, and died in 1953. In Hertie's special centenary newsletter, published in March 1982, the present-day firm glosses over the 1930s episode, laconically blaming the change of ownership on 'the economy and mass unemployment' and 'the political situation'.[9]

By the end of 1937, approximately 30,000 Jewish businesses had been 'Aryanised'. The expropriations were a source of embarrassment for many West German companies celebrating 50th anniversaries during the 1980s. In a special anniversary publication in 1986, another large department store group, Horten, doctored a facsimile of a 1936 advertisement to hide that it was founded through the 'Aryanisation' that year of Alsberg, a Jewish company. Many other present-day companies took similar action to play down or deny altogether that they had been founded originally by Jews.[10]

The Jewish takeovers of the 1930s benefited the expansion of large industrial concerns like Flick, Mannesmann and Hoesch. The process also profited the big German banks, both by giving them additional shareholdings in industry and by enabling them to take over on favourable terms the business of once-flourishing private Jewish banks. Dresdner Bank, in the 1930s the largest bank in Germany, absorbed the Berlin banking houses Bleichröder and Hardy, while Deutsche took over the business of Mendelssohn.[11] Of the 1,350 private banks – many of them Jewish – in Germany at the end of 1932, only 520 were still in existence in 1939, mainly as a result of 'Aryanisation'.[12] The full story of the banking takeovers has yet to be told, partly because of the difficulty of gaining access to the records of the Big Three West German banks for the period.

The demise of Mendelssohn illustrated how private banks were taken over on a 'voluntary' basis. Hermann Josef Abs, the Deutsche Bank veteran who was one of the bank's key executives in dealing with the Nazis during the war, explained to me the circumstances. Deutsche Bank took over the banking house's liabilities and corresponding assets as well as about a hundred employees. Abs says that he was asked to take over the business by the senior partner of Mendelssohn, Rudolf Loeb, who visited him 'very excited' in March 1938 after the Reichsbank hinted that Mendelssohn should be prepared for closure or forced liquidation. Negotiations on the takeover took place over the next eighteen months. Abs has no regrets about any actions under Nazism; an art collector of repute, he says, 'I didn't touch a thing' when liquidated Jewish property was sold off.[13]

Abs lifts the corner of a veil over the story of the Petscheks, a Jewish industrial family in eastern Germany whom he has known since 1921. The Petscheks' lignite works were expropriated by the Nazis, and the family was forced to emigrate to the US. Abs helped them to achieve compensation after the war. 'If you could help a Jew under the Third Reich, to save either his property or his life, I never found anyone in my life to be as grateful. I was a recipient of this.' Abs says the Petschek operation involved 'delicate cleverness', but goes into no details.[14]

II

Forced selling of Jewish businesses was an essential part of the machinery of state anti-Semitism. At first, to many ordinary Germans as well as to the world outside, it did not look like the countdown to the Holocaust. Horst Krüger, the author, aged 13 when Hitler came to power, has described how, in his quiet Berlin suburb of Eichkamp, 'Every Eichkamper had at least one good Jew.' His mother preferred Jewish doctors because they were 'sensitive'. No one really noticed when Jewish neighbours started to move away. In the smallest and most unwitting of ways, the Jews were even agents of their own eventual destruction. Krüger writes: 'My mother went to Hermann Tietz – it was still Jewish – and bought the first swastika pennant.'[15]

The pressure rose relentlessly. A week after a government-sponsored boycott against Jewish doctors, lawyers, shops and businesses, on 7 April 1933 the Third Reich promulgated its first anti-Jewish ordinance, banning most Jews from the civil service. Further laws and decrees removed Jews from the medical, legal and journalistic professions and from the theatre. The 1933 ordinance ended up driving from their university posts about one quarter of German physicists. Jewish scientists started to emigrate in greater numbers – giving a powerful stimulus to American and British atomic research.* The first '*Juden unerwünscht*' (Jews not wanted) signs went up in cafés, restaurants and public buildings in the summer of 1935; the noose tightened further with the promulgation of the Nuremberg racial laws in 1935.** In April 1938 the order was given for registration of all Jewish property over 5,000 RM, a prelude to systematic confiscation. Then, on the night of 9 November 1938, came the organised outbreak of arson, looting and violence of *Reichskristallnacht*, the Night of Broken Glass. The pretext for the pogrom was the fatal shooting in Paris of the German diplomat Ernst von Rath by a young Polish Jew, Herschel Grünspan (Grynszpan), whose family had just been expelled from Germany. More than 250 synagogues were set on fire and 7,000 Jewish businesses plundered. Nearly a hundred Jews died, and around 26,000 were sent to concentration camps.

The British ambassador to Berlin, Sir Nevile Henderson – the

* See Chapter 13.
** See Chapter 2.

hapless agent of Chamberlain's appeasement policies – always tried to give the Nazis the benefit of the doubt. He described the violence in his memoirs in 1940 as a 'disgusting exhibition'. In a passage which shows the success of Joseph Goebbels' propaganda in permeating diplomatic minds, he said that one of the reasons for the 'orgy of violent ill-treatment' could have been that 'the German authorities were seriously alarmed lest another Jew, emboldened by the success of Grynszpan, should follow his example and murder either Hitler or one of themselves.'[16]

No one, not even the British ambassador, could now be in doubt that the Jews faced mortal danger. In the Reichstag in 1939, Hitler promised that the result of a world war caused by 'international Jewish finance' would be 'the destruction of the Jewish race in Europe'.[17] From September 1941 onwards, Jews more than 6 years old were forced to wear a yellow star. Writing in *Das Reich* at the end of 1941, Goebbels described the Jews as 'decaying mould on the culture of healthy peoples. There is only one remedy: cut off and discard.' Goebbels expressed astonishment upon learning that his tirades were published abroad 'even in England' – paranoiacally believing that such articles would inevitably endanger Jews around the world.[18] The first mass deportations to the death camps took place in 1942. In *Mein Kampf* a decade and a half previously, Hitler had already hinted at what was to come:

> If at the beginning of the [First World] war and during the war, twelve or fifteen thousand of these Hebrew corrupters of the people had been held under poison gas, as happened to hundreds of thousands of our very best German workers in the field, the sacrifice of millions at the front would not have been in vain.[19]

Finding the right tones in which to commemorate the genocide has always been a challenge for West German politicians. In 1951 Adenauer – clinging to the view that, 'There was a predominant majority of German people who abhorred the crimes committed against the Jews' – underlined that they had been carried out 'in the name of the German people', almost as if the Germans themselves were not involved.[20] Chancellor Schmidt, speaking on the 40th anniversary of *Reichskristallnacht*, gave a more realistic version: 'Very many Germans disapproved of the crimes....(but) all this happened before the eyes of a large number of German citizens.'[21] By the time the 50th anniversary came round, Chancellor Kohl's speech-writers went to praiseworthy lengths to give a still more forthright account. On 9 November 1988, Kohl delivered a well-received address at the rebuilt West End synagogue in Frankfurt. In contrast to Adenauer, he termed the anti-Jewish crimes 'unique genocide' which had been perpetrated 'by German hand'. The November 1938 Pogrom Night 'remains with us. In pain and in shame, it is part of our present,' he said.[22]

The past's hold over the present was dramatically underlined the next day when Philipp Jenninger, the Bundestag president, delivered an ill-prepared hour-long speech which showed over-explicitly why German anti-Semitism had flourished:

> In relation to the Jews: had they not in the past – so it was said then – presumed a role to which they had no right? Should they not at last put up with restrictions? Did they not perhaps even deserve to be put in their place? And, above all, did not the propaganda – with the exception of some wild exaggerations which could not be taken seriously – correspond in the main to (one's) own suppositions and convictions?[23]

Amid a torrent of controversy in Bonn, Jenninger was forced to resign twenty-four hours later. There were some hints – even from Jewish representatives themselves[24] – that the Jews might somehow be blamed for the rumpus.

III

The inexorable point about the Jews in Germany today is that migration and murder have taken their toll. Around 40,000 Jews are estimated to live in West Germany. Approximately 28,000 are in the religious community and there are at least 10,000 non-religious Jews.[25] No more than a few thousand Jews live in East Germany, and the eight religious communities in the state are down to only about 380 members. That compares with about 525,000 Jews living in the German Reich's religious community in 1933. The Jews living in Germany are dwarfed in numbers not only by the Jews in the US – nearly 6 million – but also by those in France (slightly more than 500,000), Britain (340,000) and Hungary (100,000). In 1933 around 1 million Jews lived in the German-speaking areas of central Europe (including Austria and parts of Poland and Czechoslovakia) which were later overrun by the Nazis.

212

Today, in the whole of that area, only about 60,000 remain – a reduction of 94 per cent.

In 1933 Berlin was the fifth largest Jewish city in the world, with a Jewish population of around 160,000. Approximately 55,000 were later killed in prisons and concentration camps. The former capital is still a focal point for the Jewish community in the two halves of Germany, but the Jewish voice is fragmented and confused. An increasing proportion of Jews living in West Germany comes from eastern Europe and the Soviet Union. The influx in recent years has brought a new lease of life – the average age of the West German community had fallen to around 40 from 46 in 1970. A new generation of German Jews has grown up, representing post-war immigrants or the offspring of the victims. Many of the parents, 'displaced persons' after the war, stayed in Germany not out of choice, but because they failed to gain immigration permits, for one reason or another, to the US or Israel. Compared with their parents, those of the new generation are less defensive about living here, and quicker to speak out over real or supposed anti-Semitism. Some have been moving up the social ladder again in areas such as the legal profession, but only very few have returned to that old Jewish stronghold, banking. They wonder more loudly than their parents to what extent they are German, or Jewish, or both.

The man with the job of keeping the Jews together is Heinz Galinski, chairman of the 6,000-strong West Berlin Jewish community since 1949 and, since the beginning of 1988, chairman of the West German Jewish Council. He sits in an office in the Berlin community building in the Fasanenstrasse, erected on the site of the 1912 synagogue burnt out by the Nazis on *Reichskristallnacht*, left as a ruin until 1958. A bespectacled man of passion and bitterness, Galinski was born in Marienburg, in West Prussia (now Poland). He survived Auschwitz and Bergen-Belsen, but his mother, father and first wife were all killed by the Nazis. Galinski is well into his seventies, looks younger, but cannot throw off a shrewish, hunted look. He has a reputation for lecturing the Germans, and is not well liked.

For Galinski, 1988 is a year he will want to forget. The Jewish Council discovered that his predecessor Werner Nachmann, who died in January 1988, embezzled around DM30 million in Bonn government compensation funds. The affair came as a bombshell. At a time when Israel was receiving a bad press internationally over anti-Palestinian oppression in the occupied territories, the much-publicised revelations contributed to a general lowering of Germany's post-war sympathies for the Jewish cause. Nachmann, close to the Christian Democrats, was

213

highly regarded by the Federal Republic's politicians, partly because he did not make too many disturbing noises over the past. The Jewish Council and the government's auditors plainly failed to apply adequate controls on his business dealings. Galinski termed the Nachmann scandal the biggest setback for Germany's Jews since 1945.

Galinski receives me without warmth, not deigning to shake hands.[26] He describes himself as 'a good Jew and a good citizen (of the Federal Republic'. Defensively, overreacting to an unasked question on why he chose to settle in post-war Germany, he snaps, 'I do not have to live here.' He says that part of his job is to close gaps in German knowledge about the past: 'I sound warnings when needed. I cannot remain silent.' However, he draws a generally positive balance of post-war Germany's relationship with Jewry. Galinski praises President von Weizsäcker, and points to his regular set-piece meetings with Kohl. One focus of Galinski's warnings has been a building occupied by Left-wing squatters in the harbour area of Hamburg. Slogans scrawled prominently on the wall, as well as urging 'Destroy the International Monetary Fund', called on passers-by to 'Boycott Israel, its goods, Kibbutzim and beaches.' Galinski protested that this was reminiscent of National Socialism, and the offending inscriptions were removed.

On the other side of the Berlin Wall, only about three miles north-east from the Fasanenstrasse, sits Galinski's opposite number Peter Kirchner, the chairman of the East Berlin Jewish community. He has his offices in Oranienburger Strasse, a street full of pock-marked buildings not far from the Spree and the Alexanderplatz – a depressing urban landscape still showing unmistakable signs of wartime bombing. Kirchner's offices are next door to the famous Oranienburger Strasse synagogue, once the splendour of Germany Jewry but now reduced to a ruin. Built in 1866, with enough room for 3,000 worshippers, the temple was put to the torch on *Reichskristallnacht* in November 1938. The attack was impeded by the police (one of the few examples where the forces of law and order intervened), but the building was gutted by Allied bombs in 1943. Of the cupola-topped red brick pile, today only the façade remains. Pigeons nest amid the truncated towers, and a small tree sprouts from one of the Byzantine arches. A plaque records the synagogue's tormented history. For years, rebuilding has been discussed; in 1989, at last, the scaffolding went up and work got under way.

Kirchner, a breezy doctor in his fifties in a short-sleeved blue shirt, tells me that he now has fresh hope. It is impossible to say how much this is an act put on for my benefit (and possibly for his too).[27] He states

214

that a new plan for reconstructing the synagogue – one of the signs of the East Berlin leadership's revived interest in the Jewish community – will cost around 40 million East Marks, and that an international foundation has been set up to try to raise money. As another sign of goodwill towards the Jews, the East Berlin authorities have shelved plans mooted a few years earlier to build a road through the Weissensee cemetery. As well as announcing agreement to pay compensation to Jewish Holocaust victims, East Berlin has even been dropping hints of possibly forging diplomatic relations with Israel.

'Why this greater warmth towards the Jewish community?' I ask him. The answer is that Erich Honecker and the rest of the gerontocratic East Berlin leadership realise that the Jews in East Germany are at risk of dying out – a final demographic consequence of Hitler which seems to stir vague feelings of unease. Kirchner says: 'They [the East Berlin government] know that, in a hundred years time, there will still be a Christian community here. They want to say the same thing about the Jews.'

The East Berlin religious community is down to only about 190 people. Kirchner says hopefully that births are picking up, and that 140 younger non-religious Jews are now affiliated to the community, trying to rediscover their Jewish roots by studying Jewish literature and taking part in cultural evenings. However, breathing new life into the East Berlin community may be an impossible task. Squeezed between allegiance to religion and the all-consuming desire not to disrupt relations with an authoritarian state, the East Berlin Jews have desperately little room for manoeuvre.

One effort at revitalisation misfired badly. A Polish-born American rabbi, Isaac Neuman, came to East Berlin in autumn 1987 as the first rabbi there for twenty-two years. He tried to bring in some new ideas, but left after only nine months following well-publicised disagreements with the East Berlin community. Neuman upset the cautious and highly traditionalist Jewish leaders by pushing for reforms and more assertiveness towards the state; he wanted to create what he called 'a living Jewish community' – larger office facilities, a school, a library and a free university for adults. In East Berlin, these were plainly utopian ideals. Siegmund Rotstein, the president of the community, pained by Neuman's challenge to the accepted order, lectured the rabbi for failing to carry out his duties properly. In turn, Neuman charged the state-controlled press with anti-Semitism.

Neuman, too, is a survivor of Auschwitz. His mother, father, six sisters and one brother were murdered. He told me that he stopped being orthodox in the concentration camps.[28] 'I got clobbered when I tried to cover my head when praying,' he says. He criticises the elderly East Berlin Jews for concentrating too much on 'laying wreaths in cemeteries' and for failing to press demands for better facilities out of fear of the Communist regime's disapproval. He adds darkly that, after his experience in East Berlin, it would not be too difficult to imagine officially-sanctioned anti-Semitism again taking hold of Germany. 'Next time it will be a different colour star.' He was also simply homesick, missing American chocolate and newspapers and disturbed about East Berlin air pollution. Neuman admits he was fascinated by some of the younger members of the community: 'They know all about Marx, but not about Moses.' And his sojourn ended on a happy note. He married a lady from the East Berlin community who subsequently emigrated with him to the decidedly more relaxed environment of Champaign, Illinois.

IV

One city in Germany where rejuvenation of the Jews is going strong is in Frankfurt. The community has 5,000 members, many of them post-war immigrants from Eastern Europe. Thirty thousand Jews lived here before the Nazis took over. Forty per cent of today's community were born after the Second World War. About 15 per cent are people in their early twenties or younger, the 'third generation' of post-war Jewry. A modern community centre in the residential West End of Frankfurt, close to the city's banking skyscrapers, was opened in 1986. It cost DM30 million, with two thirds of the money put up by the *Land* of Hesse and the city authorities.

The centre boasts a kindergarten and organises a wide range of cultural activities, from films and dances to discussion evenings. The events are attended by about 35,000 people a year – most of them non-Jews. But the shadows have not totally lifted. The centre is fitted with reinforced glass doors and protected by an elaborate video-surveillance system; outside in the street a police van is parked; guards are on hand around the clock.

'We need to be protected not from Arab terrorists, but from Left- and Right-wing German extremists,' says Michel Friedman, in charge of the centre's cultural activities.[29] He says that 10 per cent of the centre's budget is spent on security. Bomb warnings are a regular occurrence, and an explosion in spring 1988 caused extensive damage, but no injuries. Thankful that sophisticated electronics make the security system relatively unobtrusive, Friedman explains that he is pleased that the centre does not need to be strung with barbed wire. The Jewish community must try to maintain its own separate identity, but also avoid looking like a fortress. 'We try to be part of this city, and of this society – not to be a ghetto, but not to be assimilated,' Friedman says. A lawyer in his early thirties, he was born in Paris; his parents survived the Warsaw ghetto and Auschwitz. Together with his family he moved to Frankfurt in the early 1960s, taking German nationality when he was 18. Friedman is a member of the Christian Democratic Union – but fiercely criticises tendencies on the Right to try to brush over the unpleasant aspects of German history. 'You can't just take Bach and Beethoven without Goebbels and Himmler and Hitler,' he says.

The Frankfurt community has a reputation for standing up for its rights. A Frankfurt Jewish group staged an on-the-spot protest during the notorious 1985 visit by Kohl and President Reagan to the Bitburg war cemetery, where it turned out that SS troopers are buried. Also in 1985, the Frankfurt community stopped performance of a controversial play *Der Müll, die Stadt und der Tod* (Rubbish, the City and Death) by the late playwright Rainer Werner Fassbinder, centering on an unscrupulous Jewish property speculator mixed up in prostitution. More recently, the community has been demonstrating against plans to construct a city building over the excavated remains of Frankfurt's medieval Jewish ghetto.

Despite mass media attention given to commemorations such as *Reichskristallnacht*, Friedman says schools do not devote enough effort to education about the past. Many young people say, 'Don't bother me,' he declares. He feels the Germans would like to wash their hands of the Nazi period: 'The Holocaust was a Jewish tragedy, but a German problem. It's their history as well.' Worried about the attraction of extreme Right-wing political groups for young people, he believes that the growth of the ultra-Right will be an increasing challenge for democracy: 'We feel more polarisation.'

Ignatz Bubis, the chairman of the Frankfurt Jewish community since the beginning of the 1980s, is himself a well-known property developer. Some believe that the figure of the 'Rich Jew' in Fassbinder's play may have been based on Bubis, who is a possible candidate to take over eventually from Galinski as the head of the country's Jewish Council. 'The Jews have changed over the past 10 to 12 years. A more active generation has come along,' says Bubis, an energetic man in his early

217

sixties with small eyes like pebbles. Coming originally from Breslau, now part of Poland, he lost his father, sister, brother, brother's wife and daughter, and grandfather at the hands of the Nazis. 'Before 1933, the Germans were less anti-Semitic than other countries,' he says. 'But things happened here which couldn't happen elsewhere. The Germans have a tendency to be narrow-minded, and to listen to authority. That's the difference.'[30]

V

The paradox about anti-Semitism in Germany is that it lives on, in spite of the lack of Jews. Its most visual form comes from the periodic scrawling of swastikas and Nazi slogans on Jewish cemeteries. Other episodes periodically make the headlines – a German military official who wrote that the mass gassing of Jews was a 'victory for the principle of efficiency',[31]; the Jewish doctor in a quiet small town in Hesse whose patients were threatened with death by Right-wing extremists[32]. According to an opinion poll in 1988, about 15 per cent of the West German population hold anti-Semitic views.[33] Another Allensbach poll a few years earlier, carried out in conjunction with surveys in other countries, showed that 20 per cent of West Germans agreed with the statement that all Jews should go back to Israel, against 24 per cent in Austria, 17 per cent in France and 9 per cent in the US. Anti-Jewish feeling in Germany does, however, seem to have lessened over the years. According to Allensbach, 37 per cent of the population in 1952 agreed with the view that it was better to have no Jews in the country.

Why do the Germans not get on with Jews? One reason is that they resemble each other so much. Henrich Heine believed that anti-Semitic virulence stemmed from spiritual kinship: 'Both peoples are so alike that one might regard ancient Palestine as an oriental Germany.'[34] The author Rudolf Walter Leonhardt wrote: 'The Jew as a type suffers somewhat in Germany from the fact that the intellectual, as a type, is not valued too highly,' although he pointed out that the academic, by contrast, meets great respect.[35] Franz Schönhuber, the leader of the ultra-Right Republican party – who disclaims being an anti-Semite by pointing out that he was once married to a Jewess and has a half-Jewish daughter – sees rivalry in terms of German perfectionism. 'Both Jews and Germans always want to be top of the class. The Germans want to be the best in everything. They are the best scholars – and the best murderers.'[36]

Because most Germans do not personally know any Jews, suspicions about Jewishness tend to be unusually paranoid. I remember one taxi-driver regaling me with a pseudo-scientific explanation of how he could spot Jews by the bone structure of their nostrils. Because of his Jewish-sounding name, Rudolf Augstein, the publisher of *Der Spiegel*, is sometimes accused by irate readers of being Jewish. Out of interest, he says that he has investigated his family history but has not unearthed evidence of a Jewish connection.[37]

Herbert Strauss, an American Jewish professor born in Würzburg who is head of the Centre for Anti-Semitic Research at the Technical University in Berlin, says anti-Semitism in Germany is probably no worse than in France or Britain. But his centre has established that – as a result of social pressure and tough post-war laws against anti-Jewish utterances – anti-Semitism has been driven underground, from where it can resurface in new, less controllable forms.[38] The legal protection against anti-Semitism is enshrined in laws banning anti-constitutional parties (such as the National Socialists) and their propaganda. Among other things, this means that bookstalls selling new editions of *Mein Kampf* are liable for prosecution. Second-hand shops can sell pre-1945 copies on the grounds that this is part of the antiquarian business. Only few of such volumes are still in circulation. About 10 million copies of *Mein Kampf* were printed during the Third Reich. Every newly-married couple after 1936 was given a copy, although only few professed to have read the book. Huge quantities of Hitler's work were burnt or buried in 1945 by Germans fearing recriminations as the Allied armies closed in.

As another form of check to anti-Semitism, in 1985 the Government brought on to the statute books the so-called 'Auschwitz-lie' bill, under which it is a criminal offence to deny or play down the importance of Nazi war crimes. The law is meant essentially to have a deterrent effect. In the first three years of application, there were about twenty prosecutions.

Ambiguities persist in official relations with Israel. Tel Aviv's veteran ambassador to Bonn, Jitzhak Ben-Ari, who returned home from Germany in 1988, tends to open conversations on the matter by saying: 'Relations with West Germany have settled down and are normal.' Then he goes on to explain why they are not.[39] West Germany is Israel's second largest trade partner after the US; about 160,000 German tourists visit the Jewish state each year. But this does not stop the ambassador, speaking in his bunker-like embassy building in Bad

219

Godesberg, from talking of his experience as a boy in Vienna, seeing old Jewish people sweep the streets with toothbrushes. To illustrate how the German people like to try to shut out their uncomfortable past, he also relates the story of his surrealistic journey by train from Vienna in 1938 to the Dachau concentration camp, where his father was being held. When he asked people for directions in 1938, they were glad enough to tell him where the Jews had been taken, he says. But when he went back to Dachau a few years after the war, in 1953, and asked to find the way there, the concentration camp had somehow been expunged from their memories. 'They didn't know where it was,' comments Ben-Ari with grim humour. He adds: 'For Germany to be accepted in the community of nations, a part is expected of them – to remember what they did. Not to open old wounds, but to remember.'

After forty years, the wounds have not healed – and an increasing number of Germans are irked by the ritual of having to remember sins committed by their fathers and grandfathers. The Israeli President, Chaim Herzog – a man who tries to do his best for international understanding – paid an emotional return visit to the site of the Bergen-Belsen concentration camp in April 1987. Herzog, who served with the British army during the war, had been to Bergen-Belsen before, as an army officer in April 1945 when the British liberated the camp and discovered its horrors. Today, the camp in which 50,000 people died has long been demolished, but the black heathland on which it stood is maintained as a memorial and a place of melancholy pilgrimage. 'I do not bring forgiveness with me, nor forgetfulness,' said Herzog in 1987. 'The grief of your death will be eternally with us.'[40] Galinski, speaking at the *Reichskristallnacht* ceremony in 1988 in Frankfurt, relentlessly warned the Germans that the Jews would not let history pass into forgetfulness. He saw the battle being carried forward by future generations: 'Driven by their own emotions, our children – the children of the victims – will carry out our task.'[41] Galinski's prescription may be necessary, but it is hardly a recipe for goodwill.

VI

'The Jewish people will probably never again play a role in German culture,' states former Chancellor Helmut Schmidt. Schmidt has revealed in recent years that his grandfather was Jewish. He says his previous reticence over admitting his ancestry stemmed above all from his wish to shield his father – who died in the early 1980s – from stigma attached to illegitimate birth[42]. The reason may however be more complicated than that: the word *Jude* (Jew) in Germany today is difficult to utter in public. As well as being used – as in other languages – as a term of abuse, the word is simply embarrassing. One of the very few Jewish politicians in West Germany today is Jutta Oesterle-Schwerin, a member of the Greens party, who came to the country from Israel in 1962. She says people prefer to use the terms 'Israeli' or 'Jewish fellow citizen', thinking these more polite. By avoiding the word 'Jew', she charges, such people are guilty of a form of 'disguised anti-Semitism'.[43]

Edgar Bronfman, the chairman of the Seagram drinks group who is president of the New York-based World Jewish Congress which links Jewish communities from seventy countries, is well accustomed to wading into the fray over anti-Semitism. Yet when he came to Bonn in the summer of 1988, partly to discuss with German politicians the controversy over the Nachmann affair, West German journalists at an hour-long press conference were too embarrassed to ask questions, leaving foreign correspondents to do nearly all the talking. 'They don't put tough questions to a Jew here,' commented Bronfman afterwards.

Under the surface of German-Jewish relations lie a lot of strained nerves. One leading company chairman says in private that he is Jewish, but asks for his name not to be revealed as this could damage his business standing. Josef Joffe, the Jewish foreign editor of the *Süddeutsche Zeitung*, is one of a handful of Jews in relatively prominent positions. He says it is healthy that younger post-war Jews are moving increasingly into mainstream society and careers, but he points to the unnatural elements of the relationship: 'Many Jews live in a ghetto, the walls of which are made of German guilt feelings.'[44] Michael Fürst, a Hanover lawyer who is chairman of the Jewish Council in Lower Saxony, says Jews in Germany have to 'show the flag that they are here – to show capacity to survive'. Although a moderate who believes Galinski adopts an over-harsh tone in rebuking the Germans for real or supposed anti-Semitism, Fürst too is wary about German xenophobia. It would be only a short step from 'Turks Out' slogans, he told me, to similar campaigns against the Jews – a warning which has since gained potency with an increase in agitation against foreigners from the far Right.[45]

In another example of uneasiness, the Jewish author Henryk Broder has accused German intellectuals of displaying 'enthusiasm for dead Jews' (such as Einstein, Freud or Marx), as a hypocritical way of covering up their 'anti-Semitic soul'.[46] The new leader of East

Germany's Socialist Unity Party at the end of 1989, Gregor Gysi, came in for some attention because of his Jewish descent. Eli Wiesel, the Nobel prize-winning Jewish novelist, voiced apprehensions that 'an anti-Semitic wave' could be sparked off by the new leader's opposition to a united Germany: 'Many Germans will simply say: "Look at this Jew! We want reunification and he, the Jew, is against it." '[47] Charlotte Knobloch, the dynamic chairwoman of the Munich Jewish Community, says she regrets – for her childrens' sake – staying in Germany after the war. 'If we had gone to the US, life would have been less complicated.' She says that when her teenage daughter told an unsuspecting friend that she was Jewish, the friend blurted out in amazement, 'I thought the Jews had horns.'[48]

At the other end of the age scale, Erich Friedenthal, a retired Jewish doctor in his eighties, is living out a quiet twilight in a modern old people's home in Neustadt an der Weinstrasse, a wine-growing town in the Rhineland Palatinate. He has known great turbulence – but now has more than enough time for reflection. Dr Friedenthal, a frail man of puckish intelligence and humour, was forced by the anti-Jewish campaigns to quit his practice in Berlin, and emigrated to Palestine in 1940. After serving with the British army during the war, he returned to Berlin in the 1950s, settling in Neustadt in the 1970s on his comfortable *Wiedergutmachung* pension. He lived with his wife (now dead) for nine years in a small Jewish old people's home in the town, but had to move out into a larger privately-run home in 1987 after most of his fellow Jewish inmates died.

The new home has the air of a luxury hotel and his room has a balcony and a fine view over the Palatinate vineyards. But the move away from the Jewish home to an institution where he has daily contact with elderly Germans was not to Friedenthal's liking.[49] He says he can spot former Nazis across the dining room: 'When I see their faces, people of my age, I can tell whether they were active [in the Nazi movement]. I didn't want to have anything to do with them then, and I don't want to have anything to do with them now,' he says. When I ask him whether he feels German or Jewish, Friedenthal replies, 'Before the arrival of Hitler, I was German. Since then, I am a Jew.'

In a few years time, in many smaller towns like Neustadt, there will be no Jews left. Across the country, with the passing of the years, the guilt which has bound together the post-war Germans and the Jews is also dying away – and there is very little else to take its place.

11

Occupied Country

Why must all these horrors come upon a fair green earth?.... It is because in the dark, cold northern plains of Germany there exists an autocracy deceiving a great people, poisoning their minds from one generation to another, and preaching the virtue and necessity of war. And until that autocracy is either wiped out or made powerless there can be no peace on earth.

James Gerard, US Ambassador to Germany, 1917[1]

A country's unconditional surrender does not give the victors the right to keep it occupied for ever.

Konrad Adenauer, 1950[2]

We are certainly sovereign, there is no question about that, but the Americans do what they like. They ask our government if they are allowed to do what they have already carried out.[3]

Dieter Hildebrandt, 1982[4]

As Allied soldiers in 1945 took possession of ruined Germany, officers pasted up notices on town walls assuring the Germans, 'We come as conquerors, but not as oppressors.'[4] The war victors were following a proliferation of partly contradictory aims, involving a mixture of coercion, correction and control. The victor powers laid down demilitarisation of Germany as an essential condition for the country's return to normal statehood but in fact – one of the most paradoxical consequences of the Cold War – the opposite happened. The Federal Republic in 1955 received its sovereignty, but only as part of a security agreement under which West Germany set up a new army and the foreign troops maintained their presence. The foreign forces on German soil have acquired the status of partners rather than armies of occupation. Yet, after more than forty years of peace the military presence is no longer a source of reassurance. Since the arrival of Mikhail Gorbachev in the Kremlin, the Germans have started to feel threatened less by the weapons aimed at them from the Warsaw Pact, more by the NATO arsenals on their own territory. The military arena holds the clues to the unravelling of the German Question.

I

Ramstein is a small town in the Palatinate on the western fringes of the Federal Republic. For centuries this wooded region on the French border has been in the path of invading and retreating armies. First mentioned in historical annals in 1215, Ramstein village was completely destroyed during the Thirty Years' War. It was occupied by the French during the Napoleonic Wars, annexed by the Bavarians in 1816 and taken over again by the French after the First World War. During the Second World War, the Luftwaffe used the local Autobahn as an airstrip. Since the 1950s, it has been the Americans' turn to take up residence; the township of 18,000 inhabitants has watched the largest US Air Force base in Europe grow up. Built under a Franco-German agreement in 1951, it carved out 3,000 acres of land from forests and pastures.

In 1972, the base was made the headquarters of the US Air Forces in Europe. It also hosts support units for the West German air force and those of five other NATO countries, and is estimated to pump $300 million annually into the local economy. Counting the collection of bases around here and the nearest large town, Kaiserslautern, a total of 70,000 Americans – 25,000 servicemen and women and 45,000 dependants – live in the region. This adds up to the largest single group of American citizens outside the US, but it is just part of the roughly 560,000-strong American forces community in West Germany, made up of 240,000 military and 30,000 civilian personnel plus 290,000 dependants.

Kaiserslautern is known in American forces jargon as 'K-Town', in line with the informal rule that any German word of more than two syllables is impossible to pronounce. The US presence in the Palatinate is underscored not only by the F.16 fighters swooping overhead, but by the roadside clusters of McDonalds and Kentucky Fried Chicken establishments, and car, video, insurance and rental agencies. Horst Gieb, the owner of the stylish Rosenhof hotel and restaurant near the Ramstein base, lamented to me at the end of 1987 about slack business from US servicemen on account of the falling dollar. For 1988, he told me, 'Forecasts are bad.'[5] Gieb's words were prophetic.

In spite of sporadic criticism from the Social Democrats and local church groups, for years the annual August air display at Ramstein was a regular attraction for aeroplane enthusiasts from all over south Germany. The show on the last Sunday of August 1988 started in brilliant sunshine, and ended in horror. At 4 o'clock in the afternoon, three aircraft of the Italian air force's *Frecce Tricolori* stunt acrobatics team collided in mid-air over the heads of more than 200,000 spectators. In the resulting inferno, more than 30 people were killed outright and 400 injured. The accident came at a particularly sensitive time. For months, opposition had been growing in the Palatinate region from politicians and local residents to the noise and safety risks of low-flying training by Ramstein jets. Rupert Scholz, the Bonn Defence Minister – still new to the job after taking over in May – announced an immediate ban on all acrobatic flying displays, including those by the Allies. Politicians from Left and Right started a public squabble over responsibility. At an emotional memorial service for the victims in Ramstein parish church, Richard Burt, the American ambassador, quoted – a little desperately – from Goethe: 'Death is an impossibility that suddenly becomes a reality.' He promised a thorough investigation and reminded the Germans that the US Air Force was flying 'for freedom'.[6]

As the death toll climbed to 70 in the following months, and the German government started to settle the tens of millions of D-Marks of compensation claims, it became clear that the Ramstein disaster marked a watershed in West Germany's dealings with its NATO allies. News filtered out of a chaotic lack of cooperation between German and American ambulance and rescue teams sent to the accident. Although caused by Italian aircraft – an air force not stationed in West Germany – the accident exacerbated political controversy over the 68,000 hours of military low-flying practice carried out annually over West Germany, one-third by the Luftwaffe and two-thirds by NATO allies. At a time when the superpowers had agreed nuclear arms cuts and the Kremlin was signalling a wish for détente, more and more Germans were chafing under the inconvenience of West Germany's defence burdens. Some people were even asking whether it was necessary to have an army at all. Ramstein reopened an old debate on whether the Federal Republic had really regained sovereignty when it joined NATO in 1955 – or whether, as some politicians on both Left and Right were beginning to proclaim, West Germany was still an 'occupied country'.

II

'When all traces of Nazism and militarism have been effectively and finally extirpated,' said Winston Churchill in 1945, 'there will be a place one day for Germans in the community of nations.'[7] Germany has entered it. Prussia and its military spirit have been expunged from the map. East and West Germany emerged out of the Allied war zones as separate states, each a partner in the military and economic alliances of its respective power bloc. All the points of the 1945 Potsdam 'purposes of occupation' were fulfilled – except the objective which was first on the list: 'The complete disarmament and demilitarisation of Germany'.* Across the cold northern plains as well as the southern valleys and forests, to the East and West, the conquerors remained. Armed forces in East and West Germany were reinforced in the early 1950s as the crisis over the Korean war heightened confrontation between the US and the Soviet Union. The soldiers stayed on – but, today, as Germany moves towards unity, they look set, before too long, to be going home.

In East Germany, the Soviet army's 'West Group' maintains 380,000 soldiers – directed from its headquarters in Zossen-Wünsdorf south of Berlin – not far from the scene of a Prussian victory over Napoleon's army at the Battle of Grossbeeren in August 1813. The Soviet air force in East Germany is thought to be around 40,000 strong. Additionally, East Germany has its own 172,000-strong armed forces (army, navy and air force), of whom 55 per cent are conscripts. In the Federal Republic, six NATO countries – the US, Britain, France, Belgium, Canada and the Netherlands – maintain about 400,000 military personnel, 344,000 soldiers and 55,600 airmen. The US, Britain and France station a further 12,000 soldiers and airmen in their sectors in West Berlin. These forces back up the 490,000 men in the West German Bundeswehr, approximately 45 per cent of whom are conscripts.[8]

Across East and West Germany, the two blocs muster the world's most concentrated array of weaponry. The forces include 21,000 main battle tanks – or nearly one third of total East and West tank deployment between the Atlantic and the Urals; 7,400 pieces of artillery and rocket launchers; 2,250 combat aircraft; and nearly 900 helicopters. More than 2,000 nuclear warheads, the bulk of them for use with artillery capable of firing either nuclear or conventional shells, are believed to be

* See Chapter 3.

stockpiled in West Germany; there are at least as many in East Germany.

The land and air forces deployed in the two halves of Germany comprise 1.4 million military personnel (not counting reserves). In the Federal Republic and West Berlin, there are 685,000 in the army and 160,000 airmen; in East Germany there are around 500,000 soldiers and 80,000 air force personnel. It is salutary to make the comparison with 1938. At the end of that year, Germany's land and air forces totalled just over 1 million men,[9] spread across an area (counting Austria) roughly 40 per cent greater than the territory of today's two Germanys. This means that the current concentration of men under arms in East and West Germany – a territory half the size of Texas – is nearly twice as high as it was during the year when Hitler was preparing for total war. It is not hard to see why West Germany – well before reunification fever broke out – was anxious for a speedy agreement on lowering forces in Europe under the Vienna disarmament talks which got under way in 1989.

As representatives of the NATO alliance, the foreign troops in the Federal Republic are guarantors of freedom and democracy. But they are also an uncomfortable hint that, in the strategic chess game between Washington and Moscow, Germany is both a pawn and the board on which any European military skirmish would be played out.

The historic agreement by the US and the Soviet Union in December 1987 to eliminate their medium-range nuclear missiles made the Germans more aware of the huge stockpiles of nuclear and conventional weapons still on their soil. The entente struck between Reagan in the White House and Gorbachev in the Kremlin impressed the Germans – and made them hungry for further steps towards disarmament.

Particular attention focused on the short-range atomic weapons remaining in Europe after the superpower accord – arsenals which the US and Britain are particularly anxious not to give up. Since these weapons have a range of less than 500 km, they would if used – as a matter of sheer geography – explode only on German soil. Egon Bahr from the Social Democratic Party is a prime advocate of negotiating the elimination of nuclear weapons from the centre of Europe – a policy which directly counters the strategy of the US and Britain. He says, 'We are not braver than the Japanese. After the first ten nuclear explosions, all will for defence would be lost.'[10] Helmut Schmidt has long doubted the value of such short-range nuclear armaments.[11] He told me: 'What you call tactical weapons will have the same psychological effect on the defenders' nation as Hiroshima had on the Japanese. Once you use one

227

of these so-called tactical weapons, the Germans will just throw up their hands.'[12]

Such views are shared on the Right. Volker Rühe, one of the Christian Democrats' leading defence experts, who in 1989 became Chancellor Kohl's right-hand-man as the CDU's general secretary, pointed out in 1987 – in a phrase which quickly became a ghoulish countrywide slogan – 'The shorter the range, the deader the Germans.' Alfred Dregger, born in 1920, the ultra-conservative leader of the Christian Democratic Union and Christian Social Union Bundestag grouping, a veteran of the Eastern Front during the Second World War, says that the Federal Republic would be the victim of its own weapons. He has a horror above all of the short-range 'battlefield' nuclear shells which can be fired from artillery deployed around the Federal Republic by various NATO armies. 'Nuclear artillery are weapons which can only be used by an expeditionary force in a desert or in a country where you don't care what happens. Think what would happen if this artillery were used by our conscript army against an undefended population (in Germany). The war would be over,' he told me.[13]

To many in both East and West Germany, the massed military might underpins a post-war order which appears to take insufficient account of Germany's own interests. The Germans are caught in a trap: the foreign armies and their weapons are both a reminder of, and a rescue from, the consequences of their history. As the barriers between East and West Germany came down, a new conundrum came into view in 1990: how could the presence of foreign troops be reconciled with German unity? Both US and Soviet forces are being reduced under the Vienna negotiations; but because of the crumbling of the Warsaw Pact, pressure is likely to build up for a complete withdrawal of Soviet troops from East Germany. Departure of the West Group would almost certainly start the countdown for NATO troops to leave West Germany too. Even if the Russians pulled out of the East, the US government would like to keep around 100,000 soldiers in the West as a guarantee against the Germans ever becoming again a source of instability in European politics. Such a policy is, however, unlikely to be accepted by American taxpayers – or by the Germans themselves.

III

Military occupation formally ended on 5 May 1955 as the Relations Convention came into force proclaiming the Federal Republic 'a sovereign state'. On 6 May, West Germany became a member of NATO. A Status of Forces convention replaced the Occupation Statute under which the Allies had based troops in the country since the foundation of the Federal Republic in 1949. The next four years were spent in negotiating a detailed agreement to codify the 'special conditions' of NATO forces on West German soil. This accord, known as the Supplementary Agreement to the general post-war NATO Status of Forces Agreement, became operational in 1963 between the Federal Republic and the six NATO countries with a military presence on its territory. In the years afterwards, most operational matters relating to troop, vehicle or aircraft movements were nearly always settled on the basis of smoothly-working cooperation. But, in the emotional aftermath of the Ramstein accident, German politicians perusing the documents started to complain that NATO forces enjoyed extra-territorial NATO rights. Although hedged with qualifications to uphold West German interests and legal procedures, the Supplementary Agreement set down that foreign forces

- have the right to cross the borders of the Federal Republic or to move within and over the federal territory in vehicles, vessels and aircraft (Article 57).
- shall have the right to conduct manoeuvres and other training exercises in the air in such measure as is necessary to the accomplishment of (their) defence missions and in accordance with orders or recommendations which the Supreme Allied Commander in Europe or any other competent authority at the North Atlantic Treaty Organisation may issue (Article 46).
- may take all the measures necessary for satisfactory fulfilment of (their) defence responsibilities (on bases and manoeuvre areas) (Article 53).

Rudolf Scharping, the Rhineland Palatinate Social Democrat leader who for several years had been leading a campaign against the heavy American military presence in the region, claimed that the NATO agreements 'restrict German sovereignty'. He was joined by voices on the Right. A week after the Ramstein accident, a bitter editorial in the conservative *Frankfurter Allgemeine Zeitung* hinted at a conspiracy to keep

German citizens in the dark: 'In contrast to its allies, the Federal Republic is not fully sovereign. This state of affairs, well known to the experts, has always been largely left unspoken by politicians.'[14]

Just as between Dregger and Bahr, there was a Left-Right consensus on the issue. An editorial in the Left-leaning magazine *Stern* lamented: 'Nearly half a century after the end of the war, the Federal Republic is still a state of lessened, limited sovereignty. Treaties which are kept secret in important passages degrade the Germans to a form of junior partner in the Alliance.'[15]

Alfred Mechtersheimer, a specialist in military strategy in the Greens parliamentary grouping in Bonn, was formerly a lieutenant in the Luftwaffe. He has uncompromising views over the Federal Republic links with NATO – but they are shared by many ordinary people too. 'If there are foreign troops in a country, that country cannot be sovereign,' he says. 'To think that the presence of foreign forces here improves our security is simply to drive unpleasant thoughts out of our minds. We would be the battle area. We would be destroyed.'[16]

Even Horst Teltschik, Chancellor Kohl's Sudetenland-born foreign policy adviser, weighed in to the fray with a light-hearted though revealing complaint to US ambassador Richard Burt. Driving home the point about inconvenience caused by American flight training, he told Burt that in 1988 during his summer break on the Tegernsee lake south of Munich his afternoon naps were spoilt by low-flying aircraft.

In 1986, in an effort to praise the West Germans for their contributions to NATO, Burt had pointed out that 'No other western country has such a density of military personnel, military installations or military activity on its soil.' Burt underlined that West Germany provided 4,000 military installations and training areas for the use of allied forces at no cost, and put up with more than 500,000 aircraft sorties a year from seven allied air forces. 'The burden on the German population in terms of noise, traffic congestion, manoeuvre damage and other inconvenience is unique.'[17]

Being unique can sometimes be uncomfortable. Just over four months after Ramstein, in December 1988, an American Thunderbolt fighter-bomber on a routine training mission crashed into the town of Remscheid near Düsseldorf, killing six people, injuring fifty and causing Blitz-like damage. It brought the 12-month total of flying accidents involving military aircraft to more than thirty, three of which had just missed West German nuclear power stations. One opinion poll showed that 89 per cent of the population wanted to end low flying. Health authority reports indicated that residents in low flying areas around the country suffered hearing and circulatory problems and high blood pressure.

The Bonn government spoke out for cuts in low flying to appease public opinion, while the NATO air forces insisted that further reductions in flying exercises below 1,500 feet would endanger operational preparedness. All the political parties supported a symbolic suspension of low flights in the period up to the New Year, and dozens of local protest movements stepped up the campaign for a permanent ban. One of the most active is based in the picturesque Palatinate wine-growing town of Deidesheim, not far from the scene of the Ramstein tragedy and directly below the flight path of many of the jets from the base. Renate Wittkugel-Hiller, the initiator of a 120-strong protest group, told me, 'This has nothing to do with anti-US feeling'; indeed, her husband is American and helps run a Palatinate vineyard. 'It's a question of principle – it's a great burden.' Because of the daytime noise, 'children wake up at night in fear'. The best outcome would be if Ramstein closed altogether, she added.[18]

That is not likely to happen. In spite of successive post-war charters aimed at normalising relations between West Germany and the war victors, occupation rights of the Americans and the other wartime powers have not been fully abrogated. The US, the Soviet Union, Britain and France still maintain rights over 'Germany as a whole'. These powers will remain as long as there is no German peace treaty; they give the forces of the US, Britain and France in the Federal Republic a different quality and status compared with those of the other three NATO members with a military presence – Belgium, the Netherlands and Canada. The West German government does not have the clear-cut legal right to ask Allied forces to leave its territory against their will, or to force reductions in troop levels or weapons systems. The limitations on West Germany's freedom of action are starting to become politically more irksome.

Foreign military rights over 'Germany as a whole' are underlined most demonstrably in Berlin, where the four wartime powers maintain supreme authority; but some vestiges of original occupation rights are also on show in East and West Germany. The Soviet Union keeps three military missions on West German soil, grouping around fifty military personnel in Frankfurt, Bünde (Westphalia) and Baden-Baden, representing the headquarters of the original US, British and French occupation zones. In East Germany, Britain, France and the US each have a mission in the royal town of Potsdam. The members of each of the missions are widely assumed to be working for their respective intelligence agencies. They are under the jurisdiction not of the German authorities but of the military commander of the corresponding victor power.

Military jurisdiction over the East-West German border is exercised not by the Bundeswehr but by the US and British armies and air forces. US bases throughout the Federal Republic for decades have been used, without the consent of the Bonn authorities, to give logistic help for foreign military operations ranging from the Vietnam war to actions in the Gulf or against Libya during the 1980s. The Allies enjoy widespread rights over the military training areas granted to them after the war. Of the twenty large manoeuvre areas in the Federal Republic – many of which were originally used by the Prussian army – thirteen are run by the Bundeswehr and seven by the Allies. One per cent of the entire territory of the Federal Republic is taken up by military bases and training grounds. West German citizens have the right to compensation for damage carried out by army manoeuvres, but the allied forces are exempt from legal action. In lawsuits over military affairs, the plaintiff has to take the Bonn government to court instead.

IV

Even before Ramstein, West Germany was already starting to feel isolated in the NATO alliance. The superpowers' 1987 nuclear disarmament agreement set off a dispute not only about the missiles which remained, but also about new ones which the US and Britain wanted deployed across German territory. In rare agreement, both the Christian Democrats and the Social Democrats came out in opposition to plans by the two senior nuclear weapons states in the alliance to deploy a new generation of upgraded missiles in the Federal Republic in the mid-1990s.

The German misgivings over the missiles cut little ice – initially at least – with either the US or Britain. General John Galvin, the American supreme commander of NATO in Europe, stoutly defended the plan to replace NATO's 120-kilometre-range Lance missiles, capable of carrying warheads of between 1 and 100 kilotons, with new weapons of 450-km range. Using one of the folksy analogies beloved of American four-star generals, he told an audience in Bonn that modernisation of nuclear weapons was basically the same as a company owner replacing part of his bus fleet when it grew old. 'The new buses will be better and more

232

comfortable than the old ones.'[19]

Margaret Thatcher, the British Prime Minister, pointed out in 1988 that Germany's sensitivities basically resulted from defeat in the Second World War. 'The Germans have the main armies on their soil because they are in the front line. That is geography combined with history,' she told a British TV interviewer, adding:

> If you are on the front line, then if they (the enemy) cross that front line then of course you would be the first victim unless you won every battle.... Look at history. You cannot deny history. You cannot deny that it was Hitler who created the last world war and had to be defeated and German freedom started the day the West won. They know that. That is their geography. It is their history. They are on the front line and the greater their resolve to deter, the greater the certainty of their peace will be.[20]

Mrs Thatcher's tactlessness over the Lance replacement was compounded by serious diplomatic errors by the Foreign Office in the winter of 1988-89. Britain failed adequately to recognise Chancellor Kohl's dilemma over the short-range nuclear missiles issue, and believed, misguidedly, that he was willing to push through a decision in early 1989 on upgrading the Lance weapons. All this amounted to a serious set-back for British influence on Bonn during a critical period of German policy-making. In spring 1989, the West German government successfully beat back a plan by the US and Britain for an immediate decision on 'modernising' the Lance missiles. NATO agreed to postpone any decision until 1992.*

In view of accelerating rapprochement between East and West, the Lance modernisation issue has effectively been buried – but it has left a scar. The row provides one reason why NATO's principles of nuclear deterrence – justifying nuclear arms as a means of dissuading the Soviet Union from attacking West Germany with conventional armies – have lost ever more credibility in West German public opinion. According to a collection of opinion polls in 1988, only 20 per cent of the population had faith in deterrence.[21] Three-quarters of West Germans said that they wanted West Germany to remain a member of NATO; a majority still believed that American troops safeguarded peace. However, a growing minority appeared to favour an allied troop pull-out: 37 per cent of the West German population said they would welcome a withdrawal of American troops, against 38 per cent who thought this

---

* See Chapter 3.

would be regrettable.[22] Only 18 per cent of the population said they were worried about the military threat from the East, compared with 49 per cent at the beginning of the 1980s and more than 60 per cent at the height of the Cold War in 1962.

As the sense of threat diminished, readiness to accept defence burdens also fell. At the end of 1988, only 67 per cent of the population had confidence in the Bundeswehr, compared with regular levels of around 75 per cent in polls during the 1970s and 1980s. Roughly 40 per cent of young men of call-up age classified soldiers in the Bundeswehr as 'potential murderers'. The percentage of the general population favouring cuts in defence spending was around 40 per cent, well above the 20-30 per cent backing in previous years going back to the 1960s. Reflecting a general increase in pacifist feeling, during 1988, the number of young men rejecting call-up on grounds of conscience grew to one in eight of the draft.

The fraying of defence consensus proved a formidable challenge for Defence Minister Rupert Scholz. Born in Grunewald in Berlin (now in the British sector) in 1937, he was the ninth holder of the job since the Ministry and the Bundeswehr were created in 1955. Donnish and bespectacled, a professor of constitutional law who had never served in the army, Scholz was one of the least warlike of Defence Ministers, seldom missing an opportunity to talk of his boyhood memories of the wartime bombs dropping on Berlin. Additionally, he was also the quickest to leave his job. In April 1989, Chancellor Kohl removed Scholz in a cabinet reshuffle. Although hardly militaristic, Scholz gained a reputation for arrogance and made himself unpopular with the electorate by refusing to take account of growing anti-military feeling in the population. He went down in the record books as the country's shortest-serving Defence Minister, holding office for just eleven months. Scholz was replaced by Gerhard Stoltenberg, previously the Finance Minister, who faced the thankless task of coping with a growing squeeze on military funding and manpower.

A prospective drop in the number of young men of call-up age, a result of the low birth-rate since the 1970s, placed a growing question mark over whether the Bundeswehr would be able to maintain its pledged total of 490,000 men under arms during the 1990s. To try to counter the impact of the falling number of draftees, in 1984 the government agreed an unpopular move to increase the period of national service to 18 months from 15 months. The longer conscription period was due to have come into effect in June 1989, but it became increasingly contested as the date for introducing the plan drew nearer.

The government shelved the plan a few days after Scholz was sacked.

Scholz may not have been very good at encouraging public support for the Bundeswehr, but he delivers a first-class analysis of the fundamental reasons behind flagging German backing for the military status quo. The post-war German defence consensus was built on the perception of threat from the East, Scholz told me half-way through his ministerial tenure, speaking in his office on the Hardthöhe, the hilltop Defence Ministry complex outside Bonn.[23] The fall in perception of threat from the Soviet Union in the wake of Gorbachev's arrival in the Kremlin increased questioning about 'the legitimacy and necessity of defence'. Scholz underlined that, 'Many Germans are not sufficiently aware that defence is a self-evident part of statehood. This reflects the fact that, over many years, the Federal Republic, through the division of Germany, had a provisional character.' The Germans have a 'sensitive psyche', Scholz added, increasing their yearning for peace and disarmament:

> The Second World War is not forgotten. It has not been purged from people's awareness. Subconsciously, that is living on still. The catastrophe of 1945, the terrible war and terrible time of National Socialism, are still present in the awareness of the people.

Scholz is a man of sensibility. In October 1988, accompanying Kohl on a trip to Moscow, he told an audience of Russian tank officers: 'I was never a soldier, but I know the horrors of war as a result of my own experiences. My father fell in Stalingrad in 1943. I was a child then. And as a child I lived through the Second World War in Berlin. I am fully aware of my responsibility today to devote my whole strength to security, preventing war, and peace.'[24] It was a statement with which few West Germans would disagree. Yet will the Germans be able to safeguard peace if they have less and less desire to put up an army?

V

NATO's forces in the Federal Republic are fanned out in eight operational sectors facing the border with East Germany and Czechoslovakia. Dutch, British, German and Belgian forces make up the Northern, and German and American troops the Central Army Group. Canadian and French forces are held in reserve in the south, with an American military brigade similarly placed in the north. Of the key components of the Soviet army on the other side of the 860-mile frontier with East Germany, the 2nd Guards Tank Army lies in the north, the 3rd Shock Army in the centre and the 8th Guards Army to the south.

The nerve centre for America's military operations in West Germany and Europe is the Baden-Württemberg capital of Stuttgart, a prosperous town where lush vineyards still sweep down to the railway station. Since 1967, the headquarters of US forces in Europe has been installed in a patch of wooded land in the Stuttgart suburb of Vaihingen, in a barracks used during the Second World War by the Wehrmacht's 7th Panzer regiment. The US European Command has a strength of 326,000 military personnel in land, sea and air forces, three-quarters of whom are in West Germany, in 211 army and 13 air force installations. The Command lists with bravado as its 'area of responsibility' 77 countries stretching over Europe, Africa and the Middle East – including all the east European members of the Warsaw Pact.

The main operational element of the American army in Europe is also based in Stuttgart, in a complex in the suburb of Möhringen. The barracks area was used during the war to billet German female troops training as air defence controllers. Today this is headquarters for the 71,000 soldiers of the VII Corps, deployed throughout Baden-Württemberg and Bavaria, who live here with 90,000 members of their families. The Corps drove through to Germany from Normandy after the D-Day landings in 1944, returned to the US in 1945, then came back to Germany in 1951 as part of the strengthening of forces touched off by the Korean war.

General Ronald Watts, the lantern-jawed commanding officer of VII Corps, tells me that Second World War experience 'teaches us to maintain a strong force in peacetime'.[25] The Germans may complain from time to time about manoeuvre damage, but Watts says his forces need a high state of readiness. 'The Washington Redskins do not go out and play without practising each week.' With military precision, he says, 'We are ready to fight if required and conclude hostilities on terms favourable to the Alliance.' To help counter belief among the German population that the Soviet menace is diminishing, Watts gives regular 'threat briefings' to businessmen and other local groups. He points out that the Warsaw Pact has 90 divisions (or 1 million men) ready to face European NATO armies. The Pact has an advantage in tanks of 3 to 1, and in artillery of between 3 and 4 to 1, says General Watts. 'We have to try to inform the public of how we see things,' he adds. 'I cannot deal in what I would like the threat to be, but how it is.'

What about integration of American soldiers into the local community? The fall in the dollar has bitten into army spending power in the last few years, both restricting the soldiers' social life and driving home to local people the decline in America's economic potency. Some taxi drivers in south German towns these days offer special fares to help out the GIs, and in 1987 the American embassy co-sponsored a funding drive to raise DM4 million from German businesses to improve the soldiers' often only meagre contacts with German people. General Watts says the US army tries to give his men a 'home from home'. He rejects the idea that American troops live in a 'ghetto', asserting, 'The quality of soldiers is the best I have seen in 32 years.... They have taken language courses – it doesn't make them linguists, but they can ask for the *Bahnhof* or order a meal.' Could the day come when American troops are no longer needed in Germany? 'Only if something occurred to take away that tremendous threat capacity which exists,' he replies firmly. 'I do not see any indication of this.'

The second core component of the US army in West Germany is the V Corps, another veteran of the First and Second World Wars. It was a unit under V Corps control which made the historic contact with the Russians on the Elbe in April 1945. The Corps returned to Europe in 1951 and has been based in Frankfurt since 1952. General John Woodmansee, the commander, directs operations from a building north-west of Frankfurt city centre with an intriguingly chequered history – the former headquarters of chemical conglomerate I.G. Farben.* Woodmansee is a lean, fast-talking extrovert, surrounded by a staff of brisk orderlies. He has just come in from a morning jogging session in the rain. During the air raids which destroyed most of Frankfurt during the war, the massive block – built in parkland on the site of a former lunatic asylum – was spared from bombing, reputedly because the Americans had already earmarked it as their post-war HQ. In 1945, the building became headquarters for Allied European forces, as well as the seat of the US military governor.

The V Corps took it over seven years later. General Woodmansee turns to a campaign map to explain why he and his 60,000 V Corps soldiers are still here. 'It is not an accident that they assigned defence of the most dangerous avenue of approach in the central region to V Corps.' The business capital of Frankfurt and the surrounding heavily built-up conurbation straddle the 'Hessian corridor' from the Thuringia Forest, which is the way the Soviet 8th Guards Army would come in the

* See Chapter 2.

event of an invasion. 'If they cut through to the Rhine-Main rivers, occupying the most important air bases, the war would be over,' he says. 'I don't think there would be much damage (to the towns and cities). If I were the 8th Army, I would not want to mess around in Frankfurt. I would want to be coordinating the parade. But I would not rubble the major installations.'[26]

Wouldn't the use of nuclear weapons cause widespread destruction? Woodmansee replies that his nuclear-capable artillery and Lance missiles, as well as the Air Force's nuclear-armed aircraft, would be 'the card of last resort'. He elaborates: 'If all else fails, we start slugging it out with nukes. We would love to be able to defend this territory convincingly and decisively with conventional forces. I believe this is an achievable goal.... If we destroy the 8th Guards Army east of the Vogelsberg mountains in the first few days, why would we be wanting to rub a little salt in by starting a nuclear war?'

Of course, there is an alternative scenario which would lead to nuclear escalation – and this is precisely the outcome that the Germans fear. Woodmansee spells out the dilemma with irrefutable logic:

> If the 8th Guards were to destroy the bulk of the V Corps force, cross the Rhine and the Main in two days, take over air space and inderdict air access, splitting the central area between north and south, and if General Saint (Commanding Officer of the US Army in Europe, based in Heidelberg) had no more reserves, then we would be in the position of saying, 'Do we surrender or do we throw nukes?'

Then, he says, the answer would be up to the politicians. Since it is a question which would decide the fate of millions of people living in one of the most built-up countries in the world, Woodmansee sensibly does not want to hazard a guess as to what the response would be.

Woodmansee makes clear that the Germans regard the activities of his men as a nuisance. Christian Democrats and Social Democrats alike are competing with each other to catch disgruntled local people's support:

> One hears increasingly of neighbourhood politicians who would prefer not to have helicopters driving down property values, asking 'Are all these manoeuvres really necessary?' or 'Do you have to shoot guns at night?' The burdens of bearing arms and being prepared appear greater than the advantage of being protected. The Germans don't want us to go away – they just don't want us in their neighbourhoods.

The Germans' mixed feelings on American troops started to come to the surface in 1990 as the US announced the first reductions in its European force presence. The US army in West Germany brings in an estimated annual cash flow of more than DM12 billion, and gives work directly and indirectly to 170,000 Germans. Ironically, one of the areas facing the greatest problems through job losses is Rhineland-Palatinate, where 22,000 Germans are employed on the state's eight NATO air bases (including Ramstein). Woodmansee says he understands German sensitivities. He adds: 'It is not normal for a country to have military forces from another country stationed on a permanent basis. It's not a stable state of affairs … So if you are in the American army, you have to be some kind of a diplomat.'

VI

When in April 1945 French troops neared Baden-Baden in the foothills of the Black Forest, some residents with a knowledge of history feared a repetition of the events of 1689, when the most famous of German spas was razed by the forces of Louis XIV. At the end of the Second World War, however, a German general was mercifully persuaded not to heed his orders to defend the town at all costs. So its elegance was virtually unspoiled when the French took it over as the seat of their military government in the zone carved out of S.W. Germany.

Baden-Baden enjoyed a long-standing reputation in Paris as a luxurious retreat. It quickly doubled in population as French army and civil service personnel poured in, naming their new acquisition a second Vichy. The French commandeered hotels, the thermal installations, garages, shops and the theatre, turned the townspeople out of villas and apartments, and felled large sections of the surrounding forest for firewood to ease the post-war French energy shortage. Local people say these episodes have not been forgotten; but General Jean-Louis Brette, a grizzled parachutist and Foreign Legion veteran of around sixty who has commanded the French forces in Germany since 1987, insists that relations with his German hosts are a model of conviviality.[27] The General has brought up his five daughters to speak German as their first foreign language. Brette is clearly a man with a well-developed taste for the good life. Speaking in his bright and spacious office at the Baden-Baden HQ, he emphasises: 'The reception is not just

239

encouraging – it is enthusiastic.' He brings out his large diary to stress the number of festive dinners and social occasions he attends in the company of local mayors.

The 48,000 French soldiers with more than 300 tanks in the Federal Republic are part of the Strasbourg-based 1st Army; a further 2,700 troops are based in West Berlin as part of the city's occupation forces. Since France left the integrated command of NATO in 1966, French forces are not allocated a specific area in NATO defence of West Germany, and their formal role is restricted to protecting approaches to French territory. Under President Mitterrand, France has undertaken to come to West German assistance in case of conflict, and French troops have taken part in manoeuvres with German and NATO forces. However, basic ambiguity about how the French would operate in wartime has not been cleared up. Regular reassuring statements from Paris have not eliminated fears in the Federal Republic that France's shorter-range nuclear missiles would be used to destroy targets on German territory.

General Brette points out that his soldiers – three-quarters of whom are conscripts – train regularly with the Bundeswehr. He plays down language problems, as well as the difficulties over harmonising different types of western weapons and equipment. 'It doesn't matter if it's a British or French cartridge, as long as it hits the target.' When I ask him about German complaints over manoeuvre damage, he replies, 'We are very careful to cause the population the smallest irritation possible. We try to explain that the French forces in Germany are here not as vigilantes but in a mission of deterrence – to defend peace, liberty, independence.'

The General seems to admire the Germans – and to find them puzzling. Take the environment, for instance: 'The French have much less fear about risks. A Frenchman will go to the first mountain spring he comes to and drink the water straight away – he doesn't have the same scepticism.' Could a time come when the French forces would no longer be required in Germany? Delivering a minor lecture on how armies have kept the peace in Europe since 1945, Brette unleashes Gallic realism to put Teutonic fantasies back in their place. 'We would all like to be in the Garden of Eden – but it won't come tomorrow, or even the day after tomorrow. We have to be wary of dreams and pious hopes.' The French rather like it in Baden-Baden – and don't want to leave just yet.

VII

After Germany's surrender in May 1945, the British set up army and air force headquarters for their occupation zone in hotels and villas in two Westphalian spa towns, Bad Oeynhausen and Bad Eilsen. Once it became likely that the military presence would be long-lasting, the British army built a new headquarters west of the Rhine near the Dutch border in 1952-54. It chose a woodland site near the town of Rheindahlen close to Mönchengladbach. There is a certain tradition behind the British presence in Mönchengladbach, going back to the War of the Spanish Succession. In 1703 the Duke of Marlborough used Rheindahlen wood as a billet for some of his 19,000 Redcoats on his way to lay siege to French-held Bonn.

Today, the Rheindahlen base is a small British town – a cluster of barracks, hostels, schools, churches, shops and sports-fields. It is headquarters for 56,000 army and 11,000 Royal Air Force personnel in West Germany, accounting for nearly one-third of the UK's peace-time army and 40 per cent of the RAF's front-line aircraft. A further 3,000 forces personnel are in Berlin. Counting civilian staff and dependants, the British community in Germany totals 180,000. General Sir Brian Kenny, wavy-haired and athletic-looking, is commander-in-chief of the British Army of the Rhine, equipped with about 600 Challenger and Chieftain tanks. He pays tribute to general relations with local communities, saying they are 'better than ever before'.[28]. But he points out, 'The lower tolerance of local people towards military training is a fact of life. The West Germans' standard of living has gone up – and experience of the war is less.'

One centre of controversy is the British training area in the rural Senne region of Westphalia, which first came into military ownership for William II's army in 1890. It was made over to the British in 1945, although it remains formally owned by the federal government. Local residents have been trying to block construction of a mock 'battle village' in the Senne for use by the army in training. However, because the British army cannot be taken to court, the residents are having to sue the Bonn government – and have become increasingly frustrated over the affair. The army is also involved in sporadic disputes with environmentalists over training on the Lüneburg Heath in north Germany, which, unlike the Senne, is not a closed manoeuvering area but open countryside. A further headache for the General comes from

241

the threat of terrorism. Security is tight, but intermittent attacks from the Irish Republican Army on barracks and off-duty soldiers have become an unpleasant fact of life.

Air Marshal Sir Anthony Skingsley, the erudite-looking commander of RAF Germany, has his own rearguard action to fight: over opposition to low flying. 'The problem brought on by developments in the Soviet Union – Gorbachev and *glasnost* – is that they have given the impression that peace has broken out,' Skingsley muses. 'This is not yet so. We have to point out that we have seen no diminution of the threat.' He is in charge of seven squadrons of Tornado fighter-bombers – and they need to practise ground-hugging flights to avoid enemy radar. He says that the RAF has already cut low flying in West Germany by 14 per cent over the past six years. In spite of German protests about the noise, he is adamant that it cannot be reduced any more.

General Kenny has a particular interest in the swirling political debate over the modernisation of the Lance nuclear missiles which form part of the British army's arsenal in the Federal Republic. He pleads for a new longer-range successor to Lance, which could then enable the British army to scrap some of its nuclear howitzers. 'Conventional arms on their own do not deter war. We need a minimum number of nuclear weapons to back up the NATO strategy of flexible response,' Kenny says. Skingsley also believes that his Tornados will need to be armed in the 1990s with new air-launched nuclear missiles. Whatever the Germans' reticence about the presence of nuclear weapons on their soil, they have probably not seen the back of them. However, in the 1990s, the question of who makes the decisions on deploying weapons in an over-militarised land will be increasingly taxing. The Germans believe in peace – in both East and West – and cannot understand why NATO seems still to be preparing for war.

12

The Arms Makers

Through its construction orders in Germany, it is the navy which from the beginning has given the shipbuilding industry the most significant and decisive impulse.

Alfred von Tirpitz, 1899.[1]

As the industry which built up the air force, you must associate yourself with the air force to the last. What importance does your work have against that of the nation? What does it matter if one day you make chamber-pots instead of aeroplanes? That is all the same!

Hermann Göring in speech to aircraft industrialists, 1938.[2]

Should the reunited Germany be the Germany of Messerschmitt-Bölkow-Blohm, Mercedes and Herrhausen?

Stefan Heym, 1989[3]

Emerging into freedom in February 1951 from the prison of Landsberg in the Bavarian countryside, Alfried Krupp von Bohlen und Halbach gave an impromptu press conference to the photographers and journalists clustering outside. Along with twenty-eight other war criminals, Krupp was released early as part of an American amnesty designed to show favour towards a German state which had now become a partner in the struggle against Communism. Krupp had spent 2½ years in Landsberg, the jail where Hitler wrote *Mein Kampf* in 1924; counting earlier custody, he had been locked up for nearly six years. The obvious question came from the waiting reporters: would Krupp be making cannon again? With his mind no doubt on the Korean war, Alfried Krupp replied that, ultimately, the question would be answered by the government. 'I hope that for Krupp, it will never again be necessary to go back to the armaments business. But the production of a factory depends in the last resort not on the will of the proprietor, but on the policy of the government.'[4]

In 1949, the young Christian Social Union politician Franz Josef

Strauss said: 'Anyone who again picks up a gun – his hand should drop off.'[5] Before he died in 1988, though, the Bavarian Prime Minister had become the most effective lobbyist for West Germany's arms exporting companies, many of them based in the electronics belt around the fast-growing Bavarian capital of Munich. Over the past thirty years, starting with the Federal Republic's entry to NATO in 1955, the Germans have gradually regained expertise in weapons manufacture. Reflecting West Germany's post-war reticence about fostering a new arms industry, the government has maintained, in formal terms, a restrictive policy on arms sales abroad. But during the 1980s, West Germany advanced to become the world's fifth largest arms exporter after the Soviet Union, US, France and Britain. The Federal Republic sold $7.6 billion worth of weaponry abroad between 1983 and 1987.[6]

Most striking of all, Daimler-Benz, the motor and engineering giant, has been driving down the road towards becoming Europe's most powerful aircraft and defence conglomerate. In a move in 1988-89, backed by the Bonn government, to take over Messerschmitt-Bölkow-Blohm (MBB), the country's biggest aerospace group, Daimler-Benz stirred up one of the country's fiercest industrial controversies. Because of the legacy of the Third Reich, the arms business in the Federal Republic is shrouded in a certain furtiveness, even embarrassment, not found in Britain, France or the US. The Germans may have become good at making war-planes, tanks and guns again; but they are not proud of it.

I

Professor Ulrich Gabler represents a well-qualified and enduring slice of the German defence industry. A master engineer and U-boat veteran of the Second World War, now well into his seventies, he is a shambling, loquacious man still with a seafaring air. More than four decades ago, he founded Ingenieurkontor Lübeck (IKL), a company which designs some of the world's most advanced conventionally-powered submarines – and symbolises post-war Germany's remarkable re-entry to the top of the armaments league.

Outside the squat offices of the Professor's submarine company, wild flowers bloom by the perimeter fence. IKL maintains its headquarters by the port-side on the outskirts of Lübeck, the idyllic medieval city in

Schleswig Holstein immortalised in Thomas Mann's novel *Budden-brooks*. The company's roots stretch back to the beginnings of the submarine age before the First World War. IKL's products now roam the seas of the northern and southern hemispheres. Twice, after defeat in 1918 and 1945, Germany's submarine-building capacity was scuttled by the war victors. Each time, the professor played a part in building it up again.

Re-established by Gabler in 1946, IKL has designed 105 military submarines for the West German navy and fifteen other countries ranging from Israel, India, Norway and Turkey to a batch of Latin American nations including Brazil, Chile and Argentina. In a murky transaction which has been the subject of a Bonn parliamentary investigation, IKL's blueprints also appear to have made their way illicitly to South Africa during the 1980s.

Gabler keeps a fatherly eye on IKL in a consultancy capacity, which brings him to the IKL offices for two or three hours a day. At the end of 1978 he sold the company to three members of his senior staff; the sales price was DM3.5 million. 'I could have sold it for three times as much to the Americans, but I wanted to keep it independent,' he says.[7]

In the early years of the Second World War, he saw active service as a deputy submarine commander harrying Allied vessels. He recalls that he had a hand in sinking 36 Allied ships: 'I was something of an ace – terrible,' he says now with a grimace. In 1942 Gabler was brought into naval construction, becoming head of the development office in submarine design headquarters near Blankenburg in the Harz mountains, over the border in what is now East Germany.

Gabler helped to design new high-powered German submarines such as the legendary Types 21 and 23 commissioned towards the end of the war, which formed the precursors of today's modern non-nuclear submarines. He also worked on the revolutionary Type 26, still under development when the war ended; it was one of the many examples of advanced German weapons technology which, if completed in time, could have changed the course of the conflict. Gabler, a respected figure for three decades on the NATO submarine circuit, has one simple comment on Type 26: 'Thank God it did not come into service.'

IKL can trace its origins back to Krupp's Germaniawerft shipbuilding company in the Schleswig Holstein capital of Kiel. In 1902 the shipyard built what ranks as the world's first fully-serviceable battery-powered underwater vessel, baptised *Forelle*. Showing the company's export acumen, the boat was sold to Russia. During the First World War, Germany built up more experience of submarine warfare than any other combatant. Although the Treaty of Versailles proscribed submarine production as part of a general ban on the German arms industry, in 1922 Krupp transferred its U-boat expertise to a company in The Hague set up for the purpose – just one illustration of how Germany circumvented the Versailles armaments provisions.

Krupp's Dutch 'front' company sold submarines to a number of navies, including those of Japan, Finland, the Netherlands, Turkey, Russia, Sweden and Romania. After Hitler denounced the Versailles Treaty and brought German rearmament into the open, the Krupp submarine company was moved to Bremen in 1935 under the name of Ingenieurkontor für Schiffbau (IFS). It was later moved to Lübeck. Gabler joined IFS in 1938 as a newly-qualified engineer before entering war service.

Gabler points out with irony that Lübeck was originally chosen as a submarine centre because it had a roughly central position on the long German coast extending all the way to Königsberg, the capital of East Prussia. After capitulation in 1945, Gabler was brought in to help the British sink remnants of the German submarine fleet off the coast at Wilhelmshaven. Now Lübeck is an outpost on the fringes of West Germany, next to the fortified border with East Germany. About 500 miles eastwards along the coast, Königsberg has been renamed Kaliningrad and is under Soviet control.

IKS was liquidated in 1946 but Gabler, released from brief internment, set up IKL on the same day and with the same personnel to carry on the business. He spent the next decade on civilian work such as the construction of masts for wireless telephones. The turning point came in 1956 when, after joining NATO, West Germany was allowed to build small coastal submarines for use in the Baltic. Three advanced wartime U-boats scuttled in 1945 – two Type 23s and one Type 21 – were refloated and played a valuable role in rebuilding the submarine arm of the freshly-established West German navy. In 1961, IKL delivered three newly-designed 201-class vessels for the Bundesmarine – and Germany was again back in the submarine business.

Ingenieurkontor Lübeck's best-selling model today is the 1,200-1,400 tonne diesel- and electric-powered 209-class. Equipped with eight torpedo tubes and designed for 50-day patrols, the submarine is constructed by IKL's main partner in the submarine field, the Kiel-based Howaldtswerke shipbuilders, part of the German state-owned Salzgitter concern. IKL is also working on developing a new 212-class boat for the West German navy; this is planned to be delivered in the mid-1990s – assuming it is not held up by defence cuts.

IKL and Howaldtswerke were involved in the suspected transfer to South Africa in 1984-85 of microfilm carrying construction plans for U-209 submarines. The transaction contravened the United Nations embargo on weapons deliveries to Pretoria, and the deal led to a political rumpus in Bonn after the opposition Social Democrats charged that the Kohl government had had a hand in organising it. A parliamentary inquiry failed to establish proof, however. IKL took part in another unconventional submarine deal during the 1970s when it supplied plans to Israel for three vessels which were built by Britain's Vickers shipyard. Federal legislation prohibits exports of weapons to 'areas of tension', a region which includes the Middle East and therefore Israel. Under a decision taken by Chancellor Brandt, however, IKL was allowed to side-step the ban in view of the Federal Republic's special links with the Jewish state. Gabler recalls whimsically: 'We spoke to Vickers and said, "We have a customer. The customer has money. Do you want to build it or not?" Of course, they said, "Yes." '

During the 1970s IKL also sold to Argentina two 209-class submarines which subsequently saw service in the 1982 Falklands war. 'We didn't know then that Argentina would start a war with England,' Gabler points out. The professor has been involved in a number of other controversial deals – including abortive attempts to sell U-boats to Pakistan, Taiwan and Saudi Arabia, all of which ran into political difficulties.

IKL had further dealings with Israel during the 1980s. These concerned a proposal to sell more submarines, to be built in both Haifa and West Germany and financed by the US government. The deal has again drawn criticism from the Social Democrats, and may well be put on ice. Gabler remembers that one Israeli defence official visiting his company was himself a German-born Jew, originating from Cologne, and a survivor of the Holocaust. But this has been no impediment to business links. 'We have no difficulties with the Israelis,' he says laconically. 'They are just normal customers.'

II

When President Dwight D. Eisenhower warned in 1961 of the 'acquisition of unwarranted influence, whether sought or unsought, by the military-industrial complex',[8] he was referring to a phenomenon which by no means existed only in the US. Close links between the government and defence establishment – and the danger of both sides falling into an unhealthy dependence – are present in all countries which have not adopted policies of state pacifism.

The foundations of William II's military-industrial complex were laid in the final years of the last century. Alfred von Tirpitz, secretary of state at the Imperial Naval Office, was the ambitious officer behind Germany's ultimately disastrous policy of building up its fleet to compete with England. The military lobby was little better loved then than it is today. In 1899 Tirpitz had to weather a storm of complaints in the Reichstag about alleged 'greed for profit' from iron and shipbuilding companies benefiting from naval orders.[9] Krupp complained to Tirpitz in 1900 over 'hateful' press allegations concerning its naval contracts to supply armoured steel plate. Just before the outbreak of the First World War, Social Democrat deputy Karl Liebknecht called Gustav Krupp, who had taken over the reins of the company in 1909, a 'matador in the blood-stained trade of death'.[10]

The armed forces did not want to see all the government's largesse concentrated on the navy; hence in 1907 the Imperial General Staff called for an industrial programme to develop German aviation. The Siemens electrical company tested a pioneering biplane on the outskirts of Berlin in 1909, and continued the construction and development of aeroplanes and aero-engines during the First World War. By 1918, the company was building large aircraft with six engines and wing-spans of up to 160 feet at its Berlin works.[11] One celebrated product of the war was Bayerische Motoren Werke (BMW), established in 1916 under the name of Bayerische Flugzeugwerke to build military aircraft and engines. The company's blue and white circular emblem which adorns its cars today dates from the First War, depicting the propellers on early German warplanes.[12]

By the end of the lost war, Germany boasted 35 aircraft factories and 20 aero-engine works. Most of the aircraft in the German air force were subsequently destroyed as part of peace conditions, but the treaty aimed at emasculating German military might proved to be full of holes. Tony Fokker, the young Dutch aircraft magnate who had made a wartime fortune supplying the German air force, fled to Holland in 1918. With the help of the Berlin War Ministry – only too pleased to find a way round the disarmament provisions – Fokker later succeeded in smuggling back by rail over the Dutch border several hundred aircraft and engines from his works in Schwerin.

Ernst Heinkel, who had built up a name in aircraft design during the war, proved supremely adept at evading the Versailles provisions. He restarted illegal production in a former gramophone factory in Travemünde on the coast near Lübeck, building a seaplane for the Swedish air force. In 1922 Heinkel set up a new company in a disused shed outside Rostock. Avoiding Allied control inspectors, he set about making aircraft for both the Reichswehr and the Japanese government. He wrote in his memoirs that, when a victor state 'tries to hold a vanquished people in a position without power and influence, then normally it succeeds in doing the opposite'.[14]

Another means by which Germany side-stepped the Versailles Treaty was through covert military collaboration with the Soviet Union. Beginning cautiously in 1919, cooperation was in hand well before the signing of the Russo-German Rapallo treaty of 1922.*[15] The Junkers company set up an aircraft factory at Fili near Moscow, and Germany also ran an air base for training pilots and testing aircraft at Lipetsk, 250 miles south-west of the Soviet capital. But a succession of difficulties prevented Russia from becoming an effective base for large-scale German arms production and later, cooperation was halted in the first three years of Hitler's dictatorship. Junkers' Russian links had an ironic epilogue when the company's aircraft works at Dessau on the Elbe north of Leipzig was dismantled by the Red Army in 1945 as part of the Soviet Union's pillage of German industry.

A more effective means of preparing German industry for the eventual armaments build-up came through the business concentration in the 1920s, above all in the chemicals** and motor sectors. A leading role was played by Emil Georg von Stauss, the dominant board member of the Deutsche Bank during the 1920s and an early advocate of the 'motorisation' of the German economy carried out under the Third Reich. Stauss masterminded the merger of Daimler and Benz in 1926,† and was one of the leading German businessmen to establish early contact with the Nazis. He struck up a particularly close relationship with Hermann Göring, who was later to become chief of the Luftwaffe and Hitler's Reichsmarshal.[16] Although Stauss failed in his effort to merge Daimler-Benz and BMW into a giant auto-trust on the lines of I.G. Farben, he made an important contribution towards switching both companies' production towards the eventual needs of a war economy, and maintained his position as supervisory board chief of both companies until his death in 1942.

* See Chapter 3.
** See Chapter 2.
† See Chapter 6.

The economic recovery under the Third Reich was driven by massive build-up of arms expenditure; this rose from 0.7 per cent of gross national product in 1933 to 15.5 per cent in 1938, a period in which GNP itself rose by more than 75 per cent.[17] Hitler's focus on the motor industry had both economic and military significance. Large-scale expansion of motor vehicle output, along with the launching of synthetic fuel and rubber production, helped lay the technological groundwork for the *Blitzkrieg*. Construction of the Autobahn network also gave Hitler a means of rapid force deployment. The Führer admitted in 1942: 'All strategic roads were built by tyrants – for the Romans, the Prussians or the French. They go straight across country. All the other roads wind like processions and waste everybody's time.'[18]

A keen racing-car fan, Hitler was an avid user of Mercedes automobiles from the 1920s onwards, profiting from sizeable Daimler discounts to equip him with luxury models. The Führer gave the opening speech at every annual Berlin Motor Exhibition from 1933 onwards; a recurring feature of such addresses was pride in Germany's achievement in inventing the motor car in the 1880s, and concern that Germany lagged behind the rest of the industrialised world in car production. The two 19th-century automobile entrepreneurs Daimler and Benz were 'among the great pioneers of humanity in the sphere of transport', he said at the Berlin Motor Show in 1935. He pointed out that 600,000 men worked in various branches of the motor industry, with a further 400,000 in road-building, adding: 'Our cars and motor cycles are not only the fastest but we can say with pride that they are also the best in the world.... Our engineers and workmen may be proud to build such cars. May the Germans be proud enough to use them!'[19]

There was no doubting the strategic importance of the motorisation effort. Lieutenant General Horst von Metzsch, one of Germany's leading military experts during the 1930s, was an arch protagonist of a large fast-moving, mechanised army. He wrote, 'An up-to-date army should possess enough motorised units to establish a base of operations on the enemy's soil, thus excluding the ground war from its own territory and protecting the homeland from counter-attacks.' He added: 'The motor will be the assassin of peace.'[20] Ironically, two US multinationals – General Motors, which purchased Adam Opel in 1929,[21] and Ford, which set up a factory in Cologne in 1930-31[22] – took part in and profited from the motorisation programme through their German subsidiaries. Opel and Daimler-Benz cooperated in building 100,000 Opel-Blitz army lorries which proved of vital importance to the Wehrmacht during the war.[23] Ford, which was eventually placed under completely German management, was also an important supplier of cross-country vehicles and army lorries for the Wehrmacht.[24]

Through the 1926 merger, Daimler-Benz became the second largest German automobile maker after Opel,[25] and was particularly well-placed to benefit from the Third Reich's economic expansion. The company's emblem of a three-pointed star framed by a circle, designed in 1909, symbolised the ubiquity of Daimler engines in air, land and sea transport. According to a Daimler-Benz advertisement in the official programme for the Nazi Party's 1936 Nuremberg congress: 'Countless are those across the whole world who place their trust in the Mercedes-Benz star – on land, in the air and on water.... The star is the mark of perfection and unconditional reliability.'[26] As the 1930s passed, the Mercedes star was seen, increasingly, side by side with the swastika.[27] Daimler-Benz became an all-round arms conglomerate, building military lorries, tanks, aero-engines, ships' motors, torpedo heads and parts of the most revolutionary of Hitler's 'secret weapons', the V-2 rockets.[28]

Hitler's furthest-reaching economic achievement was his plan for the 'People's Car'. Conceived as part of a grand strategy of bringing cheap motor vehicles within reach of ordinary people, the plan to build a car named after the Nazi slogan *Kraft durch Freude* (Strength through Joy) was never consummated. The programme nonetheless ended up by making an important contribution to the war effort. After the war, the clumsily named KdF-Auto attained world fame as the famous 'beetle' and the company producing it, Volkswagenwerk (VW), became West Germany's best-known industrial concern.

The 'People's Car' was designed from 1934 onwards by Ferdinand Porsche, the veteran vehicle engineer and founder of the Stuttgart car company which bears his name today. Born in northern Bohemia, Porsche made his name in the fledgling Austrian vehicle industry and served as technical director and board member at Daimler between 1923 and 1929. He became a member not only of the Nazi party but also of the SS. The car designer advised Hitler on tank-building during the war, but results were not always satisfactory, straining Porsche's relations with Armaments Minister Albert Speer on more than one occasion.[29] The first prototype of the 'People's Car' was produced in 1935, and the VW company was established in 1938 to build the cars at a massive new factory near the small town of Fallersleben between Hanover and Magdeburg.

Spelling out the objectives of the 'People's Car' at the VW factory's foundation ceremony at Fallersleben in May 1938, Hitler declared: 'It is for the great mass of the people that this car has been designed. Its purpose is to answer their needs in transport, and it is intended to give

251

them joy.'[30] Unfinished when the war started, the plant was swiftly adapted to military production, building 51,000 army 'bucket cars' as well as 15,000 amphibious vehicles, tank parts, bomb cases and mines. From 1943 onwards Volkswagen also produced the V.1 flying-bomb – the pilotless aircraft which caused havoc in London towards the end of the war. The 'People's' Volkswagen went into mass production only after the war when 20 million cars were eventually built, both at Wolfsburg and in VW works in Latin America.[31]

Speer complained in his memoirs that 'typically German bureaucracy' prevented the country from capitalising on its technical and industrial advances during the Second World War. He claimed that bombing raids on German cities were actually helpful because they improved improvisation.[32] On the other hand, the country's decentralised industrial structure gave clear support to war-making efforts. The machine-building industry, the single most important component in any war economy, consisted of about 6,000 mainly small firms. They could accept military orders without having to retool extensively – providing a degree of flexibility which, luckily for the Allies, was singularly missing in other areas of Nazi Germany's war machine.[33]

III

Because of Daimler-Benz's history, the company's moves to take over Messerschmitt-Bölkow-Blohm (MBB) were bound to invite comparisons with the Third Reich. Edzard Reuter, the Daimler chairman – a grizzled man of quiet intellect with close-cropped hair – has attracted a tide of criticism that his company is becoming too strong for the health of his country. The Daimler-MBB deal went through a severe tussle with the Federal Cartel Office, which ruled that pooling the two groups defence activities would give Daimler market domination. Protests were also led by the opposition Social Democratic Party. Ironically, Reuter is the son of Ernst Reuter who was the Social Democrat (SPD) post-war mayor of West Berlin – a man who fled abroad in the 1930s to escape Nazi persecution. Reuter is a friend of ex-Chancellor Helmut Schmidt, and has himself been a member of the SPD since 1946, when his family returned to Germany from exile in Turkey. But these days, he finds himself out of sympathy with his party comrades. His annual earnings are also decidedly un-socialist, estimated at about DM1.5 million.

Speaking in his spacious office suite in the company's Untertürkheim headquarters overlooking Stuttgart's industrial suburbia, Reuter explained that he finds it disturbing to see the Daimler-MBB link portrayed by critics as tantamount to 'a revival of fascism'.[34] He admits to being affected still by the experience of his family's flight from Nazi Germany: 'I have a certain aversion against words like Fatherland; I feel much more at home as a European.'

Power at the company which has now become Germany's largest corporation is impossible to attain without the support of the Deutsche Bank. In line with the bank's 60-year-old role of guiding Daimler's fortunes, the Deutsche Bank chief executive traditionally sits at the helm of the motor company's supervisory board.

Reuter joined Daimler-Benz in 1964, and became the company's finance director at the end of 1979. His membership of the SPD represents one reason why he did not climb into the Daimler driving seat earlier. Wilfried Guth, a conservative – the former Deutsche Bank chief executive who was simultaneously Daimler's supervisory board chairman – turned him down for the top job at Daimler in 1983. However, circumstances improved for Reuter when Alfred Herrhausen took over Guth's post as Deutsche Bank chief executive in 1985 – also moving into his place on Daimler's supervisory board. Herrhausen propelled Reuter to the top Daimler job in 1987 in a boardroom coup which saw the ousting of the previous chairman Werner Breitschwerdt. Asked a few months later for his views on Herrhausen's decision, Guth replied cryptically, 'I hope it will prove a good one.'[35]

Herrhausen's support was crucial in Reuter's efforts to steer Daimler on its new defence and aerospace course. Herrhausen's murder deprived Reuter of far more than merely a business acquaintance. In an emotional statement after the assassination, the Daimler chairman said the bomb blast was 'aimed against the whole of our political, economic and social order.'[36] Already in 1985, Daimler-Benz set out on the diversification path by taking under its wing three other long-established German companies with significant defence activities: the AEG electrical group, the Dornier aerospace company, and aero-engine concern MTU. With Messerschmitt, Daimler hopes to extend its empire further. A rambling defence group bearing the name of Germany's most famous aircraft designer of the Second World War, MBB has developed highly effective technology – but has suffered from poor management and a lack of financial backing. The Bonn government supported the Daimler-MBB get-together as a way of boosting the overall competitiveness of the aerospace industry.

Based in Ottobrunn outside Munich, Messerschmitt is an amalgam built up gradually over the decades through a succession of mergers bringing together most of the great names in the history of German military aviation, including Junkers, Focke-Wulfe and Heinkel. Its business is split roughly 50:50 between the defence and civilian sectors. MBB is the German partner in the four-country Airbus airliner venture.[37] Its armaments activities range from participation in the Anglo-German-Italian Tornado fighter-bomber and the new European Fighter Aircraft (being developed by Germany, Britain, Italy and Spain) to missiles and military helicopters. MBB also has a shareholding in Krauss-Maffei, the maker of West Germany's celebrated Leopard battle-tank – although this was sold in 1989 as one of the conditions for the Daimler take-over.

Even after the MBB deal, Reuter stresses that vehicles' activities would still make up around 60 per cent of its annual turnover, about DM80 billion based on 1988 figures. He believes that in ten years' time the proportion of vehicle turnover will remain little changed. Defence technology meanwhile will make up only around 10 per cent of sales. However, through the link-up Daimler-Benz's armaments operations will spread over a large range of modern non-nuclear weaponry from military aircraft, aero-engines, radar and missiles to submarine motors and military lorries. Never has the three-pointed Mercedes star looked set to extend so far.

Reuter is a great believer in combing technological expertise from the vehicle and aerospace sectors. 'System know-how revolving around micro-electronics will play a big role in future construction of motor vehicles, and also in traffic control technology,' he says. Herrhausen is also firmly wedded to the idea. 'Daimler-Benz seeks the future, Daimler-Benz seeks future markets, Daimler-Benz is not relying on simply being a motor company, because every successful motor company of the future will have to go into high technology,' Herrhausen said in 1988.[38]

To many in Germany, however, the Daimler-MBB link added up to the Federal Republic's largest-ever exercise in the acquisition of industrial power. Wolfgang Kartte, the veteran president of the Federal Cartel office, opposed the transaction on economic grounds, and also admitted deep personal unease about the concentration of economic might which would ensue. Reuter says he can 'understand emotionally, but not with my reason' Kartte's objections. The Daimler conglomerate over the medium term will absorb 60 per cent of arms procurement spending by the German Defence Ministry, and 70 per cent of new

254

weapons development. This seems to put it in a position of dangerous dominance, but Reuter claims that he will have less ability to bargain with the government than a smaller company with a greater proportion of jobs tied up with armaments.

Reuter is trying to emphasise the European dimension, claiming that the takeover will reinforce the European aerospace industry against US competition. He also believes that West Germany has to accept that, as a member of NATO, it needs its own strong defence industry. Philosophically, he told me:

> I am unhappy (over the campaign against the deal). On the other hand, perhaps it is not such a bad thing that there is a discussion in Germany which forces us to recognise that we are part of an alliance. And perhaps it is also a good thing that we have a discussion about the importance of Europe and what it means for us.

Reuter has two main headaches. If general political disillusionment with NATO and defence activities grows through West Germany, opposition to the link-up with MBB could be compounded by cancellation of major programmes such as the European Fighter Aircraft. Additionally, Reuter faces a superhuman management task in making the alliance work. Doubters within Daimler, as well as outside, believe that Reuter may have over-reached himself. Whatever happens, West Germany's top industrial manager will have to get used to occupying the headlines.

IV

The initial post-1945 ban on armaments production was gradually loosened during the 1950s after West Germany joined NATO and the Western European Union. The Adenauer government in 1961 brought in an export control regime under the Armaments Control Law which proscribed, in vaguely-worded terminology, weapons exports which would 'disturb the peaceful co-existence of people of the world'. After a boom during the 1960s in sales abroad of German naval ships, missiles and cannon, the Social Democrat-led government which came to power in 1969 decided to tighten the guidelines. A cabinet decision in June 1971 banned in principle weapons sales to 'regions of tension'. The Foreign Minister had the job of deciding which countries belonged to

255

this category, but in general the move was designed to limit the bulk of arms exports to NATO countries.

However, the 1971 action has by no means curtailed West Germany's advance in the arms business – both in standard weaponry and in so-called 'dual-use' goods which can be used for both civilian and military purposes. In particular, West German engineering companies have excelled in supplying to Third World countries machine tools for making weapons, which are not formally classified as armaments exports.

An air of unreality – not to say hypocrisy – pervades the West German arms business. When Franz Josef Strauss, the Bavarian premier, mounted a campaign before the 1987 general election to allow the Federal Republic to extend its authorised weapons sales abroad to places like Saudi Arabia, his proposals proved highly unpopular. There was a widespread perception that Strauss wanted to liberalise an export control regime which had restricted West German arms exports simply to NATO countries. In fact, between 1982 and 1986 the Federal Republic had already proved more successful than Britain in exporting arms to non-industrialised countries. According to the US government's Arms Control and Disarmament Agency (ACDA), West German sales to such countries – defined as including nations like Turkey, which is also a member of NATO – were $5.5 billion during this period, higher than Britain's $5.1 billion.[39] Much of these sales represented deliveries of naval vessels, including submarines to Latin American countries, as well as tanks to Turkey. Sales have since been falling in both categories. The chief customers during this period were Argentina ($1.4 billion), Turkey ($850 million), Colombia ($675 million) and Iraq ($625 million). Showing the ubiquity of German arms exports, the ACDA list showed that 33 developing countries were recipients of German weaponry between 1982 and 1986, although some transactions were for only very small amounts.

These figures are in fact an underestimate. Significant amounts of West German weapons exports are not covered because they are sold through consortia based abroad – the Tornado aircraft produced in partnership with Britain and Italy, for instance. Hanns Arnt Vogels, the chairman of Messerschmitt, admits that West Germany's official weapons export policies are less of a constraint than they often appear. MBB has been stepping up efforts to sell armaments such as military helicopters to Indonesia, Thailand and South Korea, and has even unveiled a military tanker version of the Airbus at a Singapore air show. 'For domestic policy reasons, the government will always push into the foreground this restrictive policy,' he told me at his heavily-guarded villa retreat in the southern German Alps. 'But in large parts of the world – either as a result of European partnership accords, or because of the opening of certain regions in South-East Asia – it does not work out in practice as especially restrictive.'[40]

MBB is one of the companies occasionally suspected to be making use of loopholes in West Germany's export control regulations. Although West Germany is by no means among the leading sources of 'grey' or 'black market' weapons, breaches of Bonn's weapons guidelines take place fairly regularly. A number of smaller German companies have faced investigations from state prosecutors in recent years for making unapproved weapons sales to Iran and Iraq. An MBB subsidiary has been suspected of helping a number of developing countries gain access to ballistic missiles technology.

West German companies hide their armaments expertise in a variety of ways. Sales of military electronics are registered in published reports and brochures under the heading 'special equipment'; MTU's tank engines are classified as 'motors for heavy vehicles'. Daimler-Benz equips countries like Iran, Iraq and South Africa with vehicles for military use, but they are invariably listed in public as civilian lorries. Anti-military German sensibilities also constrain German companies with armaments activities from aggressively displaying their wares in advertising. Executives at Daimler-Benz and Messerschmitt complain jealously of the extrovert pride with which defence companies in Britain and France promote their products. High-profile advertising of weaponry of the sort often carried out by British Aerospace, for instance, is taboo in West Germany.

One armaments company making an almost desperate attempt to change its image is Rheinmetall, based in Düsseldorf. Formerly headquartered in Berlin, the company has a long history of gun-making stretching back to Imperial Germany, but now it coyly describes armaments activities as 'defence engineering'. In its centenary celebrations in May 1989, its role as a weapons supplier in both World Wars was pointedly played down.

Rheinmetall admits that it has not completely recovered from a long-running arms-smuggling affair during the 1980s. In 1986 four executives were found guilty on charges of illegally exporting arms to Saudi Arabia, South Africa and Argentina between 1977 and 1980. The company is now diversifying as fast as possible into industrial machinery and automotive components, and has even considered changing its tradition-filled name to change its image as an armaments maker.

According to Raimund Germershausen, its director in charge of arms manufacturing, the psychological climate for weapons manufacturers has deteriorated even compared with the end of the 1970s.[41]

Krauss-Maffei, based on the outskirts of Munich, is another well-known arms concern trying to change tack. West Germany's general contractor in manufacturing Leopard tanks since the mid-1960s, the company nowadays mentions weaponry in last place in its promotional brochures, and in its advertising goes to extreme lengths to underline the purely defensive nature of its equipment. In its promotional advertising, it resorts to a large picture of a friendly-looking hedgehog set against a background of meadow flowers. Krauss-Maffei is suffering a severe shortage of tank orders both from the Bundeswehr and from clients in NATO. Hopes of approval for sales of the modern Leopard-2 tank to Saudi Arabia were buried in 1987. Burckard Wollschläger, the hearty Krauss Maffei chairman, bemoans the 'mangling' of defence spending in Bonn. To compensate for falling military business, he is busy expanding non-military production in areas ranging from environmental technology to machinery for making plastic compact discs. The company is also supplying locomotive parts for the West German railways' new high-speed train. Wollschläger says that the period of tank-making dominance which started with the delivery of the first Leopard-1 in 1965 could turn out to be no more than an 'episode' in Krauss-Maffei's long history.[42]

Arms-making in West Germany is an area where conscience starts to bite more quickly than in other countries. Even the most proficient weapons manufacturers say they would really be much happier beating swords into ploughshares.

258

13

The Nuclear Conundrum

Your radium results are very amazing.... But we have experienced so many surprises in nuclear physics that one cannot say without hesitation about anything: 'It's impossible.'

Lise Meitner to Otto Hahn, December 1938.[1]

Within a few weeks, I will make the German people atom conscious.

Franz Josef Strauss, 1955.[2]

The question after Chernobyl is not if another accident will happen, but when. Everything else is just child's belief.

Oskar Lafontaine, 1987.[3]

Germany and the atom have followed similar contorted paths. Nine months before the outbreak of the Second World War, German scientists discovered, at first unbelievingly, the splitting of the uranium nucleus. The breakthrough opened the way simultaneously to weapons of mass destruction and to nuclear reactors offering the dream of practically unlimited cheap electricity. In coming months and years, the vision and nightmare of nuclear fission spread around the world. The aftermath haunts Germany with particular virulence.

German-Jewish physicists exiled from the Third Reich helped provide the initial spark behind the US drive to build the atom bombs which destroyed Hiroshima and Nagasaki. After renouncing the production of nuclear weapons in 1954, West Germany wholeheartedly embraced the peaceful use of nuclear energy as an essential component of post-war renewal. This represented not only a break with the belligerent past, but also continuity. Leading scientists and companies involved in Germany's wartime nuclear research played a central role in the 1950s atomic programme.

Needing access to reactors, know-how and uranium supplies, the Federal Republic was an enthusiastic recipient of American assistance

259

under President Eisenhower's 1953 Atoms for Peace programme. However, the nuclear relationship with the US has never been free of strains. A streak of disgruntlement has lingered in Germany over its lost supremacy in nuclear science, and there have been sporadic complaints that its position as a non-atomic weapon state has handicapped development of the nuclear industry compared with the US, Britain and France. Suspicions have also come to the fore from time to time in the US that West Germany was assisting in the proliferation of nuclear weapons abroad – or might even want to assemble an atomic arsenal itself.

Domestic efforts in favour of nuclear power were redoubled in the 1970s under Social Democrat-led governments; this was after the sharp rise in oil prices in 1973 exposed the country's shortage of indigenous energy resources. Up to the mid-1970s, the nuclear drive was backed by broad political consensus; then it started to wither away. Reacting successively to the US reactor accident at Three Mile Island in 1979, then to the 1986 Chernobyl disaster in the Soviet Union – as well as a subsequent series of domestic nuclear scandals – West German public opinion has turned fiercely against the atom.[4]

Unease over the civil use of nuclear energy has coincided with mounting hostility to atomic weapons. Civil and military use of nuclear energy is seen increasingly as a single issue. The cooling towers of atomic power stations are no longer, as in the 1950s and 1960s, symbols of progress, but harbingers of doom. From an industrial point of view, the tide of opposition has badly, perhaps fatally, damaged West Germany's attempt to make good its late start in post-war nuclear development. Politically, the joint question of atomic power and nuclear weapons dominates the electoral debate. In a *volte-face* from its pro-nuclear stance in the 1970s, the Social Democratic Party has opted for an atomic *Ausstieg* (exit) by pledging a ten-year programme to close all nuclear power stations if it returns to office. The anti-nuclear mood has also spread deep into the ranks of the conservative parties.

The swing in public opinion has not prevented completion in recent years of light water reactors already under construction. Nuclear reactors in 1988-89 accounted for roughly 40 per cent of West Germany's electricity production, but no new orders for atomic power stations look likely for the rest of the century. Additionally, at the end of the 1980s, two highly symbolic projects marking the country's bid to close the technological gap with the three main western nuclear powers fell victim to growing political opposition and financial uncertainty. The planned reprocessing plant of Wackersdorf in Bavaria was abandoned in

June 1989, while the fast breeder reactor at Kalkar on the lower Rhine looked certain to meet the same fate. The demise of both projects delivers the most serious blow for thirty years to German supporters of atomic energy.

Crucial decisions will have to be taken later in the 1990s on whether or not to replace the first 1970s generation of nuclear power stations, which will by then be nearing the end of their operational lives. Depending on whether or not world energy prices stay low, the German anti-atom drift could then gain unstoppable momentum.

The Federal Republic however remains caught in an uncomfortable dilemma. An international move to shut down nuclear reactors would increase the burning of coal in power stations, with corresponding damage to the environment. What would be worse? The risk of more nuclear accidents? Or a worsening of the 'greenhouse effect', under which combustion of hydrocarbon fuels leads to a long-term build-up of carbon dioxide, trapping heat in the earth's atmosphere and threatening disastrous climatic changes? The Germans, more than most people, know that there are no easy options.

Ironically, France is seizing on the *Ausstieg* mood to step up efforts to export cheap nuclear electricity to the Federal Republic. But what if German-style anti-nuclearism spreads to other countries? One of the most intriguing consequences of the new links between East and West Germany is that anti-nuclear sentiment is growing across the whole of central Europe. Alarmed by revelations of catastrophic safety standards at its atomic power plants, a newly democratic East Germany has chosen comprehensively to shackle its nuclear activities. At least until the next energy crisis, the country which split the atom is leading the march away from it.

I

Karl Heinz Beckurts, a Siemens board member and for nearly thirty years one of the pillars of the West German nuclear establishment, chose sobering words to open a long article written in July 1986 on the effects of the Chernobyl nuclear disaster in the Ukraine three months earlier.

The serious reactor accident in the Soviet Union has unleashed fears and

261

worries. Nobody who thinks seriously about the use of nuclear energy can remain unaffected by Chernobyl. The unease in public opinion has been much greater in the Federal Republic than in any other country in the world.[5]

Beckurts was a 56-year-old who entered industry from the atomic research establishment at Jülich. He had risen to become board member responsible for research at Siemens, owner of the power station builder Kraftwerk Union (KWU) and one of the dominant forces in West German nuclear energy. By the time the words appeared in print, Beckurts had been dead for a week: on his way to work in a bullet-proof BMW, he and his chauffeur were blown up by a sophisticated 10-kilo bomb in a south Munich suburb.

West Germany's Red Army Faction (RAF) terrorist group claimed responsibility for the murder in a seven-page letter found after the blast. It was the latest in a string of killings of top businessmen and officials since 1970. The RAF said that Beckurts was singled out because of his role in 'western Europe's biggest high technology concern and the world's third largest atomic group'. The assassination was an extreme reminder of the criminal passion which can be unleashed by nuclear energy.[6] *Die Zeit* decided to print Beckurt's long essay posthumously to extend the debate over a nuclear *Ausstieg*. He wrote that Chernobyl increased the risk that individual West Germans would die of cancer by a mere 0.01 per cent. He warned that switching off nuclear power stations would drastically increase emissions of noxious sulphur and nitrogen oxides. He estimated that an immediate nuclear shut-down would cost the economy DM250 billion up to the end of the century. Beckurts was at pains to give a balanced view, ending his article by pleading for common sense: 'No one in the Federal Republic has a fixation with atomic power stations.... But circumspect use of nuclear energy is both responsible and necessary. Hasty renunciation would demand too high a price.'

Beckurts' careful language showed how German nuclear lobbyists have been forced to go on the defensive. When the consensus in favour of nuclear energy started to turn sour in the 1970s, Siemens at first came out fighting. The message was that unless more nuclear power stations were built, the lights would go out; in a typically exaggerated claim in 1979, Bernhard Plettner, then Siemens chairman, said the Federal Republic was 'driving on towards catastrophe' as a result of its failure to authorise new power station projects. He warned, 'We shall reach the limits of capacity by 1983-84.'[7]

By 1986, the nuclear industry had lost a lot of credibility. Chernobyl dealt a further blow. The explosion in the Ukraine directly killed 31 people, raised the risk of cancer for thousands, forced 135,000 local people to flee their homes, and sent a plume of radioactivity across more than twenty countries up to 2,000 kilometres away. The loss of life was indeed minor compared with the earthquake which shattered the Caucasus at the end of 1988, killing at least 25,000 people, but Chernobyl's shock wave travelled further – and nowhere was the alarm greater than in the Federal Republic.

Children were kept away from public playgrounds, thousands of tons of radioactive vegetables were dumped and psychiatrists registered outbreaks of panic-like anxiety. Eating of venison declined sharply because of fears of radioactive Bavarian deer. Two hundred and fifty railway wagons of contaminated milk powder had eventually to be impounded by the government. In the twelve months after the accident, the German public authorities paid out a total of DM434 million in compensation, above all to farmers.[8] The final bill faced by the West German authorities for compensation payments came to more than DM600 million.[9]

In neighbouring France life went on more or less normally. With Gallic self-confidence, the population largely accepted statements from the French authorities (which turned out to be untrue) that the radioactive cloud from the Ukraine had – through a meteorological freak – failed to cross the Rhine. Pierre Strohl, the French civil servant who is deputy director general of the Nuclear Energy Agency in Paris, explained to me the difference in reactions between France and Germany: 'The French have a tendency more than others to be confident in the authorities. They have more interest in good wine and sex than nuclear energy.'[10] In the Federal Republic, confusion was increased by a welter of conflicting information about the accident released by Federal and *Land* authorities. Just as the western Allies had intended at the end of the Second World War, political decentralisation represented a great hindrance to government control of public opinion.

The effect on general confidence was longer-lasting in the Federal Republic than in France or the UK. According to opinion polls carried out by Gallup, in the second half of 1986 more than 80 per cent of the West German population was against the building of further nuclear plants, double the proportion registered in the early 1980s. In Britain and France, meanwhile, 40 per cent of the population continued to be broadly in favour of nuclear energy.[11] Erhard Eppler, one of the Social Democratic Party's strategic thinkers and a long-time nuclear opponent, wrote a few weeks after the accident in the Ukraine that the anti-atomic swing would accelerate. In an article headlined 'The End of Acceptance', he took issue with the past economic forecasts on which SPD-supported nuclear expansion plans had been based: 'Opponents of nuclear energy have been much criticised for living from, and appealing to, people's fears. But these fears have obviously been better founded than the worry about the energy gap, about the lights which would go out, which was propagated in the second half of the 1970s.'[12]

The French magazine *Documents* termed reaction to Chernobyl east of the Rhine as 'a German apocalypse', and said the Germans were reliving 'the trauma of 1945'. Amid booming sales of home Geiger counters and a sharp increase in demand for abortions from women fearing their babies would suffer defects, a linguistically enterprising Slavonic studies professor at Münster University discovered that 'Chernobyl' was the equivalent of a Hungarian word for a type of wormwood plant, the mugwort. With morbid relish, he pointed out that the wormwood is referred to in the eighth chapter of the Apocalypse as the star which spreads death and contamination after it falls burning to earth.[13]

II

In Berlin, just before Christmas in 1938, the star rose in the firmament. After four decades in which scientists in Europe and the US had laboured to unravel the mysteries of the nucleus, the atom gave up the greatest of its secrets. It was revealed by a 58-year-old radiochemist, Otto Hahn, director of the Kaiser Wilhelm Chemistry Institute in the south-west suburb of Dahlem. In painstaking collaboration with his younger colleague Fritz Strassmann, Hahn made the experimental breakthrough which brought the atomic era to life.

For several years Hahn had been carrying out experiments to try to identify the substances produced when uranium, the heaviest naturally-occurring element, was bombarded by neutrons. Since 1934, he had been working with Lise Meitner, an Austrian Jewess who was head of the institute's physics department. She fled to Scandinavia in July 1938 to escape the consequences of Hitler's *Anschluss* with Austria in March that year, which brought her under the jurisdiction of the Nazis' anti-Jewish legislation.*

* See Chapter 10.

Late in the evening of 19 December, Hahn wrote to Meitner at her new home in Stockholm that isotopes produced from the bombardment of uranium, and presumed to be radium, were acting chemically like barium. This was inexplicable. Scientists had been working on the theory that neutron bombardment produced either slightly heavier transuranic elements through neutron capture, or slightly smaller elements formed as a neutron chipped off part of the nucleus or caused emission of a nuclear particle.

An element such as barium, of nearly half the mass of uranium, could only come about if the nucleus were split. In the draft paper prepared before Christmas for publication in the Berlin scientific journal *Naturwissenschaften*, Hahn wrote that the barium results were 'against all previous laws of nuclear physics'.[14]

Meitner, accompanied by her physicist nephew Otto Frisch who had travelled up from Denmark, reviewed Hahn's letter during a Christmas break on the Swedish coast. Together they worked out the physics explanation for Hahn's and Strassmann's results. The fundamentally unstable uranium atom had been cleaved into two smaller nuclei; the process would be accompanied by a release of energy foretold under Einstein's famous equation of 1905 establishing that mass and energy were interchangeable. Seeking a name for this entirely new phenomenon, Frisch – musing on its similarity to the division of a biological cell – suggested in January 1939 the name 'fission'.

Hahn's paper was published in Berlin on 6 January 1939. During the next few months, the experiments were repeated by scientists on both sides of the Atlantic. By the end of March, more than eighteen different research teams from France, Germany and the US had independently verified nuclear fission. Experimental data laying the groundwork for setting up nuclear chain reactions for both bombs and reactors, and the vital recognition of the fissile nature of the relatively rare uranium-235 isotope, were laid out in a flood of publications.

The world's first detailed popular exposition of the possibilities of fission came in a newspaper article in August 1939 by Siegfried Flügge, a theoretical physicist from the Kaiser Wilhelm Physics Institute near Hahn's laboratory (in the Chemistry Institute) in Berlin-Dahlem. Just over a fortnight before the German armies rolled into Poland, the article helped to stir the interest of the German authorities in the potential of nuclear research. Flügge wrote that one cubic metre of uranium contained enough energy to lift a cubic kilometre of water 27 kilometres into the sky.

As he put it, this would raise the contents of Berlin's famous Wannsee lake into the stratosphere. Although dwelling essentially on the possibilities of an energy-producing 'uranium machine', Flügge also pointed out, 'We are dealing with an explosion with the approximate force of a volcanic eruption.' He added with an undertone of grim prophecy that the discovery was likely to 'come before the eyes of all humanity'.[15]

The timing of Hahn's discovery throws up some tantalising hypotheses. If war had already broken out in the autumn of 1938, as had seemed possible before the September Munich agreement allowing Hitler to annex the Sudetenland, Hahn's results would certainly not have been published immediately, perhaps not at all. Germany would then have had a vital head start in atomic research, and the American Manhattan Project to build the bomb launched in autumn 1942 – the world's first example of big-science applied to warfare – might never have got under way. Well before revelation of the scale of the $2 billion US effort, the Nazis realised that secrecy would have bought valuable time. Hermann Göring, Hitler's Reichsmarshal, complained in a speech in July 1942 that 'our scientists' colleagues in Britain, France and America know in detail just what kind of egg their German colleagues have hatched out.'[16]

Alternatively, the fission breakthrough might easily have come years earlier. Starting with Enrico Fermi, the Italian physicist who later won the Nobel Prize, several scientists had already tried to decipher what happened after uranium was bombarded by neutrons, but only Hahn had the experimental expertise to show that barium was produced. A German woman chemist, Ida Noddack, advanced the hypothesis as early as 1934 that nuclei might break into pieces under neutron bombardment, but the suggestion was not taken seriously. If fission had been understood in the early years of the Third Reich, the war – and the rest of history – might have turned out very differently.[17]

Fears in the US and Britain that the Germans might be working on an atomic bomb lit the initial fuse which eventually led, in summer 1945, to the American test explosion of a plutonium bomb in the New Mexican desert, and then the destruction of two Japanese cities. A remarkable role in the genesis of the bomb programme was played by European scientists exiled by anti-Semitic laws. One of the many who took refuge abroad was a Jewish Hungarian physicist, Leo Szilard, who left Berlin in early 1933.[18] Szilard heard about the fission breakthrough while in New York in January 1939, and was deeply worried about the possibility of the Nazis getting the bomb first. As Hitler's armies swept into Belgium in May, he was above all concerned that the Nazis could gain access to Belgian uranium supplies in the Congo.

Szilard prevailed upon Albert Einstein to write his celebrated letter to

President Roosevelt in August 1939, pressing for a start on US fission research. Einstein had renounced his German citizenship (for the second time) six years earlier, and had taken up a post at Princeton's Institute for Advanced Study in New Jersey. Towards the end of the war, he was to say, 'Politically I hated Germany from my youth, and I always felt the dangers that threatened the world from her side.'[19] The letter prompted an interested response from the President when it was delivered in October, but significant US research efforts started only two years later.[20]

Fermi was also in the US, leaving Fascist Italy because his wife was Jewish. Enlisted by the Manhattan Project, in Chicago in December 1942 he set up the world's first working nuclear reactor. Meanwhile, the two physicists behind a crucial nuclear memorandum for the British government were also of Jewish descent. Rudolf Peierls, an émigré from Berlin, and Lise Meitner's nephew Otto Frisch – both at Birmingham University in early 1940 – worked out that a 5-kilo 'super-bomb' made by separating pure uranium-235 would have the explosive power of thousands of tons of dynamite. The memorandum grew into a government report which, passed to the US in 1941, inspired the beginnings of the Manhattan Project.[21]

Luckily for humanity, in Germany there was no equivalent. German wartime atomic research was highly fragmented in direction and organisation. The scientific, industrial and financial means poured into the Manhattan Project were in a different league altogether. German scientists continued doggedly on atomic research until just a few weeks before the country capitulated in ruins in May 1945, but they never succeeded in producing a self-sustaining chain reaction. The underlying motives early on in the war were, however, similar in the US and Germany. The story of the atomic programme under the Nazis became heavily clouded with mythology after the war, as German scientists sought to hide that they too, like the Americans and British, started out wanting to make a bomb.[22]

Even before the war started, German scientists were quick to see potential applications of nuclear energy for explosives. As early as April 1939, the German army was told by its chemical explosives consultant, Paul Harteck, a young Hamburg professor, of the possibility of using nuclear energy to make bombs 'many orders of magnitude more powerful than conventional ones'.

A nuclear research project was set up under the auspices of the army ordnance department, but the army never succeeded in its aim of completely centralising the programme at Berlin's Kaiser Wilhelm

Physics Institute. Wartime efforts were also weak in experimental flair; this was partly because of the seniority enjoyed in the scientific hierarchy by theoreticians led by Werner Heisenberg, professor at the Leipzig Institute of Theoretical Physics, who in 1932 won the Nobel Prize. Heisenberg, the leading theoretical physicist remaining in Germany after the Jewish purges, became adviser to the Kaiser Wilhelm Physics Institute and played a key role in the military research programme. Efforts to build a uranium pile in Dahlem might have been more successful had experimental scientists rather than the theoreticians been in charge.[23]

The German atomic programme also suffered from shortages of raw materials and equipment. The lack of cyclotrons, or particle accelerators, of the kind available to US scientists working on plutonium was a particular handicap; but the most conclusive reason for its failure was that the army and Nazi leadership never gave the project unrestrained support.[24] With Hitler's forces sweeping across Europe, the army believed the war would be won without any need to produce an atomic bomb. Although leading companies such as I.G. Farben (uranium hexafluoride and heavy water), Degussa (uranium), Anschütz (centrifuges) and Siemens (work on cyclotrons) were involved in the war effort, close-knit collaboration with industry was never achieved on the scale practised in the US project.

Up to 1941-42, German theoretical achievement in understanding the physics of a nuclear bomb and working towards building one ran parallel in many respects to achievements in the US and Britain. Then came the parting of the ways. At the beginning of 1942, the German army ordnance department took a basic decision that nuclear fission was irrelevant to the war drive, handing back leadership of the project to the Kaiser Wilhelm Society. Thereafter, funding for atom research continued; but the programme, ever more harried by air raids and disruption of supplies and personnel, basically marked time.

After 1945, the wartime nuclear project research was an embarrassment for the defeated Germans. The scientists who took part in the war effort – and who were in many cases leading figures in the Federal Republic's post-war civilian atomic drive – maintained falsely that they failed to exploit Hahn's discovery as a result of moral scruples. The German scientists may well have been relieved at their inability to construct a bomb for Hitler, but the reasons were political, technological and economic rather than moral.

After the war, Heisenberg claimed that his apparent collaboration with the Nazis was a cover for resistance. However, even if he was no supporter of the Nazis, this apologia was implausible at best. The author Robert Jungk, who today has become one of the fiercest opponents of the West German nuclear lobby, was responsible in the 1950s for giving credence to the misconception that the German scientists actively tried to hinder bomb development.[25] Today Jungk admits that he was misled into portraying the German scientists as 'pacifists'; he told me that he based his impression on conversations after the war both with Heisenberg (who died in 1976) and also with Carl-Friedrich von Weizsäcker.[26]

Elder brother of the West German president, Weizsäcker is today one of West Germany's foremost philosophers. He was one of Heisenberg's principal associates at the Kaiser Wilhelm Physics Institute during the war. Though not a member of the Nazi party, as the son of Ernst von Weizsäcker – Ribbentrop's state secretary in the Foreign Ministry – he was politically well-connected. Weizsäcker today has become a celebrated protagonist for world peace,[27] but under the Third Reich he appeared to have a different view of the world.

Weizsäcker played an important role in the atomic research project. In summer 1940 he worked out theoretically – partly using published US results – an alternative route to a bomb-making material, supplementing the method of boosting the concentration of uranium-235 in natural uranium. The new path was based on transmuting the heavier and more common uranium isotope, uranium 238, into a new fissile transuranic element by means of irradiation in a reactor. The Americans were to call this new element plutonium. Weizsäcker reported his findings, and their potential for making explosives, in a five-page report to army ordnance in July 1940.[28]

During the war Germany never came close to mastering either uranium-235 enrichment or the irradiation technique for manufacturing nuclear weapon material. But these two methods – producing uranium-235 at the Oak Ridge enrichment plant, and plutonium at the Hanford reactor – were the ones used in the Manhattan Project to manufacture 'Little Boy' and 'Fat Man', the bombs which destroyed Hiroshima and Nagasaki.

Weizsäcker exposed the dualism of nuclear power which has tormented politicians, scientists and regulators ever since. A 'civilian' reactor producing energy for electricity generation through a slow chain reaction also gives rise to plutonium capable of use in explosives. For the Federal Republic, a state which has forsworn nuclear weapons production but which has tried to maximise civilian use of nuclear energy, the 'dual use' conundrum was to throw up recurring problems during later decades.

On the 6 o'clock news on 6 August 1945, the BBC newsreader

announced the destruction of Hiroshima, revealing also the scale of the industrial effort in the US which had made it possible. The news was heard by ten top German nuclear scientists including Hahn, Heisenberg, Weizsäcker and Harteck, interned in Farm Hall, an English country house in Huntingdon. They had been rounded up at the end of the conflict in Europe and brought to the UK by British intelligence – partly because of the belief that the Americans might want to shoot them. British intelligence officers who had placed hidden microphones in the house overheard the scientists' reaction to the announcement,[29] but a full transcript of the scientists' conversations has never been published and the matter is treated by the UK government as a classified secret.[30]

Hahn wrote later that he was 'shocked and depressed beyond measure' after hearing the broadcast, and had to be given gin to steady his nerves.[31] One of his colleagues stayed up to watch over him that night in case he committed suicide. The Germans' shock at Farm Hall, however, was caused not only by the fearsome loss of life in Japan; it also reflected the scientists' pique that the Americans had succeeded in producing the atomic bomb which Germany had concluded was impossible.

Today, Carl-Friedrich von Weizsäcker is a commanding, silvery-haired man with a mild manner and terrifying eyebrows. He is slightly embarrassed about the post-war impression – which he helped to create – that morality held back German scientists from making a bomb. With the distance of time, Weizsäcker now is far more candid, admitting that moral scruples were irrelevant to the outcome of the atomic project. 'If we had urgently had the wish to make atomic weapons, and if the German government had given every possible help, then we would not have done it as quickly as the Americans,' he says. 'We were sure that we could not do it – we realised this around the end of 1940.'[32]

Weizsäcker says that 200 atomic scientists around the world knew by spring 1939 that an atomic bomb was possible. 'I hoped that Hitler would have no chance to use a bomb in the war. But if the bomb was going to come, it would come. Hitler would not last for ever – but the bomb would stay.' The motives of the German scientists involved in the war effort were different, he told me:

Hahn wanted to save his [Kaiser Wilhelm Chemistry] Institute. Other of us wanted to see if it [a chain reaction] would work, and, if it did, so help us God. But we came to think that the effort would be so big that no one in the world could do it. We didn't know about Oak Ridge.... We didn't think that the Americans could do such a fantastic thing [as the Manhattan Project] during the war.

Underlining his connection to the highest level of decision-making, Weizsäcker adds enigmatically: 'If I had thought that we could have made the bomb, and if I had wanted to, I could have secured an audience with Hitler [to persuade him to go ahead with it.]'

The Germans' own last fruitless effort to construct a working uranium pile was carried out in the unlikely location of a cave hewn into a rock face in a picturesque Swabian village. As bombing intensified in Berlin in early 1945, the uranium-heavy water reactor experiment was transferred from Dahlem to Haigerloch, south of Stuttgart. The region was taken in April 1945 by American troops, including members of the Alsos scientific intelligence mission looking for clues to the German nuclear project. They rounded up the cream of the German nuclear scientists in the area, dismantled the apparatus in the Haigerloch cellar and demolished it with explosives.

Before being taken off to France and then to Farm Hall with the others, Weizsäcker revealed to the Americans that important records of the atom project were suspended in a cesspit in his house. He says now of the Haigerloch experiment: 'Compared with Fermi's [reactor in 1942] it was very primitive.... The war was lost, the situation was very bad. We thought it would be good, for our country, to have a cheap energy source which could be used to advantage afterwards.'

The Haigerloch cave was renovated and opened to the public in 1980 as the 'Atom Cellar'. Today it is the township's principal tourist attraction; a guidebook for visitors skirts briefly over the military objectives of the wartime project and asserts reassuringly but misleadingly, 'The atomic bomb was not on the programme.'[33] Father Marquard Gulde, the now-retired priest of the town's church perched on the cliff above the cave, provides a bizarre footnote to the episode. He persuaded an American officer in April 1945 against carrying out his orders to blow up the whole cliff, and so succeeded in sparing his church. Father Gulde, now in his eighties and somewhat deaf, still recalls with a chuckle rebuking the 'atom professors' in 1945 for disturbing the peace of the country town with their dangerous experiments.[34]

III

In shattered post-war Germany, survival took priority over science. In 1946 the four occupation powers banned any activities in nine key fields of technology. 'Applied nuclear physics' was the first in the list.[35] In Berlin and the eastern occupied zone, scientists on the German project who had been unwilling or unable to flee westwards were rounded up by the Russians. Many went to the Soviet Union on good contracts and gave valuable assistance in the building of the Soviet atomic bomb.[36]

These included Manfred von Ardenne, who had worked on electro-magnetic isotope separation in Berlin; Gustav Hertz, who had received the Nobel Prize in 1925 for developing the gaseous separation process; and Peter-Adolf Thiessen, head of the Kaiser Wilhelm Institute for Physical Chemistry in Berlin, who had advised the government on the Third Reich's chemical research and development. Thiessen worked in the Soviet Union until 1956 and then became head of the East German Research Council. Ardenne, whose wartime design was shown after-wards to have distinct similarities with equipment developed at Oak Ridge, returned from the Soviet Union in 1955 to work at his own research establishment in Dresden. Still active in his eighties, Ardenne is today the doyen of East German science.

In the Federal Republic, the Adenauer government quickly turned attention to harnessing nuclear energy as part of economic reconstruc-tion. Even before restrictions on applied atomic research were formally lifted in 1955, the scientists who had been interned in Farm Hall took their places around the nuclear table, adapting quickly to their new political masters – and, to some extent, influencing them. On the insistence of the British occupation authorities, in 1946 the Kaiser Wilhelm Society was renamed the Max Planck Society and its manage-ment entrusted to Otto Hahn, who took over the job somewhat reluctantly because of his age. Karl Wirtz, from the Kaiser Wilhelm Physics Institute, who had also been held in Farm Hall, was made chairman of one of three specialist commissions set up in 1952 to look into the construction of nuclear reactors. He teamed up with Karl Winnacker, a top I.G. Farben executive during the war. Winnacker had been suspected of involvement in the company's poison gas programme, although the Americans brought no charges after the end of the war. Both men became driving forces behind the post-war nuclear effort.

In 1956 Heisenberg, like Hahn, became a founder member of the German Atomic Commission, a body of top scientists, businessmen and officials set up under the chairmanship of Atomic Minister Franz Josef Strauss. Its role was advisory, but it quickly became the main influence behind decision-making. One of the chief members was Hermann Josef Abs of the Deutsche Bank.[37] Siemens, AEG, Hoechst and Bayer all had representatives on the commission; it functioned until 1971, when it was wound up by the Social Democrat-led government.[38]

The Federal Republic's nuclear pioneers were torn between competing desires: a dilemma which would reassert itself at regular intervals over the next thirty years. On the one hand, the Germans wanted to establish a self-sufficient industry which could break loose from the Americans. On the other, they wanted to draw on the experience of the US in building enriched uranium reactors using light water as moderator. Germany's late post-war nuclear start proved in fact a handicap which could never fully be overcome.

A foretaste of the drawbacks of American reliance came in 1956 when the US agreed to grant the West Germans sufficient enriched uranium to build research reactors – but not enough to produce atomic piles capable of generating electricity. To avoid the need for enriched uranium, the Germans decided to construct their first home-grown reactor on the basis of natural uranium and heavy water; this was a direct continuation of the wartime experiments carried out at first in Berlin and then at Haigerloch. Called the FR2,[39] the reactor was built at the country's first full-scale nuclear research institute, opened in 1956 at Karlsruhe in Baden-Württemberg.[40] It went critical in 1961.

The West Germans also brushed with the Americans during the 1950s over the question of nuclear weapons for the Bundeswehr. Although the West Germans had renounced production of nuclear weapons, Adenauer maintained during the 1950s that the army had a right to possess the same types of weapons, i.e. nuclear ones, as the Soviet Union. As Defence Minister at the end of the 1950s, Strauss held discussions with the French on possible nuclear cooperation, although these came to nothing. Strauss suggested that atomic weapons were an 'ethical' way of deterring their use by the Soviet Union, and in 1960 raised the question of acquiring US Polaris missiles. The Americans eventually agreed during the 1960s to provide the Bundeswehr with nuclear-capable delivery systems (aircraft, rocket launchers), with the bombs and warheads remaining US-owned.

In line with the goal of maximum autonomy, in 1958 the Atomic Commission proposed the building by 1965 of five different reactor types with total capacity of 500 MW, all based on West Germany's own research and development. At the same time, AEG went ahead with licensing technology for boiling water reactor power stations from General Electric of the US. The first of a series of industrial-sized boiling water reactors (BWRs), built at Gundremmingen in Bavaria, went on stream in 1966.

The 1958 programme was clearly over-ambitious; the goal of building five 'home-grown' reactor types was never fulfilled. Siemens, however, built on the experience of FR2 and persisted along the heavy water route. Degussa, extending its wartime involvement with uranium, supplied fuel elements through its subsidiary Nukem set up close to the company's works at Hanau. In another example of historical continuity, heavy water was supplied by Hoechst and Linde using processes on which both companies had worked during the war.[41]

After FR2, Siemens built only two heavy water-moderated power stations in Germany before a decision was made to discontinue the reactor type. However, in 1962 Siemens acquired the country's first nuclear export order with a contract to build for Argentina a heavy water-natural uranium reactor at Atucha, which went on stream in 1974. Just like the Germans, the Argentinians wanted to pursue the heavy water path to avoid reliance on American supplies of enriched uranium. Argentina, which had not signed the Non-Proliferation Treaty and was also constructing uranium enrichment and reprocessing facilities, wanted to leave an option open for the possible production of nuclear weapons.

With the ending of the heavy water reactor path Siemens, like AEG, had no choice but to become a US licensee. Using pressurised water technology from Westinghouse, it built the first German PWR at Obrigheim in Baden-Württemberg; this was the first of a series which established in the Federal Republic, as in other European countries, the dominance of the American PWR. By the beginning of 1989, West German utilities counted 22 completed commercial-sized nuclear power stations, of which 13 were PWRs and 8 BWRs. Only one – the 300 MW high temperature reactor at Hamm in North Rhine Westphalia – represented home-produced technology. And, as an unhappy postscript to thirty years of German atomic development, the closure of the Hamm reactor was decided in 1989 as a result of sharply rising costs and a political row over safety.

After choosing American light water reactors, West Germany was keen to build up its own uranium enrichment capacity. Again, wartime experience came in useful. Based on experiments carried out by Paul Harteck and Wilhelm Groth in Hamburg in 1941, as well as on research by another physicist, Gerhard Zippe, in the Soviet Union, the West Germans developed a gas centrifuge method for separating uranium-235. This provided a far cheaper route than the gas diffusion technique pioneered in the US, since it needed much less energy. Reflecting American criticism that the process could provide a cheap route to a nuclear bomb, Degussa – the company at the centre of the research – was forced by the US to classify its work in 1960. The Bonn government took out rights to commercial development and in 1971 set up the Urenco company, with Britain and the Netherlands, to build centrifuge plants in the three countries.

West German planners also turned their attention to the fast breeder; this type of reactor burns plutonium formed as a by-product in an atomic pile. Because the fast breeder has the capacity continually to regenerate plutonium, it can improve the efficiency of electricity production sixty-fold compared with a first-generation nuclear reactor. Under decisions taken in the mid-1960s by the Atomic Commission, the country's first small fast breeder started operations at Karlsruhe in 1971. At the same time, a pilot reprocessing facility to separate plutonium from spent uranium fuel was also started up at Karlsruhe, and in the years since then has separated well over 1 tonne of plutonium.

Strict safeguards are applied at the Karlsruhe plants by the International Atomic Energy Agency and the European Community's atomic organisation Euratom, to ensure that no plutonium is diverted for weapons purposes. The safeguards apply under the Non-Proliferation Treaty, which Bonn signed in 1969 and finally ratified in 1974 after some controversy in parliament. Although no one wanted to renounce West Germany's commitment in 1954 against producing nuclear weapons, the treaty had a rough passage. Leading conservative deputies – including past and future Defence Ministers – complained that the treaty unfairly constrained nuclear research and development by non-nuclear-weapon states.[42]

An undertone of dissatisfaction over the treaty persists still. Scientists at Karlsruhe, for instance, claim that non-proliferation controls have prevented West Germany from carrying out research with the same secrecy guaranteed to the nuclear weapons states. One scientist I spoke to there alleged that inspectors from countries like the Soviet Union or India had been able to indulge in industrial espionage at the centre.[43] The centre certainly has a reputation for 'leakiness'. Research at Karlsruhe based on the Becker 'jet nozzle' separation process appears to have helped South Africa acquire clandestine uranium enrichment capacity in the late 1960s.[44]

With West German nuclear confidence at its peak, in 1969 Siemens and AEG set up Kraftwerk Union (KWU), a jointly owned power station manufacturer which on the nuclear side would market pressurised water reactors at home and abroad.[45] The licensing links with Westinghouse were severed.

In 1975 the Federal Republic flexed its new-found nuclear export muscles and agreed to supply Brazil with up to eight 1,300 MW reactors, together with enrichment and reprocessing technology. As in the Siemens deal with Argentina, Washington complained that Bonn was flaunting international controls by giving Brazil – another non-signatory of the Non-Proliferation Treaty – weapon-making potential.[46] Although Brazil continued to develop nuclear weapons options under a purely national research programme, American worries over the German deal subsided as the German equipment was placed under IAEA safeguards and also heavily scaled down.[47]

Another brush with the US came in 1977 when President Carter tried to force America's allies to abandon plans for nuclear reprocessing, charging that international trade in plutonium added to proliferation risks. The episode exacerbated strains between Carter and Chancellor Schmidt which had already been exposed over arms control questions. Moreover, the difficulties with the US coincided with a growing split in Schmidt's Social Democratic Party over the whole question of nuclear energy policy.

Following the sharp increase in world energy prices in 1973, in 1974 the SPD-led government in Bonn set a target of 45,000 MW for nuclear generating capacity by 1985. This proved vastly over-ambitious. Reflecting the ability of nuclear protesters to block plans through the courts, as well as a sharp slow-down in energy demand, installed West German nuclear capacity by 1985 turned out to be only 16,000 MW. As a result of new plant coming on stream, by 1989 the figure rose to 24,000 MW. Because energy consumption has risen much more slowly than expected over the past decade, utilities and nuclear plant builders agree that West Germany today has substantial generating over-capacity.

Looking back, Klaus Barthelt, the veteran Kraftwerk Union chairman, admits that the nuclear industry made mistakes.[48] Up to the beginning of the 1970s, he says, 'We had a form of euphoria over nuclear energy – it appeared a panacea. The main error was in the time before 1975. In this period, when people were basically positively disposed towards nuclear energy, we should have done more to make the technology understandable.' Talking of the national anti-nuclear mood after Chernobyl, he says, 'Nowhere apart from West Germany and perhaps Austria did any country react so hysterically.... It will take some time before we come back to the consensus which existed before. The Germans are easily aroused emotionally.' He adds, with a curious air of detachment for a man who has devoted decades to the nuclear cause, 'Whether we in Germany say farewell to nuclear energy is a matter of complete indifference to the rest of the world. If we were no longer there, there would be one less competitor on the market – and one which produces good nuclear plants.'

276

IV

In May 1986, a month after Chernobyl, President Richard von Weizsäcker made a speech urging a long-term nuclear *Ausstieg* which brought acclaim from the Greens and the SPD but did not endear him to atomic protagonists.

> I am confident that technology, which was powerful enough to lead us into nuclear energy, will also be powerful enough to lead us, in the long term, away from it and to the production of energy without radioactivity.[49]

Not all put the message so mildly. Massive post-Chernobyl protests at the sites of the planned Wackersdorf reprocessing plant, at the Brokdorf PWR in Schleswig Holstein or at the Hanau nuclear fuel factories left a trail of broken bones and injuries from water cannon. In the months after Chernobyl, the Bonn Interior Ministry estimated that a 3,000-strong 'hard core' of demonstrators armed with clubs and slings was available to lend a hand to protest action. In 1986, the Ministry registered 164 attacks on electricity supply installations – mainly the sawing-down of pylons. The number dropped to 93 in 1987 and only 43 in 1988.

According to Volker Hauff, a former SPD Technology Minister who has now become one of the party's strongest nuclear opponents, the atomic industry should be fought with economics rather than violence. In 1989 Hauff led the Social Democrats to election victory in the state of Hesse and became Mayor of Frankfurt. He argues that nuclear energy will gradually be priced out of business, as utilities have to pay mounting sums for safety precautions and radioactive waste disposal. Although electricity generated from older German nuclear plants costs considerably less than from coal-fired power stations, the anti-nuclear opposition is hoping that increasing costs for new power stations will persuade utilities against building replacements when nuclear plants come up for renewal during the 1990s.

In view of his previous ministerial responsibility for atomic research between 1978 and 1980, Hauff has a credibility problem. He says his conversion away from the nuclear cause was an almost religious experience; it took place gradually as he participated 'evening after evening' in conversations with anti-nuclear protesters in places around the country such as Wyhl, a proposed reactor site near Freiburg in

Baden-Württemberg which was shelved after strong local opposition. Another turning point, he says, was a visit to the US in 1979 during which he was told of State Department suspicions that Pakistan had acquired bomb-building material via West Germany – just one of a stream of US complaints in recent years that the Federal Republic had been a conduit for illicit nuclear weapons know-how to the Third World. 'Nuclear risks transcend the scale of humanity. That cannot be justified,' Hauff told me.[50]

The Greens point out that between 300,000 and 1 million people live within a 30-kilometre radius of most West German power stations. Evacuation in the event of a serious accident would be practically impossible, a thought which is plainly a nightmare for many. Public opinion polls show that more than 80 per cent of the population fears a severe nuclear accident in the Federal Republic.[51] Public confidence was also knocked by a scandal in 1988 over corruption at West Germany's leading radioactive waste transport company, Transnuklear, based at the Hanau nuclear fuel complex. The affair – centring on large-scale illegal consignments of nuclear material – raised an outcry and forced the Bonn government to close down and reorganise part of the Hanau operations.

One particular place to measure Germany's atomic disillusionment is the research centre in Berlin named after Hahn and Meitner. Sited on the southern fringes of West Berlin not far from the Glienicker Bridge, the publicly funded research institute was set up in 1958, when it became the home of one of the country's first research reactors. These days it concentrates on non-nuclear activities such as solar energy research and investigation of materials using neutron beams. The word 'nuclear' was dropped from its name a few years ago.

The director of the Hahn-Meitner institute, Professor Hans Stiller, warns that the phasing out of nuclear energy would damage the environment by increasing burning of hydrocarbon fuels.[52] He is obviously nervous about the strong anti-nuclear tide in Berlin. The city's Green movement has been trying to close down the centre's atomic reactor, and has charged that planned cooperation between Hahn-Meitner and East Germany's main nuclear research facility at Rossendorf near Dresden could have military implications. Professor Arnim Henglein, a nuclear physicist in charge of the institute's solar energy research, says that politicians are channelling funds into the area simply to appease public worries over nuclear power. He adds fiercely that this is 'electoral fraud': solar energy will never be economically feasible in West Germany.

278

In December 1988, West Berlin commemorated in style the 50th anniversary of Hahn's breakthrough. The city's mayor gave a speech in which he talked about nuclear weapons and disarmament, but did not mention atomic power. A few hours later, in a neo-Renaissance courtyard at the city's Technical University, anti-atomic radicals staged a commando raid on an anniversary exhibition featuring replicas of Hahn's equipment. Exhibits were smashed to pieces and red paint was splattered around. As visiting nuclear dignitaries picked their way in bewilderment through the debris, about a hundred protesters shouting 'Hiroshima' and 'Chernobyl' occupied the gallery of the building. They banged drums, blew trumpets and sang parodies of the *Deutschlandlied*. An uncertain journey into the second half-century of the nuclear era was under way – and, as could be expected, the ever-Faustian Germans were in the vanguard.

14

The Greening of the Germans

We feel uneasy about Germany, a force of the nature to which she clings so closely, a bundle of powerful yet hazy instincts.

Charles de Gaulle, 1934[1]

Even in children, tests show an alarming increase of leukaemia, cancer, rickets and blood disorders associated with air and water pollution. It is dismaying that this challenge for society, affecting the health of millions of people, has been neglected. The sky over the Ruhr must be blue again!

Willy Brandt, 1961[2]

Where many a poison factory blooms
beneath a yellow sky
where rivers flow as black as night
where we all slowly die.

Udo Lindenberg, 1982[3]

German attitudes towards the environment are shaped both by hard industrial logic and by a streak of irrationality. The debate about finding the right balance between pollution and prosperity is more passionate in Germany than anywhere else in Europe. The *Umwelt* has become the symbol for dissatisfaction with an imperfect world. The changing of attitudes has acquired its own momentum. The Greens' ecology party has remodelled the political landscape. Environmental technology has grown into an important force in the economy; as one inevitable result of the Federal Republic's dominant role in the European Community, the German ecological crusade is spreading throughout Europe. With the upheavals in East Germany, the process has been extended a step further. A Greens party in East Berlin was founded in November 1989, soon followed by the first joint East-West German demonstrations against waste transport; and, in the former no-man's-land of the East-West German border, swathes of countryside are being transformed into all-German biotopes.

I

The medieval town of Marktredwitz, in an undulating fir-tree-clad corner of Bavaria next to the Czech and East German borders, looks at first sight like an idyllic setting for Germans yearning to return to nature. In fact, it is a place where nature now is taking its revenge.

Marktredwitz lies at the hub of trunk rail lines which once criss-crossed imperial Europe. Half a century ago, the town was a bustling route centre; trains used to steam through here daily, joining Rome and Leipzig, Paris and Prague, Berlin and Barcelona. Since the Second World War it has been condemned to a backwater existence in the shadow of the Iron Curtain; when the barbed wire began to fall at the end of 1989, the region looked forward suddenly to new life. The town, with 20,000 inhabitants, still provides a home for specialist companies in fields ranging from engineering to porcelain-making. For years Hans-Achaz von Lindenfels, the veteran mayor, has concentrated his considerable energies on trying to bring more outside jobs and investment to this remote spot. Because of some recent adverse publicity, he is now having to try even harder.

As a symbol of its attractiveness as an industrial site, the town's promotional brochures have traditionally highlighted its most venerable company – the Chemische Fabrik Marktredwitz, a 200-year-old chemical works set among the houses opposite the town hall. Goethe visited the factory in 1822, and wrote admiringly of its techniques that used mercury from Spain and Mexico to make coloured glass.

Today Lindenfels no longer thinks of the firm as a prize asset and admits winsomely: 'Our image has suffered.'[4] The chemical works, ranking as Germany's oldest-established chemical company, was closed down in 1985 and has since made national headlines as the centre of an explosive pollution scandal. The affair showed how easily West Germany's strict environmental regulations can be flouted – with horrendously long-lasting consequences. Investigators looking into alarmingly high mercury concentrations in a nearby brook discovered during the 1980s that the factory site was contaminated with massive quantities of poisonous chemicals: arsenic, antimony, cadmium, cyanide, phenol and – above all – mercury. Over several decades the substances, used in weed-killer and pesticide production, had been allowed to build up in waste vessels, permeating factory buildings and equipment, in flagrant disregard of safety precautions.

281

After the shut-down, the plant was walled off and cordoned with barbed wire; it was named 'the death zone' by local people. Waste disposal specialists moved in with gas-masks and protective clothing. Around 3,000 tonnes of poisonous material were removed in sealed steel canisters, but experts reckoned that a total of 80,000 tonnes of rubble and contaminated soil needed to be carried away in coming years. Plans were laid for the entire factory to be broken up under a huge pressurised tent, to prevent the danger of poisonous dust escaping into the atmosphere.

Fears grew among the townspeople that the toxic chemicals might have spread to the water table. Pollution appears to have spread by river to the Czech town of Eger on the other side of the border, to which Marktredwitz belonged for nearly 500 years up until the end of the Napoleonic Wars. Rolf and Oskar Tropitzch, the managers of the family company, went on trial and, after a three-month court case, escaped in February 1989 with fines totalling DM190,000. The public prosecutor had demanded jail sentences, but the more serious charges were dismissed by the court on account of lack of evidence. As a political row gathered over why the town authorities had not uncovered the irregularities years earlier, experts estimated that the overall cleaning-up job would cost at least DM50 million. Since the company had filed for bankruptcy, the cost would be borne by the taxpayer.

The drums of hazardous Marktredwitz waste were transported by lorry 120 miles north-west to one of the world's most bizarre and deadly storage dumps – a disused salt mine at Herfa-Neurode near Kassel. The site is run by the Kali und Salz minerals group, part of the giant BASF chemicals concern. Since the beginning of the 1970s, it has made available deep underground caverns to store around 600,000 tonnes of industrial and household waste from West Germany and other European countries.

The mines, part of Europe's most extensive potash deposits, run across the boundary into nearby East Germany. They are connected by a warren of 150 miles of tunnels carved out by monster rock-boring vehicles. During the Second World War, the labyrinths were used for storing munitions. The poisons stockpiled here now, sealed up in their containers behind brick walls, add up to a roll-call of the most toxic substances known to mankind. Norbert Deisenroth, the jovial head of the Herfa-Neurode dump, conducts visitors on a guided tour 1,800 feet below ground in a yellow cut-down Mercedes truck. 'We call ourselves the chemists' shop,' he told me as he led me through underground chambers piled high with improbably cheerful-looking red, blue and yellow tanks bearing cyanide solutions discarded from car factories. One yellow drum has stencilled on it the helpful warning: 'Keep locked up and out of reach of children.'[5]

The dump is not particularly large as waste-tips go; around 300 million tonnes of dangerous industrial residues are generated each year from western countries, and most has to end up somewhere on a tip. But Herfa-Neurode is unique in the world on account of the range of substances it is authorised to receive: it is licensed to take 2,300 types of waste ranging from arsenic and cyanide, tars and insecticides, to toxic household rubbish such as old batteries, medicines and lamps.

The salt deposits, which are 250 million years old, are protected by a 100-yard-thick layer of clay which prevents any danger – geologists say – of water seeping into the mine. Since the poisons brought to Herfa-Neurode at the rate of about 80,000 tonnes a year are intended to stay here safely for millennia, everyone is hoping that the geology of the site is as stable as the experts claim.

An underground storage room contains shelves full of glass jars filled with samples of the consignments stacked away in the barred-off salt chambers, each one neatly labelled and dated. The aim is to give the mine's future operators an idea of the hazardous residues brought here by previous generations. Perhaps, in the future, technology will allow the substances to be hauled up out of the ground, recycled and reused? For the moment that is an illusory hope. Deisenroth ruminates, 'They are meant to be still here in 1,000 years' time.'

II

The mercury mined in Mexico, processed in Marktredwitz and then consigned again to the earth's crust at Herfa-Neurode forms one small but potent part of West Germany's tortuous environmental chain. The search for solutions is heavily laden with conflicts of interest. The confluence of wealth, high population density and intensive industrialisation makes the Germans both besotted with material progress and fearful of its consequences.

A prime cause of damage to forests is held to be oxides of nitrogen spewing from speeding German cars, but – because of the unusual emotional attachment of the Germans to their cars – no government has yet imposed what would be an obvious counter-measure: a speed limit on Autobahn drivers. Additionally, the motor industry, which directly or indirectly gives employment to about 4 million West Germans (approximately one-sixth of the work-force), tirelessly puts forward the view that less speed would somehow mean fewer jobs. Volatile public opinion puts politicians under great pressure to come up with quick results, making the *Umwelt* debate exceptionally frenetic.

West Germany's position at the European crossroads naturally turns the *Umwelt* into a question of foreign policy. The Federal Republic, depending for its livelihood on international trade, is open to pollution carried by the wind and the rivers of East and West. The Bonn government, spurred on by public opinion and given increasing backing from industry, is attempting to introduce tougher anti-pollution safeguards throughout the European Community. Smaller countries in Europe – in Scandinavia, Switzerland, the Netherlands – have also embarked on environmental programmes which in some ways are more consistent and better managed than those of West Germany. But, because of the Federal Republic's industrial muscle, it is the German ecological drive which has been crucial in encouraging greater *Umwelt* consciousness in Britain and France.

Neither of the two most dramatic European ecological disasters of recent years – the Chernobyl nuclear accident in the Ukraine and the fire at the Swiss pharmaceutical company Sandoz, both in 1986 – occurred in Germany, but the public opinion fall-out was greater in the Federal Republic than anywhere else. Efforts to fight the Sandoz blaze at Basle sluiced around 30 tonnes of dangerous agricultural chemicals, including 200 kg of mercury, into the Rhine, and brought down a storm of public criticism on West Germany's own large and powerful chemical industry.

The mishaps heightened sensitivities which had already been aroused over the Seveso chemical explosion in Italy in 1976, and the catastrophe at Bhopal in India in 1985 when 2,500 people were killed and 40,000 seriously injured by a gas leak from a Union Carbide pesticide plant. The Germans worry more than most that scientific strides are bringing the human race not towards perfection, but towards the precipice.

With many material needs sated, there is a growing feeling that damage to the ecology represents too high a price for economic growth. At the root of the questioning lies the belief that the human conquest over nature is only short-lived, for nature will get its own back. This view seemed almost entirely absent during the recovery years of the 1950s and 1960s. Now, the Germans are making up for lost time.

Efforts to protect nature from the ravages of an industrial economy have a long history in Germany. The term 'acid rain' first came into use in the early 1870s. The first widespread scientific reports of the harm caused to forests by factory pollution were in the 1880s. The almost mystical status of the forests – which as late as during the second half of the last century covered a quarter of the Reich – gives *Waldsterben* (forest death) an emotiveness not found elsewhere.

Willy Brandt's famous 'blue skies over the Ruhr' speech in 1961 represented one of the first signs of a reappearance of environmentalism. The Social Democrat-led governments of the 1970s failed to give the *Umwelt* high priority. However, the environmental cause crossed to West Germany by way of the US, bolstered by the student protest movements of the 1960s and, in the following decade, by the anti-military peace movement. The Greens were formed in 1980 out of a web of disparate protest and ecology groups; the party owes some of its roots to the back-to-the soil youth movement which sprouted around 1900, the focus of desires to attain a new ideological foundation of life after the rapid industrialisation of the final decades of the 19th century.

Concern about the environment comes second only to worries over unemployment in the league table of questions most bothering the Germans.[6] Ecology-mindedness sometimes seems a substitute for nationalism. Wrappers of chewing-gum sold in West Germany carry exhortations in several languages. In German, purchasers are entreated to 'keep the *Umwelt* clean', whereas in English the message is 'keep your country tidy'. West Germans tend to deride the lack of *Umwelt* consciousness in other EC countries and a cultural gap has opened up with Britain in particular. The British government's conversion to the cause of phasing out chlorofluorocarbons in refrigerators, aerosols and insulating materials (blamed for depleting the ozone layer in the upper atmosphere and allowing through harmful solar radiation) has been welcomed, but the Germans say that the move should have come years ago. One German student who recently visited England told me of her scorn at failing to find facilities for disposing of used batteries. She handed them dutifully over the counter in a local electrical shop. In West Germany, household batteries would be placed in a special container, headed perhaps for the catacombs of Herfa-Neurode. In England, the shop assistant took them and, without more ado, cheerfully threw them into the waste-paper basket.

Especially since the Greens entered the Bundestag in 1983, no politician – on the Right or Left – can succeed who does not swear unswerving fealty to the *Umwelt*. No household product – from electrical appliance to detergent – can be brought to market unless the manufacturer makes claims for its environmental benignancy. The Munich-based 'David against Goliath' ecology group, a regular thorn in the side of the pro-nuclear Bavarian state government, asks its members to adopt eleven commandments starting with, 'I will do everything not to pollute the air.' To show it cared just as much as the Greens, the Kohl government decided in 1987 to inscribe the sanctity of the *Umwelt* into the constitution.

Opinion polls show that 75 per cent of the population place glass in bottle banks, while 80 per cent profess to save waste paper, collected by local authorities in special *Altpapier* lorries perpetually blocking the streets. West Germany's largest religious cemetery, in Brunswick, has made the transition to ecological funerals, banning plastic urns and using only coffins made out of easily-degradable wood. Television gives regular spots to so-called 'Eco-tips', including advice on protecting woodland wild-life. Only West German television could feature a popular soap opera centring on a 12-year-old girl sick with leukaemia, pondering dead fish in the Rhine and proclaiming that she no longer had hope in the chemical industry. Customers buying Coca-Cola in plastic bottles have to pay a deposit to finance recycling. Coloured toilet paper is virtually banned from supermarket shelves on the grounds that the dyes sully the water table. Under Defence Ministry orders, the navy is given training in clearing sea pollution. Some Bonn Defence Ministry planners say that, in the coming European 'peace order', the Bundeswehr's tasks may be limited solely to environmental duties.

West German florists recommend wrapping flowers in ordinary paper rather than non-degradable cellophane. An important reason for students using spray-paint far less these days in scrawling slogans on walls is fear about aerosol propellants eating up ozone. Chlorofluorocarbons are being phased out of the plastic boxes in which hamburgers are packed; it is also noticeable that German McDonalds restaurants give as much prominence to wholesome salads as to patties of beef. In contrast to the cliché conception that the Germans are a race of militant meat-eaters,[7] the West Germans have been induced by worries about hormones and other dietary hazards to eat much less meat in recent years and more fruit and vegetables.[8] Hitler seems to have been anticipating German fastidiousness when he prophesied that 'the world of the future will be vegetarian.'[9]

Cleaning up the *Umwelt* is highly expensive, but has also developed into a major economic growth area. Konrad Henkel, owner of the family chemicals firm which bears his name, made the point in 1972 that environmental protection could bring profits. 'New tasks lead to new

286

solution; new challenges lead to new markets.'[10] Henkel led the way with non-phosphate Persil, and now three-quarters of the washing powder sold in West German stores is proudly marked as phosphate-free. During the years of post-war reconstruction, the West Germans lagged behind not only the US and Japan but also Britain in clean air legislation. During the 1980s, however, efforts to contain atmospheric pollution leaped into prominence. A law passed in 1983 requiring fossil-fuelled power stations and factories to cut down emissions of noxious sulphur and nitrogen oxides involves the investment of DM28 billion in filters and cleaning equipment up to 1993.[11] West German industry says it spends more than DM22 billion a year on overall environmental protection, while the cost of dumping household and industrial waste alone is put at DM12 billion annually.

Protecting the environment is estimated to give jobs to 450,000 people – 1.5 to 2 per cent of the West German work-force. While stronger concern about the *Umwelt* creates jobs in environmental technology sectors, it also destroys them elsewhere by encouraging industry to rationalise operations and trim costs. Peter Meurer, a board member of the Dortmund Uhde company, one of the country's foremost pollution specialists, welcomes the ecological shift in industry; nevertheless he says that, at least in the Ruhr area of traditional heavy industry, 'We can't create enough jobs to make up for those which are lost through environmental policies.'[12]

Another source of controversy comes from the European Community. Squabbling about pan-European regulations to watch over the environment has become one of the most divisive issues between Bonn and its European partners in the 1992 single market programme. The German public suspects that Bonn might have to accept more lax environmental standards as part of industrial policy harmonisation, and there is particular opposition to Community plans to allow untrammelled imports of foods which do not conform to Germany's strict purity regulations. In recent years the Federal Republic has lost hard-pitched legal battles with the European Court of Justice, trying to keep out foreign beer and sausages on the grounds that they are 'impure' for German consumers. In the defeat over beer, the European Court of Justice ruled that Community free trade principles took precedence over regulations dating back to the 16th century under which German beer could be brewed only from hops, malt and water.

The Bonn government faces a similar battle in trying to keep out imports of synthetic milk made from ingredients like soya – banned under a law dating from 1930. On the other hand, the Federal

287

Republic's less wealthy neighbours reject as a form of ecological imperialism German attempts to force through stricter Community-wide environmental standards. The nationalist 19th-century quotation much favoured by William II – '*Es mag am deutschen Wesen einmal noch die Welt genesen*' ('The German mind should edify the world')[13] has started to take on a new ecological meaning.

III

The Greens gained 5.6 per cent of the votes in the 1983 general elections, and then 8.3 per cent in the 1987 poll. The party has not lost its humourlessness, and has been lurching through a succession of internal crises while it makes up its mind whether to remain a pure protest movement, or to take part in parliamentary decision-making through sharing power with the established parties. None the less, in an increasingly fragmented political landscape, the proportional representational system gives the party leverage which is out of all proportion to its slender 42,000-strong membership.

Whatever the naïveté of some of their proposals for a reforging of industrial society, the Greens have proved a valuable catalyst in bringing environmentalism to the forefront of politics. Although often dressed up in radical verbiage, the party's philosophy recognises the reality that West Germany's economy is switching its focus away from traditional areas of heavy industry to more sophisticated, less energy-intensive manufacturing. The products of the future, made with more intelligence and less mechanical power, will be less demanding on the environment. In view of the party's amorphous structure and its *penchant* for contentious in-fighting, the Greens' policies on vital questions like West German membership of NATO or the expansion of the European Community remain shrouded by uncertainty. Their rejection of orthodox economic policies, together with their leanings towards a never-clearly-defined form of West German neutralism, up to now have ruled out the party as a serious, long-lasting coalition partner for the Social Democrats. Nevertheless, this could change in the 1990s, if the moderates in the Greens gain the upper hand.

There is still an outside chance that the Greens could simply burn themselves up in internal squabbling. With substantial parts of their basic ecology policies now taken over by the mainstream parties, their disappearance from the Bundestag would probably be no great loss. A highly disillusioned Petra Kelly, one of the party's founders, told me at the end of 1987 that the Greens had developed into 'a typical German party' beset with theoretical feuding and factional rivalry.[14] She was particularly mortified that the German Greens, through their internal bickering, were setting a bad example for the Greens parties which have sprung up in other European countries.

Otto Schily, one of the best-known Green parliamentarians, told me that the Greens' chief achievement has lain in persuading public opinion to focus not simply on the tangible benefits of economic progress but also on the costs throughout the whole gamut of production. One scientific study has estimated annual ecological damage – spreading from the costs of air pollution to the economic expense of traffic accidents – at nearly 10 per cent of the Federal Republic's gross national product.[15] Schily said:

> We are in an economic structure where we do not count the costs of clearing up the environment. We cannot accept that one industry makes the products which do the harm, and another tries to repair the damage. Gross national product goes together with dying forests. We must bring the ecological factor into growth policies. We have to carry out crisis management – but we also need to tackle the roots of the crisis.[16]

The need for a sceptical examination of the whole of the industrial cycle is now indeed accepted as part of the capitalist credo. The idea that an industrial society should accept the ruin of rivers, land or forests, and then pay to clean them up again, has been recognised as economic nonsense. It is clearly preferable to avoid the contamination in the first place. German businessmen realise that looking after the *Umwelt* by saving energy and waste can boost efficiency and profits; it can also be a source of higher morale. Gerhard Vollheim, director of applied research at Degussa, the chemical and metals firm, talks enthusiastically of his company's feat in developing catalytic converters for cars (an area where West Germany has long lagged behind the US and Japan) and phosphate substitutes in washing powders. He says that younger scientists in particular see anti-pollution research as an important motivating influence for their work. 'We are glad when we can do something positive,' he told me.[17]

Schily is a prominent figure on the pragmatic 'realo' wing of the Greens, standing in often heated contrast to the party's 'fundamentalists' who oppose all cooperation with the establishment. With the face of a quizzical pixie, Schily is a lawyer who gained a reputation for quick-wittedness in his defence of members of the Baader-Meinhof terrorist gang in the 1960s. He is sufficiently orthodox not to strike fear into the heart of the average German industrialist. Tired of strife with the 'fundis', Schily rocked the Greens boat by quitting the party in November 1989 to join the Social Democrats; his departure has not helped the Greens' survival chances.

One Green who is clearly the subject of boardroom nightmares is Jutta Ditfurth, the vivacious leader of the fundamentalist faction. Now, however, the nightmares appear to be fading. She gained national fame by composedly telling Franz Josef Strauss to 'calm down' on television just before the 1987 elections, and took over from Petra Kelly as the best-known Green media figure.

Ditfurth, a social scientist born into a liberal bourgeois Frankfurt family (she has dropped the aristocratic *von* from her surname), combines a talent for invective with a good head for facts and figures. She says she likes taking part in podium discussions with electricity utility representatives 'because I normally win'. She told me she had a simple recipe for curbing environmental risks from the country's chemical industry: 'One-third should be kept going, one-third converted to other production, and one-third closed down.'[18]

As the Greens swung round in early 1989 to a 'realo' stand on most issues, Ditfurth drew the consequences and withdrew from active Green politics. That deprived the Greens' political opponents of a valuable target. 'The Greens want to go back to the past in a postal coach,' I was told by Norbert Blüm, the tubby Social Affairs Minister who is one of the few members of Kohl's government team with a talent for political ribaldry. 'But they complain if the trains are three minutes late. And if they are ill, they want to go to the most modern hospital, don't they?'[19]

None the less, West German business shows surprising sympathy for Green-type ecological ideas running through politics. Helmut Lang, managing director of Thyssen Engineering, a subsidiary of the giant steel group which has built up important business in pollution control, says the Greens tend to over-dramatise environmental problems – but the overall effect of their activities has been positive.[20]

The West German chemical companies spend around DM5 billion a year on environmental protection, and sometimes complain about the drawbacks, but the Big Three chemical giants achieved booming profits during the 1980s. Chemical industry managers do not like it when their products are pilloried by press and politicians. 'Germans discuss the environment like a Wagner opera. We must not sacrifice everything to the *Umwelt* god,' says Herwig Hulpke, environment protection manager at the Bayer chemical company.[21] Environmental consciousness has on the whole benefited the chemical industry, however. It has forced companies to rationalise and move away from polluting bulk chemicals into cleaner, more profitable higher-value activities. 'The vitality of the German chemical industry seems to have been greater than the disadvantage it has suffered through environmental restrictions,' says Hans-Georg Peine, environmental protection director at BASF.[22]

Rudolf von Bennigsen-Foerder, chairman of the energy and chemicals giant Veba, says, 'The Germans are prone to exaggeration' and that 'a more measured approach would perhaps give industry the chance to solve the problems at less cost'. But he believes that public pressure for tough pollution regulations is ultimately salutary. Drawing a parallel with the wartime bombing of Germany which paved the way for its industrial rebirth, Bennigsen told me that environmental legislation in the long run may provide a way of keeping the Federal Republic ahead of its competitors.[23] Inevitably, Bennigsen-Foerder believes, harmonisation of industrial policies within the European Community will force countries like Britain and France to adapt to West Germany's pioneering standards. 'Strict environmental regulations bring a burden, but other countries which are not so strict will one day have to catch up. Burdens can sometimes be turned into advantages later.'

The man in the middle of conflicting pressures from industry and the public is Klaus Töpfer, appointed Environment Minister in May 1987. Chancellor Kohl set up an Environment Ministry in June 1986, in the wake of post-Chernobyl panic. Underlining Bonn's relatively late ecology start, the word *Umwelt* was first adopted in government parlance only as late as 1970, when a department for *Umweltschutz* (environmental protection) was established at the Interior Ministry. According to an Infas opinion poll carried out in 1970, only 41 per cent of West Germans that year had any idea what the word *Umweltschutz* meant – ignorance which, of course, would be inconceivable today. Töpfer is an energetic and extrovert professor from Silesia with a taste for beer and for self-publicity. His detractors among the Greens – who would favour a much tougher line on industry – accuse him of playing merely a palliative role, but at least Töpfer brings a much-needed element of good cheer into German politics. Since his responsibilities also include nuclear reactor safety, he is seldom out of the headlines. He receives more than 50,000 letters a year from concerned West Germans – the favourite topic in 1988 was the disappearance of the ozone layer – and tries to give a personal reply to as many as possible. Nicknamed 'Katastrophen-Klaus' on account of his tendency to race to the scene of ecological accidents, Töpfer even made a well-photographed swim across the Rhine in 1988 in a bid to convince doubting public opinion that water quality had improved. He was also much in evidence before the TV cameras on the German North Sea coast in 1988, when hundreds of seals died of a mysterious disease induced by pollution.

The seal deaths focused public attention on the 11,000 tonnes of lead, 28,000 tonnes of zinc, 950 tonnes of arsenic, 335 tonnes of cadmium and 75 tonnes of mercury which find their way annually into the North Sea.[24] About 100,000 tonnes of chemicals are incinerated annually at sea, around 60 per cent sent out on ships from West German harbours. North Sea pollution is also caused by the massive amounts of fertilisers consumed by European farmers: 1.5 million tonnes of nitrogenous material and 100,000 tonnes of phosphate flow into the sea each year, mostly through the Rhine and the Elbe. The North Sea coastal countries decided in 1987 to cut the amount of pollutants by 50 per cent in the period up to 1995 – but the spectre of the dying seals brought home to the German public that this was too little, too late. There is a clear conflict between intensive European Community farming produced over thirty years by the Common Agricultural Policy, and the need to cut back damaging effluents. Not surprisingly, Germany has taken in the lead in the Community in promoting 'green' farming with much less use of fertilisers – a move which, of course, needs to be financed by the taxpayers to compensate farmers for shortfalls in production.

Töpfer is surely right when he says that a vigorous environmental policy 'represents the only permanent way to safeguard jobs and industry in the modern world. All the evidence shows that countries which have lax policies on questions of the environment have to pay dearly in the end for any possible advantages this gives them.'[25] But too often Töpfer gives the impression of being forced simply to react to events rather than of mastering them. 'Why is the Federal Republic so much more worried about the environment than other countries?' I asked him. He first gave me the standard reply about population density and heavy industrialisation, then added another more fundamentally German reason: 'Under the surface, many Germans have a guilty conscience about having achieved such a high living standard in such a short time since the war.'

Töpfer recognises that the country's environment approach was inadequate until the 1970s. 'We saw this in the post-war recovery of the economy. A lot of the recovery was carried out at a cost to nature. This has produced a lot of harm – contaminated industrial sites and so on – which cost much more to clear up now than if we had tackled the

292

problems from the start.'

He can be relied upon to declare regular initiatives, spreading from cuts in chlorofluorocarbon output and reductions in imports of wood from threatened tropical forests, to efforts to bring European power station emission controls into line with those of Germany. But his main disadvantage has been lack of political weight within the cabinet to push through stricter controls, either at a federal level or throughout the European Community. The German Environment Minister has only limited influence over events in the *Länder*. The federal states, responsible for implementing environmental regulations, cannot always be relied upon to police them properly; and, as the Marktredwitz episode dramatically highlighted, infringers of *Umwelt* regulations who are brought to court often face only modest penalties.

The Environment Minister draws comfort however from the way that ecology consciousness has boosted West Germany's image abroad. It is a good way, perhaps, of erasing unpleasant memories. 'Every time I cross a border, in the West or in the East, I find that Germany is regarded and welcomed as working on the front line of environmental efforts. As a partner, we are appreciated everywhere.' Töpfer's Ministry is making a start on channelling funds and technology to East Germany and other parts of eastern Europe to reduce air and water pollution crossing from east of the Elbe. This is enlightened West German self-interest. Spreading *Umwelt* know-how eastwards extends new German ideals.

IV

When Germans talk about the *Umwelt*, the language has an apocalyptic ring. The Greens' founding policy declaration in 1980 said:

> Raw materials are becoming scarce, there is scandal after scandal over toxic waste, whole species of animals are being wiped out, varieties of plants are dying out, rivers and oceans are turning into sewers, mankind is threatening to waste away both intellectually and spiritually among an advanced industrial and consumer society, and we are heaping up a dreadful heritage for future generations.[26]

A fund-raising letter sent to thousands of households by the environmental organisation Greenpeace repeats the proverb of the Cree

Indians recited to the white man: 'When the last tree is rooted out, when the last river is poisoned, when the last fish is caught, only then will you understand: You cannot eat money.' Hans-Dietrich Genscher, the Foreign Minister, is no fundamentalist; but he talks of ecology in terms of the ending of the world:

> We face the task of protecting mankind from the danger of destruction which man himself has created. In the widest sense of the word, it is a question of the survival of the human race. The atom bombs of Hiroshima and Nagasaki, the atomic catastrophe of Chernobyl, dying lakes and forests, poisoned rivers, our endangered North Sea which washes up victims every day on the coast – these are ever greater warnings of doom written on the wall.[27]

When diplomats from Bonn's embassy in Mexico City tried to persuade the Foreign Ministry to cut posting periods in the capital on account of difficult living conditions, at first all entreaties were in vain. Appeals pointing to general stress, health problems and the high crime rate all fell on deaf ears. Only when the diplomats told Bonn that sulphur dioxide pollution in the air was so bad that birds were falling dead out of the sky did Genscher's Ministry relent and allow a cut in the period of service to two years from the normal three to four.

Jutta Ditfurth likes to term river pollution 'the continuing, suppressed catastrophe'.[28] Social Democrat politicians summon up images out of the Middle Ages to denounce the chemical companies as 'poisoners of wells'. Carl-Friedrich von Weizsäcker, the philosopher elder brother of the West German president and one of the key figures behind the German wartime atomic project,* states, 'Mankind is in a crisis, the catastrophic peak of which is probably still before us.'[29]

Certainly the statistics sound fearsome. According to figures published since 1982 in an annual ritual by the Agricultural Ministry, just over half the trees in West Germany – around 10 million acres – are damaged in some way. The deterioration of their natural habitat is the most important reason why 52 per cent of the country's bird species, 53 per cent of mammals, 71 per cent of fish and 75 per cent of reptiles are officially classified as endangered. Around 70,000 sites around the country are officially termed as potential environmental hazards because of soil contamination, which is a special problem for people living near former waste dumps and disused industrial areas. The main ecological lobbying organisation BUND has brought out a map of 72 old Third

* See Chapter 13.

Reich munitions sites in West Germany, together with a further 39 in East Germany, all said to represent a danger to health.[30] BUND has also called on West Germany's 15 million gardeners to ban insecticides and make their flower and vegetable patches 'chemical-free zones'.

In the search for a way out of the *Umwelt* dilemma, the Germans appear to be world champions at finding counter-productive solutions. Through a contorted sequence of events, Chernobyl indirectly increased *Waldsterben*. Because of fears that deer on Bavarian hunting reserves were contaminated by fall-out from the Ukraine, demand for venison fell sharply in 1986 and 1987. The consequent drop in deer-shooting sharply increased the number of animals roaming the Bavarian forests – and boosted the damage they do by gnawing at tree-trunks.

Many Germans believe that paper shopping-bags are more ecologically acceptable than those made of polythene. The Federal Environment Agency was forced to issue a warning that, when disposed of, paper bags actually unleash a greater quantity of hazardous chemicals. Regulations to reduce noxious power station emissions have often resulted simply in shifting the pollution problem rather than solving it. Equipment fitted to coal-fired power stations to remove sulphur dioxide produces several million tonnes of gypsum annually. Storing the by-product without contaminating water supplies has become almost as much a challenge for electrical utilities as the initial sulphur dioxide.

The widest-ranging environmental policy contradictions undoubtedly stem from the car industry. Opinion polls show that the Germans yearn to head back to nature ... but want to drive there as fast as possible.[31] The automobile, the symbol of the Germans' desire for self-expression and liberty, is one of the most significant sources of environmental damage. It also causes dramatic human losses which, in contrast to the media coverage of overall ecological hazards, only rarely make the headlines. In 1989 a total of 7,985 people died on the roads, a figure down 2.8 per cent from the previous year, while 449,213 were injured (up 0.2 per cent) and the number of accidents fell 1 per cent to just over 2 million.

There is little doubt, statistically at least, that driving has become safer in recent years. Annual road deaths have fallen by more than half since the beginning of the 1950s. During the 1980s there has been a clear drop both in the overall numbers of casualties and, even more marked, in the number of deaths per kilometre driven. That said, the figure for road deaths per kilometre in West Germany is still appreciably

295

higher than in Britain or the US – although the mortality rate remains below the figures in France, Italy, Austria or Spain.[32]

The government has struggled to bring in a systematic plan to control the environmental drawbacks of the automobile, partly because Europe as a whole still lags well behind the US and Japan in this respect. West Germany has had very little success in encouraging drivers to limit car pollution by slackening their speeds on motorways. Nitrogen oxides from car exhausts are blamed in particular for causing sharp increases in city ozone concentrations during the summer. Ozone high in the stratosphere acts beneficially to block ultra violet rays, but at ground level it causes asthma in humans, eats away at every kind of material from rubber bands and car tyres to textiles, and damages the growth of plants and trees.

The European Community has been struggling to clear a way through the jungle of vested interests in different countries to agree uniform rules for introducing three-way catalytic converters in new cars. Removing carbon monoxide and hydrocarbons as well as nitrogen oxides, converters have been obligatory on new cars in the US since 1981. Bonn has brought in tax incentives to favour the sale of cars with catalysts, and through lower petrol tax rates has also prompted a big increase in sales of lead-free petrol (now making up more than 50 per cent of petrol sales in West Germany). However, these limited measures have failed to soothe worries about car pollution; because of the increased number of vehicles on the roads, with no diminution in their speeds, the amount of nitrogen oxides produced by motor cars has risen rather than fallen. Additionally, Bonn's use of tax breaks to encourage sales of diesel-run cars may have been counterproductive. Diesel contains no lead additives and also gives rise to lower concentrations of nitrogen oxides and other pollutants, but there is a substantial drawback: black oily particles in diesel fumes are increasingly regarded as a significant cause of cancer.

Under pressure from public opinion, the Bonn government proposes to make US-style three-way catalysts obligatory on new West German cars from 1991 onwards. Although vehicles meeting the tough US standards make up roughly three-quarters of new registrations, only around 3 million of the 30 million cars on West German roads are fitted with three-way converters. The idea of forcing manufacturers to equip cars with these converters has met with strong resistance from the West German motor industry, on the grounds that customers not wanting to pay extra for catalysts would turn to cheaper foreign makes. None the less, the Bonn government's strategy has been vindicated by the 1989 decision of the European Community to make catalysts obligatory for small cars throughout Europe from 1992 onwards.

An even more significant stumbling block is widespread opposition to speed limits on the motorways. A government-sponsored study in 1985 stated that a limit of 100 kilometres (60 miles) per hour on West German motorways would cut the total emissions of nitrogen oxides by around 10 per cent. In contrast to other members of the European Community, West Germany has no motorway speed limit and although the authorities set a 'recommended' limit of 130 km (80 miles) per hour, German Autobahn drivers normally regard this as a minimum rather than a maximum. In the past the motoring lobby has countered proposals to introduce speed limits with the maxim: '*Freie Fahrt für freie Bürger!*' – roughly translated as, 'In a free country, let citizens drive as fast as they like!' The slogan is popular, but absurd. The US is widely held up by the German Right as a paragon of liberty – in spite of America's 55-mph speed limit. One noticeable effect of the 1989 East German revolution was a sharp increase in speeds on East German Autobahnen as Wartburg and Trabant-owners suddenly lost their fear of the Communist state's 100 km per hour speed limit. As East Germans start to exchange their puffing two-stroke roadsters for Opels, Fords and BMWs, the motoring lobby will no doubt equate reunification with freedom of the road.

The Green analyse German drivers' infatuation with speed in psychiatric terms. The headlight-flashing 120-mph Mercedes driver may indeed be, as Green authors like to say, a sexually frustrated weakling venting an urge to dominate the lesser fry on the fast lane.[33] Whatever the reason, the experts drawing up the 1985 report came to the conclusion that if a 100-km limit were introduced, only 30 per cent of the population would stick to it.

This type of resignation is mocked by the Greens. Joschka Fischer, a leading light among the Green 'realos' who sprang to prominence during his short-lived spell as Environment Minister in a coalition with the SPD in Hesse, told me sardonically: 'The Germans are an order-loving people. If you tell them to drive fast, they will do that. If you tell them to drive slowly, they will do that too.'[34] The final symbolic test of whether the Germans are really serious over the *Umwelt* may well take place on the Autobahn – in East and West.

15

A Land in Flux

Germany has an annual population increase of nearly 900,000 souls. The difficulty of nourishing this army of new citizens must increase from year to year and end in catastrophe, if ways and means are not found to head off in time this danger of pauperisation by hunger.

Adolf Hitler, 1925.[1]

Germany is not an island. No other country is in the same degree woven actively or passively into the world's destiny.... Everything that happens afar involves the heart of Germany.

Oswald Spengler, 1933.[2]

It is extremely unlikely that a society with few children will be friendly towards children.... It will be a cold-hearted society made up of many single and lonely people, and visitors to our country are already beginning to get a taste of things to come.

Wolfgang Schäuble, 1987.[3]

Germany, the pathway across Europe, has become again a land in flux. A united Germany will have to grapple with a two-fold population challenge. A stagnating birthrate during the last decade produced a steady decline in population in the Federal Republic. Simultaneously, West Germany has been making heavy weather of absorbing unexpectedly large immigration, both from eastern Europe and from strife-torn countries in the Third World. The mass exodus from East Germany into the Federal Republic from autumn 1989 onwards changed the demographic picture less dramatically than many believed. The influx brought within the space of a few months around 300,000 extra inhabitants into the western part of Germany, many of them in the 25 to 35 age group. During the whole of 1989, the population rose by more than 800,000 as a result of immigration from the East and the Third World. However, as long as the birth rate remains low, the inflow will not make much difference to general prospects for ageing.[4]

298

Reflecting its 40 years of depletion of people to the West, East Germany brings into a unified state demographic problems which if anything are worse than in the Federal Republic. Introducing an integrated social security and pensions system for a unified Germany will be one of the most pressing challenges facing a future combined German government.

Increasing life expectancy – now 70 years for men, 77 for women – will cause a growing preponderance of over-sixties. The falling, ageing population will squeeze social services, pose problems for the labour market and undermine the foundations of the high-cost pension system. It looks likely to sharpen the generation conflict by making an increasing number of elderly people dependent for their welfare on a shrinking proportion of younger wage-earners. A declining number of inhabitants may well ease environmental problems, and the government will save money in areas like education and family allowances, but the disadvantages outweigh the benefits. By dampening flexibility and mobility, the rise in the proportion of old people threatens economic dynamism. Shortage of children will make West Germany a country where people will laugh less than at present – and worry even more.

The immigration wave might look like a long-term solution to fears of depopulation. However, the new arrivals flooding into Germany at the end of the 1980s have been for the most part unwanted. Large numbers of foreign refugees have been trying to make use of the Federal Republic's liberal asylum provisions to seek a new life on West German soil. At the same time, economic difficulties in eastern Europe – together with the liberalisation of departure rules – have unleashed a tide of ethnic German emigration from Germany's formerly Communist neighbours. The refugees streaming through West Germany's portals are all potential contributors to the pensions system, but they are also costing billions of D-Marks to house, feed and train for jobs.[5] At a time when far-Right parties have started to look for scapegoats to blame for persistent unemployment and shortage of housing in big cities, the refugee intake is causing increasing political strains.

The immigration wave shows how, for 'the land in the middle', the problems of the world have an uncanny knack of knocking at its door. For reasons tied up with its history and geography, upheavals in foreign lands wash through to West Germany with surprising rapidity. It is an acute predicament. The only way to offset population decline will be to integrate more foreigners, but hosting more arrivals from abroad is something the majority of Germans do not want. East Germany has been virtually closed to the outside world for 40 years. The incorporation of 16 million citizens from the East will make a united German state less outward-looking – and, probably, a less hospitable place for people from abroad who want to make Germany their home.

I

There was more than a hint of irritation on Chancellor Kohl's broad features. Just at the time when West Germany was starting to worry seriously about its surfeit of old people, thousands of extra pensioners were streaming in from Communist Europe. In many cases the new arrivals were descended from German colonists who spread across eastern Europe in past centuries. Badly treated and forcibly resettled by the Soviet Union after Germany's Second World War defeat, by the end of the 1980s the army of Germans from the East was on the move again.

In an annexe of the West German embassy in Moscow in October 1988, Kohl was brought face to face with a small, unusually elderly sample of the *Aussiedler*, or returning settlers from the East. (The émigrés from East Germany, who have automatic claim to German nationality, are called *Übersiedler*).[6] Amounting to the largest inflows since a huge tide of refugees hit West Germany in the first few years after the war, 200,000 Soviet and east European émigrés came in during 1988 as a result of economic upheaval caused by the cracks opening up in the Communist system. In 1989, all immigration records were broken as the flows of *Aussiedler* and *Übersiedler* surged to 720,000 people.

The settlers – flotsam on the waves of history – were coming back to a land which they regarded as home, but which was greeting them with suspicion rather than with open arms. The Germans from the East are stigmatised as 'Fritzes' in Poland or the Soviet Union – and branded 'Poles' or 'Russians' when they return to the land of their forefathers. As part of his rhetorical efforts to instil a new brand of German patriotism, the Chancellor habitually made speeches at home welcoming German 'fellow-citizens' from the lands of eastern Europe.[7] But when he met a group of them in Moscow, Kohl was not in a receptive mood. The Chancellor's brusqueness underlined West Germany's dilemma over immigration: is it a blessing or a curse?

The 30-strong cluster dutifully waiting for the Chancellor was made up of ethnic Germans from various parts of the Soviet Union. Some were the descendants of German farmers and miners who had settled in Catherine the Great's Russia of the 18th century. Having just been granted their exit visas by the Soviet authorities – often after years of waiting – they were about to board a Lufthansa flight for the Federal Republic: a country they clearly regarded as the promised land.

Some of the group had already been *en route* from Soviet Asia for several days. A large proportion was over 60, although they also included some younger people and even a baby. Many of the eastern travellers were clinging to traditional ideas about Germany; they were going to be jolted when confronted with modern reality. Kohl told the émigrés that they would need 'patience' in adjusting to their new homeland. Aspirations would not be 'fulfilled overnight'. He wished them well, but underlined that the Federal Republic had changed a lot from the land of their forebears. 'You are coming from another world,' he said.

Rubin Schlack, a bent and wizened man of 73 from the Soviet central Asian province of Kazakhstan, and self-elected spokesman for the group, rose to his feet and thanked the Chancellor for Bonn's help. He pleased Kohl by recounting the old proverb: 'The German has not only rights, he has also duties,' but seemed to annoy him by taking too long with his impromptu speech. 'We are old, but we want to reach our home,' Schlack explained. His wife Antoine, aged 74, sobbed silently as her husband told me how he was caught in East Germany at the end of the Second World War and imprisoned by the Russians for seven years. During the war, he had worked for two years in one of Germany's main aircraft factories in the southern city of Würzburg, before being evacuated after American bombing.

Now, after spending forty laborious years in the Soviet Union, the Schlacks' prime wish was to spend the twilight of their lives in 'the Fatherland'. They hoped that their children, still in the Soviet Union, would be able to follow. Schlack showed me a bizarre memento cradled in the palm of his hand: a small ball-bearing component he had kept for more than four decades from his stint in the Würzburg armaments plant. It was an appropriately ambivalent souvenir of the country which was about to become his new homeland.

II

The end-1980s immigration stream marked a continuation of the great flows sweeping into West Germany after the end of the Second World War. Astonishingly, West Germany not only absorbed the influx of around 12 million fugitives from Communism in the years after 1945, but also prospered as a result. Providing both a supply of able-bodied workers and simultaneously a demand for goods, the new arrivals helped to fuel the economic miracle.

After the building of the Berlin Wall in 1961 sharply cut the intake of people fleeing from East Germany, the Federal Republic satisfied its need for cheap labour by bringing in several million 'guest workers' (*Gastarbeiter*) from southern Europe. They came predominantly from Turkey, but also from Yugoslavia, Italy, Portugal, Greece and Spain. Germany went to great lengths to show hospitality, on an official level at least: in 1964 the one-millionth *Gastarbeiter* arrival, a Portuguese, was awarded a moped in a televised welcome ceremony. The recruitment drive was stopped as the economy slowed down in 1973-74, and some of the *Gastarbeiter* were encouraged to return home with resettlement bonuses. Nevertheless the number of foreigners rose gradually – a result of the relatively high immigrant birth-rate as well as of the inflows of dependants joining their families from their home countries. At the end of the 1980s, there were about 4.3 million foreigners in West Germany – approximately 7 per cent of the population.[8]

The arrivals of the late 1980s have been coming to a land where egoism and inflexibility have risen with prosperity. The clutch of Soviet Germans whom Kohl met during his Moscow visit represented a small selection of the 47,000 Germans who left the Soviet Union to settle in the Federal Republic in 1988 – the highest figure since West Germany was established in 1949. The 200,000 Germans from eastern Europe entering the Federal Republic in 1988 included also 140,000 emigrants from Poland, as well as nearly 13,000 from Romania. In 1989 98,000 ethnic Germans came from the Soviet Union, 250,000 from Poland, 2,000 from Czechoslovakia and 23,000 from Romania. This made a total of 373,000 *Aussiedler* – in addition to 344,000 from East Germany.

Provided they can prove that at least one grandparent was German, the Germans from eastern Europe have an automatic right to West German citizenship. West Germany's Basic Law explicitly recognises as 'Germans' descendants of people deemed to have been 'of German stock' within the frontiers of the 1937 German Reich; this means that between 3.5 and 4 million inhabitants of the Soviet Union and its satellite states today have a right to German citizenship.

Perhaps half of this total of ethnic Germans can be regarded as potential emigrants. For years the Bonn government had called on Communist Europe to allow these people to depart for the Federal Republic.[9] But from 1987-88 onwards, the numbers suddenly allowed to leave were far greater than Bonn had bargained for; so too were the problems of integrating them once they reached the 'Fatherland'. The government's official line welcoming the *Aussiedler* as returning brethren started to look decidedly hollow. Significantly, Bonn changed tack in 1989 by stepping up diplomatic efforts with Moscow and Communist Europe to encourage would-be emigrants to remain in their countries of origin. It also cut social security benefits for émigrés in June 1989.

Through friends and relatives as well as through the images of West German TV, the *Aussiedler* know that in the rich West jobs and a social security safety net await them. Materially at least, life on the dole or on a pension in the Federal Republic can be far better than working in a factory in Poland. Many 'Germans' of eastern Europe have little in common with the people living in the Federal Republic. The effort to provide evidence of German descent can bring forward uncomfortable memories.

Citizens from Poland, for instance, are often given the status of *Aussiedler* after they 'discover' – following many years of hiding the fact – that their grandfathers fought for the Wehrmacht during the war. Under the post-1939 occupation of Poland, many Poles were forcibly 'Germanised' to provide soldiers for Hitler. Once they settle in the Federal Republic, elderly Poles can be a focus of rancour; under a pensions agreement with Poland in 1975, Poles have full access to German pensions rights even if they never paid into the system during their working lives. In some cases, they receive higher pensions than Germans of the same age.[10] Many of the *Aussiedler*, especially those from Poland, do not speak German. Large numbers of people in the Federal Republic regard them as foreigners rather than fellow-Germans, and they are often bracketed together in public opinion with the asylum-seekers housed in hostels and dormitories around the country. There is, indeed, a common historical origin for both types of immigration.

Just as the *Aussiedler* intake is a delayed ripple from the mighty population upheavals after the Second World War, the flood of asylum-seekers also represents an indirect consequence of Hitler. Article 16 of the Basic Law states that 'persons persecuted on political grounds shall enjoy the right of asylum.' This provision was a symbolic demonstration of the break with Nazism, an effort to lighten the guilt left by crimes against the Jews. Article 16 ensured that fugitives from oppression abroad would be sure of refuge in the new Federal Republic – just as many Jews fleeing the Third Reich had found a new home in the US. Coupled with another constitutional clause giving asylum-seekers full recourse to West Germany's weighty legal machinery, Article 16 provides temporary residence rights to foreigners declaring at the border that they are seeking asylum.

The system indeed provides a haven for genuine victims of political persecution, but is also open to misuse. Civil wars in many developing countries during the 1980s replaced the phenomenon of individual victimisation with that of mass persecution. Along with the expansion of international air travel, this greatly raised the numbers of displaced persons from the Third World seeking a bolt-hole in the West. For these new international nomads, the Federal Republic – with its wealth, open borders and all-embracing social security system – appears a natural source of shelter.

The Bonn government claims that the great majority of people seeking asylum are not genuine victims of political persecution, but are flooding in for economic reasons. Many of them live in the Federal Republic for years while they wait for their applications to go through Kafkaesque legal hurdles. In recent years, less than 10 per cent of yearly requests for asylum have been accepted.[11] Weary of their liberal reputation, the West Germans increasingly see the foreign asylum-applicants as unwelcome scroungers. Many Germans in rural areas are being confronted for the first time with black- or brown-skinned people living in their locality.

Confusion about the two types of refugees has been increased by the large number of Poles among the asylum-seekers as well as in the contingent of *Aussiedler*. In practice, an immigrant from eastern Europe will first apply to be treated as a 'German' and then, if this is turned down, will try for asylum status. Ironically, in the country which has made praiseworthy efforts to overcome the racist paranoia of the Third Reich, race is the prime determinant of people's suitability as immigrants.

Norbert von Nieding, a neatly-mannered lawyer, is head of the Federal Office for the Recognition of Foreign Refugees, based at Zirndorf near Nuremberg. He is in charge of the machinery of processing asylum requests. Families from the Middle East and Africa mill about outside his headquarters, a complex of buildings surrounded by a fence, also used to give temporary accommodation to the refugees. One Iranian family complains about the food at Zirndorf, but tells me their throats would be cut if they returned to Tehran. Nieding points out that, in war-shattered Germany in 1949, no one could have visualised that forty years later the country would be regarded as a refuge from foreign wars. 'The basis of Article 16 was the death of 6 million Jews,' he told me. 'But the fathers of the Basic Law did not think that the numbers would be so high.'[12]

Citizens from a dozen countries – led by Poland, Yugoslavia, Turkey,

Iran, Sri Lanka, Pakistan, Lebanon and Afghanistan – formed the bulk of the 250,000 asylum applications during 1986-88. A growing problem has been the mass arrival at Frankfurt airport of unaccompanied children from places like Sri Lanka or Pakistan, often with false or doctored passports. About 2,600 such arrivals came to West Germany in 1988, and the trend increased in the early months of 1989 – posing an almost insoluble problem for immigration authorities. Reflecting the bureaucratic hurdles faced by asylum-seekers, only around 80,000 have managed to attain official refugee status, thereby gaining full residence and employment rights – a similar figure to the numbers in France or Britain. Many entrants who lodge a bid for asylum stay on in West Germany even if their applications are turned down; they have recourse to lengthy legal appeal procedures, and the West German authorities in practice are often reluctant to deport refugees to civil war zones. While the wearisome asylum procedures are carried out, the immigrants are given pocket money of around DM60 a month, as well as board and lodging. Although some do find jobs in the underground economy, they are not officially allowed to work; this is partly to defuse fears that immigrants are contributing to unemployment, partly to prevent the newcomers from becoming integrated into the local population, which would make them harder eventually to dislodge.

About ten Ghanaian asylum-seekers I met in the small Bavarian town of Pressath were plainly not enjoying their stay. Living in a cramped bunk-bed hostel in the centre of the village, they declared they could not stomach the cooked food supplied by the municipality and had started to prepare their own African-style meals. 'This is not our country. We are not here for our enjoyment or entertainment, but because we have problems back home,' said Alexander, a young Ghanaian in the group. He refused to say exactly why he had left Ghana, and declined to give me his full name for fear of making his tenure in the Federal Republic still more uncertain. 'When I left, my wife was pregnant,' he said. 'They wrote me a letter to say she had the baby. We are praying to God for the future – one day a letter might arrive to say my case has been cleared.'[13]

Pressath, within firing range of a massive American training base, showed considerable tolerance towards the Ghanaians. Local citizens in the 4,000-strong community organised a petition to check the Bavarian state government's plans to move them to a larger refugee complex elsewhere. One local resident leading moves to help the Ghanaians – Richard Murr, a 24-year-old office worker – told me, 'Just because there is less guilt complex about the war, I don't see why we should do away with asylum rights.'

305

In other areas of Bavaria which I visited, the immigrants were however clearly causing some problems. In Munich, which houses hundreds of asylum-seekers in office buildings turned into makeshift dormitories in the city centre, refugee hostels have been suspected of becoming drug-dealing centres. One former government office block I visited was housing 463 people from ten countries. About 100 Tamils from Sri Lanka had been given a dispensation to work locally, mainly in Munich hamburger bars. The social worker in charge of the hostel called his charges 'a nice bunch' but admitted that homosexuality among the inmates was a problem.[14]

Hof, on the fringes of Bavaria near the East German and Czech borders, has become a major refugee area. Falling local population has made accommodation available in blocks of flats in the town centre. Residents protested when 250 coloured people were shipped into apartment blocks originally intended for trainee Bavarian functionaries; there were complaints of stealing from supermarkets and of prostitution by women from Ghana. Around the country, several asylum homes have been the object of arson attacks by far-Right extremists. Criticism also comes from the refugees. Zbigniew Szafranski, a long-bearded 63-year-old Solidarity supporter from Poland whom I met in a cramped flat in Hof, told me he had just been given official refugee status after waging a six-year legal battle. His wife was still going through an interminable application process. 'West Germany is good,' he said, 'but the bureaucracy is a hundred times worse than under Communism.'[15]

The Bonn government has been trying for several years to tighten loopholes to entry by asylum-seekers. In October 1986 it managed to persuade East Germany to block the entry of Third World refugees streaming in to the Federal Republic via Berlin. Thousands of fugitives from civil war areas, having paid large fees to unscrupulous transit companies, were being flown to East Berlin's Schönefeld airport and then crossing the divided city into the West. The East Berlin leadership would probably not be averse to opening the floodgates again in the future, if it believed this was a way of securing cash or concessions from the West.

Because it represents an important part of West Germany's liberal birthright, Article 16 is highly unlikely to be changed. This would require a two-thirds majority in the Bundestag and would cause a political furore. Bonn is exploring ways of reducing the numbers of asylum-seekers by harmonising immigration rules with the more restrictive standards of other members of the European Community, but this will probably take time to put into practice. Immigration has become a fact of life – and the government has little idea what to do about it.

306

III

The German debate on population has gone through extraordinary fluctuations. After the First World War, Germany was the youngest industrial nation in Europe. On the verge of the 1990s, both East and West Germany are on their way to becoming the oldest. During the 1930s the worries of the Nazi leadership centred on finding extra 'living-space' for the Germans. Hitler stated that Germany had to 'start where we left off 600 years ago',[16] by repossessing its old colonial areas of eastern Europe. 'If we think today of new land we can think primarily only of Russia and its subject satellite states.' Presumably Hitler drew on the population theories of Thomas Robert Malthus, under which population tended to rise geometrically but food supplies increased only arithmetically. The Führer rammed home the message that the high concentration of 140 people per square kilometre would eventually exhaust the resources of the Third Reich.[17] An expanding German population was held to be a source of vitality as well as vulnerability. Hitler said in 1942:

> It's the fall in the birth-rate that's at the bottom of everything. France with its two-children families is doomed to stagnation, and its situation can only get worse ... The overflow of our birth-rate will give us our chance. Overpopulation compels a people to look out for himself.[18]

At the end of the Second World War, Germany's frontiers contracted rather than expanded. Millions of people flowed into the supposedly already overcrowded West German state, more than making up for war deaths. Today, for the first time in history, Germany is facing a falling rather than expanding population. The Germans have a new preoccupation: two generations after Hitler, they are worried about slowly dying out.

Seen in a historical perspective, there is a strong streak of irony behind this anxiety. West Germany today has a population of 245 people per square kilometre, 75 per cent more than the density which Hitler feared would lead to catastrophe. Even in the relatively low-populated German Democratic Republic, 154 persons live on each square kilometre. As a result of the post-war immigration, and the baby boom in the late 1950s and early 1960s, the population of the geographical area taken up today by West Germany rose by 42 per cent between 1939 and 1987 – from 43 million to 61 million.

The low birth-rate will now deliver a correction to that population surge. Although birth-rates in all industrialised countries of East and West have been declining, West Germany has been in the lead.[19] For the country to maintain its population, statistically every woman would need to bear 2.1 children. In West Germany the figure has fallen to 1.3, down by a half since the 1960s. The drop reflects a combination of circumstances. They include a decline in marriages (from 1963 onwards), longer periods of education or vocational training, more effective and widespread birth control, fading family values, growing career-mindedness among married women and, inevitably, *Angst* about the sort of world future generations are going to grow up in.

An increase in the proportion of women in the population of child-bearing age (representing the baby boom generation born in the 1960s) produced a small rise in births towards the end of the 1980s. In 1988 674,000 live births were registered, well up from the low point of beneath 600,000 earlier in the 1980s, but this remains a long way below the annual total of more than 1 million births during the mid-1960s. The decline in the birth-rate may flatten out, but since the factors which have led to it are probably permanent the trend is highly unlikely to be reversed. For the population to have a chance of levelling off rather than falling in future years, the number of married couples wanting to have more than three children would have to rise to about 40 per cent – something which is virtually impossible.

The number of women of child-bearing age can be predicted fairly accurately up to about 2010, since they have mostly already been born. Although the extent of immigration remains an imponderable, population forecasts can be made for the early decades of the next century with a high degree of certainty. These all point to a dramatic reduction. According to the Interior Ministry's official projection (drawn up in 1987), the population in West Germany is likely to fall by about 20 per cent during the next forty years, from 61 million at the end of the 1980s to just over 48 million in the year 2030. The German component of the population is foreseen to fall 25 per cent, from 57 million to 42.6 million, with the number of foreigners growing from 4 million to 5.8 million and thus nearly doubling as a percentage of the population.[20]

Higher than expected immigration from developing countries, eastern Europe and the rest of the European Community will almost certainly represent a strong compensating influence. An open, rich country like West Germany can hardly expect to insulate itself from an increasingly over-populated and interdependent world. The global population will top 6 billion by the end of the century, and food and resource shortages are almost certain to spur migration from the South to the North. Further, German industry may well want to encourage an influx of cheap labour (just as during the 1960s), to offset the tightening of the labour market which would otherwise ensue during the 1990s. The Berlin-based German Economics Research Institute (DIW), assuming relatively high immigration in coming years, has concluded that by 2030 the population will total 50 million – 2 million more than predicted by the government. The difference between the two projections was due entirely to the DIW's forecast of an additional 2 million foreigners.[21]

In spite of expected immigration inflows, West Germany's prospective population drop is likely to be exceptionally severe. According to the Organisation for Economic Cooperation and Development, West Germany's population will fall by about 25 per cent over the next half a century – more than any other OECD member. By 2040 the percentage of the population aged 65 and over – which was 9.4 per cent in 1950 and 15.5 per cent in 1980 – will be 28 per cent – again, the highest of any industrialised country.[22]

The prospect creates the need for far-reaching changes in the way West Germany organises its society. But for the moment, society seems reluctant to take up the challenge. Kurt Biedenkopf, one of the intellectuals of the Christian Democrat party, has adopted the position of a lonely thinker on the fringes of his party; he says the country has been very slow to take notice of the demographic crisis:

> The social security system in the 1950s was based on a poor, relatively young, expanding population. Now the majority is wealthy, ageing and declining in numbers. A sharper contrast to reality is hardly conceivable. But we are still going ahead on the basis of the old structure.[23]

Looking at the overall consequences for West Germany in terms of his own family, Biedenkopf sees generation conflicts sharpening. 'My grandchildren will be the ones who will refuse to pay old age security for my children. When my children get close to retirement, their age groups will make up 35 to 40 per cent of the German electorate.' The burden of providing for the next generation of elderly could place intolerable financial strain on contributors, Biedenkopf predicts. 'If my children expect full old-age security, my grandchildren will break out of the system.'

West Germany's population problems will be soluble if the country makes more productive use of older people. Later, rather than earlier retirement seems inevitable. Additionally, to support an increasing proportion of old, inactive and infirm, the Federal Republic will need all the more urgently to increase dynamism and productivity among those of working age. It is here that the signs of increased immobility and inflexibility appear particularly worrying.* Inescapably, the West Germans will age not only in numbers but also in spirit. Wolfgang Schäuble, Interior Minister, points out that after the war the under-20s were twice as populous as the over-60s. Today the numbers are roughly equal and by the year 2030, there will be roughly two and a half times as many old people as young ones. This will have consequences stretching into all areas of life.

> Old people tend towards caution and fear, are afraid about losing things, hesitate to take risks, and are necessarily more concerned with themselves. You can already observe one or the other of these chararacteristics in today's society – sometimes even in the behaviour of a 25-year-old. Of course it may be good if 25-year-olds think about their security in their old age. But I would not like to say whether this is good for the future of our society, for progress and innovation. Over the long term, the Federal Republic will age not only quantitatively but also psychologically.[24]

IV

What can be done to boost the birth-rate? The government has refrained from launching full-blooded child-incentive measures through tax breaks and grants of the kind practised in France. There is a strong, almost fatalistic belief that, if society as a whole is less inclined to produce children, it would be not only futile but also wrong for the government to attempt to reverse the trend. Officially-inspired efforts to change society's views about families therefore steer clear of direct propaganda and instead tend to play on people's guilt about the treatment of the children who are already here. The Youth and Family Ministry, for instance, runs advertisement campaigns featuring plaintive pictures of single children playing by themselves. One such advertisement in newspapers and on hoardings, showing a winsome little

* See Chapter 6.

girl sitting alone on a step, bears the caption: 'I can sleep and eat by myself. But who will play with me? ... Children are glad about simple gestures. That takes away the little one's feeling of being alone.'

Politicians know that exhortations to the electorate to produce more children 'for the good of Germany' would be hopelessly burdened by memories of the motherhood programmes of the Third Reich. Ministers therefore do not like to go any further than sporadically entreating the population to be 'child-friendly' (*kinderfreundlich*). Chancellor Kohl has solemnly proclaimed that children are the 'indispensable contribution to the contract between the generations',[25] an appeal which managed simultaneously to sound jumbled, desperate and unconvincing.

Attempts have been made to encourage larger families through tinkering with the tax and pensions systems – for instance, through allowing mothers a right to a higher number of years' pension per child. But such moves largely remain half-hearted. It may be significant that the person chosen in 1988 to head the Kohl government's Youth and Family Ministry, Ursula Lehr, was a professor of gerontology specialising in the problems of the over-60s.

One problem which the West German authorities have signally failed to solve is the question of support for working mothers. Children start school at the late age of 6 or 7 and mostly go home at lunch-time, which makes it difficult for mothers to carry out even a part-time job. Partly because of the strongly-held traditional belief that the woman's place is at home with the children, crêche and kindergarten facilities for children of under school age are not nearly as developed as in France. This is one reason why fewer women go out to work in West Germany than in the US, Britain, France, Canada or Japan.[26]

The lack of nursery facilities has certainly been one factor preventing more women from entering the labour market in the last twenty years, but for married women who want to combine a career with children it has represented a further child-rearing hurdle. Ironically, in the face of a decline in births kindergarten facilities may be cut rather than expanded in coming years.

311

V

West Germany will inevitably have to learn to live a little more easily with the foreigners in its midst. Of the foreigners and their families in the Federal Republic, the Turks make up about 1.5 million, followed by the Yugoslavs, Italians and Greeks. Two-thirds have lived here for more than ten years. Seventy per cent of foreign children were born in West Germany. But foreigners who want to attain German citizenship face great obstacles. This is the result of a complex mixture of reasons, ranging from lingering suspicion towards foreigners to reticence about promoting German patriotism.

The *Gastarbeiter* of the 1960s have made a big contribution to the economy. Even after the policy of encouraging Turkish workers to return home during the 1970s and early 1980s, the steel, motor and coal sectors still rely heavily on foreign workers. In spite of grudges whipped up by the far Right that the *Gastarbeiter* have been stealing work from the Germans, most Germans recognise that foreigners are doing necessary jobs which West Germans do not want to undertake.

The *Gastarbeiter* community plays virtually no role in public life. It has few well-known spokesmen or women, hardly any representatives in politics and little or no voice in the media. More than 100,000 foreigners have started their own businesses, but there is clear evidence that foreign workers face a vicious circle by being condemned for the most part to low-paid, low-qualified and uninteresting jobs. Young Turkish people, for instance, are far less likely to find apprenticeships than young Germans. 'Membership of an ethnic group signals readiness for overtime, greater ability to be disciplined, acceptance of unqualified, monotonous, repetitive, stressful and poorly paid work; but it also signals a poor knowledge of German, imperfect command of cultural standards, and only slight ability to adapt,' according to a 1988 report on *Gastarbeiter* by the Free University in West Berlin.[27] At the beginning of 1990, the chief worry of the *Gastarbeiter* was that the new flows of East Germans on to the labour market would eventually squeeze jobs for non-German workers.

Turkish life in West Germany often seems curiously introverted – crushed by a dominant culture, hemmed in by real or imagined discrimination, constrained by worries about potential repatriation. Younger Turks born in West Germany are beset by anxieties about being caught midway between a Turkish and German way of life, suspected by both communities and belonging to neither. Second- and third-generation Turks in Germany adopt a less docile attitude towards the Germans than their parents; they are more ready to express their satisfaction with inequality.

The number of Turks in West Germany could reach 2 million by the next century, unless a Turkish economic miracle lures them back. Although the birth-rate among Turkish immigrants has been falling – a sign of how they have conformed with German attitudes – the immigrant birth-rate remains higher than among Germans, and inflows are continuing through asylum-seekers and dependants. One way to make foreigners feel more at home would be to allow more of them to have German citizenship rights. However, since the beginning of the 1980s only about 2,000 foreigners have become naturalised Germans. The main hurdles are fees of up to DM5,000 plus the requirement that the applicant's original citizenship be given up at the same time. Less than 1 per cent of Turks have taken this step. Some states run by the Social Democratic Party have tried to improve the integration of foreigners by giving them the vote in local elections, but this remains politically controversial at both local and federal level.

During the next few years, West Germany will almost certainly try to encourage more Turks, Yugoslavs, Greeks and Portuguese to become German citizens. Foreign workers, however, have noticed how the Germans have had a singular lack of pride in their own nationality. As long as this state of affairs continues, the incentive for *Gastarbeiter* to become German will probably remain low. And, if the united Germans rediscover a new and more assertive form of national identity, the *Gastarbeiter* may discover they are a great deal less welcome.

VI

The demographic trauma will force an overhaul of West Germany's elaborate pensions and health care systems, which have their roots in the social security mechanism constructed under Bismarck in the 1880s. Along with the task of integrating East Germany into the scheme, this will require considerable increases in social security contributions in coming years. The statutory retirement system ensures an employee a pension after forty years' work which comes to about 65 per cent of his gross earnings. Pensions are indexed to earnings under a scheme introduced in 1957 which assumed that high economic growth and a steady expansion of the labour force would continue almost indefinitely. Additionally, pensions are largely untaxed. A start has been made on trimming benefits and paring costs, especially over health care, causing the Bonn government a great deal of unpopularity. But more will certainly need to be done in order to bring West Germany's demand for comprehensive social security into line with the capacity to finance it.

The state pensions system, funded by levies on both employees and employers and topped up by contributions from the government, provides old age insurance for around 90 per cent of the population. Pensions are not financed – as with a private sector scheme – through the amassing of capital, but rather through a system under which the generation currently in working life pays the pensions of its fathers and grandfathers. This has worked well in previous decades, but alarming financial cracks are beginning to become apparent.

As in other countries, the market for private pensions looks set to grow. With private savings totalling well over DM2,000 billion, there is no shortage of investment resources; but the West Germans are handicapped by not having started earlier to establish British- or US-style pension funds making retirement payments out of capital rather than current income. The Federal Republic's relative lag in developing its capital markets appears to be a disadvantage here.*

The need for adjustment in the medical insurance scheme is even greater. Founded in 1883, the system has remained without radical reform with astonishing continuity during the turbulence of the past century. Shortcomings have often come to the surface, but efforts at making structural changes have regularly been blocked by political obstacles.

The growth in the numbers of elderly people requiring longer and more expensive medical care has already represented a huge financial drain. Between 1970 and 1986, annual health spending more than tripled to around DM250 billion – making up about one-seventh of West Germany's gross national product. Looking after old people at home or in old age institutions already accounts for about one-third of the social security budget, and is set to grow faster than ever in the coming years.

Because of the decentralised nature of the system, sharply rising costs have proved virtually uncontrollable. Hospital costs have been rising roughly twice as quickly as wages, while costs of drugs have been

* See Chapter 6.

increasing three times as fast. Pharmaceuticals are roughly 50 per cent more expensive in West Germany than the average in the rest of the European Community, and are double the level in France.

In the past the solution has normally been to increase charges on employees and employers. Financing limits are, however, now being reached. In spite of all the evidence that West Germany is living beyond its means, efforts at restructuring health care bring governments into a political minefield. Complaints come not only from consumers but also from an army of powerful interest groups – ranging from drugs companies to doctors' associations and hospital operators. All have profited from cosy relationships over the years, and they have no wish to see these altered. The German desire for perfection has made the health care system the envy of countries like Britain – but there are long-term doubts as to whether it can survive.

VII

If there is a solution to the financing problems of pensions and social security, one incongruous place where it is shaping up is Friedland, a small town in northern Germany offering soup, solace and bunk-beds for lost souls. Friedland is the site of a refugee transit camp a few miles to the west of the guarded border between East and West Germany, not far from the ancient university town of Göttingen. Since the end of the Second World War Friedland has been a staging post for more than 3 million displaced persons crossing to the West. It was set up in September 1945 by the British occupying forces, making use of stables owned by the university's animal experimental station.

Over four decades Friedland has been extended into a cluster of modern buildings studded with flower-beds. The end-1980s surge in the arrivals of ethnic Germans from the East has crowded the camp with newcomers. Although the arrivals – especially the older people – put initial strains on the German social services, in the long run they provide a reservoir of labour which could strengthen the country's economic backbone. The *Aussiedler* include a large number of pensioners travelling with their families, but most émigrés are between 25 and 45 years old. They are keen to work and ready to travel to find it. Afraid that the émigrés might undercut regular wage rates, some trade unionists regard the inflow with suspicion or even hostility.

315

Father Peter Görlich, the local Friedland priest, whose red-brick church on the edge of the camp overflows with refugees on Sundays, comments drily: 'Their problems start after Friedland.'[28] Father Görlich himself crossed into the West as a refugee in 1946 as the Germans were driven out of Silesia, and recalls looking back with his mother as they left their homeland. 'We had to leave,' he says. 'Now people are coming of their own free will. They are coming to a country with a foreign culture, whose language they don't understand. They must have a good reason.' In the 1940s, he says, people were united by a sense of common crisis. 'The police requisitioned rooms for us when we arrived. If they did that today, there would be an outcry.' Although he is grateful for donations from the public for refugee charities collected at the camp, Father Görlich remarks that donors are often simply trying to salve guilty consciences.

Some of the émigrés bedded down in Friedland bunks are at the end of a tortuous road and air journey from Soviet Central Asia. Unlike the Soviet émigrés, many of the Polish arrivals speak little or no German; this is above all the result of the suppression of German language teaching after the war, but it does not say much for the strength of the newcomers' ties to the Fatherland. The Poles do not have a good reputation among local shopkeepers; one described them as 'impudent', and a barman told me that they were simply after Germany's money. Several Poles I spoke to in an overcrowded gymnasium in Göttingen, functioning as a temporary dormitory, signalled total incomprehension at the simple but vital question, 'Are you German?' Language difficulties are one of the reasons why the unemployment rate for *Aussiedler* at the end of 1988 stood at around 30 per cent – three times higher than for the population as a whole.[29]

Underlining the coolness of the reception given to the newcomers from the East, 44 per cent of the West German population at the end of 1988 believed it was the country's 'duty' to accept the east European inflows, whereas 35 per cent rejected them, according to an Allensbach opinion poll. A share of 38 per cent of the population thought the *Aussiedler* were German, whereas 36 per cent branded them as foreigners.[30]

Eckart van Hooven, a veteran board member at the Deutsche Bank, was himself a post-war expellee who lost his family home on the border of Pomerania and Mecklenburg, now in East Germany. He looks back almost with nostalgia to the tough early years after the war: 'You could travel the length of Germany with an orange in your hand,' he says, 'it was proof that you had access to the Allies.' Hooven says that, compared with today, it was probably preferable being a refugee in 1945:

That time was more productive from the human point of view. We did not have a society divided by wealth; there were no differences. People's quality was put to the test, not their opportunism. I made my best friends then. Those millions of refugees were our great fortune. The people helped the whole country to become integrated after the war. Today's *Aussiedler* have romantic ideas – and they're coming up against realism.[31]

The *Aussiedler* are indeed, like Germany itself, tugged both ways – on the borderline between romanticism and realism. The émigrés are part of Germany's history, now catching up with it. The people from the East provide a unique view of where Germany has come from – and, perhaps, where it is going.

16

Across the Divide

Germany is an indivisible democratic republic, composed of German states. The republic determines all matters which are essential for the existence and the development of the German people as a whole.

Article 1 of the first East German constitution, 1949[1]

The experiment of the Socialist Unity Party will end fearfully, in a tide of moral recriminations and the destruction of all those who honestly tried to realise communist or socialist ideas.

Herbert Wehner, 1964[2]

The German empire after the Thirty Years War consisted of 300 territories. Achieving unity was so difficult. The main aim now is that the border should be permeable.

Hans Heun, mayor of Hof, 1987[3]

Over 40 years, the two Germanys learned to live with the ugly frontier between them. Then it crumbled. Both East and West would have preferred the Berlin Wall to have come down after East Germany had achieved reasonable success in improving living standards and reforming Stalinism. Instead, the collapse of the Wall, and the 860-mile long steel mesh fence coiled from the Baltic Sea to Czechoslovakia, revealed the full extent of East Germany's political and economic bankruptcy. The Germans, and the world outside, were confronted with a power vacuum. Before the breaching of the Wall, the flows of disgruntled East Germans heading westwards were fleeing to freedom; afterwards, they were simply rushing out to seek a niche in the prosperous West before it was too late. German unity was approaching; and the East Germans were departing to escape its consequences.

The East-West German border was the world's deadliest: brutal, quiet, thorough, and fortified by shear-proof chrome-nickel wire supplied by West German steel companies at DM5 per metre. There were 10 frontier posts for road crossings, eight for railways, two for

318

waterways under the terms of the 1972 treaty establishing 'good neighbourly relations' between the two Germanys. A 3-mile exclusion zone sown with sophisticated electronic and acoustic detection devices prevented approach from the eastern side. Villages along the frontier were barred off or, in some cases, simply razed to the ground.[4]

Among the border areas I visited in 1987 was the region around Hof in northern Bavaria, where the boundary ran along the slow-moving River Saale. On the eastern bank looms, fortress-like, the Hirschberg leather factory. Founded in 1741 and once Germany's largest, it was marooned after the war on the Communist side of the German cleavage. On the western side, the Saale runs into a weir supplying power for the button-making factory of the Martin family in the border township of Unter Tiefengrün. The Hirschberg factory towers surrealistically, just a hundred yards away, separated by an ugly prefabricated wall. Waltraud Martin, who has lived here since 1968 in a 600-year-old mill, told me she had grown to relish the peace and quiet. Asked when the wall was likely to come down, she said: 'We will not experience it, our children also not – and probably the grandchildren won't either.'[5]

Another border town, Philippsthal in Hesse, 100 miles north-west of Tiefengrün, had a similar haunted air. It was separated from its East German sister community of Vacha by a wall traversing a sandstone bridge across the polluted River Werra. A fence dipped down into the water like a giant lobster cage to bar off the way for swimmers. Hans Hiltrup, a printer whose workshop straddled the East-West dividing line, told me: 'I only think about the border when I'm asked about it.'[6] Reunification, he said, would be possible if the 'little people' had their say. But the 'big fish' at the helm in both East and West Germany would have to give up power – and a reunited Germany would be too big for either the US or the Soviet Union, he opined. 'None of them want us together.'

Up and down Germany, towns like Philippsthal have suddenly been reunited with the Verras on the other side; the Hirschbergs and the Tiefengrüns have come together again. The border has seemed to fade into history – and yet it has left a legacy. The story of how the Germans crossed the divide in the years before it disappeared provides a signpost towards Germany's convoluted future.

I

The road to the 1,000-year-old city of Meissen on the Elbe, the historic home of European porcelain, is paved with contradictions. It snakes along a route of dishevelled Saxon villages nestling in the mists and the mud of the East German countryside. Entering Meissen, the car skids past geese meandering into the road. The blackened spires of the Gothic cathedral loom above the state-owned *Kombinate* bearing signs exhorting workers to maintain peace 'and prevent thermonuclear catastrophe'. Fear vies with humourless fanaticism as common denominators running through East German factory placards. In September 1989, another favourite red-painted sign adorning the roads around Meissen was 'My place of work – the place I fight for freedom.'

Meissen suffers all too evidently from pollution and disrepair. But it is home to the most illustrious foreign exchange earner of the East German state. The Meissen manufactory close to the city centre has been turning out expensive fine porcelain since 1710. Its origins in the Holy Roman Empire illustrate the continuity of German history. A statue of Johann Friedrich Böttger, the alchemist who invented European porcelain in 1708, stands opposite the front door of the Meissen works. Böttger started Meissen manufacture in the Elbe-side Albrechtburg castle at the behest of August the Strong, the Elector of Saxony; the manufactury's artistic prowess and traditions have attracted hundreds of thousands of westerners to its museum.

Of Meissen's 1,900 employees, no less than 800 are highly-skilled painters, practising their delicate craft in dusty high-ceilinged rooms crammed with potted plants and soft-porn posters. A top painter earns 2,000 East Marks a month; average wage is about 1,100 Marks, and they are supposed to work 43¾ hours a week. Meissen's products, however, nearly all turn up in the homes of the wealthy in the capitalist West. In the Federal Republic, in which Meissen turns over around DM40 million a year, or half its total sales, its cheapest six-person coffee service retails at around DM1,800 – equivalent (at the black market currency rate) to more than six months salary in the East.

Hannes Walter, the Meissen managing director, a gimlet-eyed scientist born in Czechoslovakia, greets me in the wood-panelled display room. Walter, 46, took over after the previous Meissen boss, Reinhold Fichte, a highly-prized technocrat with close links to the Honecker leadership, made headlines by fleeing to the Federal Republic in February. Fichte now competes with Meissen from the other side of the wire – he is managing director of a family-owned porcelain works in Bavaria. The new chief says that Meissen's strength lies in its unbroken range of more than 150,000 different items, based on designs going back to the 18th century. He pays tribute to the Soviet general who kept Meissen going in the turbulent years between 1945 and 1949; it was briefly a Soviet joint stock company before being taken into 'people's ownership'. Walter claims that artistic quality has bloomed under Communism. 'We are a child of the German Democratic Republic.'[7] He also hails the painstaking training and apprenticeship programme. 'Our marque is quality.'

Walter has been a member of the Socialist Unity Party since 1975. He plays down both Fichte's departure and the exodus of ordinary workers leaving in the autumn emigration tide. 'Each one who leaves is one too many,' he tells me piously. Walter admits the apparent paradox that a Socialist concern should produce such exclusive goods. But he rejoins that Meissen's trading principles have always been internationalist. 'Trade has always been a significant feature of peaceful coexistence.' Meissen's world-famous symbol, hand-painted crossed swords, has graced its porcelain since 1723. 'Our swords are the most peaceful in the world,' recounts Martin, retracing a well-practised theme.

A visit to Meissen's shop in the Saxon city's restored marketplace shows how ordinary East Germans see little of the company's produce. There is a picture of a young-looking Erich Honecker by the door, but very little porcelain. When I ask the assistant where Meissen's famed figurines – retailing in the West at DM1,000 upwards – can be found, she replies gruffly: 'That is for export.'

Walter tells me that Meissen has full order books until 1990 and that delivery periods for specific items vary from two to five years. None the less, it is seeking to boost further its presence in the West with an advertising campaign in the quality West German press. It started in the autumn and is costing DM1.5million to DM2million over a year. Meissen's aim is to capture the young market – starting from the 35- to 40-year-olds. 'At some time, an older generation of customers will die out. We have to alert the younger people,' says Jochen Rotauge, who handles Meissen's sales in the Federal Republic from the trading house of Bock, based in Konstanz on the Bodensee.[8] Meissen's image in the West has remained curiously consistent in spite of four decades of Socialism, Rotauge says. 'There is a fascination which is hard to describe.' By comparison with the three centuries of history behind the Meissen name, Rotauge adds that the last forty years are 'of absolutely no importance.'

II

East Germany's income from selling porcelain figures has been dwarfed by its hard currency receipts from trading another highly-prized commodity – people. Bartering free political prisoners started in 1963, supposedly as a temporary expedient, but quickly became integrated into East Germany's planned economy. The numbers released in this way from the special prisons at Brandenburg, Cottbus, Bautzen, Naumburg, Hoheneck (for women) have ranged from between 1,000 to 2,000 a year, averaging nearer 1,000 in recent years. The going rate has been between DM90,000 and DM100,000 a head, paid in goods such as metals, fruit, cereals and oil. With the upheaval in East Germany at the end of 1989, the transactions suddenly became no longer necessary. The Bonn government for the first time revealed officially how much the practice cost. Including a variety of other shadowy 'humanitarian' transactions to release people from the East, the barter trade in the late 1980s drained the West German budget of between DM300 million and DM400 million a year.[9]

The man with a key role in organising the deals was Wolfgang Vogel, an East German lawyer with the bronzed looks of a Hollywood neuro-surgeon. In his 60s, with an alert compassionate face and penetrating blue eyes behind half-moon spectacles, Vogel has opened the way to the promised land for most of the roughly 34,000 prisoners ransomed free during the past quarter of a century. The trade has netted East Berlin well over DM1 billion over the years. Only Communist and capitalist Germany, with their peculiar twisted destinies, could succeed in perfecting such a system.

Vogel lives in some comfort on a lake an hour's drive south-east of Berlin. He runs his lawyers's practice from a green three-storey house at Reiler Strasse 4 in the Friedrichsfelde district of East Berlin, around the corner from the bleak S-bahn suburban railway station. His office is chintzy, cluttered, comfortably provincial, like the sitting room of an English boarding house. Vogel has earned no money directly from the prisoner exchanges. But his international *renommée* has helped give his practice a healthy income. He declines politely to tell me how much it is, but reveals that he pays 150 Marks in earnings-related monthly subscriptions to the East German Communist party, which he joined only as late as 1982. The cut of his checked jacket and his taste for water-skiing indicate he can afford it.

322

Vogel, a long-time confidant of Erich Honecker, has been the East German government's official representative in 'humanitarian dealings' with West Germany. His official role lasted into the final days of Honecker's stewardship; in October 1989 Vogel faced the humiliating task of trying – and failing – to persuade fugitive East Germans camped out in the West Germany embassy in Prague to return to their country. Born in Silesia in what is now Poland, Vogel has been a trusted figure for governments of both Left and Right in Bonn, and struck up a particularly close relationship with Social Democrats such as Herbert Wehner and Helmut Schmidt. A man with a taste for skiing holidays in Austria – he says the mountain republic would be his favourite country to live – Vogel slips through international boundaries with ease. One US diplomat in East Berlin who knows him well describes Vogel as 'authoritative, reliable, well connected.' He refers to the perpetual rumours that Vogel may be a Soviet spy with laughing disbelief which is almost, but not quite, total.

Vogel certainly is well known in both Moscow and Washington. He has played a central role in countless East-West spy exchanges reading like a *Who's Who* of espionage, starting with US U-2 surveillance plane pilot Francis Gary Powers downed by the Russians in 1960 and freed in 1962. Vogel also had a hand in the exchanges of British businessman/agent Greville Wynne, swapped for KGB spy Gordon Lonsdale. And he helped organise the freeing of Soviet Jewish dissident Anatoly Shcharansky in February 1986, a highly-publicised exchange which took place before whirring TV cameras at the traditional scene of East-West handovers, the Glienicke bridge south of Berlin.

Vogel's most abiding work however has been out of camera view. For years, regular busloads of ransomed political prisoners have been driven anonymously through the Wartha-Herleshausen border crossing point on their way to the West German reception camp at Giessen north of Frankfurt. The money was originally paid over in thick envelopes, but the funds were later transferred by the Bonn Ministry for Intra German Relations to a bank account in Stuttgart owned by the Diakonisches Werk, the charity organisation of the West German Protestant Church.[10] The deposit was then drawn on by East Berlin to buy pre-arranged lists of badly needed goods.

Vogel told me in 1988 that he was no longer in favour of maintaining secrecy over the ransoming.[11] 'I believe it is no longer true to say that talking will hurt people.' Vogel said he hoped that détente between the two German states would bring a 'more civilised' way of agreeing prisoner releases. 'I want to come one day to a system where there are no

323

political prisoners. It depends on the relationship between Washington and Moscow – everything depends on that.' During the frequent times of difficulties, he looks back to the early 1960s and draws comfort from the contrast. 'Prisoners were getting life sentences – that was the cold war. Everything was much worse.'

Among the fiercest critics of the transactions are, ironically, some ex-prisoners who have been bought out in what they say is a form of 20th century slave trade. Wulf Rothenbächer, a doctor originally from East Germany, was bought free from an East German prison in 1971 after being arrested in 1970 with his wife while trying to escape via Romania. 'East Germany represses, and gets paid for it,' he told me bitterly.[12] Another ex-prisoner, Sibylle Ludwig, a young woman who spent two years and 10 months in jail after applying for an exit permit, was allowed out to the West in the August 1987 amnesty. She told me she felt buying out of prisoners like 'lumps of butter' was wrong in principle. 'The opposition (to the regime) should really stay in the country. Otherwise nothing will change.'[12] The large numbers of dissidents ransomed to the West represented one reason why, after the ousting of the Honecker regime in autumn 1989, the opposition had no well-known representatives to lead an alternative government. Ottfried Hennig, state secretary in the Intra German Ministry in Bonn, put the point bluntly: 'The people who were in the resistance – we bought them free years ago.'[13]

Ludwig Rehlinger, who was state secretary at the Ministry between 1982 and 1988, had the long-time job of negotiating with Vogel over the prisoner releases and a host of other delicate arrangements – including swapping of spies. Rehlinger told me that during busy periods he would sometimes speak five times a day to Vogel by telephone, in conversations assumed to be eavesdropped by the East German secret service.[14] Rehlinger, a softly spoken Berliner two years Vogel's junior, admits the transactions smack of blackmail: 'We give money, the GDR gives people. I agree this is not moral. But the ones who give money to bring out innocent people are more moral than those who are doing the selling. I am obliged, by the constitution and as a human being, to help innocent Germans who are in trouble.'

One man who believes the ransoming can be justified is Chancellor Kohl. 'Is that not something almost immoral?' I asked him. Kohl replied:

How is that immoral? That is a theoretical consideration which you can think about in your editorial offices, because you do not have responsibility. We also pay money so that Germans in Romania can leave. Should I sit here in my office in the comfort of the Federal Republic and shut myself off from

324

the personal fate and the persecution and the terrible sacrifices of these people?[15]

III

When they arrive in the West, East German émigrés can find the clash of cultures both invigorating and unsettling. Wolfgang Mischnick, the veteran Free Democrat politician, who was Minister for Expellees and Refugees in 1961–63 under Adenauer, was born in Dresden and fled to the West in 1948. Mischnick told me in 1988 that many East Germans who came to the West regret the coldness and materialism:

> Many people (from the GDR) see more disadvantages than advantages. Everything here is very hectic. It isn't easy for them to rely on themselves. In the GDR, you are used to having a lot of things done automatically, which here you have to do yourself. Prosperity here has also brought a form of separation from people. Human warmth has suffered.[16]

The flight however also brings much relief. Anneliese Stahlbaum, a woman allowed to leave East Germany in 1984 with her husband and two young children, told me she was haunted by the bureaucratic hurdles put in the way of her emigration. The most powerful reason inciting the family to depart was discrimination against practising Christians in schools. 'We left because we thought the children would have no chance.'[17] She was full of praise for life in West Berlin. The authorities provided help in finding a flat, a DM10,000 loan for furniture and cash from social security. At the end of 1987, the East German government – after payment of a suitable sum by the West German authorities – allowed out to join them her older daughter and young son at the beginning of 1988. Frau Stahlbaum now sings twice a week in a West Berlin church choir – but misses the friends she left in the East.

A young woman dissident, Kristin Seetge, who was allowed out of East Germany in 1988 to join her brother and uncle in the Federal Republic, says of the relationship of East German citizens to the state: 'One remains a baby, hopelessly tied to its mother. You're not self-sufficient; you're not allowed to love anyone else.'[18] One young man was ransomed free into the Federal Republic from an East German

325

prison in 1983 and led an itinerant existence in the West for several years before burning down the Frankfurt Opera House in frustration in November 1987, causing DM130 million worth of damage.

Not all émigré experiences end up as expensively as that, but social problems are frequent. Newcomers from East Germany face challenges in integrating with West Germans at workplace or school, remain unemployed for above-average periods, and often run up heavy hire purchase debts. The departures in 1989 and 1990 brought to the West a heady mixture of almost boundless hope mixed with deep discontent. Dieter Schröder, head of the Chancellery in the Social Democrat-led government of West Berlin – a man with many years of experience in dealing with humanitarian problems between the two Germanys – told me that many émigrés tend to blame their personal problems on the state, not themselves. When they get to the West, he added cynically, 'They will get divorced anyway.'[19]

IV

As its role in the prisoner trading shows, the Protestant Church is an abiding bridge between East and West Germany. A symbolic cornerstone is the bishopric of Ratzeburg in Schleswig Holstein on the north-east tip of the Federal Republic. The 12th-century red brick Romanesque cathedral of Henry the Lion, surrounded by lakes, is a unique testament to ecumenicalism. It has been the only West German church still formally belonging to East Germany. Uwe Steffen, the cathedral's dean since 1976, paused to round up a straying decanal donkey from the lakeside lawn by his house before telling the story.[20] As an accident of war and geography, the parish is still part of the Evangelical-Lutheran Church of Mecklenburg in East Germany, down the road past the water meadows.

Steffen takes part in regular church events in the East. 'The link comes from the long history,' he says. Ratzeburg has raised funds from church concerts and business round-tables to provide scaffolding costing more than DM10,000 for East German churches badly needing renovation. Steffen says however the most important contact is the human one. 'Christians in the East need this more than we in the West. We live in abundance, they in uncertainty.'

The funds channelled across to Mecklenburg form a tiny part of the financial support crossing between the two arms of the Church. According to Bishop Martin Kruse, chairman of West Germany's Protestant Church Council, the money runs into 'millions of D-Marks – no one knows the total'.[21] The Protestant Churches in both parts of Germany were united until 1969, when the eight Protestant church districts in East Germany split off into a separate organisation; one of the first reactions to the breaking down of barriers after November 1989 was a decision by the two Churches to link up again.

Bishop Kruse tells me that the financial support, along with the network of church charitable services in both East and West – hospitals, homes for children and the elderly, family centres and so on – forms 'a bridge of understanding'. As an example, one-third of the Sunday collection of the West Berlin diocese goes to the East. Most of the funds for restoration of the Protestant Cathedral of East Berlin – about DM30 million – came from the West. Kruse declared that the buying out of prisoners, where the Church provides the clearing agency, 'can and must not become the general rule. These are emergency regulations which really do not stand up to thorough moral scrutiny.' He concedes though that the deals had been going on for more than a quarter of a century. 'If you look closely the GDR has an economic interest in hard currencies. Without this interest, a great deal of agreements between East and West Germany would not have come about.'

V

Plauen, a lace-making town in what used to be the hub of the German Empire, went through its apocalypse on the night of April 10 1945. An Anglo-American bombing raid, the 14th severe attack since the previous September, killed more than 500 people and destroyed three-quarters of the medieval city. The neighbouring town of Hof, 17 miles across the Vogtland plateau, sent its fire brigade to help fight the flames. A few months later, the road taken by the fire engines was intersected by the demarcation line between the Russian and American zones. The cleavage of Europe was the start of a painful separation of two communities with economic and cultural links going back nearly 900 years.

The people of the two towns have similar dialects and a similar taste in beer. Well before the opening of the border in November 1989, Hof and Plauen were taking steps to reforge links. They signed a 'twinning' agreement, and started to arrange exchange visits of orchestras, sports teams and schoolchildren.

In the rebuilt Plauen town hall, I met in 1988 the brisk mayor, Norbert Martin, 49, a member of the Communist party since 1957 and mayor of Plauen since 1981. He is waiting for me behind a large table with a Union Jack on it.[22] He states firmly that there will be no 'blurring' of different 'systems of society' in East and West. But he adds, 'Both sides have to learn to be good neighbours. Capitalism and communism may go together like fire and water, but that doesn't mean we have to shoot at each other.' Along with an impromptu breakfast of sausage sandwiches, he treats me to a pile of photos showing Plauen after the 1945 bombing. In what strikes me as remarkable politeness, he says the attack was by the Americans, not the British. The town has been reconstructed with many high rise apartment blocks and still looks a bit of a mess. Later, on a brief tour of the town, an amicable functionary points out where the bodies were found by the railway station air raid shelter, which today is the site of a travel agency offering holidays to Cuba.

Plauen's population, 126,000 before the war, is only 80,000 now. Martin stresses the positive side. 'Thanks to economic planning, Plauen has had steady economic development.' It has reconstructed its lace-making industry and also brought in electronics and specialist machinery. *Pravda* is printed on Plauen presses. 'Hof,' adds the mayor with a touch of smugness, 'has 8 per cent unemployment – that is something foreign to us.'

Sticking to the letter of the GDR constitution, twice revised to get over precisely this difficult point, Martin rejects any idea that East and West Germany are the same nation. 'National identity is more than just a common language, a piece of common history. It is a matter of the political foundations of the state.'

In the afternoon I called on Hans Heun, the mayor of Hof for 18 years, in his town hall on a busy street full of shopping pensioners.[23] The town has a population of about 52,500, down from 62,000 after the war, when it was swollen by refugees from the East. Heun, aged 60, is a rotund man from the Bavarian Christian Social Union. He paved the way for the partnership by driving to Plauen to press his case in 1986 with a coachload of local councillors.

Heun proclaims his belief in the vigour of free enterprise, but recognises winsomely that state planning has brought industries to Plauen which have not come to Hof. Before 1945, up to 80 per cent of

Hof's industrial output – above all beer and textiles – was sold in the now-lost East German hinterland of Saxony and Thuringia. Between 1928 and 1932, the Plauen theatre used to hold 60 performances a year in Hof.

Hof's sprawling, silent railway station, built to serve the far corners of the German and Austrian empires, in 1988 saw only a handful of trains a day; at the height of the unrest in autumn 1989, it was full to bursting with East German fugitives expelled by the desperate East Berlin authorities. 'We have been cut off for 50 years. We are the ones who have no visitors in our restaurants, the football ground, the theatre,' Heun told me miserably. He admitted that if a 'black cloud' passed across general relations between East and West Germany, then the Hof-Plauen partnership would wither. But he added: 'I believe a wheel has started to turn which will not be braked. People still have the feeling of being together as a nation. They know that for the moment they cannot change anything, but we have a common history which cannot be eradicated.'

VI

East and West Germany have always been fertile territory for espionage. The unplanned sharing of information via the efforts of the two states' secret services has sometimes appeared as an abstruse form of East-West confidence-building. West Germany's foreign intelligence service, the Bundesnachrichtendienst (BND), and the counter-intelligence agency, the Bundesamt für Verfassungsschutz (BfV) have traditionally faced challenges without parallel in other western secret services.

Reflecting the common border, common language, and Bonn's constitutional position that all Germans share common citizenship, the Federal Republic has been uniquely open to penetration by spies from East Berlin's Ministry of State Security (MfS) and Moscow's KGB. As a result of cross-border personal and family relationships, East German intelligence also has had great potential to acquire agents from the West through blackmail or other forms of persuasion. The same applies, of course, to the agents from the East taken up by the BND. The announcement at the end of 1989 of the winding up of the MfS – an organisation which gave work to 85,000 full-time employees and at least 109,000 part-time spies, above all to keep the East German population under control – has put a lot of jobs at risk in both East and West.

The unravelling of East Germany's apparatus of repression is also confronting East Germany with a psychological upheaval; similar to the aftermath of 1945, many who collaborated with or actively supported the previous regime suddenly found themselves on the other side. Holger Borner, the long-time Social Democrat Prime Minister of Hesse, whose father was executed by the Nazis during the 1930s, told me of the justice authorities in East Germany: 'They remind me of the people who condemned my father. For 14 years they crawled up Honecker's backside – and now they want to sit in judgement over him.'[24]

Democratic checks and balances built into the post-1949 federal system subject West German counter-espionage to greater constraints than in other western European countries like Britain – let alone the East bloc. The heads of the two security services – Hans-George Wieck, an urbane former ambassador in Teheran and Moscow, at the BND, and Gerhard Boeden, a stocky former police chief, at the BfV – are well-known figures. Boeden occasionally is interviewed on television in connection with espionage activities. In Britain, the names of the heads of the domestic and foreign branches of the intelligence services, MI5 and MI6, are official secrets, and the idea that either of them should appear on television would be unthinkable.

In the past, counter-espionage has often been hindered by competition between the BND and the BfV – rivalry which is partly due to the two agencies' very different roots. The BND, which comes under the control of the Bonn Chancellery, has its origins in an unconventional Wehrmacht intelligence service on the Eastern Front established in 1942 by Major-General Reinhard Gehlen. Realising Germany was on the way to losing the war, Gehlen in autumn 1944 hid in the Bavarian Alps microfilm files on his undercover operations in Soviet-controlled Europe. In 1946 he agreed with the American occupying forces to set up a specialised German service in the US zone to spy on eastern Europe.[25]

The service, known as the 'Organisation Gehlen', moved in 1947 to a walled settlement in the town of Pullach near Munich. The 15-acre site, containing several dozen houses and office buildings, was constructed in 1936 for staff of Hitler's deputy Rudolf Hess and was also used as the residence of Martin Bormann, the Nazi party secretary. It was not a complete coincidence that the Organisation Gehlen in its early days included, according to some estimates, as many as 50 former members of the Nazi party an the war-time secret service, the *Sicherheitsdienst* (SD).

Gehlen, who remained head of the BND until 1968, installed himself in Bormann's two-storey 'White House' in the centre of the settlement.

The BND was officially established only in April 1956, after the ending of occupation and West Germany's accession to NATO. The elegant mansion hung with is wood-panelled entrance foyer, hung with portraits of past BND chiefs, remains today the BND's nerve centre. The BND employs about 6,000 people in Pullach and in foreign posts, and has an annual budget of more than DM240 million.

The Cologne-based BfV meanwhile was set up in 1950. Under the aegis of the Interior Ministry, the BfV employs 2,300 people. A further 3,000 work for regional *Verfassungsschutz* agencies in the *Länder*, under the control of the *Land* authorities rather than Cologne. Along with keeping tabs on extreme Left- and Right-wing organisations, the BfV has to grapple with intelligence agencies from all the Communist countries. Both main arms of West German intelligence have chequered histories[26] – and both are now facing the threat of a sharp cut in budgetary entitlements from the unexpected rapprochement with the East.

At the BfV, no less than five former chiefs have had to quit in unusual circumstances. The first, Otto John, a member of the 20 July plot against Hitler in 1944, disappeared in 1954 and turned up in East Berlin. He claimed he had been drugged and driven unconscious across the border by the East German secret service. But when he mysteriously returned to the West more than a year later, the claim was disbelieved, and he was given a four-year prison sentence. John's successor, Hubert Schrübbers, had to leave after 17 years following revelations about his Nazi past. Gunther Nollau, the long-time counter-espionage expert who took over as BfV chief in 1972, was forced out in 1975 in the row over discovery the previous year that Gunter Guillaume, an aide to Chancellor Brandt, was an East German spy. Nollau left on a wave of bitterness amid a revival of accusations in the press – which were later retracted – that he was himself a Communist agent. Showing the depths of feuding between the BND and BfV, Nollau in his memoirs accused the BND of disrupting counter-espionage efforts by spreading false information.[27]

The biggest recent blow to the BfV was the defection in 1985 of Hans Joachim Tiedge, the agency's chief spy-catcher, who took with him secrets of more than 800 separate underground operations against East Berlin. Tiedge was heavily into debt and had serious drinking problems, and the BfV boss at the time, Herbert Hellenbroich, was accused of negligence for not previously informing the Interior Minister of doubts over his reliability.

Boeden, who took over at the BfV in 1987 to try to improve morale, told me it is 'terribly important' that his organisation should have 'a human face'. Tiedge defected after he found he had no one at head office with a sympathetic ear for his troubles, says Boeden. He has introduced a 'surgery' system under which he sees about three employees a week to discuss their difficulties. 'It is inevitable that in an institution like ours, employees can have problems.'[28]

Greater East-West German travel has increased East Germany's capacity to smuggle in spies. At the same time, a rising number of Communist agents have been unmasked. The BfV uncovered about 60 suspected East bloc spies in 1988 against 34 in 1987, 43 in 1986 and 18 in 1985.[29] Even after the start of dismantling of the MfS, Boeden warned that East German spying operations were continuing.[30] Like a monster which keeps writhing after its head has been removed, the East German security authorities were revealed by the Bonn government in early 1990 still to be carrying out routine telephone tapping of federal offices; the same was presumably true for BND activities in the East.

The past few years have also seen regular uncovering of a special feature of East-West German espionage: single women secretaries hired by the East Germans to spy in Bonn government offices. Many have been wooed by so-called 'Romeo' agents specially trained by the MfS to win the confidence of lonely women seeking love and companionship. The roughly 50 spy-secretaries uncovered since 1949 have given the East Germans tactical insight into Bonn political thinking, although much of the information must often have been of only routine nature.[31] The BND of course uses similar tactics. One top BND official told me, 'It is not as easy to recruit secretaries as in Bonn. But we have a good idea of what is going on in East Germany.'[32]

A good selection of the BND's agents have ended up over the years in the prison of Bautzen in Saxony, a grim five-storey building constructed at the beginning of the century – perhaps the most notorious symbol of East Germany's all-consuming police state. In a sign of new East German *glasnost*, Lt Horst Alex, the governor of Bautzen II – so called to distinguish it from another jail complex in the town – showed me round in December 1989.[33]. The Gothic prison of Bautzen, part of a building complex shared with the local justice authorities and the security service, is a place of decrepitude and decay. The waiting room into which I am ushered smells of disinfectant. There are cameras everywhere. Alex is a keen-eyed man of 38 with prematurely greying hair, clad in a gold-buttoned uniform. He is on the point of releasing most of his inmates – including a dozen convicted agents of the BND – as part of a seasonal spy swap with the Federal Republic. 'We do everything to keep to Christmas here,' he told me. Alex conducted me through the yellow-painted cell block boasting 6.4 square metre cells equipped with bed, cupboard, sink, green-seated toilet and six plastic wall hooks. He claimed that conditions in Bautzen – which traditionally has held around 200 prisoners – were better than in other East German jails. 'We have the possibility of providing for individual circumstances.'

Alex has been the governor here for 4¼ years. 'We have clean hands. I carried out our work to the best of my conscience. I distance myself from allegations that we have carried out psycho-terror.' A member of the Socialist Unity Party since 1976, Alex however acknowledges that, 'Some sentences have been overdone. I admit that. And some investigations were not carried out property.' Not yet comprehending the full extent of the changes sweeping across the two Germanys, he told me that the Bautzen prison was likely, before too long, to receive a fresh contingent of incarcerated West German spies. 'Every state needs intelligence agencies.' Like many in East Germany, Alex is struggling to prepare for a new life by separating himself from the old system he served. The prison governor told me he was not going to leave the party. 'But I have been bitterly disappointed by the gap between the grassroots and the leadership.' Alex added, almost in desperation: 'We need a new concept to escape from chaos' – an epitaph, perhaps, for the state he helped, in his own small way, to perpetuate.

17

Germany's Destiny

As for the Germans, they need neither freedom or equality. They are a speculative race, ideologists with fore- and aftersight, dreamers who live only in the past and future and have no present ... Men are strange! In our Fatherland, we grumble: every stupidity, everything that is wrong vexes us; like boys, we want to run off daily into the wide world. But when at last we really are in the wide world, we find it too wide, and often secretly yearn for the narrow stupidities and wrong things at home, and would like to sit between the old familiar walls again and, if we could, build ourselves a little house behind the stove and sit there warmly and read The Germans' General Advertiser.

Heinrich Heine, 1828[1]

I know that some people believe that one can conquer the world through economic means. That however is one of the greatest and most dire fallacies imaginable.

Adolf Hitler, 1932[2]

On 19 April 1945, a day before Hitler's 56th birthday, as the Soviet army advanced on shattered Berlin and the Third Reich drew nearer to fiery extinction, Joseph Goebbels made his last radio broadcast, delivering a vision of the idyll which would rise from the ruin:

After this war, Germany will blossom as never before. Her destroyed landscapes and provinces will be rebuilt with new and more beautiful towns and villages in which happy people will live. The whole of Europe will participate in this recovery. Once more we shall be friends with all peoples of good will. Together with them we shall let the deep wounds heal which disfigure the noble face of our continent. In rich cornfields, the daily bread will grow, banishing the hunger of millions who are needy and suffering today. There will be work in abundance, and out of it as the deepest spring of human happiness there will come bliss and strength for all. Chaos will be mastered! This continent will be ruled not by the underworld, but by order, peace and prosperity.[3]

Eighteen months later, in October/November 1946, the British publisher Victor Gollancz made a harrowing tour of northern Germany. He found that tens of thousands of Germans were slowly starving to death in the British occupied zone. One of his reports came from the town of Julich, between Aachen and Düsseldorf, 93 per cent destroyed by bombing:

> Up and across what had once been a road, a bit of a small house was standing – a ground-floor room and two rooms above it, with the staircase (now an outside staircase) intact, but the rest of the house a mess of bricks open to the sky. A mother and daughter lived and slept in the tiny ground-floor room, and I can't get them out of my mind either. The girl was a bad case of open TB, with brooding eyes and a half-open mouth: the mother looked so desolate and grey with sorrow that I oughtn't have been horrified, as I was, when she told us she wanted to die. She was a widow, and the two of them lived on something microscopic. The woman was barefoot, for she possessed only a single ruined shoe. I asked her to come into the doorway to be photographed with the shoe in her hand, but she wouldn't come far forward into the good light, saying that she didn't want to make a show of herself.[4]

Warning of the consequences of continued British neglect and wilfulness towards defeated Germany, Gollancz, a Jew of German extraction, wrote: 'If we choose the path of destruction rather than construction; if we fill the German people with despair rather than hope; if we make them hate and despise us, when they were ready for emotions of a very different kind – then the Nazis, in spite of everything, have won, and tomorrow's world will be of their pattern, and not of ours.'[5]

I

Compared with the desperate aftermath of the Second World War, today's Germany throws up a stark contrast – and some subtle parallels. In the rich Federal Republic, it is Goebbels's Arcadia which seems to have been realised; Gollancz's apocalypse remains merely a buried memory. In the East, however, the legacy of past ruin lies heavily still. The people of the GDR have spent four and a half decades repairing the ravages of war; now, they are sweeping away the rubble of Communism. Staring westwards, they yearn for something better. The breaching of the Berlin Wall has brought it into view.

335

Since 9 November 1989, reality has surged in on East Germany. The totalitarian regimes which kept the misnamed German Democratic Republic in place for 40 years were buttressed by two seemingly unshakeable external influences: the Soviet Union's desire to maintain a hold over eastern Europe, and an unspoken East-West consensus that German division represented the consequence, and the price, of Hitler's lost war. Now, the first factor has been undermined by the ousting in 1989 of a domino-like series of bankrupt Communist governments, the second by the growing self-awareness and strength of the Germans themselves. Not tanks or missiles, but an infusion of western ideas and D-Marks, have dissolved the foundations of the East German state. In rejecting Communism, Poland, Hungary and Czechoslovakia have remained intact nations; but East Germany, lacking fundamental identity and legitimacy, has seen its birthright vanish. Almost literally overnight, the alternative to the East German state has come into sight: it is called Germany.

The elections of March 1990 brought to power a government in East Berlin strongly in favour of German unity. A richer and more disturbing paradox could hardly be imagined. Within reach is the chance of lowering military tensions and spreading western values across Europe. But there is also a risk of disrupting a system of alliances which has preserved peace and stability in Europe for a longer continuous period than at any time since the Middle Ages. As Europe grapples to accommodate the German desire for self-determination, it is worthwhile recalling the lessons of the past.

Integration of the Federal Republic into the western democracies, under a policy followed by all Chancellors since 1949, was a recovery without parallel in history: an asset for the West, and a triumph for the Germans. But success has been hard-earned. Its continuation cannot be taken completely for granted. There were three basic reasons for the achievement. The West learned from the experience of the 1920s that it was dangerous and counter-productive to drive defeated Germany into a corner; antagonism between the Soviet Union and the US made the strengthening of the western part of Germany a vital precondition of American policies; and the German people showed astonishing effort and resilience in rebuilding their ravaged land.

Four decades later, the political map of Europe is being redrawn. The West as a whole has a chance of securing Germany's place on it in a way which maintains and enhances peaceful international cooperation. But West Germany and its allies will have to show evidence of the same foresight and resolution displayed, under very different conditions, during the 1950s. The balance of forces on which the stability of Germany and Europe depends is not merely military and territorial in nature, but also applies to ideas. If Germany's hopes, fears and desires become out of step with those of its neighbours, then equilibrium will be difficult to sustain – and the European architecture of which Germany is the central stone will crumble.

One reason why the challenge is so complex reflects the new perception of German strength. The post-war division of Europe ensured the Federal Republic's economic success, while simultaneously marking the political failure of the German nation. Now that superpower confrontation has ebbed, West Germany's economic vigour has given the Germans a powerful lever with which to overcome that failure. Ending partition may erase Hitler's longest-lasting legacy. But the economic power which has helped drive forward German unification simultaneously makes Germany's neighbours wary about the consequences of its realisation. It is not a complete coincidence that in 1989, the year of the East German revolution, the West German economy registered, for the first time for a decade, a growth rate higher than the average of the rest of the industrialised world. If the Federal Republic had remained locked in the growth doldrums of the early 1980s, both its magnetic appeal for the East – and also the outside fears of German dominance – would have been a great deal less.

For the Germans themselves, economic success has not banished questioning. Will the attainment of their material aims make the West Germans better or worse democrats? Can a new European security structure be found to replace a NATO alliance which no longer fulfills German needs? How does a 'junior partner' suddenly take on a more assertive 'senior' status without disrupting relations with its partners and neighbours? Can the nation be restored without renewing the conflicts which, last time, tore it apart? Fundamental questions about Germany's identity and place in the world were masked, not resolved, during four post-war decades; they are now pressing for answers.

II

The re-drawing of the East-West political map has had one obvious consequence: the Germans have rediscovered their geography. NATO membership in 1955 conferred on West Germany the status of a front-line state while simultaneously offering protection though its alliance partners' collective troops and weapons. That equilibrium has now been shattered; well before the events of autumn 1989, both East and West Germany had grown increasingly hostile to superpower policies which appear to concentrate war risks on German soil. NATO seems unlikely to reform itself thoroughly and quickly enough to satisfy German wishes for a new form of European security structure taking better account of German interests.

The Germans are tired of Cicero's maxim that those who want peace must prepare for war. Growing up under the guilt and shame bequeathed by the Third Reich, the post-1945 German electorate has tended to see armies in terms of fighting wars, and therefore has a built-in tendency to promote disarmament. For Britain and France, on the other hand, the experience of the 1930s and 1940s leads to exactly opposite conclusions. For the countries which narrowly defeated Germany, military forces are the means of preventing conflicts; their maintenance is seen as particularly necessary during times (such as the early 1990s) of political upheaval in Europe. US troops and tanks withdrawn from Europe in coming years will retreat across the Atlantic, while Soviet forces will pull back east of the Vistula. In a period when the Soviet Union is much less of an immediate threat, but remains the dominant European military power, bridging the gap between these differing perspectives may prove to be, for NATO, an impossible task.

The 1987 US-Soviet Intermediate Nuclear Forces agreement already showed that both East and West Germany realised their strategic interests did not necessarily coincide with those of their partners in the Warsaw Pact and NATO. As a result of the scrapping of all missiles of more than 500 kilometres range, US and Soviet land-based nuclear weapons in Europe are limited to those deployed in and targeted at an area roughly delineated by East and West Germany. The paradox of nuclear deterrence is that nuclear weapons prevent war by threatening a conflict of catastrophic proportions. The paradox of the division of Germany is that partition, while resented and opposed by the Germans, stabilised Europe for more than 40 years. Both precepts have been part of the post-war order; and both contain innate ambivalence which the Germans are no longer prepared to accept.

The Federal Republic now sees the Soviet Union more as a partner than as a military threat. West Germany declares regularly that it would never be so foolish as to give up its western ties. None the less, the process of German unity makes some form of German-Soviet *rapprochement* probable. The Germans are being drawn together by the tidal pull of

338

history, geography and emotion – forces which the West finds difficult to understand, let alone to master.

III

In the 1990s, the Federal Republic will have real bargaining power over the future of what was formerly Communist Europe. As the paymaster of the European Community, the Federal Republic has the financial muscle to prompt western Europe to march at the pace it judges to be consistent with its *Ost-* as well as its *Westpolitik*.

West Germany has become within the space of a few years a massive foreign creditor – the second in the world after Japan. The US has switched from being the world's banker to the largest debtor.[6] In the same way that the weakening of West Germany's faith in nuclear deterrence took years to become fully apparent, the implications of the change in economic relationships have not been fully digested. It is inconceivable that this shift will not weaken America's strategic relationship with the Federal Republic.

West Germany's desire to be protected by the US defence umbrella is decreasing along with America's capacity to pay for it. New generations of electors and political decision-makers have come to the fore in both the US and West Germany, questioning the basis of their post-war ties. Moves towards isolationism in the US and anti-Americanism in Europe could dangerously overlap. More will be heard of 'German interests'. West Germany's influence partly reflects its allies' fear of the disruption which would ensue if the country were ever to become untethered from the West. It will be up to Bonn and its partners to make sure that this influence is used wisely.

West Germany has more options than before – but it is also vulnerable. The quality of political leadership has declined. Germany may find it difficult to avoid being dragged towards the fatal temptation of trying to play off East and West against each other. In spite of being embedded in the European Community, and the international orientation of the economy, the Federal Republic during the 1980s has grown less outward-looking, more absorbed with itself. In relations with NATO, as the results of the Intermediate Nuclear Forces agreement have underlined, West Germany is increasingly prone to consider itself the victim of anti-German policies. Explicitly or implicitly, many Germans believe that the country is still unfairly carrying burdens imposed by the war victors – a mood disturbingly reminiscent of the self-pity of the 1920s.

IV

Among the pre-Second World War ruminations of Ernst von Weizsäcker, state secretary at the German Foreign Ministry, was this extraordinary blueprint for diplomatic subterfuge, written in 1937:

> Germany will be unable to improve its inadequate territorial position on the European continent without great shocks in Europe.... As a goal, one can think, at the most, quite generally of a federated Greater Germany, which would again directly link Germany with East Prussia, as well as bringing Austria and Sudeten Germany close to us and making other frontier corrections ... The condition for all these plans however is an overwhelming victory of German aims, which would in no way be attainable if these goals, or even simply the intention, were to become known in advance. Germany needs a peaceful face, to be able to act, as the case arises, with all the more surprise. It needs a wholly different position from the one it has today: military, economic, financial and political. It needs the reputation of strength, stability, reliability and dignity.[7]

More than half a century later, after experiencing crushing military defeat rather than total victory, Germany – at least, the western part of it – has indeed attained strength, stability, reliability and dignity. The achievement has come through peace, not war. The Germans have conquered the world through economic means. Yet, because of history, there is one blessing which Germany, in its dealings abroad, still does not enjoy: the benefit of the doubt. To guard against suspicions that Germany may still be prone to double games of the sort described by the elder Weizsäcker, the Federal Republic has always striven to follow foreign policies which are clear-cut and beyond reproach. At the beginning of the 1990s, however, the collapse of Communism east of the Elbe has inevitably heightened the Federal Republic's ambivalence over its international relationships. Unless West Germany and its allies succeed in jointly making up their minds on what sort of Europe they would like to see emerging from the Gorbachev era, room for mistrust and suspicion on both sides is likely to increase substantially.

340

One of the Soviet Union's policy goals has always been to drive a wedge between American and German strategic priorities. As the suggestion of a neutral unified state is brought into play, there is a risk that German reunification could come about on terms more favourable to the Soviet Union than to the West.

How should the West respond? One answer is to go back to the beginning. The initial impetus, at the end of the 1940s and the beginning of the 1950s, behind West Germany's membership of the western community came from the imperatives of the Cold War: the need to provide a counter-pole to Communist encroachment across Europe. In the 1990s, assuming that ideological and military disarmament between the superpowers continues, the Federal Republic's western bond must draw its strength far less from the requirements of defence strategy, far more from common commitment to western democratic values. A fundamental part of these values, the right to self-determination, has to apply to Germany as much as anywhere else. If the German people want to move towards some form of unity, then any attempt by the West to stand in their way would be ultimately counter-productive. Ironically, the only way of assuring the Federal Republic's ties to the West is to allow the possibility that they could be loosened.

V

In 1869, Bismarck put forward his celebrated dictum over German unity: 'We can advance our watches, but the time passes no more quickly because of that, and the ability to wait until conditions develop is a requisite of practical policy.' In an age when both the US and the Soviet Union are seeking new international roles, the clock chronicling the fate of Germany has advanced at a pace which, even in the autumn of 1989, would have been thought impossible.

The western position, laid down by treaty in 1955 and reaffirmed ever since, is that a unified German state must be integrated into the European community. There is no reason why the reemergence of a nation with 78 million people in the middle of Europe must inevitably destabilise the continent. Germany's efficiency and energy, talent and technology can prove of inestimable importance in rebuilding the shattered economies of eastern Europe. The West has always regarded

341

the goal of ending German partition as extinguishing a potential source of conflict; the lowering of military concentration on German soil will free resources for peaceful purposes. The conditions under which unification goes ahead will however be crucial. Many contemporary Germans deeply resent still being on probation as a result of Hitler's war; but the prospect of changes in borders which have been set for four decades cannot fail to raise questions among Germany's neighbours about the country's motives and ambitions.

Forty years is a long period for the people of East Germany, who bore an unjust share of the burden of division, and whose clamour for freedom set in train the 1989 revolution; but it is only a short time in the lives and the memories of nations. A neutral German state could be turned more to Moscow than to the West. To prevent this outcome, flexibility and imagination will be required within the European Community and NATO. Most difficult of all, the outside world will need to display more faith in the steadfastness and common-sense of the post-war Germans than they have often had in themselves. In any set of policies to ensure the stability and westwards orientation of the new Germany, three principles are paramount.

1. Economic integration with western Europe must not be slowed down. Fusion of East and West Germany's monetary, economic and legal systems needs to be harmonised with the European Community's progress towards a post-1992 'single market'. It is inevitable that German monetary union will take place long before European monetary union. But the best guarantee that the former does not blow off course the latter is that the whole of Europe – and not just West Germany – be closely involved in the economic rebuilding of the eastern part of the new Germany.

2. The necessary reshaping of European defence alliances needs to take full account of the security interests of all countries affected by German reunification. It would be a fatal mistake to put any of the four victor powers of the Second World War, or Germany itself, at a demonstrable disadvantage. A sensible policy would allow for the continuing presence – in far smaller numbers than in 1990 – of both US and Soviet forces in the two parts of Germany. This would apply both to the interim period leading up to full reunification and to several years afterwards. Because the Soviet Union cannot be expected to allow the GDR to join NATO, East Germany would have to be given special military status as the best possible means of blunting Moscow's campaign for complete neutrality of all of Germany. If NATO is indeed eventually to be disbanded, the four powers as well as Germany will

342

need to be joint signatories, with equal rights and responsibilities, of the European 'peace order' which takes its place. A new German army, on the West German model, will still be required as part of the guarantee force for the new European defence system, although it should be only roughly half the size of the present Bundeswehr.

3. The new Germany – a federal state, on the same decentralised lines as the successful Federal Republic – will need to enter into treaty obligations to secure its relations with the rest of Europe. Both East and West Germany must make clear during the pre-unification transition period that the forthcoming legal accord with the Second World War victors recognises the validity of the Oder-Neisse line. A timetable will be needed to phase out the four powers' responsibilities for Berlin. Even if Germany decides that Berlin should become the capital again, the Germans would be well advised to maintain a form of international status for the city, for instance, to play a special role within the Helsinki cooperation agreements. Over the past half a century, Berlin has been a source of evil and a scene of pain; to make it a city of peace, and share it with the rest of the world, would be the best possible symbol of the new Germany.

National unity has been made feasible by the Federal Republic's 40 years of prosperity, democracy and stability. The task now is to extend these accomplishments eastwards: if the process is successful, the whole continent will benefit. If it fails, all will be at risk – in West and East. Germany's destiny will shape the future of Europe.

Notes

1: On the Fault Line

1. Heine, *Deutschland*, written in summer 1840.
2. Speech to House to Commons, 13.7.34 (Churchill, *Second World War*, I, p.92).
3. Interview with author in Bonn, 9.11.87.
4. Formal independence from government is however plainly not a sufficient condition to maintain monetary stability. See Chapter 6.

2: Consequences of Catastrophe

1. Friedrich Meinecke, *Die deutsche Katastrophe*, 1946, p.5.
2. Speech to the parliamentary council in Bonn, 8.5.49.
3. Speech in Bundestag on 40th anniversary of Germany's capitulation, 8.5.85.
4. Interview with author in Frankfurt, 21.2.89.
5. Horst Krüger, *Das zerbrochene Haus: Ein Jugend in Deutschland*, 1976, (first published 1966).
6. The figure of 8 million members in 1945 has been authenticated by Prof. Jürgen Falter of West Berlin's Free University.
7. Interview with author in Ludwigsburg, 28.11.88.
8. Ralph Giordano, *Die Zweite Schuld*, 1987, p.149. Giordano, born in 1923, one of the most bitter of the many critical authors on post-war handling of Nazi crimes, suffered under the Nazis' racial laws because his mother was Jewish. He delivers a harsh judgement on thirty years of West German legal investigations into Nazi crimes. In spite of the 'immense quantitative effort' of investigators and attorneys, West Germany's bid to bring Nazi criminals to justice 'remains a farce', he wrote.
9. Symposium in Ludwigsburg, 8/9.9.88.
10. The Centre keeps around 30 million files, in somewhat primitive conditions, in a villa formerly used by the Nazi intelligence agency in Zehlendorf. It was in the headlines in 1988 after more than 10,000 files were stolen and passed on to dealers for sale as Nazi memorabilia. In January 1989, a former head of the Centre's photographic department was given a two-year prison sentence for his part. In general, the BDC files are available for examination only by authorised historians. Ultra Right-wing groups in West Germany have tried to gain access to files to use in smear campaigns against prominent German politicians with Nazi connections. The Bundestag has called on the Bonn government to take over responsibility for the archive from the Americans. One of the reasons why the government has delayed any decision is because West Germany does not want to have to decide itself whether or not files on Nazi members who may be still alive should be made available for public scrutiny.
11. Conference in Königswinter, 9.3.89.
12. The Holocaust film, by focusing on the fate of one Jewish family during the Third Reich, brought to the surface emotions which had been hidden during thirty years. German TV stations took about 30,000 telephone calls as a result of the showing.
13. The three companies each have larger turnover in chemical manufacture than Du Pont, the US chemicals giant. (Du Pont's overall sales are also boosted by its substantial energy activities.)
14. Press conference in Leverkusen, 24.11.86.
15. Press conference in Ludwigshafen, 26.11.86.
16. During the mid-1960s, Kohl at the age of 34 was offered the job as a board member of a

Notes

German chemicals company, but chose to continue his political career in the Rhineland Palatinate, of which he became Prime Minister in 1969.

17. Press conference in Bonn, 17.11.86.

18. Bayer AG, *Meilensteine*, 1988 (p.299).

19. Schrader went on after the war to become director of Bayer's insecticide research laboratories in Wuppertal.

20. Degesch supplied the gas to another firm, Tesch und Stabenow (Testa), which delivered it to the SS. Although two Testa executives were hanged by the British military government after the war for their part in the Jews' extermination, I.G. Farben directors were cleared by an American military tribunal of knowingly delivering the gas for criminal purposes.

21. Until the late 1980s, the I.G. Farben receivers, who run a shell company still quoted on the Frankfurt stock exchange from an office in a Frankfurt suburb, counted in their balance sheet a contingent liability for several million D-Marks of outstanding claims by concentration camp inmates.

22. Adenauer's decision was not popular with the electorate. According to an Allensbach survey in 1952, 44 per cent of the population termed as 'superfluous' the DM3 billion aid to Israel, while only 35 per cent agreed with the gesture.

23. Other companies which used slave labour during the war and made restitution payments include Krupp (DM10 million), AEG (DM4 million), Siemens (DM7 million) and Rheinmetall (DM2.5 million). A payment of DM5 million on behalf of the Flick company to the Jewish Claims Conference was made in 1986.

24. The company admits that it used 29,500 forced labourers at the end of 1944, around half the total work-force.

25. Interview with author in Munich, 27.11.86.

26. William Safire in the *New York Times*, 11.1.89.

27. Kohl in an interview with author in Bonn, 7.2.89. His words were: 'In chemical questions we are No. 1 in the world. When one looks at part of the reaction in the US, I don't meant the Administration, in reality it is a question of competition. We are not too blind that we cannot see what it is all about.'

28. Degesch's US subsidiary, set up in 1979, admits that the company's history 'has caused us a few difficulties' among customers. According to Donald Shaheen, one of the company's vice-presidents, 'We have had people refusing to do business with us because we're German.' (Interview with *Financial Times*, February 1989.)

29. *Brockhaus Encyclopaedia* entries for *Blausäure* (cyanide) in 1967 and 1988.

30. Höfer was in good company. Many prominent post-war journalists had worked in propaganda functions during wartime, including names as varied as Jürgen Eick (later co-publisher of the *Frankfurter Allgemeine Zeitung*) and Henri Nannen (founder of *Stern*). Otto Köhler, a Left-wing journalist who is disliked by the present-day chemical industry because of his work publicising the history of I.G. Farben, was aged 10 at the end of the war. Köhler has admitted that, stuffed full of Nazi propaganda, had he been old enough to have worked during the war he could have written the same 'dreadful' lines as Höfer. (*Die Zeit*, 15.1.88.)

31. Terence Prittie, *My Germans*, 1983, p.187.

32. Interview with author in Rodenkirchen, 17.10.88.

33. Interview with author in Hamburg, 8.12.88.

34. Interview with author in Bonn, 3.2.88.

35. According to reports in 1949, at least forty dangerous war criminals were still at large, and 61 judges and senior legal officers alone in Baden-Württemberg had served on Nazi courts. An investigation in 1951 showed that 134 officials in the Bonn Foreign Office were ex-Nazis. An official of the Auswärtiges Amt commented that this was irrelevant: 'a line should be drawn through our past.' Terence Prittie, *Germany Divided*, 1960, pp.230, 247.

36. Kiesinger's Nazi party membership made him the focus of sporadic criticism during his chancellorship. He claimed he joined to exert positive 'influence' on the Nazi movement.

37. Blessing offers an intriguing example of a well-connected financier who managed to retain his position with the Nazis yet also stay in contact with opposition figures during the war. He was a director of the Reichsbank between 1937 and 1939, when he was dismissed along with other

directors after he signed a memorandum in January 1939 opposing the government's inflationary financing of rearmament. He joined the board of the Margarine-Union, a Unilever company which controlled about 50 per cent of German margarine production. In 1941 he became chairman of Kontinentale Öl, the monopoly company set up to manage Germany's oil interests throughout occupied eastern Europe. Blessing described himself as being 'forced' to move to Kontinentale Öl. See Reinhard Vogelsang, *Der Freundeskreis Himmler*, 1972, p.74.

38. Blessing supported Himmler's SS activities with two donations of RM15,000 in 1939-40 during his time at Unilever. He explained this as necessary insurance to protect Unilever's position. (Vogelsang, op.cit. p.112/113.) After the failed 20 July plot, Blessing's name was found on two lists drawn up by the conspirators nominating him either as a future president of the Reichsbank or as a future Employment, Economy or Food Minister. Walther Funk, the Reichsbank president between 1939 and 1945, protected him from arrest after telling the secret service that Blessing was unaware that he had been earmarked for a post under the Opposition. (Funk was given a life sentence in 1946 at the Nuremberg tribunal.)

39. Fritz Stern, *Dreams and Delusions: The Drama of German History*, 1987, p.121-2.

40. Partly because he has first-class speechwriters, Kohl has learned to talk about the past in public with more sensitivity than when he first came to office. Kohl's description of himself as benefiting from 'the mercy of having been born late', used during a visit to Israel in 1984, caused protests among the Jewish community as it gave the widespread impression that the Germans had simply grown tired of commemorating the sins of the Nazis.

41. Poll by Emnid Institute, published in *Der Spiegel*, April 1989. The Allensbach Institute has posed for many years the question about assessment of Hitler. In 1955, 48 per cent of respondents said that, without the war and Jewish genocide, Hitler would have gone down in history as a great statesman. In 1960, the percentage fell to 34 per cent, and it went down to 32 per cent in 1967 and 31 per cent in 1978. *Allensbacher Jahrbuch der Demoskopie*, Vol. VIII, 1983.

42. Albert Speer, *Inside the Third Reich*, 1970.

43. The Morgenthau plan was drawn up in August/September 1944, and shelved in October.

44. Golo Mann, *Deutsche Geschichte 1919-1945*, 1968.

45. Aidan Crawley, *The Rise of Western Germany*, 1973, p.25.

46. William Manchester, *The Arms of Krupp*, 1968, introduction.

47. Hitler's private and political testaments, 29.4.45.

48. Alan Bullock, *Hitler, A Study in Tyranny*, 1963 (first published 1952), Chap. 14, VIII.

49. Office of Military Government for Germany, *Economic Developments since the Currency Reform*, November 1948.

50. Hermann Wallich, Paul Wallich, *Zwei Generationen im deutschen Bankwesen 1833-1914*, 1978, p.27.

51. Henry Wallich, *The Yale Review*, June 1955, p.503/519.

52. Speech in Stuttgart, 6.1.46.

53. Speech in New York, 16.11.87.

54. Sebastian Haffner, *Anmerkungen zu Hitler*, 1987.

55. Interview with author in Bonn, 18.7.88.

56. Sermon marking the 40th anniversary of the ending of the Second World War in St Hedwig's Cathedral, East Berlin, 5.3.85. Meisner, born in Breslau, was Roman Catholic Bishop of Berlin between 1980 and 1989, with his diocese covering both parts of the divided city and the surrounding area of Brandenburg, and with his residence in East Berlin. In 1989 he took up his duties as the new Archbishop of Cologne, appointed by the Pope under the terms of the Vatican's concordat with Prussia in 1929, which has remained in force in spite of the disappearance of the German Reich.

57. Interview with author in Düsseldorf, 14.3.89.

58. A shift in official views on Stauffenberg has also taken place in East Germany. According to the official line which persisted up to the early 1980s, the 20 July conspirators were aiming to destroy the alliance between the US, Britain and the Soviet Union and restore 'German imperialism'. More recently, however, East Berlin in its official commentaries has placed Stauffenberg on a par with the Communist resistance.

59. Another, possibly better idea, is to adopt as national day 23 May, the anniversary of the Basic Law (provisional constitution) in 1949. As Josef Joffe has observed, 'Whereas Americans or Frenchmen grow up with *The Star-Spangled Banner* or Bastille Day, the post-war West German generation did not even have a decent national holiday, or any other symbols or traditions that bind the individual to his tribe.' (*Encounter*, June 1987).

60. Interview with author at Burg Hohenzollern, 23.6.88.

61. After evidence of Rommel's implication in the 20 July plot was collected, Hitler sent a message to him offering him the choice of suicide or trial before the *Volksgerichtshof*. To spare his family, Rommel chose the former; he was said to have died of heart failure, and was given a state funeral.

62. Interview with author in Stuttgart, 23.2.88.

63. By reaching the Elbe in April 1945, American troops had penetrated much further into what is now East Germany than was thought possible in autumn 1944, when post-war occupation zones were drawn up. They retreated from Thuringia, the western part of Saxony, and Mecklenburg, and were replaced by the Red Army. This delivered up to Communism an area of 8.7 million people west of the line Wismar-Magdeburg-Torgau-Dresden, who thought that their fate was in the hands of the Americans. In accordance with the same Allied agreements, early in July 1945 British and American forces also moved into the western sectors of Berlin which, since the beginning of May 1945, had been occupied by Soviet forces.

64. During his campaign for the Chancellorship in 1980, Franz Josef Strauss had regular cause to shout at hecklers, 'You are the best Nazis who ever existed.' In a more recent example, Heiner Geissler, general secretary of the Christian Democrats, told a turbulent audience at Frankfurt university in December 1987 that they reminded him of the SA. Helmut Kohl ran into trouble in November 1988 when he accused the Social Democratic Opposition of practising *Volksverhetzung* (whipping up the people). The Nazis made the same accusations against the SPD in 1933 as a ploy for banning the party.

65. Michael Müller, an SPD deputy, has called on Bonn to cancel support for a European Community genetic engineering programme because it allegedly provided a new way of influencing racial characteristics.

66. The Institut für deutsche Sprache counts 80 books and specialist articles published on Nazi vocabulary. See Michael Kinne, NS-Wörter oder Braundeutsch von heute, *Der Sprachdienst*, January 1989.

67. Interview with author in Fehmarn, 3.5.88.

68. Speech to CDU party congress, 25.5.83.

69. Speech on 1.3.33.

70. Wolfgang Bergsdorf, *Herrschaft und Sprache*, 1983.

71. Kohl, too, has been prone to clumsy errors. In 1986, in an interview with the US magazine *Newsweek*, he indirectly compared Mikhail Gorbachev with Joseph Goebbels, Hitler's Propaganda Minister. This was a gratuitous but not fundamentally malevolent remark, illustrating above all Kohl's lack of intellectual precision. But the ensuing uproar, fanned by the Social Democrats, overshadowed Bonn's relationship with Moscow for several months.

72. Speech in Bundestag, 10.11.88.

73. After he resigned, Jenninger foolishly claimed in a TV interview that he had been sanctioned for speaking too frankly. He also claimed that his own family had suffered under the Nazis. Jenninger's father's printing works was closed by the Nazis, and the young Jenninger had been forced to work in an armaments factory.

74. Interview with author in Düsseldorf, 27.3.87.

75. Interview with author in Hamburg, 26.6.87.

76. After release, Ernst von Weizsäcker was one of the many former servants of the Third Reich to publish memoirs pretending unconvincingly to have been secret opponents of Hitler. In a rare public comment on his father, the younger Weizsäcker termed him in 1985 as 'very honest but not very strong' (*New York Times* magazine, 23.6.85).

77. *Frankfurter Allgemeine Zeitung*, 6.6.86.

78. Interview with author in Frankfurt, 3.3.88.

3: The Dilemma of East and West

1. Quoted in Gerald Freund, *Unholy Alliance: Russo-German Relations from the Treaty of Brest-Litovsk to the Treaty of Berlin*, 1957, p.245.
2. Document accompanying letter to Heinrich Weitz, the mayor of Duisburg, 31.10.45, *Adenauer Briefe 1945-47*, p.130.
3. Mikhail Gorbachev, *Perestroika*, 1987, p.262.
4. Statistic from the Geographic Survey of the Bundeswehr.
5. Interview with author in Hamburg, 1.7.88.
6. The historian Gordon Craig has written that, under Stresemann, 'the European situation made patience, ambiguity and opportunism requirements of German foreign policy' – qualities which also apply to German diplomacy in the 1980s. Craig, *Germany 1866-1945*, 1981, p.512.
7. Remark in 1927, quoted in Jon Jacobson, *Locarno Diplomacy: Germany and the West, 1925-29*, 1972, p.82.
8. Adolf Hitler, *Mein Kampf*, 1925-7, p.749.
9. Adopted in London, 12.9.44.
10. US State Department, Foreign Relations of the US: *The conferences at Malta and Yalta, 1945*, 1956.
11. Roosevelt declared that the US would take all reasonable steps to secure peace, but not at the expense of keeping a large army in Europe, 3,000 miles away from home. (Churchill, *The Second World War*, VI, p.308).
12. See note 63, Chapter 2.
13. Several months passed before the Western Allies were able to take over effective control of their Berlin city boroughs.
14. On 4.6.45 Churchill urged Truman against the withdrawal of American troops to the designated occupation zones, saying this would bring 'Soviet power into the heart of western Europe and the descent of an iron curtain between us and everything to the eastward.' (H.S. Truman, *Year of Decision*, 1955, pp.224-5.) Churchill also used the phrase 'iron curtain' in his first speech as leader of the Opposition in the House of Commons on 16.8.45. Churchill's famous speech at Fulton, Missouri, when the symbol of the Iron Curtain leapt into the headlines around the world, was not made until 1946.
15. Antagonism between Stalin and the French leader Charles de Gaulle was one reason why the provisional Paris government was not represented at Potsdam.
16. Churchill, op.cit. p.563.
17. *Documents on the Status of Berlin*, 1959, pp.34-41.
18. Some early exaggerated estimates put the number of deaths in 1945 after the German surrender among Germans living in Russia, the Soviet zone and eastern Europe at as many as 6 million.
19. The figures for refugees settling in West Germany after the war are inevitably suspect, reflecting the confused conditions in the years following 1945. The official statistics for settlement have tended to be inflated, because they also include children born of refugees after they had come to the West. The overall figures for post-war refugees include about 7 million Germans from the territories east of the Oder/Neisse line as well as 5 million from other parts of eastern Europe (above all 3 million Sudeten Germans) and 3 million from the German Democratic Republic.
20. The Foreign Ministers council was to be comprised of five powers, including France and China. China's inclusion reflected the requirement to settle post-war issues in the Far East.
21. Speech to Reichstag on 6.2.1888, quoted in C. Grant Robertson, *Bismarck*, 1918, p.47.
22. Edgar Alexander, *Adenauer*, 1957, p.17.
23. Speech in Oslo, 11.12.71.
24. Interview with author in Bonn, 3.11.86.
25. Helmut Schmidt, *Menschen und Mächte*, 1987, p.459.
26. Survey by the Infas polling organisation. According to a separate polling series by the Allensbach institute, only about 17 per cent of the population in 1987 wanted closer links with the US, compared with levels of between 40 and 60 per cent in the 1970s and early 1980s. 60 per cent said West

Germany should give equal weight to the US and the Soviet Union. In another survey, Allensbach discovered at the end of 1987 that 44 per cent favoured neutrality between East and West, compared with 31 per cent in 1980. Only 32 per cent wanted close alignment with the US – against 56 per cent in 1980. However, the proportion arguing for close cooperation with the Soviet Union remained very small – only 5 per cent.

27. Poll by ZDF television, 11.6.89.

28. According to European Community polls in the autumn of 1988, only 47 per cent of West Germans believed the Community's 1992 single market programme was a 'good thing'. This was the same result as in Britain. Luxembourg (36 per cent in favour) and Denmark (39 per cent) had lower approval scores, while the other member countries were much more enthusiastic. European Commission 'Eurobarometer' survey, March 1989.

29. As a result of the Community's budget package agreed in 1988, the Federal Republic – already by far the largest contributor to the EC – is channelling an extra amount of at least DM30 billion to Brussels during the five-year period 1988-92.

30. Interview with author in Kronberg, 7.2.89.

31. The findings are backed up by an Allensbach poll, according to which only 25 per cent of the German population in October 1988 thought that a western European political union to form a 'United States of Europe' was very important, against 33 per cent who said it was in 1983.

32. Remarks at a lunch in Bonn, 14.5.87.

33. Speech in Vienna at opening of East-West disarmament negotiations, 7.3.89.

34. Speech in Aachen, 1.11.88.

35. Speech in Leningrad, 9.7.87.

36. Genscher suffered a heart attack in July 1989 which raised speculation that he might soon step down after 15 years as Foreign Minister. But he resumed his gruelling ministerial schedule after the summer holidays.

37. The question of the boundaries of *Mitteleuropa* is a subject for dispute of theological proportions. Lorraine in eastern France, for instance, is included in the area: when a French Mirage aircraft crashed near Bar-le-Duc in April 1988, the conservative *Frankfurter Allgemeine Zeitung* wrote on its front page that this was the 'third military jet to crash in *Mitteleuropa* in the last three days'. (FAZ 2.4.88).

38. Speech in Potsdam, 11.6.88.

39. Britain's Prime Minister Margaret Thatcher, for instance, has told confidants that she does not trust him – a remark which, when transmitted to the press, deeply hurt Genscher. In the US, he has been given epithets such as 'master contortionist' (the headline in a *Washington Post* article in August 1988 which much annoyed Genscher, as it accused him of lacking 'integrity' in his dealings with the West).

40. Interview with author in Bonn, 9.11.87.

41. Interview with author in Bonn, 7.2.89.

42. The term *Sonderweg*, coined by German historians after the creation of the 1871 Reich, was used in British First World War propaganda to denote Germany's traditional authoritarianism and lack of parliamentary traditions.

43. 'For us there is no doubt that, on the basis of our origins and our feelings, we belong to the west European world.' Bundestag, 20.9.49.

44. Speech in Bundestag, 18.3.87.

45. At a press conference in Moscow, 26.10.88.

46. Interview with *Le Monde*, 20.1.88.

47. Speech in Paris, 17.1.90.

48. Interview with author in Bonn, 20.1.88.

49. Bundestag, 27.4.89.

50. Speech in Bonn, 24.5.89. Declaring that West Germany was 'irrevocably embedded' in the European Community and the NATO alliance, Weizsäcker said in the speech: 'We are not a superpower – but we are also not a plaything (*Spielball*) for others.' The word *Spielball* was used by Hitler during the 1930s to denote the Weimar Republic's lack of political virility.

51. The Relations Convention (the Bonn/Paris Conventions), which ended West Germany's

349

occupation status and allowed it to join NATO, came into force between the Federal Republic and the US, Britain and France in 1955. It pledges 'a common aim of a reunified Germany enjoying a liberal-democratic constitution like the Federal Republic, and integrated within the European Community'. The standpoint was repeated by the signatories on the 25th anniversary of the treaty in 1980.

52. The views summed up by the famous remark by François Mauriac – 'I love Germany so much that I am glad there are two of them' – have a lengthy pedigree. The French statesman Adolphe Thiers stated in the French Chamber of Deputies in 1866, 'The highest principle of European politics is that Germany shall be composed of independent states connected only by a slender federative thread. That was the principle proclaimed by all Europe at the Congress of Westphalia.'

53. Gorbachev dinner speech in the Kremlin, 24.10.88.

54. Gorbachev made the remark to President von Weizsäcker during the latter's visit to Moscow in 1987. He repeated it in *Perestroika*, p.260/261.

55. Statement in Moscow, 31.1.90.

56. Statement by Chancellor Kohl in Moscow, 10.2.90.

57. Report of the sixth discussions of the German-English Society, 14-17.4.55.

58. Paul Weymar, *Konrad Adenauer*, 1955.

59. Speech in Tutzing, 15.7.63.

60. Interview with author in Hamburg, 26.6.87.

61. The EMS was built on the European Community's 1972 'snake' currency system, which France was forced to leave twice (in 1974 and 1976) as a result of pressure on the franc.

62. At the beginning of 1989, Spain, Portugal and Greece were also non-members. Spain joined, however, with effect from 19.6.89.

63. Counting the other European countries (Austria, Switzerland, Scandinavia) whose currencies are informally linked to the EMS, almost 70 per cent of West German trade is now carried out at semi-fixed exchange rates.

64. Sofres Institute, autumn 1988.

65. Press conference in Paris, 4.2.65.

66. Interview in *Die Welt*, 18.1.88.

67. Press conference in Bonn, 3.11.89.

68. Interview in *Paris Match*, 23.11.89.

69. Press conference in East Berlin, 22.12.89.

70. French TV, 15.10.89.

71. Radio interview, 3.1.90.

72. Interview with author in Hamburg, 6.12.88.

4: Uncertain Democracy

1. Thomas Mann, *Betrachtungen eines Unpolitischen*, 1918.

2. Ralf Dahrendorf, *Gesellschaft und Demokratie in Deutschland*, 1965, p.372.

3. Speech in Gotha, 27.1.90.

4. Speech in Bundestag, 12.9.49

5. Farewell speech in Bundestag, 10.9.86.

6. Interview with author in Kiel, 19.3.87.

7. Barschel was later found to have followed almost to the letter a suicide method recommended by 'The German Society for Humane Dying', a self-help group formed to help people weary of life to kill themselves in the most efficient way. The society specifically counsels people committing suicide through an overdose of sleeping tablets to lie in a bathtub so that they will slip under water and drown.

8. Article in *Bild am Sonntag*, 18.10.87. Jenninger was the fourth Bundestag speaker to resign his post. His predecessor, Rainer Barzel, quit in 1984 over allegations that he received DM1.7 million from the Flick group in the 1970s.

9. Speech in Bundestag, 27.11.87.

10. Interview with author in Bonn, 12.11.87.
11. Infas poll, October 1987.
12. Interview with *Financial Times*, 29.11.89.
13. Speech in Frankfurt cathedral, 6.12.89.
14. Interview with author in Fehmarn, 3.5.88.
15. At the end of the Weimar period, Friedrich Flick clearly favoured the bourgeois parties supporting the Brüning coalition and backing Hindenburg in his presidential election campaign against Hitler. Flick channelled RM780,000 to the bourgeois parties in 1932, mainly for the presidential campaign, against only RM100,000 to the Nazis. In 1934 Flick became a member of the economic circle later attached to Himmler. He joined the Nazi party in 1937, on the same day as Karl Blessing, then with the Reichsbank. Flick is recorded as having contributed RM100,000 a year through the Himmler circle between 1936 and 1940. Vogelsang, op.cit.
16. Deutsche Bank already had a stake in Daimler-Benz as the result of its long-standing relationship with the company stretching back to its role in establishing the merged combine in the 1920s (see Chapter 5). Most of the 29 per cent stake was resold by Deutsche Bank to 'friendly' West German industrial and financial institutions which today maintain a large block of shares in the motor company.
17. Lambsdorff has consistently claimed that charges were brought against him over the Flick affair for political reasons, pointing out that investigations into other politicians were either dropped or settled out of court. The Flick affair left the pugilistic Lambsdorff with a smear on his honour which he was determined to remove.
18. According to estimates of *Fortune* magazine, September 1989.
19. According to the European Community's regular 'Eurobarometer' survey, 30 per cent of Germans at the end of 1988 said they were dissatisfied with the way democracy works, against levels of 20 to 25 per cent earlier in the decade. However, in the Community as a whole, an average of 47 per cent said they were dissatisfied. 50 per cent of people in Britain said they were dissatisfied, for example, and 53 per cent in France.
20. Germany has a tradition of high electoral turn-out. In the half-parliamentarian Bismarck empire, participation fluctuated between 60 and 85 per cent. In the Weimar Republic, the turn-out in national elections was never less than 75 per cent, and was above 80 per cent in the 1930s. In the Federal Republic, apart from the 1949 poll (78.5 per cent), general election turn-out has fluctuated narrowly between 84 and 91 per cent.
21. In Adenauer's third government in 1957-61, he ruled for part of the time in a nominal coalition with the German Party (Deutsche Partei).
22. John Le Carré, *A Small Town in Germany*, 1968.
23. Dahrendorf, op.cit., p. 136.
24. Churchill tells the story as related by Stalin at the Yalta conference in February 1945. According to Churchill, he repeated it at Potsdam in July. *Second World War*, VI, p.344.
25. Indicating increased fluctuations in voting patterns, an opinion poll from the Konrad Adenauer Foundation showed that in January 1987, only 48 per cent of the electorate said they had always voted for the same party. In 1980, the percentage was 60 per cent.
26. The West German *Länder* are Baden-Württemberg (formed out of Württemberg-Hohenzollern, Württemberg-Baden and Baden), Bavaria, Berlin, Bremen, Hamburg, Hesse, Lower Saxony, North-Rhine Westphalia, Rhineland Palatinate, Saarland and Schleswig Holstein. The five constituent *Länder* in the GDR when it was set up in 1949 – Brandenburg, Mecklenburg, Saxony, Saxony-Anhalt and Thuringia – were reorganised in 1952 into 14 districts as the country took the form of a centralised state.
27. Interview with author in Stuttgart, 23.2.88.
28. Allensbach poll published·30.1.89.
29. Friedrich Zimmermann, long-running Interior Minister in the Kohl government (he was demoted to Transport Minister in April 1989), said for instance, 'The fathers of our Basic Law have learned a lesson from the fate of the Weimar Republic. Influenced by the thought that a free German democracy must not again be allowed to end in dictatorship, they set up the new state order as a combative, vigorous democracy.' (Foreword to 1987 *Verfassungsschutz* report, published in June

1988.) The concept of setting up a 'vigorous democracy' (*streitbare Demokratie*) as a 'state order' (*Staatsordnung*) contains, at least to Anglo-Saxon minds, a self-contradiction.

30. Richard von Weizsäcker, *Die Deutsche Geschichte geht Weiter*, Berlin, p.158.

31. Bonn was chosen as the seat of the Parliamentary Council in August 1948 mainly because it was less badly damaged by war bombing than competitor towns. Up to the last moment of the vote by the Parliamentary Council in May 1949 on the choice of capital, Frankfurt was the favourite to be selected. Adenauer appeared to have swung the CDU (backed by some FDP representatives) behind the choice of Bonn by emphasising that a vote for 'red' Frankfurt would be a victory for the SPD. Throughout the years of Christian Democrat rule, Bonn was merely the 'provisional' capital, reflecting the official view that reunification would shift the capital to Berlin. Following conclusion of the Basic Treaty between the two Germanys, provisionality was officially brought to an end on 8.1.73.

32. Le Carré, op.cit.

33. Interview with author in Hamburg, 1.7.88.

34. Interview with author in Bonn, 11.10.88. The somewhat bizarre suggestion that the population of Berlin should be moved to the Lüneburg Heath was published in the *Guardian* in September 1960 by the Defence Correspondent, Leonard Beaton. Showing how much more attention the government paid to the foreign press in those days, the plan was received in Bonn as if it were a major diplomatic initiative.

35. Interview with author in Bonn, 13.10.88.

36. Interview with *General-Anzeiger*, 25.1.90.

37. Interview with author in Bonn, 26.1.90.

38. According to Bundestag statistics, the proportion of deputies from industry, agriculture and the professions was 37 per cent in the 1969 parliament and declined irregularly to 34 per cent in 1987. According to a wider survey in 1988 of 1,930 deputies at the Bundestag and the 11 *Land* parliaments, 40 per cent are civil servants or other public sector officials.

39. According to a survey presented by Hamm-Brücher on 5.9.88, the Bundestag has only 60 days of plenary sessions per year. For foreign parliaments the figures were Sweden 75, France 90, the US (House of Representatives) 160, Britain 180, Canada 185. Under Bundestag procedures, deputies are allowed to make speeches only if they have put their names down on an advance list.

40. Interview with author in Bonn, 16.6.88.

41. Between 1983 and 1987, the CDU drew from public funds around DM360 million, the SPD DM380 million, the CSU DM100 million, the FDP DM62 million and the Greens DM76 million. (Figures derived from annual party returns.)

42. The financing system is similar to that suggested in 1928 by Foreign Minister Gustav Stresemann. Founder of the German People's Party (DVP) in 1919, he complained that his party was becoming increasingly dependent on business donations (including from the Flick group). Stresemann proposed that the state should finance the parties in proportion to their number of seats in the Reichstag – but the idea failed to win backing.

43. The Deutsche Bank has traditionally followed a policy of donating to parties of both Right and Left, but stopped contributing to the SPD in 1987. That year it supplied DM544,000 to the CDU, DM100,000 to the CSU and DM160,000 to the FDP. In 1986, the Deutsche Bank gave DM905,000 to the CDU, DM255,000 to the FDP and DM150,000 to the SPD. The fall in donations from industry over the past few years has particularly affected the CDU. Declared donations to the Christian Democrats fell from an average of DM35 million between 1980 and 1983 to only DM29 million between 1984 and 1987. This was almost exactly compensated by an increase in state funding (from an annual average of DM53 million to DM58 million).

44. For the CDU, another form of dependence towards the private sector has grown up, namely in the form of increased indebtedness to the banks. Reflecting its overall financial squeeze, the CDU's bank debts rose to DM70 million at the end of 1987 against only DM11 million in 1984.

45. Interview with author in Düsseldorf, 11.11.88.

46. Interview with author in Munich, 25.2.88.

47. Amos Elon, *Journey through a Haunted Land*, 1967.

48. The *National Zeitung* is the successor to the *Deutsche Soldaten-Zeitung*, a newspaper founded in 1951 with US financial help to support the idea of West Germany contributing to European defence.

352

Notes

The newspaper's sharp anti-Soviet line led the US and German governments to stop supporting it in 1954. The name was changed to *National Zeitung* in 1963. The government of the Grand Coalition in 1969 tried to close down the newspaper on the grounds that it was misusing the freedom of the press, but the attempt was blocked by the Constitutional Court in 1974.

49. Using the most flimsy evidence, Irving advanced his view in his book *Hitler's War* in 1976. Condemnation of his hypothesis by most professional historians of the period has only served to strengthen Irving's contorted belief that both he and Hitler are victims of conspiracies.

50. Frey's diverse publishing activities include production of two 500-page volumes called *Prominente ohne Maske* (Celebrities without Masks), dealing with the Nazi past of leading German figures in politics, business and culture. He says he has used for source material a network of twenty agents scouring archives around the world. A particular target of Frey's campaign is President Richard von Weizsäcker. Frey and other Right-wingers like to remind the president of his soldier duties during the war, and of the role in Hitler's diplomacy of his father Ernst.

51. Telephone interview with author, March 1988.

52. Interview with author in Stuttgart, 25.11.88.

53. Interview with author in Munich, 17.7.89.

54. Interview with author in Munich, 14.11.88.

5: The German Jigsaw

1. Goethe, zu Reinhard, 1807.

2. Quoted in Aidan Crawley, *The Rise of West Germany*, p.32. The speech is also quoted by Gorbachev in his interview with *Der Spiegel*, October 1988.

3. Conversation with author in Dresden, 19.12.89.

4. Published 1987.

5. Published 1970.

6. Speech in Bonn, 23.5.86.

7. The Federal Republic today has 61.5 million people, more than 10 million higher than in 1950, and 18 million more than the numbers who lived in the area in 1939. East Germany's population is now around 16.2 million, 2 million less than in 1950 and around the same as in 1939. Comparative Figures, Ministry for Intra-German Relations.

8. The previous visits were those by Willy Brandt to Erfurt in 1970 and Helmut Schmidt to Schorfheide in 1981. The author covered Kohl's two-day visit to Dresden in December 1989 for the *Financial Times*.

9. The officials were Wolfgang Bergsdorf and Walter Neuer.

10. The visit, to Gotha, Weimar, Erfurt and Dresden, took place at the end of May 1988. Emphasising its private character, no journalists or TV cameras were taken along, although the two cars holding Kohl and his advisers were shadowed by East German state security officials.

11. Press conference in Bonn, 10.1.90. Hardly surprisingly, opinion polls carried out in East Germany on the question of reunification provided contradictory results. One poll in December carried out for *Der Spiegel* and the ZDF TV channel indicated that only 27 per cent of East Germans were in favour of unity; another one that month, for the *Bild Zeitung*, showed that 52 per cent wanted reunification.

12. Conversations with author on Dresden Christmas market, 18.12.89.

13. Conversations with author in Dresden, 7.10.89, 14.11.89.

14. Giving details of the emigration flood (possibly an under-estimate) in the Volkskammer on 11.1.90, Modrow said that 1,800 doctors and 5,000 nurses left East Germany in 1989.

15. Conversation with author in Dresden, 13.11.89.

16. Speech in East Berlin, 15.2.81.

17. Speech in East Berlin, 6.10.89. In view of the Russians' heavy dismantling of East German plant, Honecker's strictures on the 'stones placed in the way' of East Germany could also have been addressed at the Soviet Union. The Second World War was estimated to have left the GDR with a loss of productive capacity of only 15 per cent against 20 per cent suffered by West Germany.

However, the dismantling of plant and machinery by the Soviet Union was more than double that carried out by the western allies in West Germany. Because remaining plant at partly dismantled factories was in many cases useless, the total loss of productive capacity in East Germany has been estimated at roughly 50 per cent of the 1939 figure.

18. Gorbachev's comment was revealed at a press briefing by his spokesman, Genadi Gerassimov, who said dead-pan that Honecker expressed 'gratitude' for the advice.

19. The East German leader's self-confidence was also boosted by a small circle of admirers in the West. Robert Maxwell, the proprietor of the *Daily Mirror*, interviewed Honecker just a few days before the 7 October anniversary. Apparently oblivious of the growing storm clouds, Maxwell wrote that 'the great majority' of East Germans still had confidence in their leader.

20. Interview with author in Dresden, 7.10.89.

21. Willy Brandt, who has good contacts with the Kremlin, stated in December 1989 that the Soviet Union was responsible for avoiding a massacre on 9 October. He said the date would go down as 'a special day of Soviet–German friendship because on this day Soviet officers prevented a bloodbath in Leipzig.' Interview with author in Bonn, 11.12.89.

22. *Tageszeitung*, 19.10.89. Biermann said the change at the top was a 'world shattering nothingness.' He added the unflattering description of Krenz as 'the drunken veteran of the Free German Youth', 'the optimistic idiot.'

23. Interviews with author in Duisdorf, 19.10.89.

24. Speech in East Berlin, 19.1.89.

25. Conversation with author in E. Berlin, 12.11.89.

26. One of the reasons for the Soviets' interest reflected the uranium deposits in the region. The Wismut company, a Soviet–East German joint mining venture, was set up to exploit the resources, and the Soviet Union's first atomic bomb used uranium from the Schwarzenberg area.

27. Conversation in Karl-Marx-Stadt, 14.11.89.

28. Interview with author in Schwarzenberg, 14.11.89.

29. The author covered Honecker's five-day visit (7.11.9.87) for the *Financial Times*.

30. It is an ironic reflection on conditions in East Germany that identical photos of the interior of Brandenburg prison are used to illustrate both Honecker's official autobiography and brochures published during the 1980s by anti-Communist civil rights campaigners in West Germany.

31. *Die Zeit*, 24.7.87.

32. Speeches at banquet on 7.9.87.

33. Interview with author in Munich, 25.2.88.

34. Honecker, *Aus Meinem Leben*, p.68.

35. Interview with author in Wiebelskirchen, 22.6.87.

36. Allensbach, July 1986.

37. In 1988, a Cologne court dismissed a case of 'insulting the national hymn' brought against a young artist on the grounds that, legally, the national anthem did not exist. Since the *Deutschlandlied* had been established simply by an exchange of letters between Adenauer and Heuss rather than by legislation, the court established that there was no case to answer. There have been various moves to bring back the first verse of the hymn.

38. Letter from Heuss to Adenauer, 2.5.52.

39. Speech in East Berlin, 4.1.60.

40. Honecker, op. cit., p.203.

41. Statement to Volkskammer cultural committee, 28.11.89.

42. E. German radio statement, 19.8.89.

43. Interview with author in Soltau, 24.8.89.

44. Petition launched on 26.11.89. It appeared to enjoy the support of only a very small minority of the East German population, attracting the signatures of just over 1 million people.

45. Interview with author in East Berlin, 24.11.89.

46. Interview with author in East Berlin, 3.10.89.

47. Interview with author in East Berlin, 29.6.89.

48. *Deutschland Archiv*, December 1987, April 1988. A poll carried out for the magazine *Quick* in June 1989 came to the conclusion that 87 per cent of West Germans favoured reunification.

49. Estimate from Bonn Ministry for Intra German Relations.
50. Around 70 million letters a year are sent from West Germany to the rest of Europe. The next most important letter-writing destination is the US with a mere 12 million.
51. Conversation in Münster, 21.11.88.
52. Bundestag, 20.9.49.
53. Bundestag, 29.10.57.
54. Bundestag, 10.11.65.
55. Bundestag, 29.10.69.
56. Bundestag, 16.12.76.
57. Bundestag, 24.11.80.
58. Bundestag, 13.10.82.
59. Bundestag, 18.3.87.
60. Interview with author in Bonn, 7.2.89.
61. Bundestag, 28.11.89.
62. Press conference in Moscow, 26.10.88.
63. Interview with author in Bonn, 3.11.86. Brandt's views on the Fatherland seem to be ambiguous. In an impromptu aside added to his two-hour farewell speech as SPD chairman in 1987, Brandt spoke elliptically of 'our Fatherland, grown smaller.' As often the case with Brandt, however, it was not clear whether he was talking about the Federal Republic alone or the Federal Republic plus the GDR (14.6.87).
64. Interview with author in Frankfurt, 3.3.88.
65. Interview with author in Düsseldorf, 14.3.89.
66. Interview with author in Frankfurt, 22.11.88.
67. Interview with author in Stuttgart, 23.2.88.
68. Interview with author in Frankfurt, 7.2.89.
69. Interview with author in Bonn, 24.11.87.
70. Interview with author in Frankfurt, 16.9.88.
71. Interview with author in Bonn, 28.4.88.
72. Interview with author in Stuttgart, 25.11.88.
73. Interview with author in Hamburg, 1.7.88.
74. Brandt himself declared in a speech on 14.9.88 that West Germany was 'living a lie' (*eine Lebenslüge*) by proclaiming the goal of reunification. Only slightly more than a year later, he was warning the allies to beware of stoking up 'nationalism' by failure to take sufficient heed of the 'soul of the Germans' (interview with author in Bonn, 11.12.89). In similar vein, Johannes Gross, the conservative commentator, wrote in a book published in summer 1989 that 'nation' was a 'will o' the wisp ... foreign to our tradition and our political thinking.' (*Phönix in Asche*, p.159). In January 1990, in an abrupt change of tone, he warned that 'an attempt [by the allies] to hinder unification could be seen as a new Versailles and could be answered with a wave of nationalism'. (*FAZ*, 3.1.90). Rudolf Augstein hit the nail on the head when he wrote, shortly after the breaching of the Wall, that the West Germans had perennially declared that they would always prefer a united Europe to a united Germany. 'This may have been tactically clever, but it is not the truth.' (*Der Spiegel*, No. 47, 1989).

6: The Rise and Fall of the Economic Miracle

1. Speech at Unterhaching addressed to workers on the new Autobahn between Munich and the Austrian border, 21.3.34, quoted in *Hitler's Speeches, 1922-1939*, 1942.
2. Speech in Paris, 7.12.54, quoted in Ludwig Erhard, *Deutsche Wirtschaftspolitik*, 1962, p.255.
3. Interview with author in Frankfurt, 2.10.87.
4. West Germany had trade deficits only in 1950 and 1951. It has recorded deficits on current account (including invisible transactions) in six years: 1950, 1962, 1965, 1979, 1980 and 1981.
5. West Germany took over from Britain as long ago as 1958 as the world's second largest exporter (after the US). It was ranked for the first time as the biggest exporter in 1986. In 1988 it was top of the

league for the third year running, with exports totalling $323 billion. Next came the US with $322 billion and Japan with $265 billion. The Federal Republic's exports therefore had an 11.3 per cent share of world trade. In 1989, West Germany (exports of $341 bilion) was dislodged from first place by the US ($364 billion).

6. At mid 1989, West Germany had net external assets of DM427 billion.

7. Comparative figures for GNP per capita expressed in a common currency can show large annual fluctuations because of exchange rate changes. In 1988, according to OECD figures, West Germany had GNP per head of $19,575, against $19,513 in the US, $16,950 in France, $14,232 in Britain and $23,184 in Japan.

8. Average gross weekly manual wage in manufacturing industry in Britain in 1988 was about £190 (Dept of Employment statistics). Average in West Germany was DM743 or £238 at the 1988 exchange rate. (Federal Statistics Office.) West German manufacturing employees worked 1,623 hours on average in 1988, against 1,927 in Britain.

9. In 1987, industry made up 42 per cent of West Germany's gross national product, and services 56 per cent. In Britain the figures were 38 and 60 per cent; in France, 35 and 61 per cent. West Germany's industrial production was thus about 85 per cent of that of France and Britain combined.

10. New business start-ups totalled 295,000 in 1987, well up from 178,000 in 1980. Business failures have however also risen sharply – 249,000 in 1987, against 135,000 in 1980.

11. Only in three years since 1971 – in 1976, 1979 and 1989 – has the West German economy topped the OECD average. The Federal Republic's 4 per cent growth rate in 1989 compared with 3.6 per cent for the OECD as a whole.

12. West Germany's trade surpluses in the five years 1984 to 1989 respectively were DM73 billion, DM112 billion, DM118 billion, DM128 billion and DB135 billion. West Germany's current account surpluses in the same years were DM48 billion, DM85 billion, DM81 billion, DM85 billion and DM99 billion, averaging DM80 billion. The current account surplus – equivalent to the amount by which West Germany's foreign credit position has risen over this time – is less than the trade surplus because the Federal Republic runs a large deficit on 'invisible' items like tourist spending and other services and transfers abroad.

13. Derived from OECD statistics for 1980-89.

14. Erhard worked for nearly fifteen years in an economic institute in Nuremberg with strong links to the *Mittelstand* – small- and medium-sized business. Earlier in the 1930s Erhard supported state intervention to correct monopoly tendencies in industry. His observation of the Nazis' handling of the economy helped convert him to liberalism. See Norbert Walter, *Was Würde Erhard Heute Tun?*, 1986, pp.9,10.

15. One reason for the speedy recovery was that Germany was less seriously harmed by the war than its early appearance suggested. At the end of the fighting, the amount of irretrievable damage to plant was estimated at 15-20 per cent, while as a result of wartime expansion Germany's productive capacity in 1944 was 20 per cent higher than in 1936. As early as 1953, average living standards exceeded the level in 1938.

16. The Bank deutscher Länder, the Bundesbank's forerunner, was set up in 1948 under the occupation regime, before the establishment of the Federal Republic. It was subject to control by the Western Allies until 1951. The 1957 law setting up the Bundesbank gave the new central bank explicit independence from government directions, and anchored it to the overriding objective of currency stability. Article 3 of the Bundesbank Law defines the functions of the Bundesbank as follows: 'The Deutsche Bundesbank, making use of the powers in the field of monetary policy conferred upon it under this Law, shall regulate the note and coin circulation and the supply of credit to the economy with the aim of safeguarding the currency ...' Article 12 enjoins the central bank to 'support the general economic policy of the federal government' – but only if this is consistent with its functions under Article 3. Furthermore, the article states that the Bundesbank 'shall not be subject to instructions from the federal government'.

17. The strength of the traditional catholic-social position within the Christian Democratic Union can be gauged from the preamble of the party's so-called Ahlen programme in 1947, which set the groundwork for the Adenauer government's economic policies. This stated that the goal of 'social and

economic renewal' should no longer be 'capitalistic desire for profit and power' but instead 'the prosperity of our people'.

18. Interview with author in Cologne, 6.10.87.

19. Interview with author in Bonn, 15.6.88.

20. Only about 40 per cent of Germans own their own homes, against more than 60 per cent in Britain.

21. Speech in West Berlin, 16.9.87.

22. Companies' retained earnings in the Federal Republic are taxed at around 60 per cent, roughly double the rate in Britain, Spain and the Netherlands. High corporation tax rates form one reason why German companies' declared earnings are low by international standards; earnings are 'hidden' by being used to strengthen the balance sheet.

23. Of the main European countries, only Sweden, with yearly working time of 1,486 hours in manufacturing industry, seems to have shorter hours. Annual working time in Japan averages 2,163 hours (1988) – 33 per cent more than in West Germany.

24. In 1988, an average 2 days were lost through labour disputes per 1,000 employees in West Germany, against 64 in France, 164 in Britain and 44 in the US. The figure for Japan was 4.

25. In 1988, industrial companies in West Germany had to pay an extra DM83.60 in social charges for every DM100 in wage costs. According to a comparative study from the Institut der deutschen Wirtschaft, West Germany was second only to Switzerland in 1988 in a list of total labour costs in manufacturing industry.

26. Gross capital investment in the 1980s in West Germany, although recovering slightly in the last few years, made up only about 20 per cent of gross national product, compared with 25 per cent in 1970.

27. A week after the November 1918 revolution, labour and business leaders agreed to set up national and local bodies to handle cooperation between the two sides of industry. The two chief signatories of the 1918 accord were Hugo Stinnes, the most prominent Ruhr industrial magnate of the time, and Carl Legien, head of the socialist or 'free' trade union. The mood behind the *rapprochement* stemmed from a move by the imperial government in 1916 to force employers to grant *de facto* recognition to the unions and sit with their officials on boards designed to deal with wartime labour problems. The national body established in 1919 came to be known as the 'central working community' (*Zentralarbeitsgemeinschaft*).

28. J.H. Clapham, *Economic Developments in France and Germany, 1815-1914*, p.84.

29. The state industrial sector is much smaller than in Britain or France. Bonn has followed a policy of selling off some public shareholdings, the largest of which was in the Veba group, but some privatisation proposals have run into political controversy. A plan to divest the state stake in Lufthansa, the West German airline, was shelved because of opposition from the Bavarian state government.

30. Interview with author in Jesteburg, 8.10.87.

31. The current proportion of exports in gross national product of around one-third is historically very high. In imperial Germany, exports of goods made up 17.7 per cent of gross national product in 1880, 14.3 per cent in 1890, 14.8 per cent in 1900, 16.2 per cent in 1910. The percentage was 14.8 per cent in 1930, falling to 5.8 per cent in 1938 and 5.3 per cent in 1939. During the 1950s and 1960s, the proportion grew from 12 to 19 per cent.

32. Bundesbank figures, April 1989.

33. *The Siemens Company: Its Historical Role*, 1972.

34. *Financial Times*, 3.3.89.

35. J.M. Keynes, *The Economic Consequences of the Peace*, 1919.

36. Central government debt rose from 5.2 billion Marks in 1914 to 156 billion Marks in 1919. Between 1933 and 1945, it rose from 11.7 billion Reichsmarks to 380 billion Reichsmarks.

37. *Hitler's Table Talk*, 11.8.42. Hitler's flatulent remarks on future exchange rates between eastern and western zones of the Reich gave an uncanny preview of the currency regime in force today in East Germany. According to the record of his dinner monologue at field headquarters, he spoke of creating an 'Ost-Mark' for use in the eastern territories. 'We will fix the rate of exchange at five

Ost-Marks to the Reichsmark. But tourists coming here will be given only one hundred Ost-Marks for their hundred Reichsmarks … The difference will be pocketed by the state.'

38. Deutsche Bundesbank, *Währung und Wirtschaft in Deutschland, 1876-1975*, 1976.

39. The Reichsmark was introduced by the expedient of striking 12 zeros off the value of the old Marks.

40. According to figures from the Federal Statistics Office, the suicide rate in 1923 was 21.3 per 100,000 inhabitants. It rose to 23.1 in 1924, 24.5 in 1925, 26.2 in 1926, 25.3 in 1927, and reached the highest level of 28-29 under the Third Reich. By contrast, the suicide rate in the Federal Republic was also 21.3 in 1983, but fell back to 19.0 in 1986 and 1987.

41. A.J.P. Taylor, *The Course of German History*, 1945, p.228.

42. The 1948 currency reform was necessary to bring down the bloated volume of money in circulation. Since prices in occupied Germany were kept down under controls inherited from the Nazis, goods were being hoarded for black market barter sales. Disagreement between the Soviet Union and the US prevented the reform from being carried out in all four zones, partly because by 1948 the US and Britain were already making arrangements for the birth of a separate western state. Under the plan introduced on 20 June, Germans in the British, French and American zones were paid out an initial DM40 each, with DM20 paid a month later. Cash or bank deposits were exchanged at the rate of 6.5:100. The original intention had been to issue new notes in the ratio 1:10, but this would not have been sufficient to bring about the necessary reduction in volume of money. Debts were exchanged at the 1:10 ratio, so creditors did relatively well. The low rate of exchange angered savers but, by reducing the volume of the note issue, laid the basis for the D-Mark's future health. Although the Russians did not participate in the reform, they played a significant role in prompting it through heavy printing of banknotes in the Soviet zone.

43. All but two of the Reichsbank's directors were removed after the January 1939 memorandum. Schacht was serving his second period as Reichsbank president. Having already held the post between 1923 and 1930, he was recalled by Hitler in 1933. After the 1939 letter Schacht was removed and replaced by Walther Funk. Vocke went into semi-retirement during the war. Blessing, however, played an active role in the economy (see Chapter 2, Note 37). In addition to his post at Kontinentale Öl, between 1943 and 1945 Blessing was deputy supervisory board chairman of Daimler-Benz. Blessing appeared to be a member of a group at the Munitions Ministry which in 1944-5, as German defeat appeared increasingly likely, started to prepare for a post-war German economy under the aegis of the US.

44. The victor powers aimed to sever the state's influence over the Reichsbank to assure payment of war reparations. The president and directorate thus were no longer appointed by the Reich government, but by a general council, half of whose members were foreigners. Although the Reichsbank remained formally independent until 1937, in practice it came under control of central government from 1933 onwards.

45. Chancellor Adenauer, who was no supporter of an independent central bank, tried to stop the Bank deutscher Länder raising interest rates in October 1950. He took part in a meeting of the central council in Bonn, and spoke out against such an increase; after he left the meeting, however, the bank raised its discount and Lombard rates by 2 percentage points. In May 1956 he accused the central bank, which had again raised its discount rate, of bringing down a 'guillotine' on small business.

46. Difference between the Bundesbank and the Bonn government over the wisdom of D-Mark revaluations came to the surface before revaluations in 1961, in 1969, and again during the currency unrest of 1972-3. Particular bitterness was caused in the last year of the Schmidt government in 1982 over the Bundesbank's insistence on increasing interest rates to ward off depreciation of the D-Mark. (See also Chapter 8.)

47. Partly reflecting the episode related in 46. (above), ex-Chancellor Schmidt has become a persistent critic of the Bundesbank since his retirement. Schmidt already adopted a high-handed attitude towards the central bank during his period of office, on one occasion in the mid-1970s trying to force it to deposit part of Germany's monetary reserves as a loan to the Soviet state bank (see Schmidt, *Menschen und Mächte*, p.78.). During the months leading up to the establishment of the European Monetary System in 1978-9, Schmidt privately threatened the Bundesbank with a change

in the law guaranteeing its autonomy unless it agreed to the currency stabilisation scheme. In the late 1980s, Schmidt accuses the central bank of unnecessary rigidity in blocking his proposals for Europe to move towards monetary union and a common currency; he complains that the central bank artificially keeps alive inflationary fears to justify what he alleges are its over-restrictive monetary policies. There may be something in this argument, but it is not one which any other public figure has taken up.

48. Interview with author in Bonn, 19.7.87.
49. Interview with author in West Berlin, 30.9.87.
50. Interview with author in Bonn, 14.10.87.
51. Figures on savings from Federal Statistics Office, February 1989.
52. Interview with author in Cologne, 13.10.87.
53. For instance, speech in Düsseldorf, 20.4.88.
54. Interview with author in Mannheim, 17.11.88.
55. In West Germany today, 25 million of the 61 million population (40 per cent), live in small towns or villages of fewer than 20,000 inhabitants. Of these, 3.8 million live in villages of less than 2,000 people.
56. In 1870, Germany had 19,500 km of railways and Britain had 24,500 km; by 1910 Germany had 61,000 km and Britain 38,000 km.
57. Michael Balfour, *West Germany – A Contemporary History*, 1983, p.41.
58. Clapham, op.cit, p.390.
59. See Hermann J. Abs, Konzentrationsbestrebungen im deutschen Bankwesen (Lecture in 1977).
60. *Financial Times*, 23.1.90.
61. Clapham, op.cit, p.309.
62. V.I. Lenin, Imperialism, the Highest Form of Capitalism, 1916, in *Lenin on the U.S. of America.*
63. See Wilhelm Treue and Hans Pohl, *Die Konzentration in der deutschen Wirtschaft seit dem 19. Jahrhundert*, Wiesbaden, 1978.
64. Bullock, op.cit, Chapter 3, VIII. Many books have overplayed the financial role in backing Hitler of men like Fritz Thyssen. In an otherwise chillingly prophetic book written in 1934, Ernst Henri in *Hitler over Europe?* dramatically overstates Thyssen's importance by claiming: 'Not Hitler, but Thyssen, the great magnate of the Ruhr, is the real prime mover of German Fascism.'
65. For a thorough account of industry's role in politics during the Weimar period, see Henry Ashby Turner Jr, *German Big Business and the Rise of Hitler*, 1985.
66. Speech on 27.1.32, quoted in *Hitler's Speeches*, op.cit.
67. 'The so-called "free play of market forces" must be controlled by the principle of common profit which must come before individual egoistic profit.' Speech on 15.5.34.
68. Hitler, *Mein Kampf*, p.256.
69. Hermann Rauschning, *Gespräche mit Hitler*, 1940, p.179.
70. Rauschning, op.cit, p.25.
71. Speech at Wilhelmshaven, 1.4.39.
72. At dinner on 15.10.41, *Hitler's Table Talk*, op.cit.
73. Carl Krauch from I.G. Farben was enlisted by Hermann Göring in 1938 as his deputy director of the economy.
74. For instance, in some agricultural research work in areas like plastics carried out in Lower Saxony.
75. Karl Holdermann, *Im Banne der Chemie, Carl Bosch, Leben und Werk*, 1953.
76. Kurt Pritzkoleit, *Männer, Mächte, Monopole*, 1953, p.117.
77. Turner, op.cit, p.339.
78. The de-Nazification court which tried Thyssen in 1948 classified him as only slightly tainted. He was fined and allowed to emigrate to Argentina, where he died in 1951.
79. Interview with author in Kiel, 9.10.87.
80. Allensbach poll, 1.10.87.
81. Telephone interview with author, 9.1.90.
82. Survey by Portfolio Management, Munich, January 1988.

83. *Der Spiegel*, 47, 1989.
84. *Wall Street Journal*, 20.11.89.
85. *Financial Times*, 9.5.88.
86. Interview with author in Bonn, 6.7.88.
87. Abs, along with other advisers, tried to prevent Adenauer from agreeing to the revaluation which eventually took place in March 1961. Abs' anti-revaluation lobbying was repeated in 1969, but proved no more successful. The D-Mark was revalued in October 1969 after a long-running row over the currency had contributed to the break-up of the 1966-69 Grand Coalition. See Otmar Emminger, *D-Mark, Dollar, Währungskrisen*, 1986, pp.109,154.

7: Rich and Bothered

1. Madame de Staël, *De l'Allemagne*, Paris, 1813.
2. Speech in Reichstag, 9.10.1878.
3. In letter to a German school-class, 1.3.61, quoted in Erhard, op.cit.
4. Elisabeth Noelle-Neumann/Renate Köcher, *Die Verletzte Nation*, 1987. Polls based on 16,000 interviews in ten European countries and the US.
5. The funds for the ticket supplements are repaid to the Bundesbahn by the Bonn government.
6. Interview with author in Göppingen, 15.12.87.
7. Interview with author in Frankfurt, 25.2.87.
8. Emnid Institute/tourism surveys, January 1988.
9. *Thumbling's Travels*, in translation by H.B. Paull, L.A. Wheatley, London.
10. Noelle-Neumann, op.cit.
11. Interview with author in Munich, 26.2.87.
12. See C.V. Wedgwood, *The Thirty Years War*, 1938.
13. Conference in Königswinter, 9.3.89.
14. Quoted in Ursula Nuber, Heiko Ernst, Die Traurige Generation, *Psychologie Heute*, April 1989.
15. Interview with author in Frankfurt, 16.9.88.
16. Sigmund Freud, *Inhibitions, Symptoms and Anxiety*, 1926.
17. Federal study by the Max Planck Institute for Psychiatry, September 1988. It said that 7.5 per cent of adults in West Germany suffered from 'strong feelings of fear', expressing themselves in panic and chronic neurosis.
18. *Stern*, 6.4.89.
19. Poll, which may clearly have been based on some suggestive questioning, of 1,010 children by *Wiener* magazine, January 1989.
20. *Die Zeit*, 5.9.86.
21. *Financial Times*, 1.8.88.
22. *Fortune*, 11.9.89.
23. Interview with author in Hamburg, 12.7.88.
24. Interview with author at Burg Hohenzollern, 23.6.88.
25. 85 per cent said the head of state should be the president; only 8 per cent were undecided. Allensbach, September 1976.
26. Interview with author in Bonn, 9.3.89.
27. Johannes Gross, *Die Deutschen*, 1967.
28. In May 1973 West German spy-catchers poring over records of intercepted East German radio signals realised that messages sent years earlier matched up to the birthday dates of Guillaume, his wife and son. They had been transmitted in 1956-57 when he emigrated to the West at the start of his assignment. Hans-Dietrich Genscher, the then Interior Minister, did not however take the suspicions seriously enough to convince Brandt of the security risk, and Guillaume remained in the Chancellery for almost another year before he was arrested. See Günther Nollau, *Das Amt*, 1978, p.255.
29. Interview with author in Cologne, 2.3.89.
30. Dieter Hildebrandt, *Was bleibt mir übrig*, 1986.

Notes

8: Politics and the Media

1. In conversation with officers over dinner in May 1942, quoted in *Hitler's Table Talk*, p.480.
2. In valedictory speech as director-general of Nordwestdeutscher Rundfunk, November 1948.
3. Interview with author in Frankfurt, 22.11.88.
4. Interviews with author in Hamburg, 6.12.88 and 7.2.90.
5. For several years *Stern* has been trying to live down the damage to its reputation wrought by the affair, when it bought and published the 'diaries' without realising they were forged.
6. Renate Köcher, Allensbach Institute, *Spürhund und Missionar*, 1985.
7. According to an Allensbach survey in 1988, 76 per cent, 47 per cent and 38 per cent respectively said they admired doctors, priests and university professors. Less well regarded than journalists were only army officers (11 per cent) and politicians (12 per cent).
8. Interviews with author in Hamburg, 6.12.88 and 7.2.90.
9. For a description of the early newspaper years, see Wolfgang Bergsdorf, *Die vierte Gewalt*, 1980.
10. Circulation figures are for fourth quarter, 1989.
11. Günter Wallraff, *Der Aufmacher: Der Mann der bei Bild Hans Esser war*, 1977.
12. The figures are from the Bundesverband deutscher Zeitungsverleger.
13. *Media Perspektiven*, 1987.
14. Heinrich Böll, *Die verlorene Ehe der Katharine Blum*, Cologne, 1974.
15. Heinrich Böll, *Bild, Bonn, Boenisch*, 1984.
16. Interview with author in Bonn, 8.11.88.
17. Interview with author in Hamburg, 12.7.88.
18. Interview with author in Hamburg, 7.2.90.
19. Interview with author in Bonn, 14.12.88.
20. More than 500 West German journalists are accredited in Bonn as members of the official journalists association. There are about 400 foreign correspondents (not all of whom reside in the capital). After the building of the Berlin Wall in 1961, correspondents from East Germany were expelled from the former group, and officially joined the ranks of the foreign journalists in 1973.
21. Survey conducted by *Financial Times* among 19 bureau chiefs at principal newspaper and TV and radio networks. Surveys by Allensbach and a Leicester University research group (Köcher, op.cit) found that 30 per cent of a large sample of German journalists were aged more than 50, against only 17 per cent in Britain.
22. Interview with author in Bonn, 10.10.88.
23. Interview in Berlin, 27.9.88. Bölling was the longest-serving chief of the government's Press and Information Office, holding the job under Schmidt for a total of seven years, in two periods. Indicating the importance ascribed by successive Bonn governments to public information, since 1958 the post has been given the rank of state secretary.
24. Interview with author in Bonn, 11.10.88.
25. Interview with author in Hamburg, 6.12.88.
26. Interview with author in Bonn, 26.1.90.
27. There is a similar love of tradition in other journalistic areas. The system of 'embargoes', for instance, under which reporters at business press conferences have often been allowed several days to prepare stories for their newspapers, goes back to the 1880s. The system – delivering a clear invitation for illegal 'insider trading' on the stock markets – is at last slowly being phased out.
28. ARD/ZDF surveys.
29. In addition to the original *Land* stations, broadcasting networks for Berlin and Saarland were founded in the 1950s.
30. At end 1988, of the nine regional ARD networks and ZDF, two (Saarländischer Rundfunk and Radio Bremen) were run by SPD directors-general, while six were in the hands of the Christian Democrats or (in Bavaria) Christian Social Union. Two directors-general (at Westdeutscher Rundfunk and Hessischer Rundfunk) were non-party members.
31. Interview with author in Bonn, 18.7.88.
32. Interview with author in Frankfurt, 22.11.88.
33. Interview with author in Bonn, 10.11.88.

9: The Barons of Consensus

1. Speech in Munich, 31.7.32, quoted in Dr Joseph Goebbels, *Revolution der Deutschen*, 1933.
2. A.J.P. Taylor, op.cit.
3. Interview in *Neue Rhein/Neue Ruhr-Zeitung*, 5.2.88.
4. Interview with author in Kronberg, 7.2.89.
5. Funk resigned from the *Berliner Börsen-Zeitung* in 1930 and started work at the economic policy section of the Nazi party. He joined the party in June 1931.
6. Pöhl for his part has not forgotten that Schmidt's first preference as Emminger's replacement was Wilfried Guth of the Deutsche Bank. Only when, in the summer of 1979, Guth's selection proved impossible, did Schmidt turn to his former deputy at the Finance Ministry.
7. In an interview with author in Hamburg, Schmidt scornfully called Pöhl 'a technician of high calibre', 1.7.88.
8. Press conference in Bonn, 9.2.90.
9. Interview with author in Jesteburg, 8.10.87.
10. The members of the Bundesbank's directorate (including the president and vice-president) are normally selected for eight-year terms. The Governor and his deputy of the Bank of England, by contrast, are appointed for five-year terms.
11. Schlesinger is not a party member, although his sympathies lie with the Christian Democrats. Johann Wilhelm Gaddum, a CDU member, friend of Helmut Kohl and former Finance Minister in Rhineland Palatinate, entered the directorate in 1986. To give the Free Democrats a presence on the Bundesbank directorate, Günter Storch – an FDP banker also from Rhineland Palatinate – was appointed in 1987. When the director responsible for international affairs, Leonhard Gleske, reached retirement age in 1989, Tietmeyer was appointed in his place. Although Tietmeyer has served in Bonn under governments of both Left and Right, he is a CDU member and looks set to increase the conservatives' weight at the Bundesbank.
12. Before becoming Bundesbank president in 1977, Emminger for many years was the Bundesbank's 'foreign minister' responsible for international monetary affairs. He often used to cooperate with Pöhl at international financial meetings during the 1970s, but no love was lost between them. Emminger took malicious delight in slighting Pöhl in his memoirs when he wrote that the then state secretary at the Finance Ministry was absent skiing in Gstaad during a crucial period of currency unrest at the beginning of March 1973. (In fact, Pöhl was in Zermatt.) Otmar Emminger, *D-Mark, Dollar, Währungskrisen*, Stuttgart, 1986, p.240.
13. Interview with author in Bonn, 3.12.86.
14. Interview with author in Bonn, 7.2.89.
15. Interview with author in Hamburg, 6.12.88.
16. Interview with author in Hamburg, 6.12.88
17. Schmidt's book on international relations, *Menschen und Mächte*, sold more than 500,000 copies within two years of publication in 1987.
18. Interview with author in Düsseldorf, 14.3.89.
19. Apart from the Deutscher Gewerkschaftsbund (DGB), the main other union associations are the German Civil Servants' Federation or Deutscher Beamtenbund (DBB), with about 780,000 members; the German Union of Salaried Employees or Deutsche Angestellten-Gewerkschaft (DAG), with 500,000 members, and the Christian Trade Union Federation of Germany or Christlicher Gewerkschaftsbund (CGB), with 308,000 members.
20. The DGB's business participations, including Neue Heimat, were owned through a holding company, the Beteiligungsgesellschaft fur Gemeinwirtschaft (BGAG). The BGAG's prize holding, the BfG bank, was formed through a merger of six regional trade union banks in 1958.
21. Interview with author in Cologne, 14.3.89.
22. Other senior SPD civil servants under Schmidt to enter industry are Detlev Rohwedder, now chairman of the Hoesch steel group, and Ernst Pieper, chairman of the Salzgitter steel concern. Heinz Ruhnau, a Schmidt appointee as state secretary at the Transport Ministry, became chairman of Lufthansa in 1982.
23. Interview with author in Bonn, 19.9.88.

Notes

24. Interview with author in Ludwigshafen, 5.10.87.
25. Interview with author in Düsseldorf, 7.6.88.

10: Germany and the Jews

1. Luther, *Von den Juden und Ihren Lügen*, 1543.
2. Hitler, op.cit, p.335.
3. Interview with author in Munich, 14.11.88.
4. Letter to Rudolf Chritiani, 1824.
5. See description of the Jewish synagogues and cemeteries in Berlin in an invaluable companion guide, *Wegweiser durch das jüdische Berlin*, 1987.
6. For an account of the history of the Schönhauser Allee cemetery, the author is indebted to Gerd Kern.
7. The term was made popular in Germany in a book published in 1879 by Wilhelm Marr, an erstwhile Left-winger who became a populist anti-Semite.
8. Letter to Emil Ludwig, 1916, quoted in Gerhard Hecker, *Walther Rathenau und sein Verhältnis zu Militär und Krieg*, 1983.
9. *100 Jahre Hertie*, Hertie Ware- und Kaufhaus GmbH, 1982.
10. *Der Spiegel*, No. 52, 1987.
11. The official 100th anniversary histories of the two banks – *100 Jahre Deutsche Bank* (1970) and, for Dresdner, *Chiffren einer Epoche* (1972) – make no reference to the Jewish banking takeovers of the 1930s.
12. *Deutsche Bankengeschichte*, Institut für Bankhistorische Forschung, Vol. 3, p.179.
13. Interview with author, Bonn, 6.7.88.
14. The Petschek lignite works were expropriated by the Reichswerk 'Hermann Göring', an iron and steel combine which ranked as the third largest joint stock company in 1939 after I.G. Farben and United Steel.
15. Krüger, op.cit.
16. Nevile Henderson, *Failure of a Mission*, 1940.
17. Speech in Reichstag, 30.1.39.
18. Werner Stephan, *Joseph Goebbels, Dämon einer Diktatur*, 1949, p.249-50.
19. Hitler, op.cit., p.772. Hitler had been temporarily blinded by mustard gas during World War I when fighting at Ypres.
20. Speech to the Bundestag on West Germany's Jewish compensation payments, 27.9.51.
21. Speech on the 40th anniversary of *Reichskristallnacht*, Cologne, 9.11.78.
22. Speech on the 50th anniversary of *Reichskristallnacht*, Frankfurt, 9.11.88.
23. Speech to Bundestag on 10.11.88. See also Chapter 2.
24. Notably from the chairman of the Lower Saxony Jewish Council, Michael Fürst.
25. According to the Federal Statistics Office, the 65 West German Jewish communities at the end of 1987 totalled 27,612 people, slightly up from 27,533 at end-1986. Many non-religious Jews in West Germany do not register with their local communities. Other Jews, because of lingering memories of Nazism, are afraid to see their names registered on official lists of Jews.
26. Interview with author in West Berlin, 22.4.88.
27. Interview with author in East Berlin, 25.4.88.
28. Interview with author in East Berlin, 25.4.88.
29. Interview with author in Frankfurt, 11.2.88.
30. Interview with author in Frankfurt, 8.11.88.
31. The claim was made in December 1987 by a top official in the Bundeswehr administration in Munich, Rainer Reinhart. Reinhart was disciplined by the Defence Ministry, but later denied he was an anti-Semite.
32. The Jewish doctor who ran into a campaign of hate in the town of Gedern was Dan Kiesel, born in Israel of German parents who had fled the Nazis.

33. Allensbach poll carried out in conjunction with Zentrum fur Antisemitismusforschung, Technical University, Berlin.
34. Analysis of Shakespeare's Jessica, 1838.
35. Rudolf Walter Leonhardt, *This Germany*, (translation of *X-mal Deutschland*, 1961) p.150.
36. Interview with author in Munich, 14.11.88.
37. Interview with author in Hamburg, 6.12.88.
38. Interview with author in Bonn, 2.7.88.
39. Interview with author in Bonn, 17.12.87.
40. Visit to Bergen-Belsen, 6.4.87.
41. Speech in Frankfurt, 9.11.88.
42. Interview with author in Hamburg, 1.7.88. The reasons for Schmidt's revelation, published in a biography by Jonathan Carr, are obscure. Because of lack of clear evidence as to who his grandfather really was, there is some doubt whether Schmidt himself is really convinced of his Jewish heritage. Schmidt often uses the word 'Jew' – in conversation with English speakers – to denote 'scapegoat'. In an interview with Japanese journalists in September 1988, he said, 'The Japanese are in danger of being seen as the new Jews of the world.'
43. Oerstele-Schwerin made this statement in a letter to Philipp Jenninger, Bundestag president, 12.7.88.
44. Interview with author in Munich, 29.6.88.
45. Interview with author in Hanover, 4.5.88.
46. Henryk Broder; Die unheilbare Liebe deutscher Intellektuellen zu toten und totkranken Juden, 1988.
47. Interview with *Der Spiegel*, January 1990.
48. Interview with author in Munich, 14.11.88.
49. Interview with author in Neustadt, 27.11.88.

11: Occupied Country

1. James Gerard, *My Four Years in Germany*, 1917, p.317.
2. Conversation with Allied High Commissioners, December 1950, quoted in Weymar, op.cit, p.575.
3. Sketch, 14.1.82.
4. Crawley, op.cit.
5. Visit to Ramstein, 21.12.87.
6. Speech in Ramstein, 3.9.88.
7. Speech in House of Commons, 27.2.45.
8. Figures are deduced from the Military Balance 1988-89 (International Institute for Strategic Studies), as well as NATO and national publications. They do not take account of the small, unilateral cuts in Soviet and East German forces promised by end-1990.
9. According to West Germany's official military historians, the Wehrmacht on 31 October 1938 stood at 760,000 troops (including five post-*Anschluss* divisions from Austria's Bundesheer) while the Luftwaffe at end-1938 totalled 275,000 personnel – Militärisches Forschungsamt, *Handbuch zur deutschen Militärgeschichte*, Volume VII.
10. Speaking on ZDF television, 18.1.89.
11. Schmidt wrote in 1961 that using tactical nuclear weapons to repel a conventional advance from the Warsaw Pact would probably cause 'the extensive destruction of Europe, at least of Germany'. Schmidt, *Verteidigung oder Vergeltung*, 1961.
12. Interview with author in Hamburg, 26.6.87.
13. Interview with author in Bonn, 13.2.89.
14. FAZ, 5.9.88.
15. *Stern*, September 1988.
16. Interview with author in Bonn, 1.12.88.

Notes

17. Letter to *Wall Street Journal*, 12.8.86.
18. Interview in Deidersheim, 30.8.88.
19. Speech in Bonn, 2.11.88.
20. Interview on ITV news after NATO summit in Brussels, 3.3.88.
21. Allensbach, Emnid, Infas and SINUS polling institutes, compiled by Konrad Adenauer Foundation. Data also based on opinion poll survey in *Süddeutsche Zeitung*, 28.1.89 (J. Joffe).
22. In previous years going back to the early 1970s, the numbers in favour of American withdrawal remained constantly around the 20 per cent level, with between 50 and 60 per cent saying they would regret an American pull-out. Only in 1956 – at the height of controversy over the establishment of the Bundeswehr – was the opposition to US troops greater, with 51 per cent in favour of a pull-out and 22 per cent against.
23. Interview with author in Bonn, 30.9.88.
24. Speech in Moscow, 25.10.88.
25. Interview with author in Möhringen, 28.11.88.
26. Interview with author in Frankfurt, 29.11.88.
27. Interview with author in Baden-Baden, 24.11.88.
28. Interview with author in Rheindahlen, 30.5.88.

12: The Arms Makers

1. Statement to Reichstag budgetary commission on economic significance of naval fleet construction, winter 1899, quoted in Volker R. Berghahn, Wilhelm Deist, *Rüstung im Zeichen der wilhelminischen Weltpolitik*, 1988.
2. Secret speech at conference on 8.7.38, quoted in Nuremberg tribunal documents.
3. Press conference in East Berlin, 28.11.89.
4. Norman Mühlen, *Die Krupps*, 1960.
5. Quoted in Crawley, op.cit.
6. Precise figures for West German arms sales are difficult to arrive at. The Bonn government announced in April 1988 that arms exports between 1984 and 1986 amounted to about DM2 billion per year, but gave no breakdown, and said that 1987 figures were not available. Most detailed figures are available from the annual reports of the US Government's Arms Control and Disarmament Agency (ACDA) and of the Stockholm International Peace Research Institute (SIPRI). According to SIPRI's 1988 yearbook, West Germany's export total of $7.6 billion between 1983 and 1987 compared with $53 billion of exports by the Soviet Union, $52 billion from the US, $20 billion from France, $8.3 billion by the UK and $5.9 billion from China. The next biggest exporter in the list was the Netherlands, with $1 billion.
7. Interview with author in Lübeck, 12.7.88.
8. Eisenhower's farewell address, 17.1.61.
9. Berghahn, op.cit.
10. Manchester, op.cit.
11. G.W. Hadow, P.M. Grosz, *The German Giants – The story of the R-planes*, 1962.
12. Horst Mönnich, *Vor der Schallmauer, BMW – eine Jahrhundertgeschichte*, 1983.
13. Herbert Molloy Mason, *The Rise of the Luftwaffe*, 1973.
14. Ernst Heinkel, *Ein stürmisches Leben*, 1953.
15. Barton Whaley, *Covert German Rearmament, 1919-1939*.
16. Stauss won a Reichstag seat in 1930 for Stresemann's German People's Party. Göring was then deputy chairman of the Nazis' greatly-increased Reichstag grouping. Stauss was given a seat in the hand-picked Reichstag of the Third Reich and in 1934 became vice-president of the chamber. See Henry A. Turner op.cit., p.144.
17. Dietmar Keese, *Die volkswirtschaftlichen Gesamtgrossen für das Deutsche Reich in den Jahren 1925-1936*, 1967.
18. Dinner conversation on 26.2.42, quoted in *Hitler's Table Talk*.

19. Speech in Berlin, 14.2.35, quoted in Baynes, *Hitler's Speeches 1922-39*.
20. Essay published in 1932, quoted in Albert Müller, *Germany's War Machine*, 1936.
21. As part of its general expansion on European markets, in March 1929 General Motors bought 80 per cent of Opel shares, with the rest acquired in 1931. Purchase price was $33.3 million.
22. As part of a deal under which the Ford Motor Co. acquired a shareholding in the American subsidiary of I.G. Farben, the German chemical giant in 1929 took a 35 per cent stake in a newly-established Ford German subsidiary. Ford signed a contract to acquire land for a factory in Cologne with the city's mayor Konrad Adenauer in September 1929.
23. The Blitz lorry was first built in 1935 in Opel's Brandenburg works. When the US secret service discovered in 1947 the wartime link-up with Daimler Benz, General Motors was exposed to considerable criticism.
24. Hans-Peter Rosellen, *Und Trotzdem Vorwärts – Ford in Deutschland 1903-1945*, 1986.
25. The third biggest automobile group under the Third Reich was Auto-Union, based in Chemnitz in what is today East Germany. This was formed through a merger at the end of 1931 of the car factories of DKW at Zschopau, Horch of Zwickau, Audi of Chemnitz, together with the automobile department of the Chemnitz-based Wanderer company.
26. 1936 Reichsparteitag programme, Nuremberg, p.69.
27. Many of the photos of Hitler's visits to parades and rallies show the Führer arriving in a Daimler-Benz motor car. In a practice also followed by other large corporations, the swastika flag was often displayed alongside the company's own insignia on festive occasions. According to Hans Mommsen, Professor of Contemporary History at the University of Bochum and an authority on corporate history under the Third Reich: 'The Daimler-Benz managers without exception were opposed to the republican order of Weimar, welcomed Hitler's "removal" of the party-state and emphatically favoured a revision of Versailles, whereby they in no way ruled out warlike means. The acceleration of German armament, which started already in 1931-2, drove them (Daimler-Benz) with logical consistency into the arms of the Hitler regime.' *Der Spiegel*, 1987, No. 20.
28. *Das Daimler-Benz Buch*, 1987.
29. The car designer's son, Ferry, describes how Porsche, on a series of Austrian factory visits with Speer, drove by a concentration camp near Linz on the way to a quarry where prisoners were working. Speer remarked with malevolent humour: 'If you don't follow us, Herr Professor, there is still room for you here!' F. Porsche, *Porsche: Ein Traum wird Wirklichkeit*, 1978, p.227.
30. Speech in Fallersleben, 26.5.38.
31. *Eine Idee macht Geschichte: die Volkswagenchronik*, 1988.
32. Speer, op.cit.
33. Edward Zilbert, *Albert Speer and the Nazi Ministry of Arms*, 1981.
34. Interview with author in Stuttgart, 25.11.88.
35. Interview with author in Frankfurt, 2.10.87.
36. Statement on 30.11.89. In view of the list of assassinations of top West German businessmen associated with the arms industry, Reuter had already shown himself highly sensitive about the threat. In 1988 he remarked impatiently: 'I must defend myself against the idea of the famous "military-industrial complex", the alleged fraternity between the public sector and private business. That is the terminology of terrorists.' (Interview with *Stuttgarter Zeitung*, 10.9.88).
37. Partners in Airbus are France and West Germany, each with 37.9 per cent, Britain with 20 per cent and Spain with 4.2 per cent.
38. Interview in *Der Spiegel*, No. 31, 1988.
39. ACDA annual report, April 1988.
40. Interview with author in Mittenwald, 28.3.88.
41. Conversation with author in Düsseldorf, 22.6.88.
42. Interview with author in Munich, 19.7.88.

Notes

13: The Nuclear Conundrum

1. Letter to Hahn, 21.12.38, after receiving his results indicating the splitting of the nucleus.
2. Quoted by Lydia Martin-Endinghaus, *Bild der Wissenschaft*, No.4, 1977. Strauss was Minister for Atomic Affairs from the foundation of the new Ministry in October 1955 to his appointment as Defence Minister in October 1956.
3. Press conference in Bonn, 28.11.88.
4. For a description of post-war nuclear developments, see Joachim Radkau, *Aufstieg und Krise der deutschen Atomwirtschaft 1945-75*, 1983.
5. *Die Zeit*, 18.7.86.
6. Another top industrialist, Ernst Zimmermann, chairman of the aero-engine company Motoren-und Turbinen-Union (MTU), was killed by the RAF in February 1985, only miles away from the scene of the Beckurts' murder. The assassination of a symbolic representative of the nuclear industry was repeated in France in November 1986 when Georges Besse, the chairman of Renault and a former leading figure in the French atomic establishment, was gunned down in Paris.
7. *Financial Times*, 9.2.79.
8. German citizens can sue the state and claim damages under the country's Atomic Law. If a Chernobyl-type accident were to take place in West Germany, the cost would be astronomical. Britain, admittedly further away from the Ukraine, paid out only £4 million in compensation to farmers in the 12 months after the accident, mostly to cover losses caused by forced slaughter of sheep.
9. Statement by Chancellor Helmut Kohl, 31.8.88.
10. Interview with author in Paris, 12.9.86.
11. *Financial Times*, April 1987.
12. *Die Zeit*, 9.5.86.
13. Quoted in *German Comments*, Konrad Adenauer, Stiftung.
14. When the paper appeared three weeks later, Hahn, sensing that he had brought science into a new epoch, had prudently changed the wording to 'against all previous experience'. See Robert Rhodes, *The Making of the Atomic Bomb*, 1986.
15. Article in *Deutsche Allgemeine Zeitung*, 15.8.39.
16. It was clear at whom Göring's heavy sarcasm was aimed. 'Hahn' is German for 'cockerel'. David Irving, *The Virus House*, 1967.
17. Prof. Margaret Gowing, How Nuclear Power Began, CEGB Lecture, University of Southampton, 1987.
18. For an account of Leo Szilard, see Spencer Weart & Gertrud Weiss Szilard (eds), *Leo Szilard: His Version of the Facts: Selected Recollections and Correspondence*, 1978.
19. Einstein, born in Ulm in 1879, first renounced his German citizenship at the age of 15 when he moved from Milan to Zurich to finish his schooling. The quote is from Ronald W. Clarke, *Einstein, The Life and Times*, 1971, p.315.
20. Towards the end of the war, Einstein had a hand in an unsuccessful attempt to stop the use of the bomb whose development he had nurtured. Largely excluded from wartime nuclear development, he wrote his second famous letter to Roosevelt when he gave Szilard an introduction to the president in spring 1945. With Germany on the way to defeat, Szilard wanted to persuade Roosevelt not to test and use the atomic bombs whose development he had urged in 1939. Szilard's main argument was not moral but industrial – detonation would reveal the secret to the Soviet Union and could start an arms race. The president died in April 1945 before a meeting could take place. Szilard eventually succeeded in seeing Truman, but his arguments were rejected. General Leslie Groves, the head of the Manhattan Project, wrote later, 'As we poured more and more money and effort into this project, the government became increasingly committed to the ultimate use of the bomb.' (Leslie Groves, *Now It Can Be Told*, 1962, p.265.)
21. 'The Frisch-Peierls Memorandum' and 'The Maud Report', reprinted in Margaret Gowing, *Britain and Atomic Energy, 1939-45*, 1969, pp.289-436.
22. Mark Walker, *German National Socialism and the Quest for Nuclear Power, 1939-49*, 1989, contains a scholarly and painstaking account of the German atomic work and analyses critically the scientists'

post-war apologia.

23. Heisenberg did his best to keep army interest in the project alive, but at the same time played down any idea that a bomb would quickly be feasible. He told Field Marshal Milch at a conference of top armaments officials in June 1942 that the explosive charge of a nuclear bomb would be about 'as large as a pineapple'. He added that, although the Americans were working flat out and might produce a bomb within two years at the least, for Germany to produce such a bomb at the time would be economically impossible. Irving, op.cit., p.120.

24. According to Albert Speer, Hitler's Armaments Minister, nuclear fission came up only once in 2,200 recorded points of conversations with Hitler. Speer, op.cit.

25. In his book *Brighter than a Thousand Suns*, first published in 1956, Jungk wrote that Heisenberg and other leading scientists wanted to keep control of nuclear research to prevent fission being misused by the Nazis. He quotes Heisenberg's disingenuous statement that 'under a dictatorship active resistance can only be practised by those who pretend to collaborate with the regime'. Jungk misleadingly described as a 'peace feeler' Heisenberg's ambiguous conversation with the Danish physicist Niels Bohr in Copenhagen in October 1941; he claimed afterwards that he had been trying to convey to the US and Britain through Bohr that Germany had no intention of making the bomb. Bohr received the opposite impression, believing that Heisenberg was making a subtle threat.

26. Jungk now says that Weizsäcker 'sold' him the story after the war that the atomic scientists were 'pacifists' rather than 'activists'. Because the scientists could not make the bomb, Weizsäcker claimed that they did not want to. Jungk says he accepted this story partly because he wanted to believe that scientists could have freedom of action even under a totalitarian regime. In recent years, Weizsäcker has changed his own version and come nearer to admitting the truth. Jungk says, 'Actors change their story according to the outcome.' Telephone conversation with author, 19.1.89.

27. Carl-Friedrich von Weizsäcker was supported by the Social Democratic Party to run for office as federal president in 1979, but turned down the idea. His brother Richard, eight years his junior, became president in 1984. In latter years Carl-Friedrich has become a powerful voice warning that international cooperation over disarmament and the environment is the only way to prevent world catastrophe. He is a strong supporter of a peace conference of the world's Churches to ensure 'justice, peace and the integrity of creation'.

28. See Walker, op.cit.

29. R.V. Jones, the head of British scientific intelligence, explains in his book *Most Secret War* how he had the idea of installing the microphones 'so that we could hear their (the German scientists') reactions when they realised how far the Americans and ourselves had progressed'.

30. Excerpts of the scientists' reactions have been published in Groves, op.cit. The British Foreign Office appears to believe that release of the files on Farm Hall could damage Anglo-German relations.

31. Otto Hahn, *Mein Leben*, 1968.

32. Interview with author in Bonn, 14.9.87.

33. The reassuring statement came from Karl Wirtz, one of the Kaiser Wilhelm Institute physicists who went on to guide the nuclear energy programme after the war. He made it in a speech at the opening of the cellar on 16 May 1980, reprinted in the Atom Cellar guide.

34. Interview with author in Haigerloch, August 1987.

35. Other banned areas included aerodynamics, rocket motors, shipbuilding and cryptology. Control Council for Germany, Law No. 25, 30.4.46.

36. Hertz chose to go to the Soviet Union because the US already had so many top atomic physicists. He therefore believed, almost certainly correctly, that his work would be more appreciated by the Russians. See David Holloway, *The Soviet Decision to Build the Atomic Bomb, 1939-45*.

37. Abs, Heisenberg and Winnacker, who became chairman of Hoechst between 1952 and 1969, all served on the Commission continuously from 1956 to 1971.

38. For a description of post-war nuclear development, see Karl Winnacker and Karl Wirtz, *Nuclear Energy in Germany*, 1979. The book offers a highly partial view from the standpoint of atomic enthusiasts who for two decades were on the inside track of nuclear decision-making.

39. The FR1 reactor was planned to be built in Göttingen, using a core of natural uranium and heavy water and a neutron reflector of graphite. However, it was never built.
40. Karlsruhe was chosen as the site for FR2 as a result of some complex politicking by Adenauer. Heisenberg and other top physicists wanted to build it at Garching near Munich, where West Germany's fusion research is based today. In line with his policy of western integration, Adenauer wanted to construct the reactor as far away as possible from the Iron Curtain, and forced through the decision on military grounds. The reasoning appears curious today in view of the decision to build West Germany's (now abandoned) commercial reprocessing complex in eastern Bavaria close to the Czech border.
41. In 1944, after German supplies of heavy water from Norsk-Hydro's electrolysis works in Norway were cut off by Allied bombing, both IG Farben and Linde were commissioned to provide alternative sources. The war ended before the plans could be put into operation, however.
42. When the Bundestag ratified the treaty in 1974, a number of conservative deputies, including Franz Josef Strauss, Walter Wallmann (later to become Environment Minister and state premier of Hesse) and Manfred Wörner (later Defence Minister and NATO secretary general) voted against. The SPD periodically claims that elements in the conservative parties want to keep open an option for Germany to build atomic weapons, but the allegation seems far-fetched.
43. Visit to Karlsruhe Institute, 11.11.86.
44. Leonard Spector, *The Undeclared Bomb*, 1988.
45. Siemens took full control of KWU when it acquired the 50 per cent AEG stake in 1977.
46. According to Karl Kaiser, director of the research institute of the German Society for Foreign Affairs, the disagreement over the nuclear deal was 'the most serious clash in US-German relations since the war'. (*Foreign Policy*, Spring 1978.)
47. In 1985 Brazil announced that it would complete only two of the eight German reactors originally envisaged, and would postpone the reprocessing plant indefinitely. It also declared that only the first stage of the jet nozzle enrichment plant would be completed.
48. Interview with author in Erlangen, 13.3.87.
49. Speech to the German Trade Union Confederation, Hamburg, 25.5.86.
50. Interview with author in Bonn, 12.11.86.
51. Forschungsgruppe Wahlen, December 1988; Allensbach, April 1988.
52. Interviews at Hahn-Meitner Institute, 28.11.88.
53. The demonstration took place on 2.12.88. Description was provided to the author by an eye-witness.

14: The Greening of the Germans

1. Charles de Gaulle, *Vers l'armée de metier*, 1934, Chapter II.
2. Speech in Bad Godesberg, 18.4.61.
3. Pop song 'The Rats', 1982.
4. Telephone conversation with author, 23.2.89.
5. Visit to Herfa-Neurode, 26.5.87.
6. For instance, opinion polls carried out by the Emnid organisation in 1986 and 1987 showed that unemployment was counted the most pressing problems by roughly 80 per cent of the population. Between 65 and 70 per cent put the environment into this category.
7. Giving one traditional view of German habits, the US ambassador to Berlin before and during the First World War, James Gerard, wrote that 'heavy eating and large consumption of wine and beer had unfavourably affected the German national character and had made the people more aggressive and irritable, and consequently readier for war. The influence of diet on national character should not be underestimated. Meat-eating nations have always ruled vegetarians.' (*My Four Years in Germany*, p.30.)
8. According to the federal statistics office, an average four-person household in 1970 devoted 43 per cent of its food expenditure to meat, milk and other animal-based products, whereas the

Bibliography

Historical

Balfour, Michael, *West Germany, A Contemporary History*, London, 1983.
Baynes, Norman (ed.), *The Speeches of Adolf Hitler*, London, 1942.
Benz, Wolfgang, *Die Bundesrepublik Deutschland* (3 vols), Frankfurt, 1983.
———— *Von der Besatzungsherrschaft zur Bundesrepublik*, Frankfurt, 1984.
Broszat, Martin, *Nach Hitler: Der Schwierige Umgang mit unserer Geschichte*, Munich, 1986.
Bullock, Alan, *Hitler, A Study in Tyranny*, London, 1963 (first published 1952).
Churchill, Winston S., *The Second World War* (6 vols), London, 1948-54.
Craig, Gordon, *The Politics of the Prussian Army, 1640-1945*, Oxford, 1955.
———— *From Bismarck to Adenauer, Aspects of German Statecraft*, New York, 1958.
———— *Germany 1866-1945*, Oxford, 1981.
Crawley, Aidan, *The Rise of Western Germany*, London, 1973.
Dunlop, J.K., *A Short History of Germany*, Bielefeld, 1954.
Fest, Joachim, *Hitler*, Frankfurt, 1973.
François-Poncet, André, *Souvenirs d'une Ambassade à Berlin*, Paris, 1956.
Gerard, James W., *My Four Years in Germany*, London, 1917.
Goebbels, Joseph, *Revolution der Deutschen*, Oldenburg, 1933.
———— *Tagebücher 1945*, Hamburg, 1977.
Gollancz, Victor, *In Darkest Germany*, London, 1947.
Haffner, Sebastian, *Anmerkungen zu Hitler*, Frankfurt, 1987.
Henderson, Nevile, *Failure of a Mission*, London, 1940.
Henri, Ernst, *Hitler over Europe*, London, 1934.
Hitler, Adolf, *Mein Kampf*, Munich, 1925-27.
———— *Hitler's Table Talk*, London, 1953.
Kohn, Hans, *The Mind of Germany*, New York, 1960.
Mann, Golo, *Deutsche Geschichte 1919-1945*, Frankfurt, 1968.
Maser, Werner, *Deutschland: Traum oder Trauma*, Munich, 1984.
Meinecke, Friedrich, *Die deutsche Katastrophe*, Wiesbaden, 1946.
Piper Verlag, *Historikerstreit*, Munich, 1987.
Robertson, C. Grant, *Bismarck*, London, 1918.
Settel, Arthur (ed.), *This is Germany*, New York, 1950.
Shirer, William, *The Rise and Fall of the Third Reich*, New York, 1960.
Speer, Albert, *Inside the Third Reich*, London, 1970.
Spengler, Oswald, *Die Stunde der Entscheidung*, Munich, 1933.
Stephan, Werner, *Joseph Goebbels, Dämon einer Diktatur*, Stuttgart, 1949.
de Staël, Germaine, *De l'Allemagne*, Paris, 1968 (first published 1813).
Stern, Fritz, *Dreams and Delusions: The Drama of German History*, London, 1987.
Taylor, A.J.P., *The Course of German History*, London, 1945.
Wedgwood, C.V., *The Thirty Years War*, London, 1984 (first published 1938).

Political/Social

Allemann, Fritz René, *Bonn ist nicht Weimar*, Cologne, 1956.

374

Bibliography

Ardagh, John, *Germany and the Germans*, London, 1987.
Bahr, Egon, *Zum europäischen Frieden*, Berlin, 1988.
Bergsdorf, Wolfgang, *Die vierte Gewalt*, Mainz, 1980.
——— *Über die Macht der Kultur*, Stuttgart, 1988.
Bölling, Klaus, *Bonn von aussen betrachtet*, Stuttgart, 1986.
Carr, Jonathan, *Helmut Schmidt*, London, 1985.
Craig, Gordon, *The Germans*, New York, 1982.
Dahrendorf, Ralf, *Gesellschaft und Demokratie in Deutschland*, Munich, 1965.
Elon, Amos, *Journey through a Haunted Land*, London, 1967.
Engelmann, Bernt, *Deutschland ohne Juden*, Cologne, 1988.
Filmer, Werner & Schwan, Heribert, *Helmut Kohl*, Düsseldorf, 1985.
——— *Hans-Dietrich Genscher*, Düsseldorf, 1988.
Giordano, Ralph, *Die Zweite Schuld*, Hamburg, 1987.
Gross, Johannes, *Die Deutschen*, Frankfurt, 1967.
Grosser, Alfred, *Das Deutschland im Westen*, Munich, 1985.
——— *Mit Deutschen Streiten*, Munich 1987.
Koch, Peter, *Willy Brandt*, Frankfurt, 1988.
von Krockow, Christian & Lösche, Peter (eds.), *Parteien in der Krise*, Munich, 1986.
Laqueur, Walter, *Was ist los mit den Deutschen?*, Frankfurt, 1985.
Leonhardt, Rudolf Walter, *This Germany*, New York (translation of *X-mal Deutschland*, Munich 1961).
Lücke, Paul, *Ist Bonn doch Weimar*, Frankfurt, 1968.
Noelle-Neumann, Elisabeth & Köcher, Renate, *Die verletzte Nation*, Stuttgart, 1987.
Prittie, Terence, *Germany Divided*, Boston, 1960.
——— *Willy Brandt, Portrait of a Statesman*, London, 1974.
——— *My Germans*, London, 1983.
Riese, Hans-Peter, *Der Griff nach der vierten Gewalt*, Cologne, 1984.
Sauzay, Brigitte, *Die rätselhaften Deutschen*, Stuttgart, 1986.
Simonian, Haig, *The Privileged Partnership: Franco-German Relations in the European Community*, Oxford, 1985.
Schmidt, Helmut, *Eine Strategie für den Westen*, Berlin, 1985.
——— *Menschen und Mächte*, Berlin, 1987.
Schulze, Hagen, *Wir sind was wir geworden sind*, Munich, 1987.
von Weizsäcker, Richard, *Die deutsche Geschichte geht weiter*, Berlin, 1983.
Schweitzer, Carl-Christoph, et al, *Politics and Government in the Federal Republic of Germany*, Leamington, 1984.
von Westernhagen, Dörte, *Die Kinder der Täter*, Munich, 1987.
Watt, D.C., *Britain Looks to Germany*, London, 1965.
Weymar, Paul, *Konrad Adenauer*, Munich, 1955.

Two Germanys

Bundesministerium für Innerdeutsche Beziehungen, *Zahlenspiel: BRD/DDR*, 1987.
Calleo, David, *The German Problem Reconsidered*, Cambridge, 1978.
Fritsch-Bournazel, Renata, *Confronting the German Question*, New York, 1988.
Gaus, Günter, *Wo Deutschland Liegt*, Hamburg, 1983.
Honecker, Erich, *Aus Meinem Leben*, Berlin, 1980.
Merseburger, Peter, *Grenzgänger*, Munich, 1988.
Mommsen, Hans, History and National Identity: The Case of Germany, *German Studies Review*, October 1983.
Schmidthammer, Jens, *Rechtsanwalt Wolfgang Vogel*, Hamburg, 1987.
Shears, David, *The Ugly Frontier*, London, 1971.

Stürmer, Michael, Jenseits des Nationalstaats – Bemerkungen zum deutschen Kontinuitätsproblem, *Politik und Kultur*, Berlin, 1975.
————, *Deutsche Frage und europäische Integration*, Sankt-Augustin, 1988.

Economics/Business

Blessing, Karl, *Die Verteidigung des Geldwertes*, Frankfurt, 1960.
Clapham, J.H., *The Economic Development of France and Germany 1815-1914*, Cambridge, 1928.
Deutsche Bundesbank, *Währung und Wirtschaft in Deutschland, 1876-1975*, Frankfurt, 1976.
Donges, Juergen B. & Schatz, Klaus-Werner, *Staatliche Intervention in der Bundesrepublik Deutschland*, Kiel, 1986.
Erhard, Ludwig, *Deutsche Wirtschaftspolitik*, Düsseldorf, 1962.
Emminger, Otmar, *D-Mark, Dollar, Währungskrisen*, Stuttgart, 1986.
Feyerabend, *Die leisen Milliarde: Das Imperium des Friedrich Karl Flick*, Düsseldorf, 1984.
Gilbert, Milton, *Quest for World Monetary Order*, New York, 1980.
Herchenröder, K.H., et al, *Die Nachfolger der Ruhrkonzerne*, Düsseldorf, 1953.
Holtfrerich, Carl-Ludwig, *Die deutsche Inflation 1914-23*, Berlin, 1980.
Hörster-Philipps, Ulrike, *Im Schatten des grossen Geldes: Flick-Konzern und Politik*, Cologne, 1985.
Kilz, Hans Werner & Preuss, Joachim, *Flick – Die gekaufte Republik*, Reinbek, 1983.
Köhler, Otto, *Die Geschichte der IG Farben und ihrer Väter*, Hamburg, 1986.
Laitenberger, *Ludwig Erhard: Der Nationalökonom als Politiker*, Göttingen, 1986.
Lochner, Louis P., *Tycoons and Tyrant: German Industry from Hitler to Adenauer*, Chicago, 1954.
Office of Military Government for Germany, Finance Division, *Reports on IG Farben, Deutsche Bank, and Dresdner Bank Investigations, 1945, 1946, 1947* (published in German translation, Nördlingen, 1985-86).
Office of Military Government for Germany, *Economic Developments since the Currency Reform*, 1948.
Ortlieb, Heinz-Dietrich, *Glanz und Elend des deutschen Wirtschaftswunders*, Munich, 1974.
Pfeiffer, Hermannus, *Das Imperium der Deutschen Bank*, Frankfurt, 1987.
Pohl, Manfred, *Geschäft und Politik – Deutsch-russische/sowjetische Wirtschaftsbeziehungen*, Mainz, 1988.
Pritzkoleit, Kurt, *Männer, Mächte, Monopole*, Düsseldorf, 1953.
Sasuly, Richard, *I.G. Farben*, New York, 1947.
Seidenzahl, Fritz, *100 Jahre Deutsche Bank*, Frankfurt, 1970.
Treue, Wilhelm & Pohl, Hans (ed.), *Die Konzentration in der deutschen Wirtschaft seit dem 19. Jahrhundert*, Wiesbaden, 1978.
Treue, Wilhelm, *Herbert Quandt*, Bad Homburg, 1980.
Turner, Henry Ashby, *German Big Business and the Rise of Hitler*, New York, 1985.
Veblen, Thorstein, *Imperial Germany and the Industrial Revolution*, Westport, 1984 (first published 1915).
Verg, Erik, *Meilensteine: 125 Jahre Bayer*, Gütersloh, 1988.
Vocke, Wilhelm, *Memoiren*, Stuttgart, 1973.
Vogelsang, Reinard, *Der Freundeskreis Himmler*, Göttingen, 1972.
Wallich, Henry, *Mainsprings of the German Revival*, New Haven, 1955.
Walter, Norbert (ed.), *Was würde Erhard heute tun?*, Stuttgart, 1986.

Armaments

Berghahn, Volker & Deist, Wilhelm, *Rüstung im Zeichen der wilhelminischen Weltpolitik. Grundlegende Dokumente 1890-1914*, Düsseldorf, 1988.
Gabler, Ulrich, *Submarine Design*, Koblenz, 1986 (first published 1964).
Hamburger Stiftung fur Sozialgeschichte, *Das Daimler-Benz Buch*, Nördlingen, 1987.

Bibliography

Hecker, Gerhard, *Walther Rathenau und sein Verhältnis zu Militär und Krieg*, Boppard, 1983.
Heinkel, Ernst, *Ein stürmisches Leben*, Stuttgart, 1953.
International Institute for Strategic Studies, *The Military Balance 1988-89*, London, 1988.
Ishoven, Armand van, *Messerschmitt*, Munich, 1978.
Jones, R.V., *Most Secret War*, London, 1978.
Manchester, William, *The Arms of Krupp*, Boston, 1968.
Mason, Herbert Molloy, *The Rise of the Luftwaffe*, New York, 1973.
Mechtersheimer, Alfred & Barth, Peter, *Militärisierungsatlas der Bundesrepublik*, Darmstadt, 1986.
Meinck, Gerhard, *Hitler und die deutsche Aufrüstung 1933-37*, Wiesbaden, 1959.
Mühlen, Norman, *Die Krupps*, Frankfurt, 1960.
Müller, Albert, *Germany's War Machine*, London, 1936.
Spielburger, Walter, *Die Motorisierung der Deutschen Reichswehr 1920-35*, Stuttgart, 1979.
Stockholm International Peace Research Institute, *Annual Report*, Stockholm, 1988.
US Arms Control and Disarmament Agency, *World Military Expenditures and Arms Transfers*, Washington, 1988.
Zilbert, Edward, *Albert Speer and the Nazi Ministry of Arms*, London, 1981.

Nuclear

von Ardenne, Manfred, *Mein Leben für Forschung und Fortschritt*, Frankfurt, 1986.
Beyerchen, Alan, *Scientists under Hitler*, New Haven, 1977.
Clarfield, Gerald & Wiecek, William M., *Nuclear America*, New York, 1984.
Clark, Ronald W., *Einstein: The Life and Times*, New York, 1971.
Goldschmidt, Bertrand, *Le Complexe Atomique*, Paris, 1980.
Groves, Leslie, *Now It Can Be Told*, New York, 1962.
Hahn, Otto, *Mein Leben*, Munich, 1968.
Heisenberg, Werner, *Der Teil und das Ganze*, Munich, 1969.
Irving, David, *The Virus House*, London, 1967.
Jungk, Robert, *Brighter than a Thousand Suns*, London, 1958.
Lemmerich, *Die Geschichte der Entdeckung der Kernspaltung*, Berlin, 1988.
Plettner, Bernhard, *Kernkraftnutzung nach Tschernobyl?*, Munich, 1986.
Pringle, Peter & Spiegelman, James, *The Nuclear Barons*, London, 1982.
Radkau, Joachim, *Aufstieg und Krise der deutschen Atomwirtschaft 1945-75*, Reinbek, 1983.
Rhodes, Robert, *The Making of the Atomic Bomb*, New York, 1986.
Spector, Leonard, *The Undeclared Bomb*, New York, 1988.
Walker, Mark, *German National Socialism and the Quest for Nuclear Power 1939-49*, Cambridge, 1989.
Winnacker, Karl & Wirtz, Karl, *Nuclear Energy in Germany*, La Grange Park, 1979, (translation of *Das Unverstandene Wunder: Kernenergie in Deutschland*, Düsseldorf, 1975).
Wirtz, Karl, *Im Umkreis der Physik*, Karlsruhe, 1988.

Secret Services

Bauer, Ulrich, *Wozu Geheimdienste?*, Munich, 1985.
Felfe, Heinz, *Im Dienst des Gegners*, Hamburg, 1986.
Gehlen, Reinhard, *Der Dienst*, Mainz, 1971.
Nollau, Günther, *Das Amt*, Munich, 1978.
Schlomann, Friedrich-Wilhelm, *Operationsgebiet Bundesrepublik*, Munich, 1984.
Stiller, Werner, *Im Zentrum der Spionage*, Mainz, 1986.

Appendix

German Empire
Chancellor

Otto von Bismarck	1871-90
Leo von Caprivi	1890-94
Chlodwig zu Hohenlohe-Schillingsfürst	1894-1900
Bernhard von Bülow	1900-09
Theobald von Bethmann Hollweg	1909-17
Georg Michaelis	1917
Georg von Hertling	1917-18
Max von Baden	1918

Emperor

William I	1871-1888
Frederick III	1888
William II	1888-1918

Weimar Republic
Chancellor

Friedrich Ebert (Social Democratic Party)	1918-19
Philipp Scheidemann (Social Democratic Party)	1919
Gustav Bauer (Social Democratic Party)	1919-20
Hermann Müller (Social Democratic Party)	1920
Konstantin Fehrenbach (Centre Party)	1920-21
Joseph Wirth (Centre Party)	1921-22
Wilhelm Cuno (non-party)	1922-23
Gustav Stresemann (German People's Party)	1923
Wilhelm Marx (Centre Party)	1923-25
Hans Luther (non-party)	1925-26
Wilhelm Marx (Centre Party)	1926-28
Hermann Müller (Social Democratic Party)	1928-30
Heinrich Brüning (Centre Party)	1930-32
Franz von Papen (non-party)	1932
Kurt von Schleicher (non-party)	1932-33

President

Friedrich Ebert	1919-25
Paul von Hindenburg	1925-33

Third Reich
Chancellor

Adolf Hitler (National Socialist Workers Party)	1933-45

President

Paul von Hindenburg	1933-34
Adolf Hitler	1934-35
Karl Dönitz	1945

378

Appendix

Federal Republic

Chancellor

Konrad Adenauer (Christian Democratic Union)	1949-63
Ludwig Erhard (Christian Democratic Union)	1963-66
Kurt Georg Kiesinger (Christian Democratic Union)	1966-69
Willy Brandt (Social Democratic Party)	1969-74
Helmut Schmidt (Social Democratic Party)	1974-82
Helmut Kohl (Christian Democratic Union)	1982-

President

Theodor Heuss (Free Democratic Party)	1949-59
Henrich Lübke (Christian Democratic Union)	1959-69
Gustav Heinemann (Social Democratic Party)	1969-74
Walter Scheel (Free Democratic Party)	1974-79
Karl Carstens (Christian Democratic Union)	1979-84
Richard von Weizsäcker (Christian Democratic Union)	1984-

German Democratic Republic

Socialist Unity Party, First Secretary

Walter Ulbricht	1953-71
Erich Honecker	1971-89
Egon Krenz	1989

President/Head of State Council

Wilhelm Pieck	1949-60
Walter Ulbricht	1960-73
Willi Stoph	1973-76
Erich Honecker	1976-89
Egon Krenz	1989
Manfred Gerlach	1989-90

379

Index